SELECTED ENGLISH
SHORT STORIES

SELECTED ENGLISH
SHORT STORIES

XIX & XX CENTURIES

(Second Series)

By

HUMPHREY MILFORD

GYAN

Published by

Gyan Publishing House
5, Ansari Road
Daryaganj, New Delhi-110002
Phone: 011-47034999, 9811692060
E-mail: books@gyanbooks.com

Distribution Network
gyanbooks.com
India, USA, Canada, UK, Australia, France

ISBN: 978-81-212-6863-9 (HB)
First Published, 1927

2nd Impression 2023

Printed at: Gyan Press, Delhi.

**SELECTED ENGLISH SHORT STORIES,
XIX & XX CENTURIES**
Author: HUMPHREY MILFORD

SELECTED ENGLISH SHORT STORIES

XIX & XX CENTURIES

(SECOND SERIES)

NOTE

A VOLUME of Selected English Short Stories (nineteenth century) was first published in 1914, and has been often reprinted. This is a second volume selected on the same principles and from almost the same period. Of both volumes it should be noted that English means written in the English language, and that no selection from living writers has been attempted.

H. S. M.

CONTENTS

MARY ANN LAMB

1764–1847

THE SAILOR UNCLE

(From *Mrs. Leicester's School: or, The History of Several Young Ladies related by themselves.*)

My father is the curate of a village church, about five miles from Amwell. I was born in the parsonage-house, which joins the church-yard. The first thing I can remember was my father teaching me the alphabet from the letters on a tombstone that stood at the head of my mother's grave. I used to tap at my father's study-door; I think I now hear him say, 'Who is there?—What do you want, little girl?' 'Go and see mamma. Go and learn pretty letters.' Many times in the day would my father lay aside his books and his papers to lead me to this spot, and make me point to the letters, and then set me to spell syllables and words: in this manner, the epitaph on my mother's tomb being my primer and my spelling-book, I learned to read.

I was one day sitting on a step placed across the church-yard stile, when a gentleman passing by, heard me distinctly repeat the letters which formed my mother's name, and then say, *Elizabeth Villiers*, with a firm tone, as if I had performed some great matter. This gentleman was my uncle James, my mother's brother: he was a lieutenant in the navy, and had left England a few weeks after the marriage of my father and mother, and now, returned home from a long sea-voyage, he was coming to visit my mother; no tidings of her decease having reached him, though she had been dead more than a twelvemonth.

When my uncle saw me sitting on the stile, and heard me pronounce my mother's name, he looked earnestly in my face, and began to fancy a resemblance to his sister, and to think I might be her child. I was too intent on my employment to observe him, and went spelling on. 'Who has taught you to spell so prettily, my little maid?' said my uncle. 'Mamma,' I replied; for I had an idea that the words on the tombstone were somehow a part of mamma, and that she had taught me. 'And who is mamma?' asked my uncle. 'Elizabeth Villiers,' I replied; and then my uncle called me his dear little niece, and said he would go with me to mamma: he took hold of my hand, intending to lead me home, delighted that he had found out who I was, because he imagined it would be such a pleasant surprise to his sister to see her little daughter bringing home her long lost sailor uncle.

I agreed to take him to mamma, but we had a dispute about the way thither. My uncle was for going along the road which led directly up to our house; I pointed to the church-yard, and said, that was the way to mamma. Though impatient of any delay, he was not willing to contest the point with his new relation, therefore he lifted me over the stile, and was then going to take me along the path to a gate he knew was at the end of our garden; but no, I would not go that way either: letting go his hand, I said, 'You do not know the way—I will show you': and making what haste I could among the long grass and thistles, and jumping over the low graves, he said, as he followed what he called my *wayward steps*, 'What a positive soul this little niece of mine is! I knew the way to your mother's house before you were born, child.' At last I stopped at my mother's grave, and, pointing to the tombstone, said, 'Here is mamma,' in a voice of exultation, as if I had now convinced him that I knew the way best: I looked up in his face to see him acknowledge his mistake; but oh, what a face of sorrow did I see! I was so frightened, that I have but an imperfect recollection of what followed. I remember I pulled his coat, and cried, 'Sir, sir,' and tried to move him. I knew not what to do; my mind was in a strange confusion; I thought I had done something wrong in bringing the gentleman to mamma to make him cry so sadly; but what it was I could not tell. This grave had always been a scene of delight to me. In the house my father would often be weary of my prattle, and send me from him; but here he was all my own. I might say anything and be as frolicsome as I pleased here; all was cheerfulness and good humour in our visits to mamma, as we called it. My father would tell me how quietly mamma slept there, and that he and his little Betsy would one day sleep beside mamma in that grave; and when I went to bed, as I laid my little head on the pillow, I used to wish I was sleeping in the grave with my papa and mamma; and in my childish dreams I used to fancy myself there, and it was a place within the ground, all smooth, and soft, and green. I never made out any figure of mamma, but still it was the tombstone, and papa, and the smooth green grass, and my head resting upon the elbow of my father.

How long my uncle remained in this agony of grief I know not; to me it seemed a very long time: at last he took me in his arms, and held me so tight, that I began to cry, and ran home to my father, and told him, that a gentleman was crying about mamma's pretty letters.

No doubt it was a very affecting meeting between my father and my uncle. I remember that it was the first day I ever saw my father weep: that I was in sad trouble, and went into the kitchen and told Susan, our servant, that papa was crying; and she wanted to keep me with her that I might not disturb the conversation; but I would go back to the parlour to *poor papa*, and I went in softly, and crept between my father's knees. My uncle offered to take me in his arms, but I turned sullenly from him, and clung closer to my father, having conceived a dislike to my uncle because he had made my father cry.

Now I first learned that my mother's death was a heavy affliction; for I heard my father tell a melancholy story of her long illness, her death, and what he had suffered from her loss. My uncle said, what a sad thing it was for my father to be left with such a young child; but my father replied, his little Betsy was all his comfort, and that, but for me, he should have died with grief. How I could be any comfort to my father, struck me with wonder. I knew I was pleased when he played and talked with me; but I thought that was all goodness and favour done to me, and I had no notion how I could make any part of his happiness. The sorrow I now heard he had suffered, was as new and strange to me. I had no idea that he had ever been unhappy; his voice was always kind and cheerful; I had never before seen him weep, or show any such signs of grief as those in which I used to express my little troubles. My thoughts on these subjects were confused and childish; but from that time I never ceased pondering on the sad story of my dead mamma.

The next day I went by mere habit to the study-door, to call papa to the beloved grave; my mind misgave me, and I could not tap at the door. I went backwards and forwards between the kitchen and the study, and what to do with myself I did not know. My uncle met me in the passage, and said, 'Betsy, will you come and walk with me in the garden?' This I refused, for this was not what I wanted, but the old amusement of sitting on the grave, and talking to papa. My uncle tried to persuade me, but still I said, 'No, no,' and ran crying into the kitchen. As he followed me in there, Susan said, 'This child is so fretful to-day, I do not know what to do with her.' 'Aye,' said my uncle, 'I suppose my poor brother spoils her, having but one.' This reflection on my papa made me quite in a little passion of anger, for I had not forgot that with this new uncle sorrow had first come into our dwelling: I screamed loudly, till my father came out to know what it was all about. He sent my uncle into the parlour, and said, he would manage the little wrangler by himself. When my uncle was gone I ceased crying; my father forgot to lecture me for my ill humour, or to inquire into the cause, and we were soon seated by the side of the tombstone. No lesson went on that day; no talking of pretty mamma sleeping in the green grave; no jumping from the tombstone to the ground; no merry jokes or pleasant stories. I sate upon my father's knee, looking up in his face, and thinking, '*How sorry papa looks!*' till, having been fatigued with crying, and now oppressed with thought, I fell fast asleep.

My uncle soon learned from Susan that this place was our constant haunt; she told him she did verily believe her master would never get the better of the death of her mistress, while he continued to teach the child to read at the tombstone; for, though it might soothe his grief, it kept it for ever fresh in his memory. The sight of his sister's grave had been such a shock to my uncle, that he readily entered into Susan's apprehensions; and concluding, that if I were set to study by some other means, there would no longer be a pretence for these visits to the grave, away my kind uncle hastened to the nearest market-town to buy me some books.

I heard the conference between my uncle and Susan, and I did not approve of his interfering in our pleasures. I saw him take his hat and walk out, and I secretly hoped he was gone *beyond seas* again, from whence Susan had told me he had come. Where *beyond seas* was I could not tell; but I concluded it was somewhere a great way off. I took my seat on the church-yard stile, and kept looking down the road, and saying, 'I hope I shall not see my uncle again. I hope my uncle will not come from *beyond seas* any more'; but I said this very softly, and had a kind of notion that I was in a perverse ill-humoured fit. Here I sate till my uncle returned from the market-town with his new purchases. I saw him come walking very fast with a parcel under his arm. I was very sorry to see him, and I frowned, and tried to look very cross. He untied his parcel, and said, 'Betsy, I have brought you a pretty book.' I turned my head away, and said, 'I don't want a book'; but I could not help peeping again to look at it. In the hurry of opening the parcel he had scattered all the books upon the ground, and there I saw fine gilt covers and gay pictures all fluttering about. What a fine sight!—All my resentment vanished, and I held up my face to kiss him, that being my way of thanking my father for any extraordinary favour.

My uncle had brought himself into rather a troublesome office; he had heard me spell so well, that he thought there was nothing to do but to put books into my hand, and I should read; yet, notwithstanding I spelt tolerably well, the letters in my new library were so much smaller than I had been accustomed to, they were like Greek characters to me; I could make nothing at all of them. The honest sailor was not to be discouraged by this difficulty; though unused to play the schoolmaster, he taught me to read the small print, with unwearied diligence and patience; and whenever he saw my father and me look as if we wanted to resume our visits to the grave, he would propose some pleasant walk; and if my father said it was too far for the child to walk, he would set me on his shoulder, and say, 'Then Betsy shall ride'; and in this manner has he carried me many many miles.

In these pleasant excursions my uncle seldom forgot to make Susan furnish him with a luncheon which, though it generally happened every day, made a constant surprise to my papa and me, when, seated under some shady tree, he pulled it out of his pocket and began to distribute his little store ; and then I used to peep into the other pocket to see if there were not some currant wine there and the little bottle of water for me ; if, perchance, the water was forgot, then it made another joke,—that poor Betsy must be forced to drink a little drop of wine. These are childish things to tell of, and instead of my own silly history, I wish I could remember the entertaining stories my uncle used to relate of his voyages and travels, while we sate under the shady trees, eating our noontide meal.

The long visit my uncle made us was such an important event in my life, that I feel I shall tire your patience with talking of him ; but when he is gone, the remainder of my story will be but short.

The summer months passed away, but not swiftly ;—the pleasant walks, and the charming stories of my uncle's adventures, made them seem like years to me ; I remember the approach of winter by the warm great coat he bought for me, and how proud I was when I first put it on, and that he called me Little Red Riding Hood, and bade me beware of wolves, and that I laughed and said there were no such things now ; then he told me how many wolves, and bears, and tigers, and lions he had met with in uninhabited lands, that were like Robinson Crusoe's Island. Oh, these were happy days !

In the winter our walks were shorter and less frequent. My books were now my chief amusement, though my studies were often interrupted by a game of romps with my uncle, which too often ended in a quarrel because he played so roughly ; yet long before this I dearly loved my uncle, and the improvement I made while he was with us was very great indeed. I could now read very well, and the continual habit of listening to the conversation of my father and my uncle made me a little woman in understanding; so that my father said to him, 'James, you have made my child quite a companionable little being.'

My father often left me alone with my uncle; sometimes to write his sermons; sometimes to visit the sick, or give counsel to his poor neighbours; then my uncle used to hold long conversations with me, telling me how I should strive to make my father happy, and endeavour to improve myself when he was gone:—now I began justly to understand why he had taken such pains to keep my father from visiting my mother's grave, that grave which I often stole privately to look at, but now never without awe and reverence; for my uncle used to tell me what an excellent lady my mother was, and I now thought of her as having been a real mamma, which before seemed an ideal something, no way connected with life. And he told me that the ladies from the Manor-House, who sate in the best pew in the church, were not so graceful, and the best women in the village were not so good, as was my sweet mamma; and that if she had lived, I should not have been forced to pick up a little knowledge from him, a rough sailor, or to learn to knit and sew of Susan, but that she would have taught me all lady-like fine works, and delicate behaviour and perfect manners, and would have selected for me proper books, such as were most fit to instruct my mind, and of which he nothing knew. If ever in my life I shall have any proper sense of what is excellent or becoming in the womanly character, I owe it to these lessons of my rough unpolished uncle; for, in telling me what my mother would have made me, he taught me what to wish to be; and when, soon after my uncle left us, I was introduced to the ladies at the Manor-House, instead of hanging down my head with shame, as I should have done before my uncle came, like a little village rustic, I tried to speak distinctly, with ease, and a modest gentleness, as my uncle had said my mother used to do; instead of hanging down my head abashed, I looked upon them, and thought what a pretty sight a fine lady was, and thought how well my mother must have appeared, since she was so much more graceful than these ladies were; and when I heard them compliment my father on the admirable behaviour of his child, and say how well he had brought me up, I thought to myself, 'Papa does not much mind my manners, if I am but a good girl; but it was my uncle that taught me to behave like mamma.'—I cannot now think my uncle was so rough and unpolished as he said he was, for his lessons were so good and so impressive that I shall never forget them, and I hope they will be of use to me as long as I live: he would explain to me the meaning of all the words he used, such as grace and elegance, modest diffidence and affectation, pointing out instances of what he meant by those words, in the manners of the ladies and their young daughters who came to our church; for, besides the ladies of the Manor-House, many of the neighbouring families came to our church because my father preached so well.

It must have been early in the spring when my uncle went away, for the crocuses were just blown in the garden, and the primroses had begun to peep from under the young budding hedge-rows. I cried as if my heart would break, when I had the last sight of him through a little opening among the trees, as he went down the road. My father accompanied him to the market-town, from whence he was to proceed in the stage-coach to London. How tedious I thought all Susan's endeavours to comfort me were. The stile where I first saw my uncle came into my mind, and I thought I would go and sit there, and think about that day; but I was no sooner seated there, than I remembered how I had frightened him by taking him so foolishly to my mother's grave, and then again how naughty I had been when I sate muttering to myself at this same stile, wishing that he, who had gone so far to buy me books, might never come back any more: all my little quarrels with my uncle came into my mind, now that I could never play with him again, and it almost broke my heart. I was forced to run into the house to Susan for that consolation I had just before despised.

Some days after this, as I was sitting by the fire with my father, after it was dark, and before the candles were lighted, I gave him an account of my troubled conscience at the church-stile, where I remembered how unkind I had been to my uncle when he first came, and how sorry I still was whenever I thought of the many quarrels I had had with him.

My father smiled and took hold of my hand, saying, 'I will tell you all about this, my little penitent. This is the sort of way in which we all feel, when those we love are taken from us.—When our dear friends are with us, we go on enjoying their society, without much thought or consideration of the blessings we are possessed of, nor do we too nicely weigh the measure of our daily actions;—we let them freely share our kind or our discontented moods; and, if any little bickerings disturb our friendship, it does but the more endear us to each other when we are in a happier temper. But these things come over us like grievous faults when the object of our affection is gone for ever. Your dear mamma and I had no quarrels; yet in the first days of my lonely sorrow, how many things came into my mind that I might have done to have made her happier. It is so with you, my child. You did all a child could do to please your uncle, and dearly did he love you; and these little things which now disturb your tender mind, were remembered with delight by your uncle. He was telling me in our last walk, just perhaps as you were thinking about it with sorrow, of the difficulty he had in getting into your good graces when he first came; he will think of these things with pleasure when he is far away. Put away from you this unfounded grief; only let it be a lesson to you to be as kind as possible to those you love; and remember, when they are gone from you, you will never think you had been kind enough. Such feelings as you have now described are the lot of humanity. So you will feel when I am no more; and so will your children feel when you are dead. But your uncle will come back again, Betsy, and we will now think of where we are to get the cage to keep the talking parrot in, he is to bring home; and go and tell Susan to bring the candles, and ask her if the nice cake is almost baked, that she promised to give us for our tea.'

CHARLES LAMB

1775—1834

FIRST GOING TO CHURCH

(From *Mrs. Leicester's School: or, The History of Several Young Ladies related by themselves.*)

I WAS born and brought up, in a house in which my parents had all their lives resided, which stood in the midst of that lonely tract of land called the Lincolnshire fens. Few families besides our own lived near the spot, both because it was reckoned an unwholesome air, and because its distance from any town or market made it an inconvenient situation. My father was in no very affluent circumstances, and it was a sad necessity which he was put to, of having to go many miles to fetch anything he wanted from the nearest village, which was full seven miles distant, through a sad miry way that at all times made it heavy walking, and after rain was almost impassable. But he had no horse or carriage of his own.

The church which belonged to the parish in which our house was situated, stood in this village; and its distance being, as I said before, seven miles from our house, made it quite an impossible thing for my mother or me to think of going to it. Sometimes, indeed, on a fine dry Sunday, my father would rise early, and take a walk to the village, just to see how *goodness thrived*, as he used to say; but he would generally return tired, and the worse for his walk. It is scarcely possible to explain to any one who has not lived in the fens, what difficult and dangerous walking it is. A mile is as good as four, I have heard my father say, in those parts. My mother, who in the early part of her life had lived in a more civilized spot, and had been used to constant church-going, would often lament her situation. It was from her I early imbibed a great curiosity and anxiety to see that thing, which I had heard her call a church, and so often lament that she could never go to. I had seen houses of various structures, and had seen in pictures the shapes of ships and boats, and palaces and temples, but never rightly anything that could be called a church, or that could satisfy me about its form. Sometimes I thought it must be like our house, and sometimes I fancied it must be more like the house of our neighbour, Mr. Sutton, which was bigger and handsomer than ours. Sometimes I thought it was a great hollow cave, such as I have heard my father say the first inhabitants of the earth dwelt in. Then I thought it was like a waggon, or a cart, and that it must be something moveable. The shape of it ran in my mind strangely, and one day I ventured to ask my mother, what was that foolish thing that she was always longing to go to, and which she called a church. Was it anything to eat or drink, or was it only like a great huge plaything, to be seen and stared at?—I was not quite five years of age when I made this inquiry.

This question, so oddly put, made my mother smile; but in a little time she put on a more grave look, and informed me, that a church was nothing that I had supposed it, but it was a great building, far greater than any house which I had seen, where men, and women, and children, came together, twice a day, on Sundays, to hear the Bible read, and make good resolutions for the week to come. She told me, that the fine music which we sometimes heard in the air, came from the bells of St. Mary's church, and that we never heard it but when the wind was in a particular point. This raised my wonder more than all the rest; for I had somehow conceived that the noise which I heard was occasioned by birds up in the air, or that it was made by the angels, whom (so ignorant I was till that time) I had always considered to be a sort of birds: for before this time I was totally ignorant of anything like religion, it being a principle of my father, that young heads should not be told too many things at once, for fear they should get confused ideas, and no clear notions of anything. We had always indeed so far observed Sundays, that no work was done upon that day, and upon that day I wore my best muslin frock, and was not allowed to sing, or to be noisy; but I never understood why that day should differ from any other. We had no public meetings:—indeed, the few straggling houses which were near us, would have furnished but a slender congregation; and the loneliness of the place we lived in, instead of making us more sociable, and drawing us closer together, as my mother used to say it ought to have done, seemed to have the effect of making us more distant and averse to society than other people. One or two good neighbours indeed we had, but not in numbers to give me an idea of church attendance.

But now my mother thought it high time to give me some clearer instruction in the main points of religion, and my father came readily in to her plan. I was now permitted to sit up half an hour later on a Sunday evening, that I might hear a portion of Scripture read, which had always been their custom, though by reason of my tender age, and my father's opinion on the impropriety of children being taught too young, I had never till now been an auditor. I was taught my prayers, and those things which you, ladies, I doubt not, had the benefit of being instructed in at a much earlier age.

The clearer my notions on these points became, they only made me more passionately long for the privilege of joining in that social service, from which it seemed that we alone, of all the inhabitants of the land, were debarred; and when the wind was in that point which favoured the sound of the distant bells of St. Mary's to be heard over the great moor which skirted our house, I have stood out in the air to catch the sounds which I almost devoured; and the tears have come in my eyes, when sometimes they seemed to speak to me almost in articulate sounds, to *come to church*, and because of the great moor which was between me and them I could not come; and the too tender apprehensions of these things have filled me with a religious melancholy. With thoughts like these I entered into my seventh year.

And now the time has come, when the great moor was no longer to separate me from the object of my wishes and of my curiosity. My father having some money left him by the will of a deceased relation, we ventured to set up a sort of a carriage—no very superb one, I assure you, ladies; but in that part of the world it was looked upon with some envy by our poorer neighbours. The first party of pleasure which my father proposed to take in it, was to the village where I had so often wished to go, and my mother and I were to accompany him; for it was very fit, my father observed, that little Susan should go to church, and learn how to behave herself, for we might some time or other have occasion to live in London, and not always be confined to that out of the way spot.

It was on a Sunday morning that we set out, my little heart beating with almost breathless expectation. The day was fine, and the roads as good as they ever are in those parts. I was so happy and so proud. I was lost in dreams of what I was going to see. At length the tall steeple of St. Mary's church came in view. It was pointed out to me by my father, as the place from which that music had come which I had heard over the moor, and had fancied to be angels singing. I was wound up to the highest pitch of delight at having visibly presented to me the spot from which had proceeded that unknown friendly music; and when it began to peal, just as we approached the village, it seemed to speak, *Susan is come*, as plainly as it used to invite me *to come*, when I heard it over the moor. I pass over our alighting at the house of a relation, and all that passed till I went with my father and mother to church.

St. Mary's church is a great church for such a small village as it stands in. My father said it was a cathedral, and that it had once belonged to a monastery, but the monks were all gone. Over the door there was stone work, representing saints and bishops, and here and there, along the sides of the church, there were figures of men's heads, made in a strange, grotesque way: I have since seen the same sort of figures in the round tower of the Temple church in London. My father said they were very improper ornaments for such a place, and so I now think them; but it seems the people who built these great churches in old times, gave themselves more liberties than they do now; and I remember that when I first saw them, and before my father had made this observation, though they were so ugly and out of shape, and some of them seemed to be grinning and distorting their features with pain or with laughter, yet being placed upon a church, to which I had come with such serious thoughts, I could not help thinking they had some serious meaning; and I looked at them with wonder, but without any temptation to laugh. I somehow fancied they were the representation of wicked people set up as a warning.

When we got into the church, the service was not begun, and my father kindly took me round, to show me the monuments and everything else remarkable. I remember seeing one of a venerable figure, which my father said had been a judge. The figure was kneeling as if it was alive, before a sort of desk, with a book, I suppose the Bible, lying on it. I somehow fancied the figure had a sort of life in it, it seemed so natural, or that the dead judge that it was done for, said his prayers at it still. This was a silly notion, but I was very young, and had passed my little life in a remote place, where I had never seen anything nor knew anything; and the awe which I felt at first being in a church, took from me all power but that of wondering. I did not reason about anything, I was too young. Now I understand why monuments are put up for the dead, and why the figures which are upon them, are described as doing the actions which they did in their life-times, and that they are a sort of pictures set up for our instruction. But all was new and surprising to me on that day; the long windows with little panes, the pillars, the pews made of oak, the little hassocks for the people to kneel on, the form of the pulpit with the sounding-board over it, gracefully carved in flower work. To you, who have lived all your lives in populous places, and have been taken to church from the earliest time you can remember, my admiration of these things must appear strangely ignorant. But I was a lonely young creature, that had been brought up in remote places, where there was neither church nor church-going inhabitants. I have since lived in great towns, and seen the ways of churches and of worship, and I am old enough now to distinguish between what is essential in religion, and what is merely formal or ornamental.

When my father had done pointing out to me the things most worthy of notice about the church, the service was almost ready to begin; the parishioners had most of them entered, and taken their seats; and we were shown into a pew where my mother was already seated. Soon after the clergyman entered, and the organ began to play what is called the voluntary. I had never seen so many people assembled before. At first I thought that all eyes were upon me, and that because I was a stranger. I was terribly ashamed and confused at first; but my mother helped me to find out the places in the Prayer-book, and being busy about that, took off some of my painful apprehensions. I was no stranger to the order of the service, having often read in a Prayer-book at home; but my thoughts being confused, it puzzled me a little to find out the responses and other things, which I thought I knew so well; but I went through it tolerably well. One thing which has often troubled me since, is, that I am afraid I was too full of myself, and of thinking how happy I was, and what a privilege it was for one that was so young to join in the service with so many grown people, so that I did not attend enough to the instruction which I might have received. I remember, I foolishly applied everything that was said to myself, so as it could mean nobody but myself, I was so full of my own thoughts. All that assembly of people seemed to me as if they were come together only to show me the way of a church. Not but I received some very affecting impressions from some things which I heard that day; but the standing up and the sitting down of the people; the organ; the singing;—the way of all these things took up more of my attention than was proper; or I thought it did. I believe I behaved better and was more serious when I went a second time, and a third time; for now we went as a regular thing every Sunday, and continued to do so, till, by a still further change for the better in my father's circumstances, we removed to London. Oh! it was a happy day for me my first going to St. Mary's church: before that day I used to feel like a little outcast in the wilderness, like one that did not belong to the world of Christian people. I have never felt like a little outcast since. But I never can hear the sweet noise of bells, that I don't think of the angels singing, and what poor but pretty thoughts I had of angels in my uninstructed solitude.

NATHANIEL HAWTHORNE

1804—1864

THE MAYPOLE OF MERRY MOUNT

There is an admirable foundation for a philosophic romance, in the curious history of the early settlement of Mount Wollaston, or Merry Mount. In the slight sketch here attempted, the facts, recorded on the grave pages of our New England annalists, have wrought themselves, almost spontaneously, into a sort of allegory. The masques, mummeries, and festive customs, described in the text, are in accordance with the manners of the age. Authority on these points may be found in Strutt's Book of English Sports and Pastimes.

BRIGHT were the days at Merry Mount, when the Maypole was the banner-staff of that gay colony! They who reared it, should their banner be triumphant, were to pour sunshine over New England's rugged hills, and scatter flower-seeds throughout the soil. Jollity and gloom were contending for an empire. Midsummer eve had come, bringing deep verdure to the forest, and roses in her lap, of a more vivid hue than the tender buds of Spring. But May, or her mirthful spirit, dwelt all the year round at Merry Mount, sporting with the Summer months, and revelling with Autumn, and basking in the glow of Winter's fireside. Through a world of toil and care she flitted with a dreamlike smile, and came hither to find a home among the lightsome hearts of Merry Mount.

Never had the Maypole been so gaily decked as at sunset on Midsummer eve. This venerated emblem was a pine-tree, which had preserved the slender grace of youth, while it equalled the loftiest height of the old wood monarchs. From its top streamed a silken banner, coloured like the rainbow. Down nearly to the ground the pole was dressed with birchen boughs, and others of the liveliest green, and some with silvery leaves, fastened by ribands that fluttered in fantastic knots of twenty different colours, but no sad ones. Garden flowers, and blossoms of the wilderness, laughed gladly forth amid the verdure, so fresh and dewy, that they must have grown by magic on that happy pine-tree. Where this green and flowery splendour terminated, the shaft of the Maypole was stained with the seven brilliant hues of the banner at its top. On the lowest green bough hung an abundant wreath of roses, some that had been gathered in the sunniest spots of the forest, and others, of still richer blush, which the colonists had reared from English seed. O people of the Golden Age, the chief of your husbandry was to raise flowers!

But what was the wild throng that stood hand in hand about the Maypole? It could not be, that the fauns and nymphs, when driven from their classic groves and homes of ancient fable, had sought refuge, as all the persecuted did, in the fresh woods of the West. These were Gothic monsters, though perhaps of Grecian ancestry. On the shoulders of a comely youth, uprose the head and branching antlers of a stag; a second, human in all other points, had the grim visage of a wolf; a third, still with the trunk and limbs of a mortal man, showed the beard and horns of a venerable he-goat. There was the likeness of a bear erect, brute in all but his hind legs, which were adorned with pink silk stockings. And here again, almost as wondrous, stood a real bear of the dark forest, lending each of his fore-paws to the grasp of a human hand, and as ready for the dance as any in that circle. His inferior nature rose halfway to meet his companions as they stooped. Other faces wore the similitude of man or woman, but distorted or extravagant, with red noses pendulous before their mouths, which seemed of awful depth, and stretched from ear to ear in an eternal fit of laughter. Here might be seen the Salvage Man, well known in heraldry, hairy as a baboon, and girdled with green leaves. By his side, a nobler figure, but still a counterfeit, appeared an Indian hunter, with feathery crest and wampum belt. Many of this strange company wore fools-caps, and had little bells appended to their garments, tinkling with a silvery sound, responsive to the inaudible music of their gleesome spirits. Some youths and maidens were of soberer garb, yet well maintained their places in the irregular throng, by the expression of wild revelry upon their features. Such were the colonists of Merry Mount, as they stood in the broad smile of sunset, round their venerated Maypole.

Had a wanderer, bewildered in the melancholy forest, heard their mirth, and stolen a half-affrighted glance, he might have fancied them the crew of Comus, some already transformed to brutes, some midway between man and beast, and the others rioting in the flow of tipsy jollity that foreran the change. But a band of Puritans, who watched the scene, invisible themselves, compared the masques to those devils and ruined souls with whom their superstition peopled the black wilderness.

Within the ring of monsters, appeared the two airiest forms that had ever trodden on any more solid footing than a purple and golden cloud. One was a youth in glistening apparel, with a scarf of the rainbow pattern crosswise on his breast. His right hand held a gilded staff, the ensign of high dignity among the revellers, and his left grasped the slender fingers of a fair maiden, not less gaily decorated than himself. Bright roses glowed in contrast with the dark and glossy curls of each, and were scattered round their feet, or had sprung up spontaneously there. Behind this lightsome couple, so close to the Maypole that its boughs shaded his jovial face, stood the figure of an English priest, canonically dressed, yet decked with flowers, in heathen fashion, and wearing a chaplet of the native vine leaves. By the riot of his rolling eye, and the pagan decorations of his holy garb, he seemed the wildest monster there, and the very Comus of the crew.

'Votaries of the Maypole,' cried the flower-decked priest, 'merrily, all day long, have the woods echoed to your mirth. But be this your merriest hour, my hearts! Lo, here stand the Lord and Lady of the May, whom I, a clerk of Oxford, and high priest of Merry Mount, am presently to join in holy matrimony. Up with your nimble spirits, ye morris-dancers, green men, and glee-maidens, bears and wolves, and horned gentlemen! Come; a chorus now, rich with the old mirth of Merry England, and the wilder glee of this fresh forest; and then a dance, to show the youthful pair what life is made of, and how airily they should go through it! All ye that love the Maypole, lend your voices to the nuptial song of the Lord and Lady of the May!'

This wedlock was more serious than most affairs of Merry Mount, where jest and delusion, trick and fantasy, kept up a continual carnival. The Lord and Lady of the May, though their titles must be laid down at sunset, were really and truly to be partners for the dance of life, beginning the measure that same bright eve. The wreath of roses, that hung from the lowest green bough of the Maypole, had been twined for them, and would be thrown over both their heads, in symbol of their flowery union. When the priest had spoken, therefore, a riotous uproar burst from the rout of monstrous figures.

'Begin you the stave, reverend Sir,' cried they all; 'and never did the woods ring to such a merry peal as we of the Maypole shall send up!'

Immediately a prelude of pipe, cithern, and viol, touched with practised minstrelsy, began to play from a neighbouring thicket, in such a mirthful cadence, that the boughs of the Maypole quivered to the sound. But the May Lord, he of the gilded staff, chancing to look into his Lady's eyes, was wonder-struck at the almost pensive glance that met his own.

'Edith, sweet Lady of the May,' whispered he, reproachfully, 'is yon wreath of roses a garland to hang above our graves, that you look so sad? Oh, Edith, this is our golden time! Tarnish it not by any pensive shadow of the mind; for it may be, that nothing of futurity will be brighter than the mere remembrance of what is now passing.'

'That was the very thought that saddened me! How came it in your mind too?' said Edith, in a still lower tone than he; for it was high treason to be sad at Merry Mount. 'Therefore do I sigh amid this festive music. And besides, dear Edgar, I struggle as with a dream, and fancy that these shapes of our jovial friends are visionary, and their mirth unreal, and that we are no true Lord and Lady of the May. What is the mystery in my heart?'

Just then, as if a spell had loosened them, down came a shower of withering rose leaves from the Maypole. Alas for the young lovers! No sooner had their hearts glowed with real passion, than they were sensible of something vague and unsubstantial in their former pleasures, and felt a dreary presentiment of inevitable change. From the moment that they truly loved, they had subjected themselves to earth's doom of care and sorrow, and troubled joy, and had no more a home at Merry Mount. That was Edith's mystery. Now leave we the priest to marry them, and the masquers to sport round the Maypole, till the last sunbeam be withdrawn from its summit, and the shadows of the forest mingle gloomily in the dance. Meanwhile, we may discover who these gay people were.

Two hundred years ago, and more, the old world and its inhabitants became mutually weary of each other. Men voyaged by thousands to the West; some to barter glass beads, and such like jewels, for the furs of the Indian hunter; some to conquer virgin empires; and one stern band to pray. But none of these motives had much weight with the colonists of Merry Mount. Their leaders were men who had sported so long with life, that when Thought and Wisdom came, even these unwelcome guests were led astray by the crowd of vanities which they should have put to flight. Erring Thought and perverted Wisdom were made to put on masques, and play the fool. The men of whom we speak, after losing the heart's fresh gaiety, imagined a wild philosophy of pleasure, and came hither to act out their latest day-dream. They gathered followers from all that giddy tribe, whose whole life is like the festal days of soberer men. In their train were minstrels, not unknown in London streets; wandering players, whose theatres had been the halls of noblemen; mummers, rope-dancers, and mountebanks, who would long be missed at wakes, church ales, and fairs; in a word, mirth-makers of every sort, such as abounded in that age, but now began to be discountenanced by the rapid growth of Puritanism. Light had their footsteps been on land, and as lightly they came across the sea. Many had been maddened by their previous troubles into a gay despair; others were as madly gay in the flush of youth, like the May Lord and his Lady; but whatever might be the quality of their mirth, old and young were gay at Merry Mount. The young deemed themselves happy. The elder spirits, if they knew that mirth was but the counterfeit of happiness, yet followed the false shadow wilfully, because at least her garments glittered brightest. Sworn triflers of a lifetime, they would not venture among the sober truths of life, not even to be truly blest.

All the hereditary pastimes of Old England were transplanted hither. The King of Christmas was duly crowned, and the Lord of Misrule bore potent sway. On the eve of Saint John, they felled whole acres of the forest to make bonfires, and danced by the blaze all night, crowned with garlands, and throwing flowers into the flame. At harvest-time, though their crop was of the smallest, they made an image with the sheaves of Indian corn, and wreathed it with autumnal garlands, and bore it home triumphantly. But what chiefly characterized the colonists of Merry Mount, was their veneration for the Maypole. It has made their true history a poet's tale. Spring decked the hallowed emblem with young blossoms and fresh green boughs; Summer brought roses of the deepest blush, and the perfected foliage of the forest; Autumn enriched it with that red and yellow gorgeousness, which converts each wildwood leaf into a painted flower; and Winter silvered it with sleet, and hung it round with icicles, till it flashed in the cold sunshine, itself a frozen sunbeam. Thus each alternate season did homage to the Maypole, and paid it a tribute of its own richest splendour. Its votaries danced round it, once, at least, in every month; sometimes they called it their religion, or their altar; but always, it was the banner-staff of Merry Mount.

Unfortunately, there were men in the new world, of a sterner faith than these Maypole worshippers. Not far from Merry Mount was a settlement of Puritans, most dismal wretches, who said their prayers before daylight, and then wrought in the forest or the cornfield, till evening made it prayer-time again. Their weapons were always at hand to shoot down the straggling savage. When they met in conclave, it was never to keep up the old English mirth, but to hear sermons three hours long, or to proclaim bounties on the heads of wolves and the scalps of Indians. Their festivals were fast-days, and their chief pastime the singing of psalms. Woe to the youth or maiden who did but dream of a dance! The selectman nodded to the constable; and there sat the light-heeled reprobate in the stocks; or if he danced, it was round the whipping-post, which might be termed the Puritan Maypole.

A party of these grim Puritans, toiling through the difficult woods, each with a horseload of iron armour to burden his footsteps, would sometimes draw near the sunny precincts of Merry Mount. There were the silken colonists, sporting round their Maypole; perhaps teaching a bear to dance, or striving to communicate their mirth to the grave Indian; or masquerading in the skins of deer and wolves, which they had hunted for that especial purpose. Often, the whole colony were playing at blindman's buff, magistrates and all with their eyes bandaged, except a single scape-goat, whom the blinded sinners pursued by the tinkling of the bells at his garments. Once, it is said, they were seen following a flower-decked corpse, with merriment and festive music, to his grave. But did the dead man laugh? In their quietest times, they sang ballads and told tales, for the edification of their pious visitors; or perplexed them with juggling tricks; or grinned at them through horse-collars; and when sport itself grew wearisome, they made game of their own stupidity, and began a yawning match. At the very least of these enormities, the men of iron shook their heads and frowned so darkly, that the revellers looked up, imagining that a momentary cloud had overcast the sunshine, which was to be perpetual there. On the other hand, the Puritans affirmed, that, when a psalm was pealing from their place of worship, the echo which the forest sent them back seemed often like the chorus of a jolly catch, closing with a roar of laughter. Who but the fiend, and his bond-slaves, the crew of Merry Mount, had thus disturbed them? In due time, a feud arose, stern and bitter on one side, and as serious on the other as anything could be among such light spirits as had sworn allegiance to the Maypole. The future complexion of New England was involved in this important quarrel. Should the grizzly saints establish their jurisdiction over the gay sinners, then would their spirits darken all the clime, and make it a land of clouded visages, of hard toil, of sermon and psalm for ever. But should the banner-staff of Merry Mount be fortunate, sunshine would break upon the hills, and flowers would beautify the forest, and late posterity do homage to the Maypole.

After these authentic passages from history, we return to the nuptials of the Lord and Lady of the May. Alas! we have delayed too long, and must darken our tale too suddenly. As we glance again at the Maypole, a solitary sunbeam is fading from the summit, and leaves only a faint, golden tinge, blended with the hues of the rainbow banner. Even that dim light is now withdrawn, relinquishing the whole domain of Merry Mount to the evening gloom, which has rushed so instantaneously from the black surrounding woods. But some of these black shadows have rushed forth in human shape.

Yes, with the setting sun, the last day of mirth had passed from Merry Mount. The ring of gay masquers was disordered and broken; the stag lowered his antlers in dismay; the wolf grew weaker than a lamb; the bells of the morris-dancers tinkled with tremulous affright. The Puritans had played a characteristic part in the Maypole mummeries. Their darksome figures were intermixed with the wild shapes of their foes, and made the scene a picture of the moment, when waking thoughts start up amid the scattered fantasies of a dream. The leader of the hostile party stood in the centre of the circle, while the rout of monsters cowered around him, like evil spirits in the presence of a dread magician. No fantastic foolery could look him in the face. So stern was the energy of his aspect, that the whole man, visage, frame, and soul, seemed wrought of iron, gifted with life and thought, yet all of one substance with his headpiece and breastplate. It was the Puritan of Puritans; it was Endicott himself!

'Stand off, priest of Baal!' said he, with a grim frown, and laying no reverent hand upon the surplice. 'I know thee, Blackstone! Thou art the man, who couldst not abide the rule even of thine own corrupted church, and hast come hither to preach iniquity, and to give example of it in thy life. But now shall it be seen that the Lord hath sanctified this wilderness for his peculiar people. Woe unto them that would defile it! And first, for this flower-decked abomination, the altar of thy worship!'

And with his keen sword Endicott assaulted the hallowed Maypole. Nor long did it resist his arm. It groaned with a dismal sound; it showered leaves and rosebuds upon the remorseless enthusiast; and finally, with all its green boughs, and ribands, and flowers, symbolic of departed pleasures, down fell the banner-staff of Merry Mount. As it sank, tradition says, the evening sky grew darker, and the woods threw forth a more sombre shadow.

'There,' cried Endicott, looking triumphantly on his work, 'there lies the only Maypole in New England! The thought is strong within me, that, by its fall, is shadowed forth the fate of light and idle mirth-makers, amongst us and our posterity. Amen, saith John Endicott.'

'Amen!' echoed his followers.

But the votaries of the Maypole gave one groan for their idol. At the sound, the Puritan leader glanced at the crew of Comus, each a figure of broad mirth, yet, at this moment, strangely expressive of sorrow and dismay.

'Valiant captain,' quoth Peter Palfrey, the Ancient of the band, 'what order shall be taken with the prisoners?'

'I thought not to repent me of cutting down a Maypole,' replied Endicott, 'yet now I could find in my heart to plant it again, and give each of these bestial pagans one other dance round their idol. It would have served rarely for a whipping-post!'

'But there are pine-trees enow,' suggested the lieutenant.

'True, good Ancient,' said the leader. 'Wherefore, bind the heathen crew, and bestow on them a small matter of stripes apiece, as earnest of our future justice. Set some of the rogues in the stocks to rest themselves, so soon as Providence shall bring us to one of our own well-ordered settlements, where such accommodations may be found. Further penalties, such as branding and cropping of ears, shall be thought of hereafter.'

'How many stripes for the priest?' inquired Ancient Palfrey.

'None as yet,' answered Endicott, bending his iron frown upon the culprit. 'It must be for the Great and General Court to determine, whether stripes and long imprisonment, and other grievous penalty, may atone for his transgressions. Let him look to himself! For such as violate our civil order, it may be permitted us to show mercy. But woe to the wretch that troubleth our religion!'

'And this dancing bear,' resumed the officer. 'Must he share the stripes of his fellows?'

'Shoot him through the head!' said the energetic Puritan. 'I suspect witchcraft in the beast.'

'Here be a couple of shining ones,' continued Peter Palfrey, pointing his weapon at the Lord and Lady of the May. 'They seem to be of high station among these misdoers. Methinks their dignity will not be fitted with less than a double share of stripes.'

Endicott rested on his sword, and closely surveyed the dress and aspect of the hapless pair. There they stood, pale, downcast, and apprehensive. Yet there was an air of mutual support, and of pure affection, seeking aid and giving it, that showed them to be man and wife, with the sanction of a priest upon their love. The youth, in the peril of the moment, had dropped his gilded staff, and thrown his arm about the Lady of the May, who leaned against his breast, too lightly to burden him, but with weight enough to express that their destinies were linked together, for good or evil. They looked first at each other, and then into the grim captain's face. There they stood, in the first hour of wedlock, while the idle pleasures, of which their companions were the emblems, had given place to the sternest cares of life, personified by the dark Puritans. But never had their youthful beauty seemed so pure and high, as when its glow was chastened by adversity.

'Youth,' said Endicott, 'ye stand in an evil case, thou and thy maiden wife. Make ready presently; for I am minded that ye shall both have a token to remember your wedding-day!'

'Stern man,' cried the May Lord, 'how can I move thee? Were the means at hand, I would resist to the death. Being powerless, I entreat! Do with me as thou wilt, but let Edith go untouched!'

'Not so,' replied the immitigable zealot. 'We are not wont to show an idle courtesy to that sex, which requireth the stricter discipline. What sayest thou, maid? Shall thy silken bridegroom suffer thy share of the penalty, besides his own?'

'Be it death,' said Edith, 'and lay it all on me!'

Truly, as Endicott had said, the poor lovers stood in a woeful case. Their foes were triumphant, their friends captive and abased, their home desolate, the benighted wilderness around them, and a rigorous destiny, in the shape of the Puritan leader, their only guide. Yet the deepening twilight could not altogether conceal that the iron man was softened; he smiled at the fair spectacle of early love; he almost sighed for the inevitable blight of early hopes.

'The troubles of life have come hastily on this young

couple,' observed Endicott. 'We will see how they comport themselves under their present trials, ere we burden them with greater. If, among the spoil, there be any garments of a more decent fashion, let them be put upon this May Lord and his Lady, instead of their glistening vanities. Look to it, some of you.'

'And shall not the youth's hair be cut?' asked Peter Palfrey, looking with abhorrence at the love-lock and long glossy curls of the young man.

'Crop it forthwith, and that in the true pumpkin-shell fashion,' answered the captain. 'Then bring them along with us, but more gently than their fellows. There be qualities in the youth, which may make him valiant to fight, and sober to toil, and pious to pray; and in the maiden, that may fit her to become a mother in our Israel, bringing up babes in better nurture than her own hath been. Nor think ye, young ones, that they are the happiest, even in our lifetime of a moment, who misspend it in dancing round a Maypole!'

And Endicott, the severest Puritan of all who laid the rock foundation of New England, lifted the wreath of roses from the ruin of the Maypole, and threw it, with his own gauntleted hand, over the heads of the Lord and Lady of the May. It was a deed of prophecy. As the moral gloom of the world overpowers all systematic gaiety, even so was their home of wild mirth made desolate amid the sad forest. They returned to it no more. But, as their flowery garland was wreathed of the brightest roses that had grown there, so, in the tie that united them, were intertwined all the purest and best of their early joys. They went heavenward, supporting each other along the difficult path which it was their lot to tread, and never wasted one regretful thought on the vanities of Merry Mount.

THE GREY CHAMPION

THERE was once a time when New England groaned under the actual pressure of heavier wrongs than those threatened ones which brought on the Revolution. James II, the bigoted successor of Charles the Voluptuous, had annulled the charters of all the colonies, and sent a harsh and unprincipled soldier to take away our liberties and endanger our religion. The administration of Sir Edmund Andros lacked scarcely a single characteristic of tyranny: a Governor and Council, holding office from the King, and wholly independent of the country; laws made and taxes levied without concurrence of the people, immediate or by their representatives; the rights of private citizens violated, and the titles of all landed property declared void; the voice of complaint stifled by restrictions on the press; and, finally, disaffection overawed by the first band of mercenary troops that ever marched on our free soil. For two years our ancestors were kept in sullen submission, by that filial love which had invariably secured their allegiance to the mother country, whether its head chanced to be a Parliament, Protector, or Popish Monarch. Till these evil times, however, such allegiance had been merely nominal, and the colonists had ruled themselves, enjoying far more freedom than is even yet the privilege of the native subjects of Great Britain.

At length, a rumour reached our shores that the Prince of Orange had ventured on an enterprise, the success of which would be the triumph of civil and religious rights and the salvation of New England. It was but a doubtful whisper; it might be false, or the attempt might fail; and, in either case, the man that stirred against King James would lose his head. Still the intelligence produced a marked effect. The people smiled mysteriously in the streets, and threw bold glances at their oppressors; while, far and wide, there was a subdued and silent agitation, as if the slightest signal would rouse the whole land from its sluggish despondency. Aware of their danger, the rulers resolved to avert it by an imposing display of strength, and perhaps to confirm their despotism by yet harsher measures. One afternoon in April, 1689, Sir Edmund Andros and his favourite councillors, being warm with wine, assembled the red-coats of the Governor's Guard, and made their appearance in the streets of Boston. The sun was near setting when the march commenced.

The roll of the drum, at that unquiet crisis, seemed to go through the streets, less as the martial music of the soldiers, than as a muster call to the inhabitants themselves. A multitude, by various avenues, assembled in King Street, which was destined to be the scene, nearly a century afterwards, of another encounter between the troops of Britain and a people struggling against her tyranny. Though more than sixty years had elapsed since the Pilgrims came, this crowd of their descendants still showed the strong and sombre features of their character, perhaps more strikingly in such a stern emergency than on happier occasions. There were the sober garb, the general severity of mien, the gloomy but undismayed expression, the scriptural forms of speech, and the confidence in Heaven's blessing on a righteous cause, which would have marked a band of the original Puritans, when threatened by some peril of the wilderness. Indeed, it was not yet time for the old spirit to be extinct; since there were men in the street, that day, who had worshipped there beneath the trees, before a house was reared to the God for whom they had become exiles. Old soldiers of the Parliament were here, too, smiling grimly at the thought, that their aged arms might strike another blow against the house of Stuart. Here, also, were the veterans of King Philip's war, who had burned villages and slaughtered young and old, with pious fierceness, while the godly souls throughout the land were helping them with prayer. Several ministers were scattered among the crowd, which, unlike all other mobs, regarded them with such reverence, as if there were sanctity in their very garments. These holy men exerted their influence to quiet the people, but not to disperse them. Meantime, the purpose of the Governor, in disturbing the peace of the town, at a period when the slightest commotion might throw the country into a ferment, was almost the universal subject of inquiry, and variously explained.

'Satan will strike his master-stroke presently,' cried some, 'because he knoweth that his time is short. All our godly pastors are to be dragged to prison! We shall see them at a Smithfield fire in King Street!'

Hereupon the people of each parish gathered closer round their minister, who looked calmly upwards and assumed a more apostolic dignity, as well befitted a candidate for the highest honour of his profession, the crown of martyrdom. It was actually fancied, at that period, that New England might have a John Rogers of her own, to take the place of that worthy in the Primer.

'The Pope of Rome has given orders for a new St. Bartholomew!' cried others. 'We are to be massacred, man and male child!'

Neither was this rumour wholly discredited, although the wiser class believed the Governor's object somewhat less atrocious. His predecessor under the old charter, Bradstreet, a venerable companion of the first settlers, was known to be in town. There were grounds for conjecturing that Sir Edmund Andros intended, at once, to strike terror, by a parade of military force, and to confound the opposite faction, by possessing himself of their chief.

'Stand firm for the old charter, Governor!' shouted

the crowd, seizing upon the idea. 'The good old Governor Bradstreet!'

While this cry was at the loudest, the people were surprised by the well-known figure of Governor Bradstreet himself, a patriarch of nearly ninety, who appeared on the elevated steps of a door, and, with characteristic mildness, besought them to submit to the constituted authorities.

'My children,' concluded this venerable person, 'do nothing rashly. Cry not aloud, but pray for the welfare of New England, and expect patiently what the Lord will do in this matter!'

The event was soon to be decided. All this time, the roll of the drum had been approaching through Cornhill, louder and deeper, till with reverberations from house to house, and the regular tramp of martial footsteps, it burst into the street. A double rank of soldiers made their appearance, occupying the whole breadth of the passage, with shouldered matchlocks, and matches burning, so as to present a row of fires in the dusk. Their steady march was like the progress of a machine, that would roll irresistibly over everything in its way. Next, moving slowly, with a confused clatter of hoofs on the pavement, rode a party of mounted gentlemen, the central figure being Sir Edmund Andros, elderly, but erect and soldier-like. Those around him were his favourite councillors, and the bitterest foes of New England. At his right hand rode Edward Randolph, our arch-enemy, that 'blasted wretch,' as Cotton Mather calls him, who achieved the downfall of our ancient government, and was followed with a sensible curse, through life and to his grave. On the other side was Bullivant, scattering jests and mockery as he rode along. Dudley came behind, with a downcast look, dreading, as well he might, to meet the indignant gaze of the people, who beheld him, their only countryman by birth, among the oppressors of his native land. The captain of a frigate in the harbour, and two or three civil officers under the Crown, were also there. But the figure which most attracted the public eye, and stirred up the deepest feeling, was the Episcopal clergyman of King's Chapel, riding haughtily among the magistrates in his priestly vestments, the fitting representative of prelacy and persecution, the union of church and state, and all those abominations which had driven the Puritans to the wilderness. Another guard of soldiers, in double rank, brought up the rear.

The whole scene was a picture of the condition of New England, and its moral, the deformity of any government that does not grow out of the nature of things and the character of the people. On one side the religious multitude, with their sad visages and dark attire, and on the other, the group of despotic rulers, with the High Churchman in the midst, and here and there a crucifix at their bosoms, all magnificently clad, flushed with wine, proud of unjust authority, and scoffing at the universal groan. And the mercenary soldiers, waiting but the word to deluge the street with blood, showed the only means by which obedience could be secured.

'O Lord of Hosts,' cried a voice among the crowd, 'provide a Champion for Thy people!'

This ejaculation was loudly uttered, and served as a herald's cry, to introduce a remarkable personage. The crowd had rolled back, and were now huddled together nearly at the extremity of the street, while the soldiers had advanced no more than a third of its length. The intervening space was empty—a paved solitude, between lofty edifices, which threw almost a twilight shadow over it. Suddenly, there was seen the figure of an ancient man, who seemed to have emerged from among the people, and was walking by himself along the centre of the street, to confront the armed band. He wore the old Puritan dress, a dark cloak and a steeple-crowned hat, in the fashion of at least fifty years befóre, with a heavy sword upon his thigh, but a staff in his hand to assist the tremulous gait of age.

When at some distance from the multitude, the old man turned slowly round, displaying a face of antique majesty, rendered doubly venerable by the hoary beard that descended on his breast. He made a gesture at once of encouragement and warning, then turned again, and resumed his way.

'Who is this grey patriarch?' asked the young men of their sires.

'Who is this venerable brother?' asked the old men among themselves.

But none could make reply. The fathers of the people, those of fourscore years and upwards, were disturbed, deeming it strange that they should forget one of such evident authority, whom they must have known in their early days, the associates of Winthrop, and all the old councillors, giving laws, and making prayers, and leading them against the savage. The elderly men ought to have remembered him, too, with locks as grey in their youth, as their own were now. And the young! How could he have passed so utterly from their memories—that hoary sire, the relic of long-departed times, whose awful benediction had surely been bestowed on their uncovered heads in childhood?

'Whence did he come? What is his purpose? Who can this old man be?' whispered the wondering crowd.

Meanwhile, the venerable stranger, staff in hand, was pursuing his solitary walk along the centre of the street. As he drew near the advancing soldiers, and as the roll of the drum came full upon his ear, the old man raised himself to a loftier mien, while the decrepitude of age seemed to fall from his shoulders, leaving him in grey but unbroken dignity. Now, he marched onward with a warrior's step, keeping time to the military music. Thus the aged form advanced on one side, and the whole parade of soldiers and magistrates on the other, till, when scarcely twenty yards remained between, the old man grasped his staff by the middle, and held it before him like a leader's truncheon.

'Stand!' cried he.

The eye, the face, and attitude of command; the solemn, yet warlike peal of that voice, fit either to rule a host in the battle field or be raised to God in prayer, were irresistible. At the old man's word and outstretched arm, the roll of the drum was hushed at once, and the advancing line stood still. A tremulous enthusiasm seized upon the multitude. That stately form, combining the leader and the saint, so grey, so dimly seen, in such an ancient garb, could only belong to some old champion of the righteous cause, whom the oppressor's drum had summoned from his grave. They raised a shout of awe and exultation, and looked for the deliverance of New England.

The Governor, and the gentlemen of his party, perceiving themselves brought to an unexpected stand, rode hastily forward, as if they would have pressed their snorting and affrighted horses right against the hoary apparition. He, however, blenched not a step, but glancing his severe eye round the group, which half encompassed him, at last bent it sternly on Sir Edmund Andros. One would have thought that the dark old man was chief ruler there, and that the Governor and Council, with soldiers at their back, representing the whole power and authority of the Crown, had no alternative but obedience.

'What does this old fellow here?' cried Edward Randolph, fiercely. 'On, Sir Edmund! Bid the soldiers forward, and give the dotard the same choice that you give all his countrymen—to stand aside or be trampled on!'

'Nay, nay, let us show respect to the good grandsire,' said Bullivant, laughing. 'See you not, he is some old round-headed dignitary, who hath lain asleep these thirty years, and knows nothing of the change of times? Doubtless, he thinks to put us down with a proclamation in Old Noll's name!'

'Are you mad, old man?' demanded Sir Edmund Andros, in loud and harsh tones. 'How dare you stay the march of King James's Governor?'

'I have stayed the march of a King himself, ere now,' replied the grey figure, with stern composure. 'I am here, Sir Governor, because the cry of an oppressed people hath disturbed me in my secret place; and beseeching this favour earnestly of the Lord, it was vouchsafed me to appear once again on earth, in the good old cause of His saints. And what speak ye of James? There is no longer a Popish tyrant on the throne of England, and by to-morrow noon, his name shall be a byword in this very street, where ye would make it a word of terror. Back, thou that wast a Governor, back! With this night thy power is ended—to-morrow the prison!—back lest I foretell the scaffold!'

The people had been drawing nearer and nearer, and drinking in the words of their champion, who spoke in accents long disused, like one unaccustomed to converse, except with the dead of many years ago. But his voice stirred their souls. They confronted the soldiers, not wholly without arms, and ready to convert the very stones of the street into deadly weapons. Sir Edmund Andros looked at the old man; then he cast his hard and cruel eye over the multitude, and beheld them burning with that lurid wrath, so difficult to kindle or to quench; and again he fixed his gaze on the aged form, which stood obscurely in an open space, where neither friend nor foe had thrust himself. What were his thoughts, he uttered no word which might discover. But whether the oppressor were overawed by the Grey Champion's look, or perceived his peril in the threatening attitude of the people, it is certain that he gave back, and ordered his soldiers to commence a slow and guarded retreat. Before another sunset, the Governor, and all that rode so proudly with him, were prisoners, and long ere it was known that James had abdicated, King William was proclaimed throughout New England.

But where was the Grey Champion? Some reported, that when the troops had gone from King Street, and the people were thronging tumultuously in their rear, Bradstreet, the aged Governor, was seen to embrace a form more aged than his own. Others soberly affirmed, that while they marvelled at the venerable grandeur of his aspect, the old man had faded from their eyes, melting slowly into the hues of twilight, till, where he stood, there was an empty space. But all agreed that the hoary shape was gone. The men of that generation watched for his reappearance, in sunshine and in twilight, but never saw him more, nor knew when his funeral passed, nor where his gravestone was.

And who was the Grey Champion? Perhaps his name might be found in the records of that stern Court of Justice which passed a sentence, too mighty for the age, but glorious in all after times, for its humbling lesson to the monarch and its high example to the subject. I have heard, that whenever the descendants of the Puritans are to show the spirit of their sires, the old man appears again. When eighty years had passed, he walked once more in King Street. Five years later, in the twilight of an April morning, he stood on the green, beside the meeting-house, at Lexington, where now the obelisk of granite, with a slab of slate inlaid, commemorates the first fallen of the Revolution. And when our fathers were toiling at the breastwork on Bunker's Hill, all through that night the old warrior walked his rounds. Long, long may it be ere he comes again! His hour is one of darkness, and adversity, and peril. But should domestic tyranny oppress us, or the invader's step pollute our soil, still may the Grey Champion come; for he is the type of New England's hereditary spirit: and his shadowy march, on the eve of danger, must ever be the pledge that New England's sons will vindicate their ancestry.

ROGER MALVIN'S BURIAL

ONE of the few incidents of Indian warfare naturally susceptible of the moonlight of romance was that expedition undertaken for the defence of the frontiers in the year 1725, which resulted in the well-remembered 'Lovell's Fight.' Imagination, by casting certain circumstances judicially into the shade, may see much to admire in the heroism of a little band who gave battle to twice their number in the heart of the enemy's country. The open bravery displayed by both parties was in accordance with civilized ideas of valour; and chivalry itself might not blush to record the deeds of one or two individuals. The battle, though so fatal to those who fought, was not unfortunate in its consequences to the country; for it broke the strength of a tribe and conduced to the peace which subsisted during several ensuing years. History and tradition are unusually minute in their memorials of this affair; and the captain of a scouting party of frontier men has acquired as actual a military renown as many a victorious leader of thousands. Some of the incidents contained in the following pages will be recognized, notwithstanding the substitution of fictitious names, by such as have heard, from old men's lips, the fate of the few combatants who were in a condition to retreat after 'Lovell's Fight.'

. . . . .

The early sunbeams hovered cheerfully upon the tree-tops, beneath which two weary and wounded men had stretched their limbs the night before. Their bed of withered oak-leaves was strewn upon the small level space, at the foot of a rock, situated near the summit of one of the gentle swells by which the face of the country is there diversified. The mass of granite, rearing its smooth, flat surface fifteen or twenty feet above their heads, was not unlike a gigantic gravestone, upon which the veins seemed to form an inscription in forgotten characters. On a tract of several acres around this rock, oaks and other hard-wood trees had supplied the place of the pines, which were the usual growth of the land; and a young and vigorous sapling stood close beside the travellers.

The severe wound of the elder man had probably deprived him of sleep; for, so soon as the first ray of sunshine rested on the top of the highest tree, he reared himself painfully from his recumbent posture and sat erect. The deep lines of his countenance and the scattered grey of his hair marked him as past the middle age; but his muscular frame would, but for the effects of his wound, have been as capable of sustaining fatigue as in the early vigour of life. Languor and exhaustion now sat upon his haggard features; and the despairing glance which he sent forward through the depths of the forest proved his own conviction that his pilgrimage was at an end. He next turned his eyes to the companion who reclined by his side. The youth—for he had scarcely attained the years of manhood—lay, with his head upon his arm, in the embrace of an unquiet sleep, which a thrill of pain from his wounds seemed each moment on the point of breaking. His right hand grasped a musket; and, to judge from the violent action of his features, his slumbers were bringing back a vision of the conflict of which he was one of the few survivors. A shout—deep and loud in his dreaming fancy—found its way in an imperfect murmur to his lips; and, starting even at the slight sound of his own voice, he suddenly awoke. The first act of reviving recollection was to make anxious inquiries respecting the condition of his wounded fellow traveller. The latter shook his head.

'Reuben, my boy,' said he, 'this rock beneath which we sit will serve for an old hunter's gravestone. There is many and many a long mile of howling wilderness before us yet; nor would it avail me anything if the smoke of my own chimney were but on the other side of that swell of land. The Indian bullet was deadlier than I thought.'

'You are weary with our three days' travel,' replied the youth, 'and a little longer rest will recruit you. Sit you here while I search the woods for the herbs and roots that must be our sustenance; and, having eaten, you shall lean on me, and we will turn our faces homeward. I doubt not that, with my help, you can attain to some one of the frontier garrisons.'

'There is not two days' life in me, Reuben,' said the other, calmly, 'and I will no longer burden you with my useless body, when you can scarcely support your own. Your wounds are deep and your strength is failing fast; yet, if you hasten onward alone, you may be preserved. For me there is no hope, and I will await death here.'

'If it must be so, I will remain and watch by you,' said Reuben, resolutely.

'No, my son, no,' rejoined his companion. 'Let the wish of a dying man have weight with you; give me one grasp of your hand, and get you hence. Think you that my last moments will be eased by the thought that I leave you to die a more lingering death? I have loved you like a father, Reuben; and at a time like this I should have something of a father's authority. I charge you to be gone, that I may die in peace.'

'And because you have been a father to me, should I therefore leave you to perish and to lie unburied in the wilderness?' exclaimed the youth. 'No; if your end be in truth approaching, I will watch by you and receive your parting words. I will dig a grave here by the rock, in which, if my weakness overcome me, we will rest together; or, if Heaven gives me strength, I will seek my way home.'

'In the cities and wherever men dwell,' replied the other, 'they bury their dead in the earth; they hide them from the sight of the living; but here, where no step may pass perhaps for a hundred years, wherefore should I not rest beneath the open sky, covered only by the oak-leaves when the autumn winds shall strew them? And for a monument, here is this grey rock, on which my dying hand shall carve the name of Roger Malvin; and the traveller in days to come will know that here sleeps a hunter and a warrior. Tarry not, then, for a folly like this, but hasten away, if not for your own sake, for hers who will else be desolate.'

Malvin spoke the last few words in a faltering voice, and their effect upon his companion was strongly visible.

They reminded him that there were other and less questionable duties than that of sharing the fate of a man whom his death could not benefit. Nor can it be affirmed that no selfish feeling strove to enter Reuben's heart, though the consciousness made him more earnestly resist his companion's entreaties.

'How terrible to wait the slow approach of death in this solitude!' exclaimed he. 'A brave man does not shrink in the battle; and, when friends stand round the bed, even women may die composedly; but here——'

'I shall not shrink even here, Reuben Bourne,' interrupted Malvin. 'I am a man of no weak heart; and, if I were, there is a surer support than that of earthly friends. You are young, and life is dear to you. Your last moments will need comfort far more than mine; and when you have laid me in the earth, and are alone, and night is settling on the forest, you will feel all the bitterness of the death that may now be escaped. But I will urge no selfish motive to your generous nature. Leave me for my sake, that, having said a prayer for your safety, I may have space to settle my account undisturbed by worldly sorrows.'

'And your daughter,—how shall I dare to meet her eye?' exclaimed Reuben. 'She will ask the fate of her father, whose life I vowed to defend with my own. Must I tell her that he travelled three days' march with me from the field of battle, and that then I left him to perish in the wilderness? Were it not better to lie down and die by your side than to return safe and say this to Dorcas?'

'Tell my daughter,' said Roger Malvin, 'that, though yourself sore wounded, and weak, and weary, you led my tottering footsteps many a mile, and left me only at my earnest entreaty, because I would not have your blood upon my soul. Tell her that through pain and danger you were faithful, and that, if your lifeblood could have saved me, it would have flowed to its last drop; and tell her that you will be something dearer than a father, and that my blessing is with you both, and that my dying eyes can see a long and pleasant path in which you will journey together.'

As Malvin spoke he almost raised himself from the ground, and the energy of his concluding words seemed to fill the wild and lonely forest with a vision of happiness; but, when he sank exhausted upon his bed of oak-leaves, the light which had kindled in Reuben's eye was quenched. He felt as if it were both sin and folly to think of happiness at such a moment. His companion watched his changing countenance, and sought with generous art to wile him to his own good.

'Perhaps I deceive myself in regard to the time I have to live,' he resumed. 'It may be that, with speedy assistance, I might recover of my wound. The foremost fugitives must, ere this, have carried tidings of our fatal battle to the frontiers, and parties will be out to succour those in like condition with ourselves. Should you meet one of these and guide them hither, who can tell but that I may sit by my own fireside again ?'

A mournful smile strayed across the features of the dying man as he insinuated that unfounded hope; which, however, was not without its effect on Reuben. No merely selfish motive, nor even the desolate condition of Dorcas could have induced him to desert his companion at such a moment—but his wishes seized upon the thought that Malvin's life might be preserved, and his sanguine nature heightened almost to certainty the remote possibility of procuring human aid.

'Surely there is reason, weighty reason, to hope that friends are not far distant,' he said, half aloud. 'There fled one coward, unwounded, in the beginning of the fight, and most probably he made good speed. Every true man on the frontier would shoulder his musket at the news; and, though no party may range so far into the woods as this, I shall perhaps encounter them in one day's march. Counsel me faithfully,' he added, turning to Malvin, in distrust of his own motives. 'Were your situation mine, would you desert me while life remained ?'

'It is now twenty years,' replied Roger Malvin, sighing, however, as he secretly acknowledged the wide dissimilarity between the two cases,—'it is now twenty years since I escaped with one dear friend from Indian captivity near Montreal. We journeyed many days through the woods till at length, overcome with hunger and weariness, my friend lay down and besought me to leave him; for he knew that, if I remained, we both must perish; and, with but little hope of obtaining succour, I heaped a pillow of dry leaves beneath his head and hastened on.'

'And did you return in time to save him ?' asked Reuben, hanging on Malvin's words as if they were to be prophetic of his own success.

'I did,' answered the other. 'I came upon the camp of a hunting party before sunset of the same day. I guided them to the spot where my comrade was expecting death; and he is now a hale and hearty man upon his own farm, far within the frontiers, while I lie wounded here in the depths of the wilderness.'

This example, powerful in effecting Reuben's decision, was aided, unconsciously to himself, by the hidden strength of many another motive. Roger Malvin perceived that the victory was nearly won.

'Now, go, my son, and Heaven prosper you!' he said. 'Turn not back with your friends when you meet them, lest your wounds and weariness overcome you; but send hitherward two or three, that may be spared, to search for me; and believe me, Reuben, my heart will be lighter with every step you take towards home.' Yet there was, perhaps, a change both in his countenance and voice as he spoke thus; for, after all, it was a ghastly fate to be left expiring in the wilderness.

Reuben Bourne, but half convinced that he was acting rightly, at length raised himself from the ground and prepared himself for his departure. And first, though contrary to Malvin's wishes, he collected a stock of roots and herbs, which had been their only food during the last two days. This useless supply he placed within reach of the dying man, for whom, also, he swept together a fresh bed of dry oak leaves. Then climbing to the summit of the rock, which on one side was rough and broken, he bent the oak sapling downward, and bound his handkerchief to the topmost branch. This precaution was not unnecessary to direct any who might come in search of Malvin; for every part of the rock, except its broad, smooth front, was concealed at a little distance by the dense undergrowth of the forest. The handkerchief had been the bandage of a wound upon Reuben's arm; and, as he bound it to the tree, he vowed by the blood that stained it that he would return, either to save his companion's life, or to lay his body in the grave. He then descended, and stood, with down-cast eyes, to receive Roger Malvin's parting words.

The experience of the latter suggested much and minute advice respecting the youth's journey through the trackless forest. Upon this subject he spoke with calm earnestness, as if he were sending Reuben to the battle or the chase while he himself remained secure at home, and not as if the human countenance that was about to leave him were the last he would ever behold. But his firmness was shaken before he concluded.

'Carry my blessing to Dorcas, and say that my last prayer shall be for her and you. Bid her to have no hard thoughts because you left me here,'—Reuben's heart smote him,—'for that your life would not have weighed with you if its sacrifice could have done me good. She will marry you after she has mourned a little while for her father; and Heaven grant you long and happy days, and may your children's children stand round your deathbed! And, Reuben,' he added, as the weakness of mortality made its way at last, 'return, when your wounds are healed and your weariness refreshed,—return to this wild rock, and lay my bones in the grave, and say a prayer over them.'

An almost superstitious regard, arising perhaps from the customs of the Indians, whose war was with the dead as well as the living, was paid by the frontier inhabitants to the rites of sepulture; and there are many instances of the sacrifice of life in the attempt to bury those who had fallen by the 'sword of the wilderness.' Reuben, therefore, felt the full importance of the promise which he most solemnly made to return and perform Roger Malvin's obsequies. It was remarkable that the latter, speaking his whole heart in his parting words, no longer endeavoured to persuade the youth that even the speediest succour might avail to the preservation of his life. Reuben was internally convinced that he should see Malvin's living face no more. His generous nature would fain have delayed him, at whatever risk, till the dying scene were past; but the desire of existence and the hope of happiness had strengthened in his heart, and he was unable to resist them.

'It is enough,' said Roger Malvin, having listened to Reuben's promise. 'Go, and God speed you!'

The youth pressed his hand in silence, turned, and was departing. His slow and faltering steps, however, had borne him but a little way before Malvin's voice recalled him.

'Reuben, Reuben,' said he, faintly; and Reuben returned and knelt down by the dying man.

'Raise me, and let me lean against the rock,' was his last request. 'My face will be turned towards home, and I shall see you a moment longer as you pass among the trees.'

Reuben, having made the desired alteration in his companion's posture, again began his solitary pilgrimage. He walked more hastily at first than was consistent with his strength; for a sort of guilty feeling, which sometimes torments men in their most justifiable acts, caused him to seek concealment from Malvin's eyes; but after he had trodden far upon the rustling forest leaves he crept back, impelled by a wild and painful curiosity, and, sheltered by the earthy roots of an uptorn tree, gazed earnestly at the desolate man. The morning sun was unclouded, and the trees and shrubs imbibed the sweet air of the month of May; yet there seemed a gloom on Nature's face, as if she sympathized with mortal pain and sorrow. Roger Malvin's hands were uplifted in a fervent prayer, some of the words of which stole through the stillness of the woods and entered Reuben's heart, torturing it with an unutterable pang. They were the broken accents of a petition for his own happiness and that of Dorcas; and, as the youth listened, conscience, or something in its similitude, pleaded strongly with him to return and lie down again by the rock. He felt how hard was the doom of the kind and generous being whom he had deserted in his extremity. Death would come like the slow approach of a corpse, stealing gradually towards him through the forest, and showing its ghastly and motionless features from behind a nearer and yet a nearer tree. But such must have been Reuben's own fate had he tarried another sunset; and who shall impute blame to him if he shrank from so useless a sacrifice? As he gave a parting look, a breeze waved the little banner upon the sapling oak and reminded Reuben of his vow.

. . . . .

Many circumstances contributed to retard the wounded traveller in his way to the frontiers. On the second day the clouds, gathering densely over the sky, precluded the possibility of regulating his course by the position of the sun; and he knew not but that every effort of his almost exhausted strength was removing him farther from the home he sought. His scanty sustenance was supplied by the berries and other spontaneous products of the forest. Herds of deer, it is true, sometimes bounded past him, and partridges frequently whirred up before his footsteps; but his ammunition had been expended in the fight, and he had no means of slaying them. His wounds, irritated by the constant exertion in which lay the only hope of life, wore away his strength and at intervals confused his reason. But, even in the wanderings of intellect, Reuben's young heart clung strongly to existence; and it was only through absolute incapacity of motion that he at last sank down beneath a tree, compelled there to await death.

In this situation he was discovered by a party who, upon the first intelligence of the fight, had been dispatched to the relief of the survivors. They conveyed him to the nearest settlement, which chanced to be that of his own residence.

Dorcas, in the simplicity of the olden time, watched by the bedside of her wounded lover and administered all those comforts that are in the sole gift of woman's heart and hand. During several days Reuben's recollection strayed drowsily among the perils and hardships through which he had passed, and he was incapable of returning definite answers to the inquiries with which many were eager to harass him. No authentic particulars of the battle had yet been circulated; nor could mothers, wives, and children tell whether their loved ones were detained by captivity or by the stronger chain of death. Dorcas nourished her apprehensions in silence till one afternoon when Reuben awoke from an unquiet sleep and seemed to recognize her more perfectly than at any previous time. She saw that his intellect had become composed, and she could no longer restrain her filial anxiety.

'My father, Reuben?' she began; but the change in her lover's countenance made her pause.

The youth shrank as if with a bitter pain, and the blood gushed vividly into his wan and hollow cheeks. His first impulse was to cover his face; but, apparently with a desperate effort, he half raised himself and spoke vehemently, defending himself against an imaginary accusation.

'Your father was sore wounded in the battle, Dorcas; and he bade me not burden myself with him, but only to lead him to the lakeside, that he might quench his thirst and die. But I would not desert the old man in his extremity, and, though bleeding myself, I supported him; I gave him half my strength, and led him away with me. For three days we journeyed on together, and your father was sustained beyond my hopes; but, awaking at sunrise on the fourth day, I found him faint and exhausted; he was unable to proceed; his life had ebbed away fast; and——'

'He died!' exclaimed Dorcas, faintly.

Reuben felt it impossible to acknowledge that his selfish love of life had hurried him away before her father's fate was decided. He spoke not; he only bowed his head; and, between shame and exhaustion, sank back and hid his face in the pillow. Dorcas wept when her fears were thus confirmed; but the shock, as it had been long anticipated, was on that account the less violent.

'You dug a grave for my poor father in the wilderness, Reuben?' was the question by which her filial piety manifested itself.

'My hands were weak; but I did what I could,' replied the youth in a smothered tone. 'There stands a noble tombstone above his head; and I would to Heaven I slept as soundly as he!'

Dorcas, perceiving the wildness of his latter words, inquired no further at the time; but her heart found ease in the thought that Roger Malvin had not lacked such funeral rites as it was possible to bestow. The tale of Reuben's courage and fidelity lost nothing when she communicated it to her friends; and the poor youth, tottering from his sick chamber to breathe the sunny air, experienced from every tongue the miserable and humiliating torture of unmerited praise. All acknowledged that he might worthily demand the hand of the fair maiden to whose father he had been 'faithful unto death'; and, as my tale is not of love, it shall suffice to say that in the space of a few months Reuben became the husband of Dorcas Malvin. During the marriage ceremony the bride was covered with blushes; but the bridegroom's face was pale.

There was now in the breast of Reuben Bourne an incommunicable thought—something which he was to conceal most heedfully from her whom he most loved and trusted. He regretted, deeply and bitterly, the moral cowardice that had restrained his words when he was about to disclose the truth to Dorcas; but pride, the fear of losing her affection, the dread of universal scorn, forbade him to rectify this falsehood. He felt that for leaving Roger Malvin he deserved no censure. His presence, the gratuitous sacrifice of his own life, would have added only another and a needless agony to the last moments of the dying man; but concealment had imparted to a justifiable act much of the secret effect of guilt; and Reuben, while reason told him that he had done right, experienced in no small degree the mental horrors which punish the perpetrator of undiscovered crime. By a certain association of ideas, he at times almost imagined himself a murderer. For years, also, a thought would occasionally recur, which, though he perceived all its folly and extravagance, he had not power to banish from his mind. It was a haunting and torturing fancy that his father-in-law was yet sitting at the foot of the rock, on the withered forest leaves, alive, and awaiting his pledged assistance. These mental deceptions, however, came and went, nor did he ever mistake them for realities; but in the calmest and clearest moods of his mind he was conscious that he had a deep vow unredeemed, and that an unburied corpse was calling to him out of the wilderness. Yet such was the consequence of his prevarication that he could not obey the call. It was now too late to require the assistance of Roger Malvin's friends in performing his long-deferred sepulture; and superstitious fears, of which none were more susceptible than the people of the outward settlements, forbade Reuben to go alone. Neither did he know where in the pathless and illimitable forest to seek that smooth and lettered rock at the base of which the body lay; his remembrance of every portion of his travel thence was indistinct, and the latter part had left no impression upon his mind. There was, however, a continual impulse, a voice audible only to himself, commanding him to go forth and redeem his vow; and he had a strange impression that, were he to make the trial, he would be led straight to Malvin's bones. But year after year that summons, unheard but felt, was disobeyed. His one secret thought became like a chain binding down his spirit and like a serpent gnawing into his heart; and he was transformed into a sad and downcast yet irritable man.

In the course of a few years after their marriage changes began to be visible in the external prosperity of Reuben and Dorcas. The only riches of the former had been his stout heart and strong arm; but the latter, her father's sole heiress, had made her husband master of a farm, under older cultivation, larger, and better stocked than most of the frontier establishments. Reuben Bourne, however, was a neglectful husbandman; and, while the lands of the other settlers became annually more fruitful, his deteriorated in the same proportion. The discouragements to agriculture were greatly lessened by the cessation of Indian war, during which men held the plough in one hand and the musket in the other, and were fortunate if the products of their dangerous labour were not destroyed, either in the field or in the barn, by the savage enemy. But Reuben did not profit by the altered condition of the country; nor can it be denied that his intervals of industrious attention to his affairs were but scantily rewarded with success. The irritability by which he had recently become distinguished was another cause of his declining prosperity, as it occasioned frequent quarrels in his unavoidable intercourse with the neighbouring settlers. The results of these were innumerable lawsuits; for the people of New England, in the earliest stages and wildest circumstances of the country, adopted, whenever attainable, the legal mode of deciding their differences. To be brief, the world did not go well with Reuben Bourne; and, though not till many years after his marriage, he was finally a ruined man, with but one remaining expedient against the evil fate that had pursued him. He was to throw sunlight into some deep recess of the forest, and seek subsistence from the virgin bosom of the wilderness.

The only child of Reuben and Dorcas was a son,

now arrived at the age of fifteen years, beautiful in youth, and giving promise of a glorious manhood. He was peculiarly qualified for, and already began to excel in, the wild accomplishments of frontier life. His foot was fleet, his aim true, his apprehension quick, his heart glad and high; and all who anticipated the return of Indian war spoke of Cyrus Bourne as a future leader in the land. The boy was loved by his father with a deep and silent strength, as if whatever was good and happy in his own nature had been transferred to his child, carrying his affections with it. Even Dorcas, though loving and beloved, was far less dear to him; for Reuben's secret thoughts and insulated emotions had gradually made him a selfish man, and he could no longer love deeply except where he saw or imagined some reflection or likeness of his own mind. In Cyrus he recognized what he had himself been in other days; and at intervals he seemed to partake of the boy's spirit and to be revived with a fresh and happy life. Reuben was accompanied by his son in the expedition, for the purpose of selecting a tract of land and felling and burning the timber, which necessarily preceded the removal of the household gods. Two months of autumn were thus occupied; after which Reuben Bourne and his young hunter returned to spend their last winter in the settlements.

. . . . .

It was early in the month of May that the little family snapped asunder whatever tendrils of affections had clung to inanimate objects, and bade farewell to the few who, in the blight of fortune, called themselves their friends. The sadness of the parting moment had, to each of the pilgrims, its peculiar alleviations. Reuben, a moody man, and misanthropic because unhappy, strode onward with his usual stern brow and downcast eye, feeling few regrets and disdaining to acknowledge any. Dorcas, while she wept abundantly over the broken ties by which her simple and affectionate nature had bound itself to everything, felt that the inhabitants of her inmost heart moved on with her, and that all else would be supplied wherever she might go. And the boy dashed one teardrop from his eye, and thought of the adventurous pleasures of the untrodden forest.

Oh ! who, in the enthusiasm of a daydream, has not wished that he were a wanderer in a world of summer wilderness, with one fair and gentle being hanging lightly on his arm ? In youth his free and exulting step would know no barrier but the rolling ocean or the snow-topped mountains ; calmer manhood would choose a home where Nature had strewn a double wealth in the vale of some transparent stream ; and when hoary age, after long, long years of that pure life, stole on and found him there, it would find him the father of a race, the patriarch of a people, the founder of a mighty nation yet to be. When death, like the sweet sleep which we welcome after a day of happiness, came over him, his far descendants would mourn over the venerated dust. Enveloped by tradition in mysterious attributes, the men of future generations would call him godlike ; and remote posterity would see him standing dimly glorious, far up the valley of a hundred centuries.

The tangled and gloomy forest through which the personages of my tale were wandering differed widely from the dreamer's land of fantasy ; yet there was something in their way of life that Nature asserted as her own, and the gnawing cares which went with them from the world were all that now obstructed their happiness. One stout and shaggy steed, the bearer of all their wealth, did not shrink from the added weight of Dorcas ; although her hardy breeding sustained her, during the latter part of each day's journey, by her husband's side. Reuben and his son, their muskets on their shoulders and their axes slung behind them, kept an unwearied pace, each watching with a hunter's eye for the game that supplied their food. When hunger bade, they halted and prepared their meal on the bank of some unpolluted forest brook, which, as they knelt down with thirsty lips to drink, murmured a sweet unwillingness, like a maiden at love's first kiss. They slept beneath a hut of branches, and awoke at peep of light refreshed for the toils of another day. Dorcas and the boy went on joyously, and even Reuben's spirit shone at intervals with an outward gladness; but inwardly there was a cold, cold sorrow, which he compared to the snow-drifts lying deep in the glens and hollows of the rivulets while the leaves were brightly green above.

Cyrus Bourne was sufficiently skilled in the travel of the woods to observe that his father did not adhere to the course they had pursued in their expedition of the preceding autumn. They were now keeping farther to the north, striking out more directly from the settlements, and into a region of which savage beasts and savage men were as yet the sole possessors. The boy sometimes hinted his opinions upon the subject, and Reuben listened attentively, and once or twice altered the direction of their march in accordance with his son's counsel; but, having so done, he seemed ill at ease. His quick and wandering glances were sent forward, apparently in search of enemies lurking behind the tree-trunks; and, seeing nothing there, he would cast his eyes backwards as if in fear of some pursuer. Cyrus, perceiving that his father gradually resumed the old direction, forbore to interfere; nor, though something began to weigh upon his heart, did his adventurous nature permit him to regret the increased length and the mystery of their way.

On the afternoon of the fifth day they halted, and made their simple encampment nearly an hour before sunset. The face of the country, for the last few miles, had been diversified by swells of land resembling huge waves of a petrified sea; and in one of the corresponding hollows, a wild and romantic spot, had the family reared their hut and kindled their fire. There is something chilling, and yet heart-warming, in the thought of these three, united by strong bands of love and insulated from all that breathe beside. The dark and gloomy pines looked down upon them, and, as the wind swept through their tops, a pitying sound was heard in the forest; or did those old trees groan in fear that men were come to lay the axe to their roots at last? Reuben and his son, while Dorcas made ready their meal, proposed to wander out in search of game, of which that day's march had afforded no supply. The boy, promising not to quit the vicinity of the encampment, bounded off with a step as light and elastic as that of the deer he hoped to slay; while his father, feeling a transient happiness as he gazed after him, was about to pursue an opposite direction. Dorcas, in the meanwhile, had seated herself near their fire of fallen branches, upon the mossgrown and mouldering trunk of a tree uprooted years before. Her employment, diversified by an occasional glance at the pot, now beginning to simmer over the blaze, was the perusal of the current year's Massachusetts Almanac, which, with the exception of an old black-letter Bible, comprised all the literary wealth of the family. None pay a greater regard to arbitrary divisions of time than those who are excluded from society; and Dorcas mentioned, as if the information were of importance, that it was now the twelfth of May. Her husband started.

'The twelfth of May! I should remember it well,' muttered he, while many thoughts occasioned a momentary confusion in his mind. 'Where am I? Whither am I wandering? Where did I leave him?'

Dorcas, too well accustomed to her husband's wayward moods to note any peculiarity of demeanour, now laid aside the almanac and addressed him in that mournful tone which the tender-hearted appropriate to griefs long cold and dead.

'It was near this time of the month, eighteen years ago, that my poor father left this world for a better. He had a kind arm to hold his head and a kind voice to cheer him, Reuben, in his last moments; and the thought of the faithful care you took of him has comforted me many a time since. Oh, death would have been awful to a solitary man in a wild place like this!'

'Pray Heaven, Dorcas,' said Reuben, in a broken voice,—'pray Heaven that neither of us three dies solitary and lies unburied in this howling wilderness!' And he hastened away, leaving her to watch the fire beneath the gloomy pines.

Reuben Bourne's rapid pace gradually slackened as the pang, unintentionally inflicted by the words of Dorcas, became less acute. Many strange reflections, however, thronged upon him; and, straying onward rather like a sleep-walker than a hunter, it was attributable to no care of his own that his devious course kept him in the vicinity of the encampment. His steps were imperceptibly led almost in a circle; nor did he observe that he was on the verge of a tract of land heavily timbered, but not with pine-trees. The place of the latter was here supplied by oaks and other of the harder woods; and around their roots clustered a dense and bushy undergrowth, leaving, however, barren spaces between the trees, thick-strewn with withered leaves. Whenever the rustling of the branches or the creaking of the trunks made a sound, as if the forest were waking from slumber, Reuben instinctively raised the musket that rested on his arm, and cast a quick, sharp glance on every side; but, convinced by a partial observation that no animal was near, he would again give himself up to his thoughts. He was musing on the strange influence that had led him away from his premeditated course and so far into the depths of the wilderness. Unable to penetrate to the secret place of his soul where his motives lay hidden, he believed that a supernatural voice had called him onward and that a supernatural power had obstructed his retreat. He trusted that it was Heaven's intent to afford him an opportunity of expiating his sin; he hoped that he might find the bones so long unburied; and that, having laid the earth over them, peace would throw its sunlight into the sepulchre of his heart. From these thoughts he was aroused by a rustling in the forest at some distance from the spot to which he had wandered. Perceiving the motion of some object behind a thick veil of undergrowth, he fired, with the instinct of a hunter and the aim of a practised marksman. A low moan, which told his success, and by which even animals can express their dying agony, was unheeded by Reuben Bourne. What were the recollections now breaking upon him?

The thicket into which Reuben had fired was near the summit of a swell of land, and was clustered around the base of a rock, which, in the shape and smoothness of one of its surfaces, was not unlike a gigantic gravestone. As if reflected in a mirror, its likeness was in Reuben's memory. He even recognized the veins which seemed to form an inscription in forgotten characters: everything remained the same, except that a thick covert of bushes shrouded the lower part of the rock, and would have hidden Roger Malvin had he still been sitting there. Yet in the next moment Reuben's eye was caught by another change that time had effected since he last stood where he was now standing again behind the earthy roots of the uptorn tree. The sapling to which he had bound the bloodstained symbol of his vow had increased and strengthened into an oak, far indeed from its maturity, but with no mean spread of shadowy branches. There was one singularity observable in this tree which made Reuben tremble. The middle and lower branches were in luxuriant life, and an excess of vegetation had fringed the trunk almost to the ground; but a blight had apparently stricken the upper part of the oak, and the very topmost bough was withered, sapless, and utterly dead. Reuben remembered how the little banner had fluttered on that topmost bough, when it was green and lovely, eighteen years before. Whose guilt had blasted it?

. . . . .

Dorcas, after the departure of the two hunters, continued her preparations for their evening repast. Her sylvan table was the moss-covered trunk of a large fallen tree, on the broadest part of which she had spread a snow-white cloth and arranged what were left of the bright pewter vessels that had been her pride in the settlements. It had a strange aspect, that one little spot of homely comfort in the desolate heart of Nature. The sunshine yet lingered upon the higher branches of the trees that grew on rising ground; but the shadows of evening had deepened into the hollow where the encampment was made, and the firelight began to redden as it gleamed up the tall trunks of the pines or hovered on the dense and obscure mass of foliage that circled round the spot. The heart of Dorcas was not sad; for she felt that it was better to journey in the wilderness with two whom she loved than to be a lonely woman in a crowd that cared not for her. As she busied herself in arranging seats of mouldering wood, covered with leaves, for Reuben and her son, her voice danced through the gloomy forest in the measure of a song that she had learned in youth. The rude melody, the production of a bard who won no name, was descriptive of a winter evening in a frontier cottage, when, secured from savage inroad by the high-piled snow-drifts, the family rejoiced by their own fireside. The whole song possessed the nameless charm peculiar to unborrowed thought; but four continually-recurring lines shone out from the rest like the blaze of the hearth whose joys they celebrated. Into them, working magic with a few simple words, the poet had instilled the very essence of domestic love and household happiness, and they were poetry and picture joined in one. As Dorcas sang, the walls of her forsaken home seemed to encircle her; she no longer saw the gloomy pines, nor heard the wind, which still, as she began each verse, sent a heavy breath through the branches and died away in a hollow moan from the burden of the song. She was aroused by the report of a gun in the vicinity of the encampment; and either the sudden sound or her loneliness by the glowing fire caused her to tremble violently. The next moment she laughed in the pride of a mother's heart.

'My beautiful young hunter! My boy has slain a deer!' she exclaimed, recollecting that in the direction whence the shot proceeded Cyrus had gone to the chase.

She waited a reasonable time to hear her son's light step bounding over the rustling leaves to tell of his success. But he did not immediately appear; and she sent her cheerful voice among the trees in search of him.

'Cyrus! Cyrus!'

His coming was still delayed; and she determined, as the report had apparently been very near, to seek for him in person. Her assistance, also, might be necessary in bringing home the venison which she flattered herself he had obtained. She therefore set forward, directing her steps by the long-past sound, and singing as she went, in order that the boy might be aware of her approach and run to meet her. From behind the trunk of every tree and from every hiding-place in the thick foliage of the undergrowth she hoped to discover the countenance of her son, laughing with the sportive mischief that is born of affection. The sun was now beneath the horizon, and the light that came down among the trees was sufficiently dim to create many illusions in her expecting fancy. Several times she seemed indistinctly to see his face gazing out from among the leaves; and once she imagined that he stood beckoning to her at the base of a craggy rock. Keeping her eyes on this object, however, it proved to be no more than the trunk of an oak, fringed to the very ground with little branches, one of which, thrust out farther than the rest, was shaken by the breeze. Making her way round the foot of the rock, she suddenly found herself close to her husband, who had approached in another direction. Leaning upon the butt of his gun, the muzzle of which rested upon the withered leaves, he was apparently absorbed in the contemplation of some object at his feet.

'How is this, Reuben? Have you slain the deer and fallen asleep over him?' exclaimed Dorcas, laughing cheerfully, on her first slight observation of his posture and appearance.

He stirred not, neither did he turn his eyes towards her; and a cold, shuddering fear, indefinite in its source and object, began to creep into her blood. She now perceived that her husband's face was ghastly pale, and his features were rigid, as if incapable of assuming any other expression than the strong despair which had hardened upon them. He gave not the slightest evidence that he was aware of her approach.

'For the love of Heaven, Reuben, speak to me!' cried Dorcas; and the strange sound of her own voice affrighted her even more than the dead silence.

Her husband started, stared into her face, drew her to the front of the rock, and pointed with his finger.

Oh, there lay the boy, asleep, but dreamless, upon the fallen forest leaves! His cheek rested upon his arm—his curled locks were thrown back from his brow—his limbs were slightly relaxed. Had a sudden weariness overcome the youthful hunter? Would his mother's voice arouse him? She knew that it was death.

'This broad rock is the gravestone of your near kindred, Dorcas,' said her husband. 'Your tears will fall at once over your father and your son.'

She heard him not. With one wild shriek, that seemed to force its way from the sufferer's inmost soul, she sank insensible by the side of her dead boy. At that moment the withered topmost bough of the oak loosened itself in the stilly air, and fell in soft, light fragments upon the rock, upon the leaves, upon Reuben, upon his wife and child, and upon Roger Malvin's bones. Then Reuben's heart was stricken, and the tears gushed out like water from a rock. The vow that the wounded youth had made the blighted man had come to redeem. His sin was expiated—the curse was gone from him; and in the hour when he had shed blood dearer to him than his own, a prayer, the first for years, went up to Heaven from the lips of Reuben Bourne.

OLD ESTHER DUDLEY

OUR host having resumed the chair, he, as well as Mr. Tiffany and myself, expressed much eagerness to be made acquainted with the story to which the loyalist had alluded. That venerable man first of all saw fit to moisten his throat with another glass of wine, and then, turning his face towards our coal fire, looked steadfastly for a few moments into the depths of its cheerful glow. Finally, he poured forth a great fluency of speech. The generous liquid that he had imbibed, while it warmed his age-chilled blood, likewise took off the chill from his heart and mind, and gave him an energy to think and feel, which we could hardly have expected to find beneath the snows of fourscore winters. His feelings, indeed, appeared to me more excitable than those of a younger man; or, at least, the same degree of feeling manifested itself by more visible effects, than if his judgement and will had possessed the potency of meridian life. At the pathetic passages of his narrative, he readily melted into tears. When a breath of indignation swept across his spirit, the blood flushed his withered visage even to the roots of his white hair; and he shook his clinched fist at the trio of peaceful auditors, seeming to fancy enemies in those who felt very kindly towards the desolate old soul. But ever and anon, sometimes in the midst of his most earnest talk, this ancient person's intellect would wander vaguely, losing its hold of the matter in hand, and groping for it amid misty shadows. Then would he cackle forth a feeble laugh, and express a doubt whether his wits—for by that phrase it pleased our ancient friend to signify his mental powers—were not getting a little the worse for wear.

Under these disadvantages, the old loyalist's story required more revision to render it fit for the public eye, than those of the series which have preceded it; nor should it be concealed, that the sentiment and tone of the affair may have undergone some slight, or perchance more than slight metamorphosis, in its transmission to the reader through the medium of a thorough-going democrat. The tale itself is a mere sketch, with no involution of plot, nor any great interest of events, yet possessing, if I have rehearsed it aright, that pensive influence over the mind, which the shadow of the old Province House flings upon the loiterer in its courtyard.

. . . . .

The hour had come—the hour of defeat and humiliation—when Sir William Howe was to pass over the threshold of the Province House, and embark with no such triumphal ceremonies as he once promised himself, on board the British fleet. He bade his servants and military attendants go before him, and lingered a moment in the loneliness of the mansion, to quell the fierce emotions that struggled in his bosom as with a death-throb. Preferable, then, would he have deemed his fate, had a warrior's death left him a claim to the narrow territory of a grave, within the soil which the King had given him to defend. With an ominous perception that, as his departing footsteps echoed adown the staircase, the sway of Britain was passing for ever from New England, he smote his clinched hand on his brow, and cursed the destiny that had flung the shame of a dismembered empire upon him.

'Would to God,' cried he, hardly repressing his tears of rage, 'that the rebels were even now at the door-step! A blood-stain upon the floor should then bear testimony that the last British ruler was faithful to his trust.'

The tremulous voice of a woman replied to his exclamation.

'Heaven's cause and the King's are one,' it said. 'Go forth, Sir William Howe, and trust in Heaven to bring back a Royal Governor in triumph.'

Subduing at once the passion to which he had yielded only in the faith that it was unwitnessed, Sir William Howe became conscious that an aged woman, leaning on a gold-headed staff, was standing betwixt him and the door. It was old Esther Dudley, who had dwelt almost immemorial years in this mansion until her presence seemed as inseparable from it as the recollections of its history. She was the daughter of an ancient and once eminent family, which had fallen into poverty and decay, and left its last descendant no resource save the bounty of the King, nor any shelter except within the walls of the Province House. An office in the household, with merely nominal duties, had been assigned to her as a pretext for the payment of a small pension, the greater part of which she expended in adorning herself with an antique magnificence of attire. The claims of Esther Dudley's gentle blood were acknowledged by all the successive Governors; and they treated her with the punctilious courtesy which it was her foible to demand, not always with success, from a neglectful world. The only actual share which she assumed in the business of the mansion, was to glide through its passages and public chambers late at night, to see that the servants had dropped no fire from their flaring torches, nor left embers crackling and blazing on the hearths. Perhaps it was this invariable custom of walking her rounds in the hush of midnight, that caused the superstition of the times to invest the old woman with attributes of awe and mystery; fabling that she had entered the portal of the Province House, none knew whence, in the train of the first Royal Governor, and that it was her fate to dwell there till the last should have departed. But Sir William Howe, if he ever heard this legend, had forgotten it.

'Mistress Dudley, why are you loitering here?' asked he, with some severity of tone. 'It is my pleasure to be the last in this mansion of the King.'

'Not so, if it please your Excellency,' answered the time-stricken woman. 'This roof has sheltered me long. I will not pass from it until they bear me to the tomb of my forefathers. What other shelter is there for old Esther Dudley, save the Province House or the grave?'

'Now Heaven forgive me!' said Sir William Howe to himself. 'I was about to leave this wretched old creature to starve or beg. Take this, good Mistress Dudley,' he added, putting a purse into her hands, 'King George's head on these golden guineas is sterling yet, and will continue so, I warrant you, even should the rebels crown John Hancock their king. That purse will buy a better shelter than the Province House can now afford.'

'While the burden of life remains upon me, I will have no other shelter than this roof,' persisted Esther Dudley, striking her staff upon the floor, with a gesture that expressed immovable resolve. 'And when your Excellency returns in triumph, I will totter into the porch to welcome you.'

'My poor old friend!' answered the British General, —and all his manly and martial pride could no longer restrain a gush of bitter tears. 'This is an evil hour for you and me. The province which the King intrusted to my charge is lost. I go hence in misfortune —perchance in disgrace—to return no more. And you, whose present being is incorporated with the past—who have seen Governor after Governor in stately pageantry ascend these steps—whose whole life has been an observance of majestic ceremonies, and a worship of the King—how will you endure the change? Come with us! Bid farewell to a land that has shaken off its allegiance, and live still under a Royal government at Halifax.'

'Never, never!' said the pertinacious old dame. 'Here will I abide; and King George shall still have one true subject in his disloyal province.'

'Beshrew the old fool!' muttered Sir William Howe, growing impatient of her obstinacy, and ashamed of the emotion into which he had been betrayed. 'She is the very moral of old-fashioned prejudice, and could exist nowhere but in this musty edifice. Well, then, Mistress Dudley, since you will needs tarry, I give the Province House in charge to you. Take this key, and keep it safe until myself, or some other Royal Governor, shall demand it of you.'

Smiling bitterly at himself and her, he took the heavy key of the Province House, and delivering it into the old lady's hands, drew his cloak around him for departure. As the General glanced back at Esther Dudley's antique figure, he deemed her well-fitted for such a charge, as being so perfect a representative of the decayed past—of an age gone by, with its manners, opinions, faith, and feelings, all fallen into oblivion or scorn—of what had once been a reality, but was now merely a vision of faded magnificence. Then Sir William Howe strode forth, smiting his clinched hands together, in the fierce anguish of his spirit; and old Esther Dudley was left to keep watch in the lonely Province House, dwelling there with memory; and if Hope ever seemed to flit around her, still it was Memory in disguise.

The total change of affairs that ensued on the departure of the British troops did not drive the venerable lady from her stronghold. There was not, for many years afterwards, a Governor of Massachusetts; and the magistrates, who had charge of such matters, saw no objection to Esther Dudley's residence in the Province House, especially as they must otherwise have paid a hireling for taking care of the premises, which with her was a labour of love. And so they left her the undisturbed mistress of the old historic edifice. Many and strange were the fables which the gossips whispered about her, in all the chimney-corners of the town. Among the time-worn articles of furniture that had been left in the mansion, there was a tall, antique mirror, which was well worthy of a tale by itself, and perhaps may hereafter be the theme of one. The gold of its heavily-wrought frame was tarnished, and its surface was so blurred, that the old woman's figure, whenever she passed before it, looked indistinct and ghost-like. But it was the general belief that Esther could cause the Governors of the overthrown dynasty, with the beautiful ladies who had once adorned their festivals, the Indian chiefs who had come up to the Province House to hold council or swear allegiance, the grim Provincial warriors, the severe clergyman—in short, all the pageantry of gone days—all the figures that ever swept across the broad plate of glass in former times—she could cause the whole to reappear, and people the inner world of the mirror with shadows of old life. Such legends as these, together with the singularity of her isolated existence, her age, and the infirmity that each added winter flung upon her, made

Mistress Dudley the object both of fear and pity; and it was partly the result of either sentiment, that, amid all the angry licence of the times, neither wrong nor insult ever fell upon her unprotected head. Indeed, there was so much haughtiness in her demeanour towards intruders, among whom she reckoned all persons acting under the new authorities, that it was really an affair of no small nerve to look her in the face. And to do the people justice, stern republicans as they had now become, they were well content that the old gentlewoman, in her hoop petticoat and faded embroidery, should still haunt the palace of ruined pride and overthrown power, the symbol of a departed system, embodying a history in her person. So Esther Dudley dwelt, year after year, in the Province House, still reverencing all that others had flung aside, still faithful to her King, who, so long as the venerable dame yet held her post, might be said to retain one true subject in New England, and one spot of the empire that had been wrested from him.

And did she dwell there in utter loneliness? Rumour said, not so. Whenever her chill and withered heart desired warmth, she was wont to summon a black slave of Governor Shirley's from the blurred mirror, and send him in search of guests who had long ago been familiar in those deserted chambers. Forth went the sable messenger, with the starlight or the moonshine gleaming through him, and did his errand in the burial ground, knocking at the iron doors of tombs, or upon the marble slabs that covered them, and whispering to those within: 'My mistress, old Esther Dudley, bids you to the Province House at midnight.' And punctually as the clock of the Old South told twelve, came the shadows of the Olivers, the Hutchinsons, the Dudleys, all the grandees of a by-gone generation, gliding beneath the portal into the well-known mansion, where Esther mingled with them as if she likewise were a shade. Without vouching for the truth of such traditions, it is certain that Mistress Dudley sometimes assembled a few of the stanch, though crestfallen old Tories, who had lingered in the rebel town during those days of wrath and tribulation. Out of a cobwebbed bottle, containing liquor that a Royal Governor might have smacked his lips over, they quaffed healths to the King, and babbled treason to the Republic, feeling as if the protecting shadow of the throne were still flung around them. But, draining the last drops of their liquor, they stole timorously homeward, and answered not again, if the rude mob reviled them in the street.

Yet Esther Dudley's most frequent and favoured guests were the children of the town. Towards them she was never stern. A kindly and loving nature, hindered elsewhere from its free course by a thousand rocky prejudices, lavished itself upon these little ones. By bribes of gingerbread of her own making, stamped with a royal crown, she tempted their sunny sportiveness beneath the gloomy portal of the Province House, and would often beguile them to spend a whole play day there, sitting in a circle round the verge of her hoop petticoat, greedily attentive to her stories of a dead world. And when these little boys and girls stole forth again from the dark mysterious mansion, they went bewildered, full of old feelings that graver people had long ago forgotten, rubbing their eyes at the world around them as if they had gone astray into ancient times, and become children of the past. At home, when their parents asked where they had loitered such a weary while, and with whom they had been at play, the children would talk of all the departed worthies of the Province, as far back as Governor Belcher, and the haughty dame of Sir William Phipps. It would seem as though they had been sitting on the knees of these famous personages, whom the grave had hidden for half a century, and had toyed with the embroidery of their rich waistcoats, or roguishly pulled the long curls of their flowing wigs. 'But Governor Belcher has been dead this many a year,' would the mother say to her little boy. 'And did you really see him at the Province House?' 'Oh yes, dear mother! yes!' the half-dreaming child would answer. 'But when old Esther had done speaking about him he faded away out of his chair.' Thus, without affrighting her little guests, she led them by the hand into the chambers of her own desolate heart, and made childhood's fancy discern the ghosts that haunted there.

Living so continually in her own circle of ideas, and never regulating her mind by a proper reference to present things, Esther Dudley appears to have grown partially crazed. It was found that she had no right sense of the progress and true state of the Revolutionary war, but held a constant faith that the armies of Britain were victorious on every field, and destined to be ultimately triumphant. Whenever the town rejoiced for a battle won by Washington, or Gates, or Morgan, or Greene, the news, in passing through the door of the Province House, as through the ivory gate of dreams, became metamorphosed into a strange tale of the prowess of Howe, Clinton, or Cornwallis. Sooner or later, it was her invincible belief, the colonies would be prostrate at the footstool of the King. Sometimes she seemed to take for granted that such was already the case. On one occasion, she startled the town's people by a brilliant illumination of the Province House, with candles at every pane of glass, and a transparency of the King's initials and a crown of light, in the great balcony window. The figure of the aged woman, in the most gorgeous of her mildewed velvets and brocades, was seen passing from casement to casement, until she paused before the balcony, and flourished a huge key above her head. Her wrinkled visage actually gleamed with triumph, as if the soul within her were a festal lamp.

'What means this blaze of light? What does old Esther's joy portend?' whispered a spectator. 'It is frightful to see her gliding about the chambers, and rejoicing there without a soul to bear her company.'

'It is as if she were making merry in a tomb,' said another.

'Pshaw! It is no such mystery,' observed an old man, after some brief exercise of memory. 'Mistress Dudley is keeping jubilee for the King of England's birthday.'

Then the people laughed aloud, and would have thrown mud against the blazing transparency of the King's crown and initials, only that they pitied the poor old dame, who was so dismally triumphant amid the wreck and ruin of the system to which she appertained.

Oftentimes it was her custom to climb the weary staircase that wound upward to the cupola, and thence strain her dimmed eyesight seaward and countryward, watching for a British fleet, or for the march of a grand procession, with the King's banner floating over it. The passengers in the street below would discern her anxious visage, and send up a shout—'When the golden Indian on the Province House shall shoot his arrow, and when the cock on the Old South spire shall crow, then look for a Royal Governor again!'—for this had grown a byword through the town. And at last, after long, long years, old Esther Dudley knew, or perchance she only dreamed, that a Royal Governor was on the eve of returning to the Province House, to receive the heavy key which Sir William Howe had committed to her charge. Now it was the fact, that intelligence bearing some faint analogy to Esther's version of it, was current among the town's people. She set the mansion in the best order that her means allowed, and arraying herself in silks and tarnished gold, stood long before the blurred mirror to admire her own magnificence. As she gazed, the grey and withered lady moved her ashen lips, murmuring half aloud, talking to shapes that she saw within the mirror, to shadows of her own fantasies, to the household friends of memory, and bidding them rejoice with her, and come forth to meet the Governor. And while absorbed in this communion, Mistress Dudley heard the tramp of many footsteps in the street, and looking out of the window, beheld what she construed as the Royal Governor's arrival.

'O happy day! O blessed, blessed hour!' she exclaimed. 'Let me but bid him welcome within the portal, and my task in the Province House, and on earth, is done!'

Then with tottering feet, which age and tremulous joy caused to tread amiss, she hurried down the grand staircase, her silks sweeping and rustling as she went, so that the sound was as if a train of spectral courtiers were thronging from the dim mirror. And Esther Dudley fancied, that as soon as the wide door should be flung open, all the pomp and splendour of bygone times would pace majestically into the Province House, and the gilded tapestry of the past would be brightened by the sunshine of the present. She turned the key—withdrew it from the lock—unclosed the door—and stepped across the threshold. Advancing up the court-yard appeared a person of most dignified mien, with tokens, as Esther interpreted them, of gentle blood, high rank, and long-accustomed authority, even in his walk and every gesture. He was richly dressed, but wore a gouty shoe, which, however, did not lessen the stateliness of his gait. Around and behind him were people in plain civic dresses, and two or three war-worn veterans, evidently officers of rank, arrayed in a uniform of blue and buff. But Esther Dudley, firm in the belief that had fastened its roots about her heart, beheld only the principal personage, and never doubted that this was the long-looked-for Governor, to whom she was to surrender up her charge. As he approached, she involuntarily sank down on her knees, and tremblingly held forth the heavy key.

'Receive my trust! take it quickly!' cried she; 'for methinks Death is striving to snatch away my triumph. But he comes too late. Thank Heaven for this blessed hour! God save King George!'

'That, Madam, is a strange prayer to be offered up at such a moment,' replied the unknown guest of the Province House, and courteously removing his hat, he offered his arm to raise the aged woman. 'Yet, in reverence for your grey hairs and long-kept faith, Heaven forbid that any here should say you nay. Over the realms which still acknowledge his sceptre, God save King George!'

Esther Dudley started to her feet, and hastily clutching back the key, gazed with fearful earnestness at the stranger; and dimly and doubtfully, as if suddenly awakened from a dream, her bewildered eyes half recognized his face. Years ago, she had known him among the gentry of the province. But the ban of the King had fallen upon him! How, then, came the doomed victim here? Proscribed, excluded from mercy, the monarch's most dreaded and hated foe, this New England merchant had stood triumphantly against a kingdom's strength; and his foot now trod upon humbled Royalty, as he ascended the steps of the Province House, the people's chosen Governor of Massachusetts.

'Wretch, wretch that I am!' muttered the old woman, with such a heart-broken expression, that the tears gushed from the stranger's eyes. 'Have I bidden a traitor welcome? Come, Death! come quickly!'

'Alas, venerable lady!' said Governor Hancock, lending her his support with all the reverence that a courtier would have shown to a queen. 'Your life has been prolonged until the world has changed around you. You have treasured up all that time has rendered worthless—the principles, feelings, manners, modes of being and acting, which another generation has flung aside—and you are a symbol of the past.

And I, and these around me—we represent a new race of men—living no longer in the past, scarcely in the present—but projecting our lives forward into the future. Ceasing to model ourselves on ancestral superstitions, it is our faith and principle to press onward, onward! Yet,' continued he, turning to his attendants, 'let us reverence, for the last time, the stately and gorgeous prejudices of the tottering Past!'

While the Republican Governor spoke, he had continued to support the helpless form of Esther Dudley; her weight grew heavier against his arm; but at last, with a sudden effort to free herself, the ancient woman sank down beside one of the pillars of the portal. The key of the Province House fell from her grasp, and clanked against the stone.

'I have been faithful unto death,' murmured she. 'God save the King!'

'She hath done her office!' said Hancock, solemnly. 'We will follow her reverently to the tomb of her ancestors; and then, my fellow-citizens, onward—onward! We are no longer children of the Past!'

As the old loyalist concluded his narrative, the enthusiasm which had been fitfully flashing within his sunken eyes, and quivering across his wrinkled visage, faded away, as if all the lingering fire of his soul were extinguished. Just then, too, a lamp upon the mantelpiece threw out a dying gleam, which vanished as speedily as it shot upward, compelling our eyes to grope for one another's features by the dim glow of the hearth. With such a lingering fire, methought, with such a dying gleam, had the glory of the ancient system vanished from the Province House, when the spirit of old Esther Dudley took its flight. And now, again, the clock of the Old South threw its voice of ages on the breeze, knolling the hourly knell of the Past, crying out far and wide through the multitudinous city, and filling our ears, as we sat in the dusky chamber, with its reverberating depth of tone. In that same mansion—in that very chamber—what a volume of history had been told off into hours, by the same voice that was now trembling in the air. Many a Governor had heard those midnight accents, and longed to exchange his stately cares for slumber. And as for mine host, and Mr. Bela Tiffany, and the old loyalist, and me, we had babbled about dreams of the past, until we almost fancied that the clock was still striking in a bygone century. Neither of us would have wondered, had a hoop-petticoated phantom of Esther Dudley tottered into the chamber, walking her rounds in the hush of midnight, as of yore, and motioned us to quench the fading embers of the fire, and leave the historic precincts to herself and her kindred shades. But as no such vision was vouchsafed, I retired unbidden, and would advise Mr. Tiffany to lay hold of another auditor, being resolved not to show my face in the Province House for a good while hence—if ever.

EDGAR ALLAN POE

1809—1849

THE PURLOINED LETTER

'Nil sapientiae odiosius acumine nimio.'—SENECA.

AT Paris, just after dark one gusty evening in the autumn of 18—, I was enjoying the twofold luxury of meditation and a meerschaum, in company with my friend, C. Auguste Dupin, in his little back library or book-closet, *au troisième*, No. 33 Rue Dunôt, Faubourg St. Germain. For one hour at least we had maintained a profound silence; while each, to any casual observer, might have seemed intently and exclusively occupied with the curling eddies of smoke that oppressed the atmosphere of the chamber. For myself, however, I was mentally discussing certain topics which had formed matter for conversation between us at an earlier period of the evening; I mean the affair of the Rue Morgue, and the mystery attending the murder of Marie Rogêt. I looked upon it, therefore, as something of a coincidence, when the door of our apartment was thrown open and admitted our old acquaintance, Monsieur G——, the Prefect of the Parisian police.

We gave him a hearty welcome; for there was nearly half as much of the entertaining as of the contemptible about the man, and we had not seen him for several years. We had been sitting in the dark, and Dupin now arose for the purpose of lighting a lamp, but sat down again, without doing so, upon G.'s saying that he had called to consult us, or rather to ask the opinion of my friend, about some official business which had occasioned a great deal of trouble.

'If it is any point requiring reflection,' observed Dupin, as he forbore to enkindle the wick, 'we shall examine it to better purpose in the dark.'

'That is another of your odd notions,' said the Prefect, who had a fashion of calling everything 'odd' that was beyond his comprehension, and thus lived amid an absolute legion of 'oddities.'

'Very true,' said Dupin, as he supplied his visitor with a pipe, and rolled towards him a comfortable chair.

'And what is the difficulty now?' I asked. 'Nothing more in the assassination way, I hope?'

'Oh, no; nothing of that nature. The fact is, the business is *very* simple indeed, and I make no doubt that we can manage it sufficiently well ourselves; but then I thought Dupin would like to hear the details of it, because it is so excessively *odd*.'

'Simple and odd,' said Dupin.

'Why, yes; and not exactly that, either. The fact is, we have all been a good deal puzzled because the affair *is* so simple, and yet baffles us altogether.'

'Perhaps it is the very simplicity of the thing which puts you at fault,' said my friend.

'What nonsense you *do* talk!' replied the Prefect, laughing heartily.

'Perhaps the mystery is a little *too* plain,' said Dupin.

'Oh, good heavens! who ever heard of such an idea?'

'A little *too* self-evident.'

'Ha! ha! ha!—ha! ha! ha!—ho! ho! ho!' roared our visitor, profoundly amused; 'O Dupin, you will be the death of me yet!'

'And what, after all, *is* the matter on hand?' I asked.

'Why, I will tell you,' replied the Prefect, as he gave a long, steady, and contemplative puff, and settled himself in his chair. 'I will tell you in a few words; but, before I begin, let me caution you that this is an affair demanding the greatest secrecy, and that I should most probably lose the position I now hold, were it known that I confided it to any one.'

'Proceed,' said I.

'Or not,' said Dupin.

'Well, then; I have received personal information, from a very high quarter, that a certain document of the last importance has been purloined from the royal apartments. The individual who purloined it is known; this beyond a doubt; he was seen to take it. It is known, also, that it still remains in his possession.'

'How is this known?' asked Dupin.

'It is clearly inferred,' replied the Prefect, 'from the nature of the document, and from the non-appearance of certain results which would at once arise from its passing *out* of the robber's possession—that is to say, from his employing it as he must design in the end to employ it.'

'Be a little more explicit,' I said.

'Well, I may venture so far as to say that the paper gives its holder a certain power in a certain quarter where such power is immensely valuable.' The Prefect was fond of the cant of diplomacy.

'Still I do not quite understand,' said Dupin.

'No? Well; the disclosure of the document to a third person, who shall be nameless, would bring in question the honour of a personage of most exalted station; and this fact gives the holder of the document an ascendancy over the illustrious personage whose honour and peace are so jeopardized.'

'But this ascendancy,' I interposed, 'would depend upon the robber's knowledge of the loser's knowledge of the robber. Who would dare——'

'The thief,' said G., 'is the Minister D——, who dares all things, those unbecoming as well as those becoming a man. The method of the theft was not less ingenious than bold. The document in question —a letter, to be frank—had been received by the personage robbed while alone in the royal *boudoir*. During its perusal she was suddenly interrupted by the entrance of the other exalted personage from whom especially it was her wish to conceal it. After a hurried and vain endeavour to thrust it into a drawer, she was forced to place it, open as it was, upon a table. The address, however, was uppermost, and, the contents thus unexposed, the letter escaped notice. At this juncture enters the Minister D——. His lynx eye immediately perceives the paper, recognizes the handwriting of the address, observes the confusion of the personage addressed, and fathoms her secret. After some business transactions, hurried through in his ordinary manner, he produces a letter somewhat similar to the one in question, opens it, pretends to read it, and then places it in close juxtaposition to the other. Again he converses, for some fifteen minutes, upon the public affairs. At length, in taking leave, he takes also from the table the letter to which he had no claim. Its rightful owner saw, but, of course, dared not call attention to the act, in the presence of the third personage who stood at her elbow. The Minister decamped, leaving his own letter—one of no importance—upon the table.'

'Here, then,' said Dupin to me, 'you have precisely what you demand to make the ascendancy complete—the robber's knowledge of the loser's knowledge of the robber.'

'Yes,' replied the Prefect; 'and the power thus attained has, for some months past, been wielded, for political purposes, to a very dangerous extent. The personage robbed is more thoroughly convinced, every day, of the necessity of reclaiming her letter. But this, of course, cannot be done openly. In fine, driven to despair, she has committed the matter to me.'

'Than whom,' said Dupin, amid a perfect whirlwind of smoke, 'no more sagacious agent could, I suppose, be desired, or even imagined.'

'You flatter me,' replied the Prefect; 'but it is possible that some such opinion may have been entertained.'

'It is clear,' said I, 'as you observe, that the letter is still in the possession of the Minister; since it is this possession, and not any employment of the letter, which bestows the power. With the employment the power departs.'

'True,' said G.; 'and upon this conviction I proceeded. My first care was to make thorough search of the Minister's hotel; and here my chief embarrassment lay in the necessity of searching without his knowledge. Beyond all things, I have been warned of the danger which would result from giving him reason to suspect our design.'

'But,' said I, 'you are quite *au fait* in these investigations. The Parisian police have done this thing often before.'

'Oh yes; and for this reason I did not despair. The habits of the Minister gave me, too, a great advantage. He is frequently absent from home all night. His servants are by no means numerous. They sleep at a distance from their master's apartment, and, being chiefly Neapolitans, are readily made drunk. I have keys, as you know, with which I can open any chamber or cabinet in Paris. For three months a night has not passed, during the greater part of which I have not been engaged, personally, in ransacking the D—— Hotel. My honour is interested, and, to mention a great secret, the reward is enormous. So I did not abandon the search until I had become fully satisfied that the thief is a more astute man than myself. I fancy that I have investigated every nook and corner of the premises in which it is possible that the paper can be concealed.'

'But is it not possible,' I suggested, 'that although the letter may be in possession of the Minister, as it unquestionably is, he may have concealed it elsewhere than upon his own premises?'

'This is barely possible,' said Dupin. 'The present peculiar condition of affairs at court, and especially of those intrigues in which D—— is known to be involved, would render the instant availability of the document—its susceptibility of being produced at a moment's notice—a point of nearly equal importance with its possession.'

'Its susceptibility of being produced?' said I.

'That is to say, of being *destroyed*,' said Dupin.

'True,' I observed; 'the paper is clearly then upon the premises. As for its being upon the person of the Minister, we may consider that as out of the question.'

'Entirely,' said the Prefect. 'He has been twice waylaid, as if by footpads, and his person rigorously searched under my own inspection.'

'You might have spared yourself this trouble,' said Dupin. 'D——, I presume, is not altogether a fool, and, if not, must have anticipated these waylayings, as a matter of course.'

'Not *altogether* a fool,' said G.; 'but then he's a poet, which I take to be only one remove from a fool.'

'True,' said Dupin, after a long and thoughtful whiff from his meerschaum, 'although I have been guilty of certain doggerel myself.'

'Suppose you detail,' said I, 'the particulars of your search.'

'Why, the fact is we took our time, and we searched *everywhere*. I have had long experience in these affairs. I took the entire building, room by room; devoting the nights of a whole week to each. We examined, first, the furniture of each apartment. We opened every possible drawer; and I presume you know that, to a properly trained police agent, such a thing as a *secret* drawer is impossible. Any man is a dolt who permits a "secret" drawer to escape him in a search of this kind. The thing is *so* plain. There is a certain amount of bulk—of space—to be accounted for in every cabinet. Then we have accurate rules. The fiftieth part of a line could not escape us. After the cabinets we took the chairs. The cushions we probed with the fine long needles you have seen me employ. From the tables we removed the tops.'

'Why so?'

'Sometimes the top of a table, or other similarly arranged piece of furniture, is removed by the person wishing to conceal an article; then the leg is excavated, the article deposited within the cavity, and the top replaced. The bottoms and tops of bedposts are employed in the same way.'

'But could not the cavity be detected by sounding?' I asked.

'By no means, if, when the article is deposited, a sufficient wadding of cotton be placed around it. Besides, in our case, we were obliged to proceed without noise.'

'But you could not have removed—you could not have taken to pieces *all* articles of furniture in which it would have been possible to make a deposit in the manner you mention. A letter may be compressed into a thin spiral roll, not differing much in shape or bulk from a large knitting-needle, and in this form it might be inserted into the rung of a chair, for example. You did not take to pieces all the chairs?'

'Certainly not; but we did better—we examined the rungs of every chair in the hotel, and, indeed, the jointings of every description of furniture, by the aid of a most powerful microscope. Had there been any traces of recent disturbance we should not have failed to detect it instantly. A single grain of gimlet-dust, for example, would have been as obvious as an apple. Any disorder in the glueing—any unusual gaping in the joints—would have sufficed to ensure detection.'

'I presume you looked to the mirrors, between the boards and the plates, and you probed the beds and the bedclothes, as well as the curtains and carpets.'

'That of course; and when we had absolutely completed every particle of the furniture in this way, then we examined the house itself. We divided its entire surface into compartments, which we numbered, so that none might be missed; then we scrutinized each individual square inch throughout the premises, including the two houses immediately adjoining, with the microscope, as before.'

'The two houses adjoining!' I exclaimed; 'you must have had a great deal of trouble.'

'We had; but the reward offered is prodigious.'

'You include the *grounds* about the houses?'

'All the grounds are paved with brick. They gave us comparatively little trouble. We examined the moss between the bricks, and found it undisturbed.'

'You looked among D——'s papers, of course, and into the books of the library?'

'Certainly; we opened every package and parcel; we not only opened every book, but we turned over every leaf in each volume, not contenting ourselves with a mere shake, according to the fashion of some of our police officers. We also measured the thickness of every book-*cover*, with the most accurate admeasurement, and applied to each the most jealous scrutiny of the microscope. Had any of the bindings been recently meddled with, it would have been utterly impossible that the fact should have escaped observation. Some five or six volumes, just from the hands of the binder, we carefully probed longitudinally, with the needles.'

'You explored the floors beneath the carpets?'

'Beyond doubt. We removed every carpet, and examined the boards with the microscope.'

'And the paper on the walls?'

'Yes.'

'You looked into the cellars?'

'We did.'

'Then,' I said, 'you have been making a miscalculation, and the letter is *not* upon the premises, as you suppose.'

'I fear you are right there,' said the Prefect. 'And now, Dupin, what would you advise me to do?'

'To make a thorough research of the premises.'

'That is absolutely needless,' replied G——. 'I am not more sure that I breathe than I am that the letter is not at the hotel.'

'I have no better advice to give you,' said Dupin. 'You have, of course, an accurate description of the letter?'

'Oh yes!' And here the Prefect, producing a memorandum-book, proceeded to read aloud a minute account of the internal, and especially of the external appearance of the missing document. Soon after finishing the perusal of this description, he took his departure more entirely depressed in spirits than I had ever known the good gentleman before.

In about a month afterwards he paid us another visit, and found us occupied very nearly as before. He took a pipe and a chair and entered into some ordinary conversation. At length I said—

'Well, but G——, what of the purloined letter? I presume you have at last made up your mind that there is no such thing as overreaching the Minister?'

'Confound him, say I—yes; I made the re-examination, however, as Dupin suggested—but it was all labour lost, as I knew it would be.'

'How much was the reward offered, did you say?' asked Dupin.

'Why, a very great deal—a *very* liberal reward—I don't like to say how much, precisely; but I *will* say, that I wouldn't mind giving my individual cheque for fifty thousand francs to any one who could obtain me that letter. The fact is, it is becoming of more and more importance every day; and the reward has been lately doubled. If it were trebled, however, I could do no more than I have done.'

'Why, yes,' said Dupin drawlingly, between the whiffs of his meerschaum, 'I really—think, G——, you have not exerted yourself—to the utmost—in this matter. You might—do a little more, I think, eh?'

'How?—in what way?'

'Why—puff, puff—you might—puff, puff—employ counsel in the matter, eh?—puff, puff, puff. Do you remember the story they tell of Abernethy?'

'No; hang Abernethy!'

'To be sure! hang him and welcome. But once upon a time, a certain rich miser conceived the design of sponging upon this Abernethy for a medical opinion. Getting up, for this purpose, an ordinary conversation in a private company, he insinuated his case to the physician, as that of an imaginary individual.

'"We will suppose," said the miser, "that his symptoms are such and such; now, doctor, what would *you* have directed him to take?"

'"Take!" said Abernethy, "why, take *advice*, to be sure."'

'But,' said the Prefect, a little discomposed, 'I am *perfectly* willing to take advice, and to pay for it. I would *really* give fifty thousand francs to any one who would aid me in the matter.'

'In that case,' replied Dupin, opening a drawer, and producing a cheque-book, 'you may as well fill me up a cheque for the amount mentioned. When you have signed it, I will hand you the letter.'

I was astounded. The Prefect appeared absolutely thunderstricken. For some minutes he remained speechless and motionless, looking incredulously at my friend with open mouth, and eyes that seemed starting from their sockets; then, apparently recovering himself in some measure, he seized a pen, and after several pauses and vacant stares, finally filled up and signed a cheque for fifty thousand francs, and handed it across the table to Dupin. The latter examined it carefully and deposited it in his pocket-book; then, unlocking an *escritoire*, took thence a letter and gave it to the Prefect. This functionary grasped it in a perfect agony of joy, opened it with a trembling hand, cast a rapid glance at its contents, and then, scrambling and struggling to the door, rushed at length unceremoniously from the room and from the house, without having uttered a syllable since Dupin had requested him to fill up the cheque.

When he had gone, my friend entered into some explanations.

'The Parisian police,' he said, 'are exceedingly able in their way. They are persevering, ingenious, cunning, and thoroughly versed in the knowledge which their duties seem chiefly to demand. Thus, when G—— detailed to us his mode of searching the premises at the Hôtel D——, I felt entire confidence in his having made a satisfactory investigation—so far as his labours extended.'

'So far as his labours extended?' said I.

'Yes,' said Dupin. 'The measures adopted were not only the best of their kind, but carried out to absolute perfection. Had the letter been deposited within the range of their search, these fellows would, beyond a question, have found it.'

I merely laughed—but he seemed quite serious in all that he said.

'The measures, then,' he continued, 'were good in their kind, and well executed; their defect lay in their being inapplicable to the case, and to the man. A certain set of highly ingenious resources are, with the Prefect, a sort of Procrustean bed, to which he forcibly adapts his designs. But he perpetually errs by being too deep or too shallow for the matter in hand; and many a schoolboy is a better reasoner than he. I knew one about eight years of age, whose success at guessing in the game of "even and odd" attracted universal admiration. This game is simple, and is played with marbles. One player holds in his hand a number of these toys, and demands of another whether that number is even or odd. If the guess is right, the guesser wins one; if wrong, he loses one. The boy to whom I allude won all the marbles of the school. Of course he had some principle of guessing; and this lay in mere observation and admeasurement of the astuteness of his opponents. For example, an arrant simpleton is his opponent, and, holding up his closed hand, asks, "Are they even or odd?" Our schoolboy replies, "Odd," and loses; but upon the second trial he wins, for he then says to himself, "The simpleton had them even upon the first trial, and his amount of cunning is just sufficient to make him have them odd upon the second; I will therefore guess odd"—he guesses odd, and wins. Now, with a simpleton a degree above the first, he would have reasoned thus: "This fellow finds that in the first instance I guessed odd, and, in the second, he will propose to himself, upon the first impulse, a simple variation from even to odd, as did the first simpleton; but then a second thought will suggest that this is too simple a variation, and finally he will decide upon putting it even as before. I will therefore guess even"—he guesses even, and wins. Now this mode of reasoning in the schoolboy, whom his fellows termed "lucky"—what, in its last analysis, is it?"

'It is merely,' I said, 'an identification of the reasoner's intellect with that of his opponent.'

'It is,' said Dupin; 'and upon inquiring of the boy by what means he effected the *thorough* identification in which his success consisted, I received answer as follows: "When I wish to find out how wise, or how stupid, or how good, or how wicked is anyone, or what are his thoughts at the moment, I fashion the expression of my face, as accurately as possible, in accordance with the expression of his, and then wait to see what thoughts or sentiments arise in my mind or heart, as if to match or correspond with the expression." This response of the schoolboy lies at the bottom of all the spurious profundity which has been attributed to Rochefoucauld, to La Bruyère, to Machiavelli, and to Campanella.'

'And the identification,' I said, 'of the reasoner's intellect with that of his opponent, depends, if I understand you aright, upon the accuracy with which the opponent's intellect is admeasured.'

'For its practical value it depends upon this,' replied Dupin; 'and the Prefect and his cohort fail so frequently, first, by default of his identification, and, secondly, by ill-admeasurement, or rather through non-admeasurement, of the intellect with which they are engaged. They consider only their *own* ideas of ingenuity; and, in searching for anything hidden, advert only to the modes in which *they* would have hidden it. They are right in this much—that their own ingenuity is a faithful representative of that of *the mass*; but when the cunning of the individual felon is diverse in character from their own, the felon foils them, of course. This always happens when it is above their own, and very usually when it is below. They have no variation of principle in their investigations; at best, when urged by some unusual emergency—by some extraordinary reward—they extend or exaggerate their old modes of *practice*, without touching their principles. What, for example, in this case of D——, has been done to vary the principle of action? What is all this boring, and probing, and sounding, and scrutinizing with the microscope, and dividing the surface of the building into registered square inches—what is it all but an exaggeration *of the application* of the one principle or set of principles of search, which are based upon the one set of notions regarding human ingenuity, to which the Prefect, in the long routine of his duty, has been accustomed ? Do you not see he has taken it for granted that *all* men proceed to conceal a letter—not exactly in a gimlet-hole bored in a chair-leg—but, at least, in *some* out-of-the-way hole or corner suggested by the same tenor of thought which would urge a man to secrete a letter in a gimlet-hole bored in a chair-leg ? And do you not see also, that such *recherchés* nooks for concealment are adapted only for ordinary occasions, and would be adopted only by ordinary intellects ; for, in all cases of concealment, a disposal of the article concealed—a disposal of it in this *recherché* manner—is, in the very first instance, presumable and presumed ; and thus its discovery depends, not at all upon the acumen, but altogether upon the mere care, patience, and determination of the seekers ; and where the case is of importance—or, what amounts to the same thing in the policial eyes, when the reward is of magnitude—the qualities in question have *never* been known to fail. You will now understand what I meant in suggesting that, had the purloined letter been hidden anywhere within the limits of the Prefect's examination—in other words, had the principle of its concealment been comprehended within the principles of the Prefect—its discovery would have been a matter altogether beyond question. This functionary, however, has been thoroughly mystified ; and the remote source of his defeat lies in the supposition that the Minister is a fool, because he has acquired renown as a poet. All fools are poets—this the Prefect *feels* ; and he is merely guilty of a *non distributio medii* in thence inferring that all poets are fools.'

'But is this really the poet ?' I asked. 'There are two brothers, I know ; and both have attained reputation in letters. The Minister, I believe, has written learnedly on the Differential Calculus. He is a mathematician, and no poet.'

'You are mistaken; I know him well; he is both. As poet *and* mathematician, he would reason well; as mere mathematician, he could not have reasoned at all, and thus would have been at the mercy of the Prefect.'

'You surprise me,' I said, 'by these opinions, which have been contradicted by the voice of the world. You do not mean to set at naught the well-digested idea of centuries. The mathematical reason has long been regarded as *the* reason *par excellence*.'

'"*Il y a à parier*,"' replied Dupin, quoting from Chamfort, '"*que toute idée publique, toute convention reçue, est une sottise, car elle a convenue au plus grand nombre*." The mathematicians, I grant you, have done their best to promulgate the popular error to which you allude, and which is none the less an error for its promulgation as truth. With an art worthy a better cause, for example, they have insinuated the term "analysis" into application to algebra. The French are the originators of this particular deception; but if a term is of any importance—if words derive any value from applicability—then "analysis" conveys "algebra" about as much as, in Latin, "*ambitus*" implies "ambition," "*religio*" "religion," or "*homines honesti*" a set of *honourable* men.'

'You have a quarrel on hand, I see,' said I, 'with some of the algebraists of Paris; but proceed.'

'I dispute the availability, and thus the value, of that reason which is cultivated in any especial form other than the abstractly logical. I dispute, in particular, the reason educed by mathematical study. The mathematics are the science of form and quantity; mathematical reasoning is merely logic applied to observation upon form and quantity. The great error lies in supposing that even the truths of what is called *pure* algebra, are abstract or general truths. And this error is so egregious that I am confounded at the universality with which it has been received. Mathematical axioms are *not* axioms of general truth. What is true of *relation*—of form and quantity—is often grossly false in regard to morals, for example. In this latter science it is very usually *un*true that the aggregated parts are equal to the whole. In chemistry also the axiom fails. In the consideration of motive it fails; for two motives, each of a given value, have not, necessarily, a value when united, equal to the sum of their values apart. There are numerous other mathematical truths which are only truths within the limits of *relation*. But the mathematician argues, from his *finite truths*, through habit, as if they were of an absolutely general applicability—as the world indeed imagines them to be. Bryant, in his very learned *Mythology*, mentions an analogous source of error, when he says that "although the Pagan fables are not believed, yet we forget ourselves continually, and make inferences from them as existing realities." With the algebraists, however, who are Pagans themselves, the "Pagan fables" *are* believed, and the inferences are made, not so much through lapse of memory, as through an unaccountable addling of the brains. In short, I never yet encountered the mere mathematician who could be trusted out of equal roots, or one who did not clandestinely hold it as a point of his faith that $x^2 + px$ was absolutely and unconditionally equal to q. Say to one of these gentlemen, by way of experiment, if you please, that you believe occasions may occur where $x^2 + px$ is *not* altogether equal to q, and, having made him understand what you mean, get out of his reach as speedily as convenient, for, beyond doubt, he will endeavour to knock you down.

'I mean to say,' continued Dupin, while I merely laughed at his last observations, 'that if the Minister had been no more than a mathematician, the Prefect would have been under no necessity of giving me this cheque. I knew him, however, as both mathematician and poet, and my measures were adapted to his capacity, with reference to the circumstances by which he was surrounded. I knew him as a courtier, too, and as a bold *intriguant.* Such a man, I considered, could not fail to be aware of the ordinary policial modes of action. He could not have failed to anticipate—and events have proved that he did not fail to anticipate—the waylayings to which he was subjected. He must have foreseen, I reflected, the secret investigations of his premises. His frequent absences from home at night, which were hailed by the Prefect as certain aids to his success, I regarded only as ruses, to afford opportunity for thorough search to the police, and thus the sooner to impress them with the conviction to which G——, in fact, did finally arrive—the conviction that the letter was not upon the premises. I felt, also, that the whole train of thought, which I was at some pains in detailing to you just now, concerning the invariable principle of policial action in searches for articles concealed—I felt that this whole train of thought would necessarily pass through the mind of the Minister. It would imperatively lead him to despise all the ordinary *nooks* of concealment. *He* could not, I reflected, be so weak as not to see that the most intricate and remote recess of his hotel would be as open as his commonest closets to the eyes, to the probes, to the gimlets, and to the microscopes of the Prefect. I saw, in fine, that he would be driven, as a matter of course, to *simplicity,* if not deliberately induced to it as a matter of choice. You will remember, perhaps, how desperately the Prefect laughed when I suggested, upon our first interview, that it was just possible this mystery troubled him so much on account of its being so *very* self-evident.'

'Yes,' said I, 'I remember his merriment well. I really thought he would have fallen into convulsions.'

'The material world,' continued Dupin, 'abounds with very strict analogies to the immaterial; and thus some colour of truth has been given to the rhetorical dogma, that metaphor, or simile, may be made to strengthen an argument, as well as to embellish a description. The principle of the *vis inertiæ*, for example, seems to be identical in physics and metaphysics. It is not more true in the former, that a large body is with more difficulty set in motion than a smaller one, and that its subsequent momentum is commensurate with this difficulty, than it is, in the latter, that intellects of the vaster capacity, while more forcible, more constant, and more eventful in their movements than those of inferior grade, are yet the less readily moved, and more embarrassed and full of hesitation in the first few steps of their progress. Again, have you ever noticed which of the street signs over the shop-doors are the most attractive of attention?'

'I have never given the matter a thought,' I said.

'There is a game of puzzles,' he resumed, 'which is played upon a map. One party playing requires another to find a given word—the name of town, river, state or empire—any word, in short, upon the motley and perplexed surface of the chart. A novice in the game generally seeks to embarrass his opponents by giving them the most minutely lettered names; but the adept selects such words as stretch, in large characters, from one end of the chart to the other. These, like the over-largely lettered signs and placards of the street, escape observation by dint of being excessively obvious; and here the physical oversight is precisely analogous with the moral inapprehension by which the intellect suffers to pass unnoticed those considerations which are too obtrusively and too palpably self-evident. But this is a point, it appears, somewhat above or beneath the understanding of the Prefect. He never once thought it probable, or possible, that the Minister had deposited the letter immediately beneath the nose of the whole world, by way of best preventing any portion of that world from perceiving it.

'But the more I reflected upon the daring, dashing, and discriminating ingenuity of D—— ; upon the fact that the document must always have been *at hand*, if he intended to use it to good purpose ; and upon the decisive evidence, obtained by the Prefect, that it was not hidden within the limits of that dignitary's ordinary search—the more satisfied I became that, to conceal this letter, the Minister had resorted to the comprehensive and sagacious expedient of not attempting to conceal it at all.

'Full of these ideas, I prepared myself with a pair of green spectacles, and called one fine morning, quite by accident, at the Ministerial hotel. I found D—— at home, yawning, lounging, and dawdling, as usual, and pretending to be in the last extremity of *ennui*. He is, perhaps, the most really energetic human being now alive—but that is only when nobody sees him.

'To be even with him, I complained of my weak eyes, and lamented the necessity of the spectacles, under cover of which I cautiously and thoroughly surveyed the whole apartment, while seemingly intent only upon the conversation of my host.

'I paid especial attention to a large writing-table near which he sat, and upon which lay confusedly some miscellaneous letters and other papers, with one or two musical instruments and a few books. Here, however, after a long and very deliberate scrutiny, I saw nothing to excite particular suspicion.

'At length my eyes, in going the circuit of the room, fell upon a trumpery filigree card-rack of pasteboard, that hung dangling by a dirty blue ribbon, from a little brass knob just beneath the middle of the mantelpiece. In this rack, which had three or four compartments, were five or six visiting cards and a solitary letter. This last was much soiled and crumpled. It was torn nearly in two, across the middle—as if a design, in the first instance, to tear it entirely up as worthless, had been altered, or stayed, in the second. It had a large black seal, bearing the D—— cipher *very* conspicuously, and was addressed, in a diminutive female hand, to D——, the Minister, himself. It was thrust carelessly, and even, as it seemed, contemptuously, into one of the uppermost divisions of the rack.

'No sooner had I glanced at this letter, than I concluded it to be that of which I was in search. To be sure, it was, to all appearance, radically different from the one of which the Prefect had read us so minute a description. Here the seal was large and black, with the D—— cipher; there it was small and red, with the ducal arms of the S—— family. Here, the address, to the Minister, was diminutive and feminine; there the superscription, to a certain royal personage, was markedly bold and decided; the size alone formed a point of correspondence. But then the *radicalness* of these differences, which was excessive; the dirt; the soiled and torn condition of the paper, so inconsistent with the *true* methodical habits of D——, and so suggestive of a design to delude the beholder into an idea of the worthlessness of the document; these things, together with the hyper-obtrusive situation of this document, full in the view of every visitor, and thus exactly in accordance with the conclusions to which I had previously arrived; these things, I say, were strongly corroborative of suspicion, in one who came with the intention to suspect.

'I protracted my visit as long as possible, and, while I maintained a most animated discussion with the Minister, upon a topic which I knew well had never failed to interest and excite him, I kept my attention really riveted upon the letter. In this examination, I committed to memory its external appearance and arrangement in the rack; and also fell, at length, upon a discovery, which set at rest whatever trivial doubt I might have entertained. In scrutinizing the edges of the paper, I observed them to be more *chafed* than seemed necessary. They presented the *broken* appearance which is manifested when a stiff paper, having been once folded and pressed with a folder, is refolded in a reverse direction, in the same creases or edges which had formed the original fold. This discovery was sufficient. It was clear to me that the letter had been turned, as a glove, inside out, redirected and resealed. I bade the Minister good-morning, and took my departure at once, leaving a gold snuff-box upon the table.

'The next morning I called for the snuff-box, when we resumed, quite eagerly, the conversation of the preceding day. While thus engaged, however, a loud report, as if of a pistol, was heard immediately beneath the windows of the hotel, and was succeeded by a series of fearful screams, and the shoutings of a terrified mob. D—— rushed to a casement, threw it open, and looked out. In the meantime, I stepped to the card-rack, took the letter, put it in my pocket, and replaced it by a fac-simile (so far as regards externals) which I had carefully prepared at my lodgings—imitating the D—— cipher, very readily, by means of a seal formed of bread.

'The disturbance in the street had been occasioned by the frantic behaviour of a man with a musket. He had fired it among a crowd of women and children. It proved, however, to have been without ball, and the fellow was suffered to go his way as a lunatic or a drunkard. When he had gone, D—— came from the window, whither I had followed him immediately upon securing the object in view. Soon afterwards I bade him farewell. The pretended lunatic was a man in my own pay.'

'But what purpose had you,' I asked, 'in replacing the letter by a fac-simile? Would it not have been better, at the first visit, to have seized it openly, and departed?'

'D——,' replied Dupin, 'is a desperate man, and a man of nerve. His hotel, too, is not without attendants devoted to his interests. Had I made the wild attempt you suggest, I might never have left the Ministerial presence alive. The good people of Paris might have heard of me no more. But I had an object apart from these considerations. You know my political prepossessions. In this matter, I act as a partisan of the lady concerned. For eighteen months the Minister has had her in his power. She has now him in hers—since, being unaware that the letter is not in his possession, he will proceed with his exactions as if it was. Thus will he inevitably commit himself, at once, to his political destruction. His downfall, too, will not be more precipitate than awkward. It is all very well to talk about the *facilis descensus Averni*; but in all kinds of climbing, as Catalani said of singing, it is far more easy to get up than to come down. In the present instance I have no sympathy—at least no pity—for him who descends. He is that *monstrum horrendum*, an unprincipled man of genius. I confess, however, that I should like very well to know the precise character of his thoughts, when, being defied by her whom the Prefect terms "a certain personage," he is reduced to opening the letter which I left for him in the card-rack.'

'How? did you put anything particular in it?'

'Why—it did not seem altogether right to leave the interior blank—that would have been insulting. D——, at Vienna once, did me an evil turn, which I told him, quite good-humouredly, that I should remember. So, as I knew he would feel some curiosity in regard to the identity of the person who had outwitted him, I thought it a pity not to give him a clue. He is well acquainted with my MS., and I just copied into the middle of the blank sheet the words:—

'"——Un dessein si funeste,
S'il n'est digne d'Atrée, est digne de Thyeste."

They are to be found in Crébillon's "Atrée."'

THE CASK OF AMONTILLADO

THE thousand injuries of Fortunato I had borne as I best could; but when he ventured upon insult, I vowed revenge. You, who so well know the nature of my soul, will not suppose, however, that I gave utterance to a threat. *At length* I would be avenged; this was a point definitely settled—but the very definitiveness with which it was resolved, precluded the idea of risk. I must not only punish, but punish with impunity. A wrong is unredressed when retribution overtakes its redresser. It is equally unredressed when the avenger fails to make himself felt as such to him who has done the wrong.

It must be understood, that neither by word nor deed had I given Fortunato cause to doubt my good-will. I continued, as was my wont, to smile in his face, and he did not perceive that my smile *now* was at the thought of his immolation.

He had a weak point—this Fortunato—although in other regards he was a man to be respected and even feared. He prided himself on his connoisseurship in wine. Few Italians have the true virtuoso spirit. For the most part their enthusiasm is adapted to suit the time and opportunity—to practise imposture upon the British and Austrian millionaires. In painting and gemmary Fortunato, like his countrymen, was a quack—but in the matter of old wines he was sincere. In this respect I did not differ from him materially: I was skilful in the Italian vintages myself, and bought largely whenever I could.

It was about dusk, one evening during the supreme madness of the Carnival season, that I encountered my friend. He accosted me with excessive warmth, for he had been drinking much. The man wore motley. He had on a tight-fitting parti-striped dress, and his head was surmounted by the conical cap and bells. I was so pleased to see him, that I thought I should never have done wringing his hand.

I said to him, 'My dear Fortunato, you are luckily met. How remarkably well you are looking to-day! But I have received a pipe of what passes for Amontillado, and I have my doubts.'

'How?' said he; 'Amontillado? A pipe? Impossible! And in the middle of the Carnival!'

'I have my doubts,' I replied; 'and I was silly enough to pay the full Amontillado price without consulting you in the matter. You were not to be found, and I was fearful of losing a bargain.'

'Amontillado!'

'I have my doubts.'

'Amontillado!'

'And I must satisfy them.'

'Amontillado!'

'As you are engaged, I am on my way to Luchesi. If any one has a critical turn, it is he. He will tell me——'

'Luchesi cannot tell Amontillado from Sherry.'

'And yet some fools will have it that his taste is a match for your own.'

'Come, let us go.'

'Whither?'

'To your vaults.'

'My friend, no; I will not impose upon your good-nature. I perceive you have an engagement. Luchesi——'

'I have no engagement; come.'

'My friend, no. It is not the engagement, but the severe cold with which I perceive you are afflicted. The vaults are insufferably damp. They are encrusted with nitre.'

'Let us go nevertheless. The cold is merely nothing. Amontillado! You have been imposed upon. And as for Luchesi—he cannot distinguish Sherry from Amontillado.'

Thus speaking, Fortunato possessed himself of my arm. Putting on a mask of black silk, and drawing a *roquelaire* closely about my person, I suffered him to hurry me to my palazzo.

There were no attendants at home; they had absconded to make merry in honour of the time. I had told them that I should not return until the morning, and had given them explicit orders not to stir from the house. These orders were sufficient, I well knew, to ensure their immediate disappearance, one and all, as soon as my back was turned.

I took from their sconces two flambeaux, and giving one to Fortunato, bowed him through several suites of rooms to the archway that led into the vaults. I passed down a long and winding staircase, requesting him to be cautious as he followed. We came at length to the foot of the descent, and stood together on the damp ground of the catacombs of the Montresors.

The gait of my friend was unsteady, and the bells upon his cap jingled as he strode.

'The pipe,' said he.

'It is farther on,' said I; 'but observe the white webwork which gleams from these cavern walls.'

He turned towards me, and looked into my eyes with two filmy orbs that distilled the rheum of intoxication.

'Nitre?' he asked, at length.

'Nitre,' I replied. 'How long have you had that cough?'

'Ugh! ugh! ugh!—ugh! ugh! ugh!—ugh! ugh! ugh!—ugh! ugh! ugh!—ugh! ugh! ugh!'

My poor friend found it impossible to reply for many minutes.

'It is nothing,' he said at last.

'Come,' I said, with decision, 'we will go back; your health is precious. You are rich, respected, admired, beloved; you are happy, as once I was. You are a man to be missed. For me it is no matter. We will go back; you will be ill, and I cannot be responsible. Besides, there is Luchesi——'

'Enough,' he said, 'the cough is a mere nothing; it will not kill me. I shall not die of a cough.'

'True—true,' I replied; 'and, indeed, I had no intention of alarming you unnecessarily—but you should use all proper caution. A draught of this Médoc will defend us from the damps.'

Here I knocked off the neck of a bottle which I drew from a long row of its fellows that lay upon the mould.

'Drink,' I said, presenting him the wine.

He raised it to his lips with a leer. He paused and nodded to me familiarly, while his bells jingled.

'I drink,' he said, 'to the buried that repose around us.'

'And I to your long life.'

He again took my arm, and we proceeded.

'These vaults,' he said, 'are extensive.'

'The Montresors,' I replied, 'were a great and numerous family.'

'I forget your arms.'

'A huge human foot d'or, in a field azure; the foot crushes a serpent rampant whose fangs are embedded in the heel.'

'And the motto?'

'*Nemo me impune lacessit.*'

'Good!' he said.

The wine sparkled in his eyes and the bells jingled. My own fancy grew warm with the Médoc. We had passed through walls with piled bones, with casks and puncheons intermingling, into the inmost recesses of the catacombs. I paused again, and this time I made bold to seize Fortunato by an arm above the elbow.

'The nitre!' I said; 'see, it increases. It hangs like moss upon the vaults. We are below the river's bed. The drops of moisture trickle among the bones.

Come, we will go back ere it is too late. Your cough——'

'It is nothing,' he said; 'let us go on. But first, another draught of the Médoc.'

I broke and reached him a flagon of De Grâve. He emptied it at a breath. His eyes flashed with a fierce light. He laughed and threw the bottle upwards with a gesticulation I did not understand.

I looked at him in surprise. He repeated the movement—a grotesque one.

'You do not comprehend?' he said.

'Not I,' I replied.

'Then you are not of the brotherhood.'

'How?'

'You are not of the masons.'

'Yes, yes,' I said; 'yes, yes.'

'You? Impossible! A mason?'

'A mason,' I replied.

'A sign,' he said.

'It is this,' I answered, producing a trowel from beneath the folds of my *roquelaire.*

'You jest,' he exclaimed, recoiling a few paces. 'But let us proceed to the Amontillado.'

'Be it so,' I said, replacing the tool beneath the cloak, and again offering him my arm. He leaned upon it heavily. We continued our route in search of the Amontillado. We passed through a range of low arches, descended, passed on, and descending again, arrived at a deep crypt, in which the foulness of the air caused our flambeaux rather to glow than flame.

At the most remote end of the crypt there appeared another less spacious. Its walls had been lined with human remains, piled to the vault overhead, in the fashion of the great catacombs of Paris. Three sides of this interior crypt were still ornamented in this manner. From the fourth the bones had been thrown down, and lay promiscuously upon the earth, forming at one point a mound of some size. Within the wall thus exposed by the displacing of the bones, we perceived a still interior recess, in depth about four feet, in width three, in height six or seven. It seemed to have been constructed for no especial use within itself, but formed merely the interval between two of the colossal supports of the roof of the catacombs, and was backed by one of their circumscribing walls of solid granite.

It was in vain that Fortunato, uplifting his dull torch, endeavoured to pry into the depth of the recess. Its termination the feeble light did not enable us to see.

'Proceed,' I said; 'herein is the Amontillado. As for Luchesi——'

'He is an ignoramus,' interrupted my friend, as he stepped unsteadily forward, while I followed immediately at his heels. In an instant he had reached the extremity of the niche, and finding his progress arrested by the rock, stood stupidly bewildered. A moment more and I had fettered him to the granite. In its surface were two iron staples, distant from each other about two feet, horizontally. From one of these depended a short chain, from the other a padlock. Throwing the links about his waist, it was but the work of a few seconds to secure it. He was too much astounded to resist. Withdrawing the key, I stepped back from the recess.

'Pass your hand,' I said, 'over the wall; you cannot help feeling the nitre. Indeed it is *very* damp. Once more let me *implore* you to return. No? Then I must positively leave you. But I must first render you all the little attentions in my power.'

'The Amontillado!' ejaculated my friend, not yet recovered from his astonishment.

'True,' I replied, 'the Amontillado.'

As I said these words I busied myself among the pile of bones of which I have before spoken. Throwing them aside, I soon uncovered a quantity of building stone and mortar. With these materials, and with the aid of my trowel, I began vigorously to wall up the entrance of the niche.

I had scarcely laid the first tier of the masonry when I discovered that the intoxication of Fortunato had in a great measure worn off. The earliest indication I had of this was a low moaning cry from the depth of the recess. It was *not* the cry of a drunken man. There was then a long and obstinate silence. I laid the second tier, and the third, and the fourth; and then I heard the furious vibrations of the chain. The noise lasted for several minutes, during which, that I might hearken to it with the more satisfaction, I ceased my labours and sat down upon the bones. When at last the clanking subsided, I resumed the trowel, and finished without interruption the fifth, the sixth, and the seventh tier. The wall was now nearly upon a level with my breast. I again paused, and holding the flambeaux over the mason-work, threw a few feeble rays upon the figure within.

A succession of loud and shrill screams, bursting suddenly from the throat of the chained form, seemed to thrust me violently back. For a brief moment I hesitated—I trembled. Unsheathing my rapier, I began to grope with it about the recess; but the thought of an instant reassured me. I placed my hand upon the solid fabric of the catacombs, and felt satisfied. I reapproached the wall. I replied to the yells of him who clamoured. I re-echoed—I aided—I surpassed them in volume and in strength. I did this, and the clamourer grew still.

It was now midnight, and my task was drawing to a close. I had completed the eighth, the ninth, and the tenth tier. I had finished a portion of the last and the eleventh; there remained but a single stone to be fitted and plastered in. I struggled with its weight; I placed it partially in its destined position. But now there came from out the niche a low laugh that erected the hairs upon my head. It was succeeded by a sad voice, which I had difficulty in recognizing as that of the noble Fortunato. The voice said—

'Ha! ha! ha!—he! he!—a very good joke indeed—an excellent jest. We will have many a rich laugh about it at the palazzo—he! he! he!—over our wine—he! he! he!'

'The Amontillado!' I said.

'He! he! he!—he! he! he!—yes, the Amontillado. But is it not getting late? Will not they be awaiting us at the palazzo, the Lady Fortunato and the rest? Let us be gone.'

'Yes,' I said, 'let us be gone.'

'*For the love of God, Montresor!*'

'Yes,' I said, 'for the love of God!'

But to these words I hearkened in vain for a reply. I grew impatient. I called aloud—

'Fortunato!'

No answer. I called again—

'Fortunato!'

No answer still. I thrust a torch through the remaining aperture and let it fall within. There came forth in return only a jingling of the bells. My heart grew sick on account of the dampness of the catacombs. I hastened to make an end of my labour. I forced the last stone into its position; I plastered it up. Against the new masonry I re-erected the old rampart of bones. For the half of a century no mortal has disturbed them. *In pace requiescat!*

CHARLES DICKENS

1812–1870

THE HOLLY-TREE

Three Branches

FIRST BRANCH

MYSELF

I HAVE kept one secret in the course of my life. I am a bashful man. Nobody would suppose it, nobody ever does suppose it, nobody ever did suppose it, but I am naturally a bashful man. This is the secret which I have never breathed until now.

I might greatly move the reader by some account of the innumerable places I have not been to, the innumerable people I have not called upon or received, the innumerable social evasions I have been guilty of, solely because I am by original constitution and character a bashful man. But I will leave the reader unmoved, and proceed with the object before me.

That object is to give a plain account of my travels and discoveries in the Holly-Tree Inn; in which place of good entertainment for man and beast I was once snowed up.

It happened in the memorable year when I parted for ever from Angela Leath, whom I was shortly to have married, on making the discovery that she preferred my bosom friend. From our school-days I had freely admitted Edwin, in my own mind, to be far superior to myself; and, though I was grievously wounded at heart, I felt the preference to be natural, and tried to forgive them both. It was under these circumstances that I resolved to go to America—on my way to the Devil.

Communicating my discovery neither to Angela nor to Edwin, but resolving to write each of them an affecting letter conveying my blessing and forgiveness, which the steam-tender for shore should carry to the post when I myself should be bound for the New World, far beyond recall,—I say, locking up my grief in my own breast, and consoling myself as I could with the prospect of being generous, I quietly left all I held dear, and started on the desolate journey I have mentioned.

The dead winter-time was in full dreariness when I left my chambers for ever, at five o'clock in the morning. I had shaved by candle-light, of course, and was miserably cold, and experienced that general all-pervading sensation of getting up to be hanged which I have usually found inseparable from untimely rising under such circumstances.

How well I remember the forlorn aspect of Fleet-street when I came out of the Temple! The street-lamps flickering in the gusty north-east wind, as if the very gas were contorted with cold; the white-topped houses; the bleak, star-lighted sky; the market people and other early stragglers, trotting to circulate their almost frozen blood; the hospitable light and warmth of the few coffee-shops and public-houses that were open for such customers; the hard, dry, frosty rime with which the air was charged (the wind had already beaten it into every crevice), and which lashed my face like a steel whip.

It wanted nine days to the end of the month, and end of the year. The Post-office packet for the United States was to depart from Liverpool, weather permitting, on the first of the ensuing month, and I had the intervening time on my hands. I had taken this into consideration, and had resolved to make a visit to a certain spot (which I need not name) on the farther borders of Yorkshire. It was endeared to me by my having first seen Angela at a farmhouse in that place, and my melancholy was gratified by the idea of taking a wintry leave of it before my expatriation. I ought to explain, that, to avoid being sought out before my resolution should have been rendered irrevocable by being carried into full effect, I had written to Angela overnight, in my usual manner, lamenting that urgent business, of which she should know all particulars by-and-by—took me unexpectedly away from her for a week or ten days.

There was no Northern Railway at that time, and in its place there were stage-coaches; which I occasionally find myself, in common with some other people, affecting to lament now, but which everybody dreaded as a very serious penance then. I had secured the box-seat on the fastest of these, and my business in Fleet-street was to get into a cab with my portmanteau, so to make the best of my way to the Peacock at Islington, where I was to join this coach. But when one of our Temple watchmen, who carried my portmanteau into Fleet-street for me, told me about the huge blocks of ice that had for some days past been floating in the river, having closed up in the night, and made a walk from the Temple Gardens over to the Surrey shore, I began to ask myself the question, whether the box-seat would not be likely to put a sudden and a frosty end to my unhappiness. I was heart-broken, it is true, and yet I was not quite so far gone as to wish to be frozen to death.

When I got up to the Peacock,—where I found everybody drinking hot purl, in self-preservation,—I asked if there were an inside seat to spare. I then discovered that, inside or out, I was the only passenger. This gave me a still livelier idea of the great inclemency of the weather, since that coach always loaded particularly well. However, I took a little purl (which I found uncommonly good), and got into the coach. When I was seated, they built me up with straw to the waist, and, conscious of making a rather ridiculous appearance, I began my journey.

It was still dark when we left the Peacock. For a little while, pale, uncertain ghosts of houses and trees appeared and vanished, and then it was hard, black, frozen day. People were lighting their fires; smoke was mounting straight up high into the rarefied air; and we were rattling for Highgate Archway over the hardest ground I have ever heard the ring of iron shoes on. As we got into the country, everything seemed to have grown old and grey. The roads, the trees, thatched roofs of cottages and homesteads, the ricks in farmers' yards. Out-door work was abandoned, horse-troughs at roadside inns were frozen hard, no stragglers lounged about, doors were close shut, little turnpike houses had blazing fires inside, and children (even turnpike people have children, and seem to like them) rubbed the frost from the little panes of glass with their chubby arms, that their bright eyes might catch a glimpse of the solitary coach going by. I don't know when the snow began to set in; but I know that we were changing horses somewhere when I heard the guard remark, 'That the old lady up in the sky was picking her geese pretty hard to-day.' Then, indeed, I found the white down falling fast and thick.

The lonely day wore on, and I dozed it out, as a lonely traveller does. I was warm and valiant after eating and drinking,—particularly after dinner; cold and depressed at all other times. I was always bewildered as to time and place, and always more or less out of my senses. The coach and horses seemed to execute in chorus Auld Lang Syne, without a moment's intermission. They kept the time and tune with the greatest regularity, and rose into the swell at the beginning of the Refrain, with a precision that worried me to death. While we changed horses, the guard and coachman went stumping up and down the road, printing off their shoes in the snow, and poured so much liquid consolation into themselves without being any the worse for it, that I began to confound them, as it darkened again, with two great white casks standing on end. Our horses tumbled down in solitary places, and we got them up,—which was the pleasantest variety *I* had, for it warmed me. And it snowed and snowed, and still it snowed, and never left off snowing. All night long we went on in this manner. Thus we came round the clock, upon the Great North Road, to the performance of Auld Lang Syne all day again. And it snowed and snowed, and still it snowed, and never left off snowing.

I forget now where we were at noon on the second day, and where we ought to have been; but I know that we were scores of miles behindhand, and that our case was growing worse every hour. The drift was becoming prodigiously deep; landmarks were getting snowed out; the road and the fields were all one; instead of having fences and hedge-rows to guide us, we went crunching on over an unbroken surface of ghastly white that might sink beneath us at any moment and drop us down a whole hillside. Still the coachman and guard—who kept together on the box, always in council, and looking well about them—made out the track with astonishing sagacity.

When we came in sight of a town, it looked, to my fancy, like a large drawing on a slate, with abundance of slate-pencil expended on the churches and houses where the snow lay thickest. When we came within a town, and found the church clocks all stopped, the dial-faces choked with snow, and the inn-signs blotted out, it seemed as if the whole place were overgrown with white moss. As to the coach, it was a mere snowball; similarly, the men and boys who ran along beside us to the town's end, turning our clogged wheels and encouraging our horses, were men and boys of snow; and the bleak wild solitude to which they at last dismissed us was a snowy Sahara. One would have thought this enough: notwithstanding which, I pledge my word that it snowed and snowed, and still it snowed, and never left off snowing.

We performed Auld Lang Syne the whole day; seeing nothing, out of towns and villages, but the track of stoats, hares, and foxes, and sometimes of birds. At nine o'clock at night, on a Yorkshire moor, a cheerful burst from our horn, and a welcome sound of talking, with a glimmering and moving about of lanterns, roused me from my drowsy state. I found that we were going to change.

They helped me out, and I said to a waiter, whose bare head became as white as King Lear's in a single minute, 'What Inn is this?'

'The Holly-Tree, Sir,' said he.

'Upon my word, I believe,' said I, apologetically, to the guard and coachman, 'that I must stop here.'

Now the landlord, and the landlady, and the ostler, and the postboy, and all the stable authorities, had already asked the coachman, to the wide-eyed interest of all the rest of the establishment, if he meant to go on. The coachman had already replied, 'Yes, he'd take her through it,'—meaning by Her the coach,—'if so be as George would stand by him.' George was the guard, and he had already sworn that he *would* stand by him. So the helpers were already getting the horses out.

My declaring myself beaten, after this parley, was not an announcement without preparation. Indeed, but for the way to the announcement being smoothed by the parley, I more than doubt whether, as an innately bashful man, I should have had the confidence to make it. As it was, it received the approval even of the guard and coachman. Therefore, with many confirmations of my inclining, and many remarks from one bystander to another, that the gentleman could go for'ard by the mail to-morrow, whereas to-night he would only be froze, and where was the good of a gentleman being froze ?—ah ! let alone buried alive (which latter clause was added by a humorous helper as a joke at my expense, and was extremely well received), I saw my portmanteau got out stiff, like a frozen body ; did the handsome thing by the guard and coachman ; wished them good-night and a prosperous journey ; and, a little ashamed of myself, after all, for leaving them to fight it out alone, followed the landlord, landlady, and waiter of the Holly-Tree upstairs.

I thought I had never seen such a large room as that into which they showed me. It had five windows, with dark red curtains that would have absorbed the light of a general illumination ; and there were complications of drapery at the top of the curtains, that went wandering about the wall in a most extraordinary manner. I asked for a smaller room, and they told me there was no smaller room. They could screen me in, however, the landlord said. They brought a great old japanned screen, with natives (Japanese, I suppose) engaged in a variety of idiotic pursuits all over it ; and left me roasting whole before an immense fire.

My bedroom was some quarter of a mile off, up a great staircase at the end of a long gallery ; and nobody knows what a misery this is to a bashful man who would rather not meet people on the stairs. It was the grimmest room I have ever had the nightmare in ; and all the furniture, from the four posts of the bed to the two old silver candlesticks, was tall, high-shouldered, and spindle-waisted. Below, in my sitting-room, if I looked round my screen, the wind rushed at me like a mad bull ; if I stuck to my armchair, the fire scorched me to the colour of a new brick. The chimney-piece was very high, and there was a bad glass —what I may call a wavy glass—above it, which, when I stood up, just showed me my anterior phrenological developments,—and these never look well, in any subject, cut short off at the eyebrow. If I stood with my back to the fire, a gloomy vault of darkness above and beyond the screen insisted on being looked at; and, in its dim remoteness, the drapery of the ten curtains of the five windows went twisting and creeping about, like a nest of gigantic worms.

I suppose that what I observe in myself must be observed by some other men of similar character in *themselves*; therefore I am emboldened to mention, that, when I travel, I never arrive at a place but I immediately want to go away from it. Before I had finished my supper of broiled fowl and mulled port, I had impressed upon the waiter in detail my arrangements for departure in the morning. Breakfast and bill at eight. Fly at nine. Two horses, or, if needful, even four.

Tired though I was, the night appeared about a week long. In cases of nightmare, I thought of Angela, and felt more depressed than ever by the reflection that I was on the shortest road to Gretna Green. What had *I* to do with Gretna Green? I was not going *that* way to the Devil, but by the American route, I remarked in my bitterness.

In the morning I found that it was snowing still, that it had snowed all night, and that I was snowed up. Nothing could get out of that spot on the moor, or could come at it, until the road had been cut out by labourers from the market-town. When they might cut their way to the Holly-Tree nobody could tell me.

It was now Christmas-eve. I should have had a dismal Christmas-time of it anywhere, and consequently that did not so much matter; still, being snowed up was like dying of frost, a thing I had not bargained for. I felt very lonely. Yet I could no more have proposed to the landlord and landlady to admit me to their society (though I should have liked it very much) than I could have asked them to present me with a piece of plate. Here my great secret, the real bashfulness of my character, is to be observed. Like most bashful men, I judge of other people as if they were bashful too. Besides being far too shame-faced to make the proposal myself, I really had a delicate misgiving that it would be in the last degree disconcerting to them.

Trying to settle down, therefore, in my solitude, I first of all asked what books there were in the house. The waiter brought me a *Book of Roads*, two or three old Newspapers, a little Song-Book, terminating in a collection of Toasts and Sentiments, a little Jest-Book, an odd volume of *Peregrine Pickle*, and the *Sentimental Journey*. I knew every word of the two last already, but I read them through again, then tried to hum all the songs (Auld Lang Syne was among them); went entirely through the jokes,—in which I found a fund of melancholy adapted to my state of mind; proposed all the toasts, enunciated all the sentiments, and mastered the papers. The latter had nothing in them but stock advertisements, a meeting about a county rate, and a highway robbery. As I am a greedy reader, I could not make this supply hold out until night; it was exhausted by tea-time. Being then entirely cast upon my own resources, I got through an hour in considering what to do next. Ultimately, it came into my head (from which I was anxious by any means to exclude Angela and Edwin), that I would endeavour to recall my experience of Inns, and would try how long it lasted me. I stirred the fire, moved my chair a little to one side of the screen,—not daring to go far, for I knew the wind was waiting to make a rush at me, I could hear it growling,—and began.

My first impressions of an Inn dated from the Nursery; consequently I went back to the Nursery for a starting-point, and found myself at the knee of a sallow woman with a fishy eye, an aquiline nose, and a green gown, whose speciality was a dismal narrative of a landlord by the roadside, whose visitors unaccountably disappeared for many years, until it was discovered that the pursuit of his life had been to convert them into pies. For the better devotion of himself to this branch of industry, he had constructed a secret door behind the head of the bed; and when the visitor (oppressed with pie) had fallen asleep, this wicked landlord would look softly in with a lamp in one hand and a knife in the other, would cut his throat, and would make him into pies; for which purpose he had coppers, underneath a trap-door, always boiling; and rolled out his pastry in the dead of the night. Yet even he was not insensible to the stings of conscience, for he never went to sleep without being heard to mutter, 'Too much pepper!' which was eventually the cause of his being brought to justice. I had no sooner disposed of this criminal than there started up another of the same period, whose profession was originally housebreaking; in the pursuit of which art he had had his right ear chopped off one night, as he was burglariously getting in at a window, by a brave and lovely servant-maid (whom the aquiline-nosed woman, though not at all answering the description, always mysteriously implied to be herself). After several years, this brave and lovely servant-maid was married to the landlord of a country Inn; which landlord had this remarkable characteristic, that he always wore a silk nightcap, and never would on any consideration take it off. At last, one night, when he was fast asleep, the brave and lovely woman lifted up his silk nightcap on the right side, and found that he had no ear there; upon which she sagaciously perceived that he was the clipped housebreaker, who had married her with the intention of putting her to death. She immediately heated the poker and terminated his career, for which she was taken to King George upon his throne, and received the compliments of royalty on her great discretion and valour. This same narrator, who had a Ghoulish pleasure, I have long been persuaded, in terrifying me to the utmost confines of my reason, had another authentic anecdote within her own experience, founded, I now believe, upon *Raymond and Agnes, or the Bleeding Nun.* She said it happened to her brother-in-law, who was immensely rich,—which my father was not; and immensely tall,—which my father was not. It was always a point with this Ghoul to present my dearest relations and friends to my youthful mind under circumstances of disparaging contrast. The brother-in-law was riding once through a forest on a magnificent horse (we had no magnificent horse at our house), attended by a favourite and valuable Newfoundland dog (we had no dog), when he found himself benighted, and came to an Inn. A dark woman opened the door, and he asked her if he could have a bed there. She answered yes, and put his horse in the stable, and took him into a room where there were two dark men. While he was at supper, a parrot in the room began to talk, saying, 'Blood, blood! Wipe up the blood!' Upon which one of the dark men wrung the parrot's neck, and said he was fond of roasted parrots, and he meant to have this one for breakfast in the morning. After eating and drinking heartily, the immensely rich, tall brother-in-law went up to bed; but he was rather vexed, because they had shut his dog in the stable, saying that they never allowed dogs in the house. He sat very quiet for more than an hour, thinking and thinking, when, just as his candle was burning out, he heard a scratch at the door. He opened the door, and there was the Newfoundland dog! The dog came softly in, smelt about him, went straight to some straw in the corner which the dark men had said covered apples, tore the straw away, and disclosed two sheets steeped in blood. Just at that moment the candle went out, and the brother-in-law, looking through a chink in the door, saw the two dark men stealing upstairs; one armed with a dagger that long (about five feet); the other carrying a chopper, a sack, and a spade. Having no remembrance of the close of this adventure, I suppose my faculties to have been always so frozen with terror at this stage of it, that the power of listening stagnated within me for some quarter of an hour.

These barbarous stories carried me, sitting there on the Holly-Tree hearth, to the Roadside Inn, renowned in my time in a sixpenny book with a folding plate, representing in a central compartment of oval form the portrait of Jonathan Bradford, and in four corner compartments four incidents of the tragedy with which the name is associated,—coloured with a hand at once so free and economical, that the bloom of Jonathan's complexion passed without any pause into the breeches of the ostler, and, smearing itself off into the next division, became rum in a bottle. Then I remembered how the landlord was found at the murdered traveller's bedside, with his own knife at his feet, and blood upon his hand; how he was hanged for the murder, notwithstanding his protestation that he had indeed come there to kill the traveller for his saddle-bags, but had been stricken motionless on finding him already slain; but how the ostler, years afterwards, owned the deed. By this time I had made myself quite uncomfortable. I stirred the fire, and stood with my back to it as long as I could bear the heat, looking up at the darkness beyond the screen, and at the wormy curtains creeping in and creeping out, like the worms in the ballad of Alonzo the Brave and the Fair Imogene.

There was an Inn in the cathedral town where I

went to school, which had pleasanter recollections about it than any of these. I took it next. It was the Inn where friends used to put up, and where we used to go to see parents, and to have salmon and fowls, and be tipped. It had an ecclesiastical sign,—the Mitre,—and a bar that seemed to be the next best thing to a bishopric, it was so snug. I loved the landlord's youngest daughter to distraction,—but let that pass. It was in this Inn that I was cried over by my rosy little sister, because I had acquired a black eye in a fight. And though she had been, that Holly-Tree night, for many a long year where all tears are dried, the Mitre softened me yet.

'To be continued to-morrow,' said I, when I took my candle to go to bed. But my bed took it upon itself to continue the train of thought that night. It carried me away, like the enchanted carpet, to a distant place (though still in England), and there, alighting from a stage-coach at another Inn in the snow, as I had actually done some years before, I repeated in my sleep a curious experience I had really had here. More than a year before I made the journey in the course of which I put up at that Inn, I had lost a very near and dear friend by death. Every night since, at home or away from home, I had dreamed of that friend; sometimes as still living; sometimes as returning from the world of shadows to comfort me; always as being beautiful, placid, and happy, never in association with any approach to fear or distress. It was at a lonely Inn in a wide moorland place, that I halted to pass the night. When I had looked from my bedroom window over the waste of snow on which the moon was shining, I sat down by my fire to write a letter. I had always, until that hour, kept it within my own breast that I dreamed every night of the dear lost one. But in the letter that I wrote I recorded the circumstance, and added that I felt much interested in proving whether the subject of my dream would still be faithful to me, travel-tired, and in that remote place. No. I lost the beloved figure of my vision in parting with the secret. My sleep has never looked upon it since, in sixteen years, but once. I was in Italy, and awoke (or seemed to awake), the well-remembered voice distinctly in my ears, conversing with it. I entreated it, as it rose above my bed and soared up to the vaulted roof of the old room, to answer me a question I had asked touching the Future Life. My hands were still outstretched towards it as it vanished, when I heard a bell ringing by the garden wall, and a voice in the deep stillness of the night calling on all good Christians to pray for the souls of the dead; it being All Souls' Eve.

To return to the Holly-Tree. When I awoke next day, it was freezing hard, and the lowering sky threatened more snow. My breakfast cleared away, I drew my chair into its former place, and, with the fire getting so much the better of the landscape that I sat in twilight, resumed my Inn remembrances.

That was a good Inn down in Wiltshire where I put up once, in the days of the hard Wiltshire ale, and before all beer was bitterness. It was on the skirts of Salisbury Plain, and the midnight wind that rattled my lattice window came moaning at me from Stonehenge. There was a hanger-on at that establishment (a supernaturally preserved Druid I believe him to have been, and to be still), with long white hair, and a flinty blue eye always looking afar off; who claimed to have been a shepherd, and who seemed to be ever watching for the reappearance, on the verge of the horizon, of some ghostly flock of sheep that had been mutton for many ages. He was a man with a weird belief in him that no one could count the stones of Stonehenge twice, and make the same number of them; likewise, that any one who counted them three times nine times, and then stood in the centre and said, 'I dare!' would behold a tremendous apparition, and be stricken dead. He pretended to have seen a bustard (I suspect him to have been familiar with the dodo), in manner following: He was out upon the plain at the close of a late autumn day, when he dimly discerned, going on before him at a curious fitfully bounding pace, what he at first supposed to be a gig-umbrella that had been blown from some conveyance, but what he presently believed to be a lean dwarf man upon a little pony. Having followed this object for some distance without gaining on it, and having called to it many times without receiving any answer, he pursued it for miles and miles, when, at length coming up with it, he discovered it to be the last bustard in Great Britain, degenerated into a wingless state, and running along the ground. Resolved to capture him or perish in the attempt, he closed with the bustard; but the bustard, who had formed a counter-resolution that he should do neither, threw him, stunned him, and was last seen making off due west. This weird man, at that stage of metempsychosis, may have been a sleep-walker or an enthusiast or a robber; but I awoke one night to find him in the dark at my bedside, repeating the Athanasian Creed in a terrific voice. I paid my bill next day, and retired from the county with all possible precipitation.

That was not a commonplace story which worked itself out at a little Inn in Switzerland, while I was staying there. It was a very homely place, in a village of one narrow zigzag street, among mountains, and you went in at the main door through the cow-house, and among the mules and the dogs and the fowls, before ascending a great bare staircase to the rooms; which were all of unpainted wood, without plastering or papering,—like rough packing-cases. Outside there was nothing but the straggling street, a little toy church with a copper-coloured steeple, a pine forest, a torrent, mists, and mountain sides. A young man belonging to this Inn had disappeared eight weeks before (it was winter-time), and was supposed to have had some undiscovered love affair, and to have gone for a soldier. He had got up in the night, and dropped into the village street from the loft in which he slept with another man; and he had done it so quietly, that his companion and fellow-labourer had heard no movement when he was awakened in the morning, and they said, 'Louis, where is Henri?' They looked for him high and low, in vain, and gave him up. Now, outside this Inn, there stood, as there stood outside every dwelling in the village, a stack of firewood; but the stack belonging to the Inn was higher than any of the rest, because the Inn was the richest house, and burnt the most fuel. It began to be noticed, while they were looking high and low, that a Bantam cock, part of the live stock of the Inn, put himself wonderfully out of his way to get to the top of this wood-stack; and that he would stay there for hours and hours, crowing, until he appeared in danger of splitting himself. Five weeks went on,—six weeks,—and still this terrible Bantam, neglecting his domestic affairs, was always on the top of the wood-stack, crowing the very eyes out of his head. By this time it was perceived that Louis had become inspired with a violent animosity towards the terrible Bantam, and one morning he was seen by a woman, who sat nursing her goitre at a little window in a gleam of sun, to catch up a rough billet of wood, with a great oath, hurl it at the terrible Bantam crowing on the wood-stack, and bring him down dead. Hereupon the woman, with a sudden light in her mind, stole round to the back of the wood-stack, and, being a good climber, as all those women are, climbed up, and soon was seen upon the summit, screaming, looking down the hollow within, and crying, 'Seize Louis, the murderer! Ring the church bell! Here is the body!' I saw the murderer that day, and I saw him as I sat by my fire at the Holly-Tree Inn, and I see him now, lying shackled with cords on the stable litter, among the mild eyes and the smoking breath of the cows, waiting to be taken away by the police, and stared at by the fearful village. A heavy animal,—the dullest animal in the stables,—with a stupid head, and a lumpish face devoid of any trace of sensibility, who had been, within the knowledge of the murdered youth, an embezzler of certain small moneys belonging to his master, and who had taken this hopeful mode of putting a possible accuser out of his way. All of which he confessed next day, like a sulky wretch who couldn't be troubled any more, now that they had got hold of him, and meant to make an end of him. I saw him once again, on the day of my departure from the Inn. In that Canton the headsman still does his office with a sword; and I came upon this murderer sitting bound to a chair, with his eyes bandaged, on a scaffold in a little market-place. In that instant, a great sword (loaded with quicksilver in the thick part of the blade) swept round him like a gust of wind or fire, and there was no such creature in the world. My wonder was, not that he was so suddenly dispatched, but that any head was left unreaped, within a radius of fifty yards of that tremendous sickle.

That was a good Inn, too, with the kind, cheerful landlady and the honest landlord, where I lived in the shadow of Mont Blanc, and where one of the apartments has a zoological papering on the walls, not so accurately joined but that the elephant occasionally rejoices in a tiger's hind legs and tail, while the lion puts on a trunk and tusks, and the bear, moulting as it were, appears as to portions of himself like a leopard. I made several American friends at that Inn, who all called Mont Blanc Mount Blank,—except one good-humoured gentleman, of a very sociable nature, who became on such intimate terms with it that he spoke of it familiarly as 'Blank'; observing, at breakfast, 'Blank looks pretty tall this morning'; or considerably doubting in the courtyard in the evening, whether there warn't some go-ahead naters in our country, Sir, that would make out the top of Blank in a couple of hours from the first start—now!

Once I passed a fortnight at an Inn in the North of England, where I was haunted by the ghost of a tremendous pie. It was a Yorkshire pie, like a fort,—an abandoned fort with nothing in it; but the waiter had a fixed idea that it was a point of ceremony at every meal to put the pie on the table. After some days I tried to hint, in several delicate ways, that I considered the pie done with; as, for example, by emptying fag-ends of glasses of wine into it; putting cheese-plates and spoons into it, as into a basket; putting wine-bottles into it, as into a cooler; but always in vain, the pie being invariably cleaned out again and brought up as before. At last, beginning to be doubtful whether I was not the victim of a spectral illusion, and whether my health and spirits might not sink under the horrors of an imaginary pie, I cut a triangle out of it, fully as large as the musical instrument of that name in a powerful orchestra. Human prevision could not have foreseen the result—but the waiter mended the pie. With some effectual species of cement, he adroitly fitted the triangle in again, and I paid my reckoning and fled.

The Holly-Tree was getting rather dismal. I made an overland expedition beyond the screen, and penetrated as far as the fourth window. Here I was driven back by stress of weather. Arrived at my winter-quarters once more, I made up the fire, and took another Inn.

It was in the remotest part of Cornwall. A great annual Miners' Feast was being holden at the Inn, when I and my travelling companions presented ourselves at night among the wild crowd that were dancing before it by torchlight. We had had a break-down in the dark, on a stony morass some miles away; and I had the honour of leading one of the unharnessed post-horses. If any lady or gentleman, on perusal of the present lines, will take any very tall post-horse with his traces hanging about his legs, and will conduct him by the bearing-rein into the heart of a country dance of a hundred and fifty couples, that lady or gentleman will then, and only then, form an adequate idea of the extent to which that post-horse will tread on his conductor's toes. Over and above which, the post-horse, finding three hundred people whirling about him, will probably rear, and also lash out with his hind legs, in a manner incompatible with dignity or self-respect on his conductor's part. With such little drawbacks on my usually impressive aspect, I appeared at this Cornish Inn, to the unutterable wonder of the Cornish Miners. It was full, and twenty times full, and nobody could be received but the post-horse,—though to get rid of that noble animal was something. While my fellow-travellers and I were discussing how to pass the night and so much of the next day as must intervene before the jovial blacksmith and the jovial wheelwright would be in a condition to go out on the morass and mend the coach, an honest man stepped forth from the crowd and proposed his unlet floor of two rooms, with supper of eggs and bacon, ale and punch. We joyfully accompanied him home to the strangest of clean houses, where we were well entertained to the satisfaction of all parties. But the novel feature of the entertainment was, that our host was a chairmaker, and that the chairs assigned to us were mere frames, altogether without bottoms of any sort; so that we passed the evening on perches. Nor was this the absurdest consequence; for when we unbent at supper, and any one of us gave way to laughter, he forgot the peculiarity of his position, and instantly disappeared. I myself, doubled up into an attitude from which self-extrication was impossible, was taken out of my frame, like a clown in a comic pantomime who has tumbled into a tub, five times by the taper's light during the eggs and bacon.

The Holly-Tree was fast reviving within me a sense of loneliness. I began to feel conscious that my subject would never carry on until I was dug out. I might be a week here,—weeks!

There was a story with a single idea in it, connected with an Inn I once passed a night at in a picturesque old town on the Welsh border. In a large double-bedded room of this Inn there had been a suicide committed by poison, in one bed, while a tired traveller slept unconscious in the other. After that time, the suicide bed was never used, but the other constantly was; the disused bedstead remaining in the room empty, though as to all other respects in its old state. The story ran, that whosoever slept in this room, though never so entire a stranger, from never so far off, was invariably observed to come down in the morning with an impression that he smelt Laudanum, and that his mind always turned upon the subject of suicide; to which, whatever kind of man he might be, he was certain to make some reference if he conversed with anyone. This went on for years, until it at length induced the landlord to take the disused bedstead down, and bodily burn it,—bed, hangings, and all. The strange influence (this was the story) now changed to a fainter one, but never changed afterwards. The occupant of that room, with occasional but very rare exceptions, would come down in the morning, trying to recall a forgotten dream he had had in the night. The landlord, on his mentioning his perplexity, would suggest various commonplace subjects, not one of which, as he very well knew, was the true subject. But the moment the landlord suggested 'Poison,' the traveller started, and cried, 'Yes!' He never failed to accept that suggestion, and he never recalled any more of his dream.

This reminiscence brought the Welsh Inns in general

before me; with the women in their round hats, and the harpers with their white beards (venerable, but humbugs, I am afraid), playing outside the door while I took my dinner. The transition was natural to the Highland Inns, with the oatmeal bannocks, the honey, the venison steaks, the trout from the loch, the whisky, and perhaps (having the materials so temptingly at hand) the Athol brose. Once was I coming south from the Scottish Highlands in hot haste, hoping to change quickly at the station at the bottom of a certain wild historical glen, when these eyes did with mortification see the landlord come out with a telescope and sweep the whole prospect for the horses; which horses were away picking up their own living, and did not heave in sight under four hours. Having thought of the loch-trout, I was taken by quick association to the Anglers' Inns of England (I have assisted at innumerable feats of angling by lying in the bottom of the boat, whole summer days, doing nothing with the greatest perseverance; which I have generally found to be as effectual towards the taking of fish as the finest tackle and the utmost science), and to the pleasant white, clean, flower-pot-decorated bedrooms of those inns, overlooking the river, and the ferry, and the green ait, and the church-spire, and the country bridge; and to the peerless Emma with the bright eyes and the pretty smile, who waited, bless her! with a natural grace that would have converted Blue-Beard. Casting my eyes upon my Holly-Tree fire, I next discerned among the glowing coals the pictures of a score or more of those wonderful English posting-inns which we are all so sorry to have lost, which were so large and so comfortable, and which were such monuments of British submission to rapacity and extortion. He who would see these houses pining away, let him walk from Basingstoke, or even Windsor, to London, by way of Hounslow, and moralize on their perishing remains; the stables crumbling to dust; unsettled labourers and wanderers bivouacking in the outhouses; grass growing in the yards; the rooms, where erst so many hundred beds of down were made up, let off to Irish lodgers at eighteenpence a week; a little ill-looking beer-shop shrinking in the tap of former days, burning coach-house gates for firewood, having one of its two windows bunged up, as if it had received punishment in a fight with the Railroad; a low, bandy-legged, brick-making bulldog standing in the doorway. What could I next see in my fire so naturally as the new railway-house of these times near the dismal country station; with nothing particular on draught but cold air and damp, nothing worth mentioning in the larder but new mortar, and no business doing beyond a conceited affectation of luggage in the hall? Then I came to the Inns of Paris, with the pretty apartment of four pieces up one hundred and seventy-five waxed stairs, the privilege of ringing the bell all day long without influencing anybody's mind or body but your own, and the not-too-much-for-dinner, considering the price. Next, to the provincial Inns of France, with the great church-tower rising above the courtyard, the horse-bells jingling merrily up and down the street beyond, and the clocks of all descriptions in all the rooms, which are never right, unless taken at the precise minute when, by getting exactly twelve hours too fast or too slow, they unintentionally become so. Away I went, next, to the lesser roadside Inns of Italy; where all the dirty clothes in the house (not in wear) are always lying in your ante-room; where the mosquitoes make a raisin pudding of your face in summer, and the cold bites it blue in winter; where you get what you can, and forget what you can't; where I should again like to be boiling my tea in a pocket-handkerchief dumpling, for want of a teapot. So to the old palace Inns and old monastery Inns, in towns and cities of the same bright country; with their massive quadrangular staircases, whence you may look from among clustering pillars high into the blue vault of heaven; with their stately banqueting-rooms, and vast refectories; with their labyrinths of ghostly bedchambers, and their glimpses into gorgeous streets that have no appearance of reality or possibility. So to the close little Inns of the Malaria districts, with their pale attendants, and their peculiar smell of never letting in the air. So to the immense, fantastic Inns of Venice, with the cry of the gondolier below, as he skims the corner; the grip of the watery odours on one particular little bit of the bridge of your nose (which is never released while you stay there); and the great bell of St. Mark's Cathedral tolling midnight. Next I put up for a minute at the restless Inns upon the Rhine, where your going to bed, no matter at what hour, appears to be the tocsin for everybody else's getting up; and where, in the table-d'hôte room at the end of the long table (with several Towers of Babel on it at the other end, all made of white plates), one knot of stoutish men, entirely dressed in jewels and dirt, and having nothing else upon them, *will* remain all night, clinking glasses, and singing about the river that flows, and the grape that grows, and Rhine wine that beguiles, and Rhine woman that smiles and hi drink drink my friend and ho drink drink my brother, and all the rest of it. I departed thence, as a matter of course, to other German Inns, where all the eatables are sodden down to the same flavour, and where the mind is disturbed by the apparition of hot puddings, and boiled cherries, sweet and slab, at awfully unexpected periods of the repast. After a draught of sparkling beer from a foaming glass jug, and a glance of recognition through the windows of the student beer-houses at Heidelberg and elsewhere, I put out to sea for the Inns of America, with their four hundred beds apiece, and their eight or nine hundred ladies and gentlemen at dinner every day. Again I stood in the bar-rooms thereof, taking my evening cobbler, julep, sling, or cocktail. Again I listened to my friend the General,—whom I had known for five minutes, in the course of which period he had made me intimate for life with two Majors, who again had made me intimate for life with three Colonels, who again had made me brother to twenty-two civilians,—again, I say, I listened to my friend the General, leisurely expounding the resources of the establishment, as to gentlemen's morning-room, Sir; ladies' morning-room, Sir; gentlemen's evening-room, Sir; ladies' evening-room, Sir; ladies' and gentlemen's evening reuniting-room, Sir; music-room, Sir; reading-room, Sir; over four hundred sleeping-rooms, Sir; and the entire planned and finished within twelve calendar months from the first clearing off of the old encumbrances on the plot, at a cost of five hundred thousand dollars, Sir. Again I found, as to my individual way of thinking, that the greater, the more gorgeous, and the more dollarous the establishment was, the less desirable it was. Nevertheless, again I drank my cobbler, julep, sling, or cocktail, in all good-will, to my friend the General, and my friends the Majors, Colonels, and civilians all; full well knowing that, whatever little motes my beamy eyes may have descried in theirs, they belong to a kind, generous, large-hearted, and great people.

I had been going on lately at a quick pace to keep my solitude out of my mind; but here I broke down for good, and gave up the subject. What was I to do? What was to become of me? Into what extremity was I submissively to sink? Supposing that, like Baron Trenck, I looked out for a mouse or spider, and found one, and beguiled my imprisonment by training it? Even that might be dangerous with a view to the future. I might be so far gone when the road did come to be cut through the snow, that, on my way forth, I might burst into tears, and beseech, like the prisoner who was released in his old age from the Bastille, to be taken back again to the five windows, the ten curtains, and the sinuous drapery.

A desperate idea came into my head. Under any other circumstances I should have rejected it; but, in the strait at which I was, I held it fast. Could I so far overcome the inherent bashfulness which withheld me from the landlord's table and the company I might find there, as to call up the Boots, and ask him to take a chair,—and something in a liquid form,—and talk to me? I could. I would. I did.

SECOND BRANCH

THE BOOTS

WHERE had he been in his time? he repeated, when I asked him the question. Lord, he had been everywhere! And what had he been? Bless you, he had been everything you could mention a'most!

Seen a good deal? Why, of course he had. I should say so, he could assure me, if I only knew about a twentieth part of what had come in *his* way. Why, it would be easier for him, he expected, to tell what he hadn't seen than what he had. Ah! A deal, it would.

What was the curiousest thing he had seen? Well! He didn't know. He couldn't momently name what was the curiousest thing he had seen,—unless it was a Unicorn,—and he see *him* once at a Fair. But supposing a young gentleman not eight year old was to run away with a fine young woman of seven, might I think *that* a queer start? Certainly. Then that was a start as he himself had had his blessed eyes on, and he had cleaned the shoes they run away in—and they was so little he couldn't get his hands into 'em.

Master Harry Walmers' father, you see, he lived at the Elmses, down away by Shooter's Hill there, six or seven miles from Lunnon. He was a gentleman of spirit, and good-looking, and held his head up when he walked, and had what you may call Fire about him. He wrote poetry, and he rode, and he ran, and he cricketed, and he danced, and he acted, and he done it all equally beautiful. He was uncommon proud of Master Harry as was his only child; but he didn't spoil him neither. He was a gentleman that had a will of his own and a eye of his own, and that would be minded. Consequently, though he made quite a companion of the fine bright boy, and was delighted to see him so fond of reading his fairy books, and was never tired of hearing him say My name is Norval, or hear him sing his songs about Young May Moons is beaming love, and When he as adores thee has left but the name, and that; still he kept the command over the child, and the child *was* a child, and it's to be wished more of 'em was!

How did Boots happen to know all this? Why, through being under-gardener. Of course he couldn't be under-gardener, and be always about, in the summer-time, near the windows on the lawn, a-mowing, and sweeping, and weeding, and pruning, and this and that, without getting acquainted with the ways of the family. Even supposing Master Harry hadn't come to him one morning early, and said, 'Cobbs, how should you spell Norah, if you was asked?' and then began cutting it in print all over the fence.

He couldn't say he had taken particular notice of children before that; but really it was pretty to see them two mites a-going about the place together, deep in love. And the courage of the boy! Bless your soul, he'd have throwed off his little hat, and tucked up his little sleeves, and gone in at a Lion, he would, if they had happened to meet one, and she had been frightened of him. One day he stops, along with her, where Boots was hoeing weeds in the gravel, and says, speaking up, 'Cobb,' he says, 'I like *you*.' 'Do you, Sir? I'm proud to hear it.' 'Yes, I do, Cobbs. Why do I like you, do you think, Cobbs?' 'Don't know, Master Harry, I am sure.' 'Because Norah likes you, Cobbs.' 'Indeed, Sir? That's very gratifying.'

'Gratifying, Cobbs? It's better than millions of the brightest diamonds to be liked by Norah.' 'Certainly, Sir.' 'You're going away, ain't you, Cobbs?' 'Yes, Sir.' 'Would you like another situation, Cobbs?' 'Well, Sir, I shouldn't object, if it was a good 'un.' 'Then, Cobbs,' says he, 'you shall be our Head Gardener when we are married.' And he tucks her, in her little sky-blue mantle, under his arm, and walks away.

Boots could assure me that it was better than a picter, and equal to a play, to see them babies, with their long, bright, curling hair, their sparkling eyes, and their beautiful light tread, a rambling about the garden, deep in love. Boots was of opinion that the birds believed they was birds, and kept up with 'em, singing to please 'em. Sometimes they would creep under the Tulip-tree, and would sit there with their arms round one another's necks, and their soft cheeks touching, a-reading about the Prince and the Dragon, and the good and bad enchanters, and the king's fair daughter. Sometimes he would hear them planning about having a house in a forest, keeping bees and a cow, and living entirely on milk and honey. Once he came upon them by the pond, and heard Master Harry say, 'Adorable Norah, kiss me, and say you love me to distraction, or I'll jump in head-foremost.' And Boots made no question he would have done it if she hadn't complied. On the whole, Boots said it had a tendency to make him feel as if he was in love himself—only he didn't exactly know who with.

'Cobbs,' said Master Harry, one evening, when Cobbs was watering the flowers, 'I am going on a visit, this present Midsummer, to my grandmamma's at York.'

'Are you indeed, Sir? I hope you'll have a pleasant time. I am going into Yorkshire myself, when I leave here.'

'Are you going to your grandmamma's, Cobbs?'

'No, Sir. I haven't got such a thing.'

'Not as a grandmamma, Cobbs?'

'No, Sir.'

The boy looked on at the watering of the flowers for a little while, and then said, 'I shall be very glad indeed to go, Cobbs,—Norah's going.'

'You'll be all right then, Sir,' says Cobbs, 'with your beautiful sweetheart by your side.'

'Cobbs,' returned the boy, flushing, 'I never let anybody joke about it, when I can prevent them.'

'It wasn't a joke, Sir,' says Cobbs, with humility,—'wasn't so meant.'

'I am glad of that, Cobbs, because I like you, you know, and you're going to live with us.—Cobbs!'

'Sir.'

'What do you think my grandmamma gives me when I go down there?'

'I couldn't so much as make a guess, Sir.'

'A Bank of England five-pound note, Cobbs.'

'Whew!' says Cobbs, 'that's a spanking sum of money, Master Harry.'

'A person could do a good deal with such a sum of money as that,—couldn't a person, Cobbs?'

'I believe you, Sir!'

'Cobbs,' said the boy, 'I'll tell you a secret. At Norah's house, they have been joking her about me, and pretending to laugh at our being engaged,—pretending to make game of it, Cobbs!'

'Such, Sir,' says Cobbs, 'is the depravity of human natur.'

The boy, looking exactly like his father, stood for a few minutes with his glowing face towards the sunset, and then departed with, 'Good-night, Cobbs. I'm going in.'

If I was to ask Boots how it happened that he was a-going to leave that place just at that present time, well, he couldn't rightly answer me. He did suppose he might have stayed there till now if he had been anyways inclined. But, you see, he was younger then, and he wanted change. That's what he wanted,—change. Mr. Walmers, he said to him when he gave him notice of his intentions to leave, 'Cobbs,' he says, 'have you anythink to complain of? I make the inquiry because if I find that any of my people really has anythink to complain of, I wish to make it right if I can.' 'No, 'Sir, says Cobbs; 'thanking you, Sir, I find myself as well sitiwated here as I could hope to be anywheres. The truth is, Sir, that I am a-going to seek my fortun'.' 'O, indeed, Cobbs!' he says; 'I hope you may find it.' And Boots could assure me—which he did, touching his hair with his bootjack, as a salute in the way of his present calling—that he hadn't found it yet.

Well, Sir! Boots left the Elmses when his time was up, and Master Harry, he went down to the old lady's at York, which old lady would have given that child the teeth out of her head (if she had had any), she was so wrapped up in him. What does that Infant do,—for Infant you may call him and be within the mark,—but cut away from that old lady's with his Norah, on a expedition to go to Gretna Green and be married!

Sir, Boots was at this identical Holly-Tree Inn (having left it several times since to better himself, but always come back through one thing or another), when, one summer afternoon, the coach drives up, and out of the coach gets them two children. The Guard says to our Governor, 'I don't quite make out these little passengers, but the young gentleman's words was, that they was to be brought here.' The young gentleman gets out; hands his lady out; gives the Guard something for himself; says to our Governor, 'We're to stop here to-night, please. Sitting-room and two bedrooms will be required. Chops and cherry-pudding for two!' and tucks her, in her little sky-blue mantle, under his arm, and walks into the house much bolder than Brass.

Boots leaves me to judge what the amazement of

that establishment was, when these two tiny creatures all alone by themselves was marched into the Angel,—much more so, when he, who had seen them without their seeing him, give the Governor his views of the expedition they was upon. 'Cobbs,' says the Governor, 'if this is so, I must set off myself to York, and quiet their friends' minds. In which case you must keep your eye upon 'em, and humour 'em, till I come back. But before I take these measures, Cobbs, I should wish you to find from themselves whether your opinion is correct. 'Sir, to you,' says Cobbs, 'that shall be done directly.'

So Boots goes upstairs to the Angel, and there he finds Master Harry on a e-normous sofa,—immense at any time, but looking like the Great Bed of Ware, compared with him,—a-drying the eyes of Miss Norah with his pocket-hankecher. Their little legs was entirely off the ground, of course, and it really is not possible for Boots to express to me how small them children looked.

'It's Cobbs! It's Cobbs!' cried Master Harry, and comes running to him, and catching hold of his hand. Miss Norah comes running to him on t'other side and catching hold of his t'other hand, and they both jump for joy.

'I see you a-getting out, Sir,' says Cobbs. 'I thought it was you. I thought I couldn't be mistaken in your height and your figure. What's the object of your journey, Sir?—Matrimonial?'

'We are going to be married, Cobbs, at Gretna Green,' returned the boy. 'We have run away on purpose. Norah has been in rather low spirits, Cobbs; but she'll be happy, now we have found you to be our friend.'

'Thank you, Sir, and thank *you*, Miss,' says Cobbs, 'for your good opinion. *Did* you bring any luggage with you, Sir?'

If I will believe Boots when he gives me his word and honour upon it, the lady had got a parasol, a smelling-bottle, a round and a half of cold buttered toast, eight peppermintdrops, and a hair-brush,—seemingly a doll's. The gentleman had got about half-a-dozen yards of string, a knife, three or four sheets of writing-paper folded up surprising small, a orange, and a Chaney mug with his name upon it.

'What may be the exact natur' of your plans, Sir ?' says Cobbs.

'To go on,' replied the boy,—which the courage of that boy was something wonderful !—'in the morning, and be married to-morrow.'

'Just so, Sir,' says Cobbs. 'Would it meet your views, Sir, if I was to accompany you ?'

When Cobbs said this, they both jumped for joy again, and cried out, 'Oh, yes, yes, Cobbs ! Yes !'

'Well, Sir,' says Cobbs. 'If you will excuse my having the freedom to give an opinion, what I should recommend would be this. I'm acquainted with a pony, Sir, which, put in a pheayton that I could borrow, would take you and Mrs. Harry Walmers, Junior, (myself driving, if you approved,) to the end of your journey in a very short space of time. I am not altogether sure, Sir, that this pony will be at liberty to-morrow, but even if you had to wait over to-morrow for him, it might be worth your while. As to the small account here, Sir, in case you was to find yourself running at all short, that don't signify ; because I'm a part proprietor of this inn, and it could stand over.'

Boots assures me that when they clapped their hands, and jumped for joy again, and called him 'Good Cobbs !' and 'Dear Cobbs !' and bent across him to kiss one another in the delight of their confiding hearts, he felt himself the meanest rascal for deceiving 'em that was ever born.

'Is there anything you want just at present, Sir ?' says Cobbs, mortally ashamed of himself.

'We should like some cakes after dinner,' answered Master Harry, folding his arms, putting out one leg, and looking straight at him, 'and two apples,—and jam. With dinner we should like to have toast-and-water. But Norah has always been accustomed to half a glass of currant wine at dessert. And so have I.'

'It shall be ordered at the bar, Sir,' says Cobbs; and away he went.

Boots has the feeling as fresh upon him at this minute of speaking as he had then, that he would far rather have had it out in half-a-dozen rounds with the Governor than have combined with him; and that he wished with all his heart there was any impossible place where those two babies could make an impossible marriage, and live impossibly happy ever afterwards. However, as it couldn't be, he went into the Governor's plans, and the Governor set off for York in half-an-hour.

The way in which the women of that house—without exception—every one of 'em—married *and* single—took to that boy when they heard the story, Boots considers surprising. It was as much as he could do to keep 'em from dashing into the room and kissing him. They climbed up all sorts of places, at the risk of their lives, to look at him through a pane of glass. They was seven deep at the keyhole. They was out of their minds about him and his bold spirit.

In the evening, Boots went into the room to see how the runaway couple was getting on. The gentleman was on the window-seat, supporting the lady in his arms. She had tears upon her face, and was lying, very tired and half asleep, with her head upon his shoulder.

'Mrs. Harry Walmers, Junior, fatigued, Sir?' says Cobbs.

'Yes, she is tired, Cobbs; but she is not used to be away from home, and she has been in low spirits again. Cobbs, do you think you could bring a biffin, please?'

'I ask your pardon, Sir,' says Cobbs. 'What was it you——?'

'I think a Norfolk biffin would rouse her, Cobbs. She is very fond of them.'

Boots withdrew in search of the required restorative, and, when he brought it in, the gentleman handed it to the lady, and fed her with a spoon, and took a little himself; the lady being heavy with sleep, and rather cross. 'What should you think, Sir,' says Cobbs, 'of a chamber candlestick?' The gentleman approved; the chambermaid went first, up the great staircase; the lady, in her sky-blue mantle, followed, gallantly escorted by the gentleman; the gentleman embraced her at her door, and retired to his own apartment, where Boots softly locked him up.

Boots couldn't but feel with increased acuteness what a base deceiver he was, when they consulted him at breakfast (they had ordered sweet milk-and-water, and toast and currant jelly, overnight) about the pony. It really was as much as he could do, he don't mind confessing to me, to look them two young things in the face, and think what a wicked old father of lies he had grown up to be. Howsomever, he went on a-lying like a Trojan about the pony. He told 'em that it did so unfort'nately happen that the pony was half clipped, you see, and that he couldn't be taken out in that state, for fear it should strike to his inside. But that he'd be finished clipping in the course of the day, and that to-morrow morning at eight o'clock the pheayton would be ready. Boots's view of the whole case, looking back on it in my room, is, that Mrs. Harry Walmers, Junior, was beginning to give in. She hadn't had her hair curled when she went to bed, and she didn't seem quite up to brushing it herself, and its getting in her eyes put her out. But nothing put out Master Harry. He sat behind his breakfast-cup, a-tearing away at the jelly, as if he had been his own father.

After breakfast, Boots is inclined to consider that they drawed soldiers,—at least, he knows that many such was found in the fireplace, all on horseback. In the course of the morning, Master Harry rang the bell,—it was surprising how that there boy did carry on,—and said, in a sprightly way, 'Cobbs, is there any good walks in this neighbourhood ?'

'Yes, Sir,' says Cobbs. 'There's Love-lane.'

'Get out with you, Cobbs !'—that was that there boy's expression,—'you're joking.'

'Begging your pardon, Sir,' says Cobbs, 'there really is Love-lane. And a pleasant walk it is, and proud shall I be to show it to yourself and Mrs. Harry Walmers, Junior.'

'Norah, dear,' said Master Harry, 'this is curious. We really ought to see Love-lane. Put on your bonnet, my sweetest darling, and we will go there with Cobbs.'

Boots leaves me to judge what a Beast he felt himself to be, when that young pair told him, as they all three jogged along together, that they had made up their minds to give him two thousand guineas a year as head-gardener, on accounts of his being so true a friend to 'em. Boots could have wished at the moment that the earth would have opened and swallowed him up, he felt so mean, with their beaming eyes a-looking at him, and believing him. Well, Sir, he turned the conversation as well as he could, and he took 'em down Love-lane to the water-meadows, and there Master Harry would have drowned himself in half a moment more, a-getting out a water-lily for her,—but nothing daunted that boy. Well, Sir, they was tired out. All being so new and strange to 'em, they was tired as tired could be. And they laid down on a bank of daisies, like the children in the wood, leastways meadows, and fell asleep.

Boots don't know—perhaps I do,—but never mind, it don't signify either way—why it made a man fit to make a fool of himself to see them two pretty babies a-lying there in the clear still sunny day, not dreaming half so hard when they was asleep as they done when they was awake. But Lord ! when you come to think of yourself, you know, and what a game you have been up to ever since you was in your own cradle, and what a poor sort of a chap you are, and how it's always either Yesterday with you, or else To-morrow, and never To-day, that's where it is!

Well, Sir, they woke up at last, and then one thing was getting pretty clear to Boots, namely, that Mrs. Harry Walmerses, Junior's, temper was on the move. When Master Harry took her round the waist, she said he 'teased her so'; and when he says, 'Norah, my young May Moon, your Harry tease you?' she tells him, 'Yes; and I want to go home!'

A biled fowl, and baked bread-and-butter pudding, brought Mrs. Walmers up a little; but Boots could have wished, he must privately own to me, to have seen her more sensible of the woice of love, and less abandoning of herself to currants. However, Master Harry, he kept up, and his noble heart was as fond as ever. Mrs. Walmers turned very sleepy about dusk, and began to cry. Therefore, Mrs. Walmers went off to bed as per yesterday; and Master Harry ditto repeated.

About eleven or twelve at night comes back the Governor in a chaise, along with Mr. Walmers and a elderly lady. Mr. Walmers looks amused and very serious, both at once, and says to our missis, 'We are much indebted to you, ma'am, for your kind care of our little children, which we can never sufficiently acknowledge. Pray, ma'am, where is my boy?' Our missis says, 'Cobbs has the dear child in charge, Sir. Cobbs, show Forty!' Then he says to Cobbs, 'Ah, Cobbs, I am glad to see *you*! I understood you was here!' And Cobbs says, 'Yes, Sir. Your most obedient, Sir.'

I may be surprised to hear Boots say it, perhaps; but Boots assures me that his heart beat like a hammer, going upstairs. 'I beg your pardon, Sir,' says he, while unlocking the door; 'I hope you are not angry with Master Harry. For Master Harry is a fine boy,

Sir, and will do you credit and honour.' And Boots signifies to me, that, if the fine boy's father had contradicted him in the daring state of mind in which he then was, he thinks he should have 'fetched him a crack,' and taken the consequences.

But Mr. Walmers only says, 'No, Cobbs. No, my good fellow. Thank you!' And, the door being opened, goes in.

Boots goes in too, holding the light, and he sees Mr. Walmers go up to the bedside, bend gently down, and kiss the little sleeping face. Then he stands looking at it for a minute, looking wonderfully like it (they do say he ran away with Mrs. Walmers); and then he gently shakes the little shoulder.

'Harry, my dear boy! Harry!'

Master Harry starts up and looks at him. Looks at Cobbs too. Such is the honour of that mite, that he looks at Cobbs, to see whether he has brought him into trouble.

'I am not angry, my child. I only want you to dress yourself and come home.'

'Yes, pa.'

Master Harry dresses himself quickly. His breast begins to swell when he has nearly finished, and it swells more and more as he stands, at last, a-looking at his father: his father standing a-looking at him, the quiet image of him.

'Please may I'—the spirit of that little creatur, and the way he kept his rising tears down!—'please, dear pa—may I—kiss Norah before I go?'

'You may, my child.'

So he takes Master Harry in his hand, and Boots leads the way with the candle, and they come to that other bedroom, where the elderly lady is seated by the bed, and poor little Mrs. Harry Walmers, Junior, is fast asleep. There the father lifts the child up to the pillow, and he lays his little face down for an instant by the little warm face of poor unconscious little Mrs. Harry

Walmers, Junior, and gently draws it to him,—a sight so touching to the chambermaids who are peeping through the door, that one of them calls out, 'It's a shame to part 'em!' But this chambermaid was always, as Boots informs me, a soft-hearted one. Not that there was any harm in that girl. Far from it.

Finally, Boots says, that's all about it. Mr. Walmers drove away in the chaise, having hold of Master Harry's hand. The elderly lady and Mrs. Harry Walmers, Junior, that was never to be (she married a Captain long afterwards, and died in India), went off next day. In conclusion, Boots put it to me whether I hold with him in two opinions: firstly, that there are not many couples on their way to be married who are half as innocent of guile as those two children; secondly, that it would be a jolly good thing for a great many couples on their way to be married, if they could only be stopped in time, and brought back separately.

THIRD BRANCH

THE BILL

I HAD been snowed up a whole week. The time had hung so lightly on my hands, that I should have been in great doubt of the fact but for a piece of documentary evidence that lay upon my table.

The road had been dug out of the snow on the previous day, and the document in question was my bill. It testified emphatically to my having eaten and drunk, and warmed myself, and slept among the sheltering branches of the Holly-Tree, seven days and nights.

I had yesterday allowed the road twenty-four hours to improve itself, finding that I required that additional margin of time for the completion of my task. I had ordered my bill to be upon the table, and a chaise to be at the door, 'at eight o'clock to-morrow evening.' It was eight o'clock to-morrow evening when I buckled up my travelling writing-desk in its leather case, paid my bill, and got on my warm coats and wrappers. Of course, no time now remained for my travelling on to add a frozen tear to the icicles which were doubtless hanging plentifully about the farmhouse where I had first seen Angela. What I had to do was to get across to Liverpool by the shortest open road, there to meet my heavy baggage and embark. It was quite enough to do, and I had not an hour too much time to do it in.

I had taken leave of all my Holly-Tree friends—almost, for the time being, of my bashfulness too—and was standing for half a minute at the Inn door watching the ostler as he took another turn at the cord which tied my portmanteau on the chaise, when I saw lamps coming down towards the Holly-Tree. The road was so padded with snow that no wheels were audible; but all of us who were standing at the Inn door saw lamps coming on, and at a lively rate too, between the walls of snow that had been heaped up on either side of the track. The chambermaid instantly divined how the case stood, and called to the ostler, 'Tom, this is a Gretna job!' The ostler, knowing that her sex instinctively scented a marriage, or anything in that direction, rushed up the yard bawling, 'Next four out!' and in a moment the whole establishment was thrown into commotion.

I had a melancholy interest in seeing the happy man who loved and was beloved; and therefore, instead of driving off at once, I remained at the Inn door when the fugitives drove up. A bright-eyed fellow, muffled in a mantle, jumped out so briskly that he almost overthrew me. He turned to apologize, and, by Heaven, it was Edwin!

'Charley!' said he, recoiling. 'Gracious powers, what do you do here?'

'Edwin,' said I, recoiling, 'gracious powers, what do *you* do here?' I struck my forehead as I said it, and an insupportable blaze of light seemed to shoot before my eyes.

He hurried me into the little parlour (always kept with a slow fire in it and no poker), where posting company waited while their horses were putting to, and, shutting the door, said:

'Charley, forgive me!'

'Edwin!' I returned. 'Was this well? When I loved her so dearly! When I had garnered up my heart so long!' I could say no more.

He was shocked when he saw how moved I was, and made the cruel observation, that he had not thought I should have taken it so much to heart.

I looked at him. I reproached him no more. But I looked at him.

'My dear, dear Charley,' said he, 'don't think ill of me, I beseech you! I know you have a right to my utmost confidence, and, believe me, you have ever had it until now. I abhor secrecy. Its meanness is intolerable to me. But I and my dear girl have observed it for your sake.'

He and his dear girl! It steeled me.

'You have observed it for my sake, Sir?' said I, wondering how his frank face could face it out so.

'Yes!—and Angela's,' said he.

I found the room reeling round in an uncertain way, like a labouring humming-top. 'Explain yourself,' I said, holding on by one hand to an armchair.

'Dear old darling Charley!' returned Edwin, in his cordial manner, 'consider! When you were going on so happily with Angela, why should I compromise you with the old gentleman by making you a party to our engagement, and (after he had declined my proposals) to our secret intention? Surely it was better that you should be able honourably to say, 'He never took counsel with me, never told me, never breathed a word of it.' If Angela suspected it, and showed me all the favour and support she could—God bless her for a precious creature and a priceless wife!—I couldn't help that. Neither I nor Emmeline ever told her, any more than we told you. And for the same good reason, Charley; trust me, for the same good reason, and no other upon earth!'

Emmeline was Angela's cousin. Lived with her. Had been brought up with her. Was her father's ward. Had property.

'Emmeline is in the chaise, my dear Edwin!' said I, embracing him with the greatest affection.

'My good fellow!' said he, 'do you suppose I should be going to Gretna Green without her?'

I ran out with Edwin, I opened the chaise door, I took Emmeline in my arms, I folded her to my heart. She was wrapped in soft white fur, like the snowy landscape: but was warm, and young, and lovely. I put their leaders to with my own hands, I gave the boys a five-pound note apiece, I cheered them as they drove away, I drove the other way myself as hard as I could pelt.

I never went to Liverpool, I never went to America, I went straight back to London, and I married Angela. I have never until this time, even to her, disclosed the secret of my character, and the mistrust and the mistaken journey into which it led me. When she, and they, and our eight children and their seven—I mean Edwin's and Emmeline's, whose eldest girl is old enough now to wear white for herself, and to look very like her mother in it—come to read these pages, as of course they will, I shall hardly fail to be found out at last. Never mind! I can bear it. I began at the Holly-Tree, by idle accident, to associate the Christmas-time of year with human interest, and with some inquiry into, and some care for, the lives of those by whom I find myself surrounded. I hope that I am none the worse for it, and that no one near me or afar off is the worse for it. And I say, May the green Holly-Tree flourish, striking its roots deep into our English ground, and having its germinating qualities carried by the birds of Heaven all over the world!

WILLIAM WILKIE COLLINS

1824—1889

THE TRAVELLER'S STORY OF A TERRIBLY STRANGE BED

SHORTLY after my education at college was finished, I happened to be staying at Paris with an English friend. We were both young men then, and lived, I am afraid, rather a wild life, in the delightful city of our sojourn. One night we were idling about the neighbourhood of the Palais Royal, doubtful to what amusement we should next betake ourselves. My friend proposed a visit to Frascati's; but his suggestion was not to my taste. I knew Frascati's, as the French saying is, by heart; had lost and won plenty of five-franc pieces there, merely for amusement's sake, until it was amusement no longer, and was thoroughly tired, in fact, of all the ghastly respectabilities of such a social anomaly as a respectable gambling-house. 'For Heaven's sake,' said I to my friend, 'let us go somewhere where we can see a little genuine, blackguard, poverty-stricken gaming, with no false gingerbread glitter thrown over it at all. Let us get away from fashionable Frascati's, to a house where they don't mind letting in a man with a ragged coat, or a man with no coat, ragged or otherwise.'—'Very well,' said my friend, 'we needn't go out of the Palais Royal to find the sort of company you want. Here's the place just before us; as blackguard a place, by all report, as you could possibly wish to see.' In another minute we arrived at the door, and entered the house, the back of which you have drawn in your sketch.[1]

When we got upstairs, and left our hats and sticks with the doorkeeper, we were admitted into the chief gambling-room. We did not find many people assembled there. But, few as the men were who looked up at us on our entrance, they were all types—lamentably true types—of their respective classes.

We had come to see blackguards; but these men were something worse. There is a comic side, more or less appreciable, in all blackguardism—here there was nothing but tragedy—mute, weird tragedy. The quiet in the room was horrible. The thin, haggard, long-haired young man, whose sunken eyes fiercely watched the turning up of the cards, never spoke; the flabby, fat-faced, pimply player, who pricked his piece of pasteboard perseveringly, to register how often black won, and how often red—never spoke; the dirty, wrinkled old man, with the vulture eyes and the darned greatcoat, who had lost his last *sou*, and still looked on desperately, after he could play no longer—never spoke. Even the voice of the croupier sounded as if it were strangely dulled and thickened in the atmosphere of the room. I had entered the place to laugh, but the spectacle before me was something to weep over. I soon found it necessary to take refuge in excitement from the depression of spirits which was fast stealing on me. Unfortunately I sought the nearest excitement, by going to the table, and beginning to play. Still more unfortunately, as the event will show, I won—won prodigiously; won incredibly; won at such a rate, that the regular players at the table crowded round me; and staring at my stakes with hungry, superstitious eyes, whispered to one another that the English stranger was going to break the bank.

The game was *Rouge et Noir*. I had played at it in

1 [The story is supposed to be narrated by its chief actor, to the artist who is painting his portrait.]

every city in Europe, without, however, the care or the wish to study the Theory of Chances—that philosopher's stone of all gamblers! And a gambler, in the strict sense of the word, I had never been. I was heart-whole from the corroding passion for play. My gaming was a mere idle amusement. I never resorted to it by necessity, because I never knew what it was to want money. I never practised it so incessantly as to lose more than I could afford, or to gain more than I could coolly pocket without being thrown off my balance by my good luck. In short, I had hitherto frequented gambling-tables—just as I frequented ball-rooms and opera-houses—because they amused me, and because I had nothing better to do with my leisure hours.

But on this occasion it was very different—now, for the first time in my life, I felt what the passion for play really was. My success first bewildered, and then, in the most literal meaning of the word, intoxicated me. Incredible as it may appear, it is nevertheless true, that I only lost when I attempted to estimate chances, and played according to previous calculation. If I left everything to luck, and staked without any care or consideration, I was sure to win—to win in the face of every recognized probability in favour of the bank. At first, some of the men present ventured their money safely enough on my colour; but I speedily increased my stakes to sums which they dared not risk. One after another they left off playing, and breathlessly looked on at my game.

Still, time after time, I staked higher and higher, and still won. The excitement in the room rose to fever pitch. The silence was interrupted by a deep-muttered chorus of oaths and exclamations in different languages, every time the gold was shovelled across to my side of the table—even the imperturbable croupier dashed his rake on the floor in a (French) fury of astonishment at my success. But one man present preserved his self-possession; and that man was my friend. He came to my side, and whispering in English, begged me to leave the place, satisfied with what I had already gained. I must do him the justice to say that he repeated his warnings and entreaties several times, and only left me and went away, after I had rejected his advice (I was to all intents and purposes gambling-drunk) in terms which rendered it impossible for him to address me again that night.

Shortly after he had gone, a hoarse voice behind me cried: 'Permit me, my dear sir!—permit me to restore to their proper place two Napoleons which you have dropped. Wonderful luck, sir! I pledge you my word of honour, as an old soldier, in the course of my long experience in this sort of thing, I never saw such luck as yours!—never! Go on, sir—*Sacré mille bombes!* Go on boldly, and break the bank!'

I turned round and saw, nodding and smiling at me with inveterate civility, a tall man, dressed in a frogged and braided surtout.

If I had been in my senses, I should have considered him, personally, as being rather a suspicious specimen of an old soldier. He had goggling blood-shot eyes, mangy mustachios, and a broken nose. His voice betrayed a barrack-room intonation of the worst order, and he had the dirtiest pair of hands I ever saw—even in France. These little personal peculiarities exercised, however, no repelling influence on me. In the mad excitement, the reckless triumph of that moment, I was ready to 'fraternize' with anybody who encouraged me in my game. I accepted the old soldier's offered pinch of snuff; clapped him on the back, and swore he was the honestest fellow in the world—the most glorious relic of the Grand Army that I had ever met with. 'Go on!' cried my military friend, snapping his fingers in ecstasy,—'Go on, and win! Break the Bank—*Mille tonnerres!* my gallant English comrade, break the bank!'

And I *did* go on—went on at such a rate, that in

another quarter of an hour the croupier called out: 'Gentlemen! the bank has discontinued for to-night.' All the notes, and all the gold in that 'bank,' now lay in a heap under my hands; the whole floating capital of the gambling-house was waiting to pour into my pockets!

'Tie up the money in your pocket-handkerchief, my worthy sir,' said the old soldier, as I wildly plunged my hands into my heap of gold. 'Tie it up, as we used to tie up a bit of dinner in the Grand Army; your winnings are too heavy for any breeches pockets that ever were sewed. There! that's it!—shovel them in, notes and all! *Credié!* what luck!—Stop! another Napoleon on the floor! *Ah! sacré petit polisson de Napoléon!* have I found thee at last? Now then, sir—two tight double knots each way with your honourable permission, and the money's safe. Feel it! feel it, fortunate sir! hard and round as a cannon ball—*Ah, bah!* if they had only fired such cannon balls at us at Austerlitz—*nom d'une pipe!* if they only had! And now, as an ancient grenadier, as an ex-brave of the French army, what remains for me to do? I ask what? Simply this: to entreat my valued English friend to drink a bottle of champagne with me, and toast the goddess Fortune in foaming goblets before we part!'

Excellent ex-brave! Convivial ancient grenadier! Champagne by all means! An English cheer for an old soldier! Hurrah! hurrah! Another English cheer for the goddess Fortune! Hurrah! hurrah! hurrah!

'Bravo! the Englishman; the amiable, gracious Englishman, in whose veins circulates the vivacious blood of France! Another glass? *Ah, bah!*—the bottle is empty! Never mind! *Vive le vin!* I, the old soldier, order another bottle, and half-a-pound of *bonbons* with it!'

'No, no, ex-brave; never—ancient grenadier!

Your bottle last time; *my* bottle this. Behold it! Toast away! The French Army!—the great Napoleon!—the present company! the croupier! the honest croupier's wife and daughters—if he has any! the Ladies generally! Everybody in the world!'

By the time the second bottle of champagne was emptied, I felt as if I had been drinking liquid fire—my brain seemed all a-flame. No excess in wine had ever had this effect on me before in my life. Was it the result of a stimulant acting upon my system when I was in a highly excited state? Was my stomach in a particularly disordered condition? Or was the champagne amazingly strong?

'Ex-brave of the French Army!' cried I, in a mad state of exhilaration, '*I* am on fire! how are *you*? You have set me on fire! Do you hear, my hero of Austerlitz? Let us have a third bottle of champagne to put the flame out!'

The old soldier wagged his head, rolled his goggle eyes, until I expected to see them slip out of their sockets; placed his dirty forefinger by the side of his broken nose; solemnly ejaculated 'Coffee!' and immediately ran off into an inner room.

The word pronounced by the eccentric veteran seemed to have a magical effect on the rest of the company present. With one accord they all rose to depart. Probably they had expected to profit by my intoxication; but finding that my new friend was benevolently bent on preventing me from getting dead drunk, had now abandoned all hope of thriving pleasantly on my winnings. Whatever their motive might be, at any rate they went away in a body. When the old soldier returned, and sat down again opposite to me at the table, we had the room to ourselves. I could see the croupier, in a sort of vestibule which opened out of it, eating his supper in solitude. The silence was now deeper than ever.

A sudden change, too, had come over the 'ex-brave.' He assumed a portentously solemn look; and when he spoke to me again, his speech was ornamented by no oaths, enforced by no finger-snapping, enlivened by no apostrophes or exclamations.

'Listen, my dear sir,' said he, in mysteriously confidential tones—'listen to an old soldier's advice. I have been to the mistress of the house (a very charming woman, with a genius for cookery!) to impress on her the necessity of making us some particularly strong and good coffee. You must drink this coffee in order to get rid of your little amiable exaltation of spirits before you think of going home—you *must*, my good and gracious friend! With all that money to take home to-night, it is a sacred duty to yourself to have your wits about you. You are known to be a winner to an enormous extent by several gentlemen present to-night, who, in a certain point of view, are very worthy and excellent fellows, but they are mortal men, my dear sir, and they have their amiable weaknesses! Need I say more? Ah, no, no! you understand me! Now, this is what you must do—send for a cabriolet when you feel quite well again—draw up all the windows when you get into it—and tell the driver to take you home only through the large and well-lighted thoroughfares. Do this; and you and your money will be safe. Do this; and to-morrow you will thank an old soldier for giving you a word of honest advice.'

Just as the ex-brave ended his oration in very lachrymose tones, the coffee came in, ready poured out in two cups. My attentive friend handed me one of the cups with a bow. I was parched with thirst, and drank it off at a draught. Almost instantly afterwards, I was seized with a fit of giddiness, and felt more completely intoxicated than ever. The room whirled round and round furiously; the old soldier seemed to be regularly bobbing up and down before me like the piston of a steam-engine. I was half deafened by a violent singing in my ears; a feeling of utter bewilderment, helplessness, idiocy, overcame me. I rose from my chair, holding on by the table to keep my balance; and stammered out, that I felt dreadfully unwell—so unwell that I did not know how I was to get home.

'My dear friend,' answered the old soldier—and even his voice seemed to be bobbing up and down as he spoke—'my dear friend, it would be madness to go home in *your* state; you would be sure to lose your money; you might be robbed and murdered with the greatest ease. *I* am going to sleep here: do *you* sleep here, too—they make up capital beds in this house—take one; sleep off the effects of the wine, and go home safely with your winnings to-morrow—to-morrow, in broad daylight.'

I had but two ideas left:—one, that I must never let go hold of my handkerchief full of money; the other, that I must lie down somewhere immediately, and fall off into a comfortable sleep. So I agreed to the proposal about the bed, and took the offered arm of the old soldier, carrying my money with my disengaged hand. Preceded by the croupier, we passed along some passages and up a flight of stairs into the bedroom which I was to occupy. The ex-brave shook me warmly by the hand, proposed that we should breakfast together, and then, followed by the croupier, left me for the night.

I ran to the wash-hand stand; drank some of the water in my jug; poured the rest out, and plunged my face into it; then sat down in a chair and tried to compose myself. I soon felt better. The change for my lungs, from the fetid atmosphere of the gambling-room to the cool air of the apartment I now occupied; the almost equally refreshing change for my eyes, from the glaring gas-lights of the 'Salon' to the dim, quiet flicker of one bedroom candle, aided wonderfully the restorative effects of cold water. The giddiness left me, and I began to feel a little like a reasonable being again. My first thought was of the risk of sleeping all night in a gambling-house; my second, of the still greater risk of trying to get out after the house was closed, and of going home alone at night, through the streets of Paris, with a large sum of money about me. I had slept in worse places than this on my travels; so I determined to lock, bolt, and barricade my door, and take my chance till the next morning.

Accordingly, I secured myself against all intrusion; looked under the bed, and into the cupboard; tried the fastening of the window; and then, satisfied that I had taken every proper precaution, pulled off my upper clothing, put my light, which was a dim one, on the hearth among a feathery litter of wood ashes, and got into bed, with the handkerchief full of money under my pillow.

I soon felt not only that I could not go to sleep, but that I could not even close my eyes. I was wide awake, and in a high fever. Every nerve in my body trembled—every one of my senses seemed to be preternaturally sharpened. I tossed and rolled, and tried every kind of position, and perseveringly sought out the cold corners of the bed, and all to no purpose. Now, I thrust my arms over the clothes; now, I poked them under the clothes; now, I violently shot my legs straight out down to the bottom of the bed; now, I convulsively coiled them up as near my chin as they would go; now, I shook out my crumpled pillow, changed it to the cool side, patted it flat, and lay down quietly on my back; now, I fiercely doubled it in two, set it up on end, thrust it against the board of the bed, and tried a sitting posture. Every effort was in vain; I groaned with vexation, as I felt that I was in for a sleepless night.

What could I do? I had no book to read. And yet, unless I found out some method of diverting my mind, I felt certain that I was in the condition to imagine all sorts of horrors; to rack my brain with forebodings of every possible and impossible danger; in short, to pass the night in suffering all conceivable varieties of nervous terror.

I raised myself on my elbow, and looked about the room—which was brightened by a lovely moonlight pouring straight through the window—to see if it contained any pictures or ornaments that I could at all clearly distinguish. While my eyes wandered from wall to wall, a remembrance of Le Maistre's delightful little book, *Voyage autour de ma Chambre*, occurred to me. I resolved to imitate the French author, and find occupation and amusement enough to relieve the tedium of my wakefulness, by making a mental inventory of every article of furniture I could see, and by following up to their sources the multitude of associations which even a chair, a table, or a wash-hand stand may be made to call forth.

In the nervous unsettled state of my mind at that moment, I found it much easier to make my inventory than to make my reflections, and thereupon soon gave up all hope of thinking in Le Maistre's fanciful track—or, indeed, of thinking at all. I looked about the room at the different articles of furniture, and did nothing more.

There was, first, the bed I was lying in; a four-post bed, of all things in the world to meet with in Paris!—yes, a thorough clumsy British four-poster, with the regular top lined with chintz—the regular fringed valance all round—the regular stifling unwholesome curtains, which I remembered having mechanically drawn back against the posts without particularly noticing the bed when I first got into the room. Then there was the marble-topped wash-hand stand, from which the water I had spilt, in my hurry to pour it out, was still dripping, slowly and more slowly, on to the brick floor. Then two small chairs, with my coat, waistcoat, and trousers flung on them. Then a large elbow-chair covered with dirty-white dimity, with my cravat and shirt-collar thrown over the back. Then a chest of drawers with two of the brass handles off, and a tawdry, broken china inkstand placed on it by way of ornament for the top. Then the dressing-table, adorned by a very small looking-glass, and a very large pincushion. Then the window—an unusually large window. Then a dark old picture, which the feeble candle dimly showed me. It was the picture of a fellow in a high Spanish hat, crowned with a plume of towering feathers. A swarthy sinister ruffian, looking upward, shading his eyes with his hand, and looking intently upward—it might be at some tall gallows at which he was going to be hanged. At any rate, he had the appearance of thoroughly deserving it.

This picture put a kind of constraint upon me to look upward too—at the top of the bed. It was a gloomy and not an interesting object, and I looked back at the picture. I counted the feathers in the man's hat—they stood out in relief—three white, two green. I observed the crown of his hat, which was of a conical shape, according to the fashion supposed to have been favoured by Guido Fawkes. I wondered what he was looking up at. It couldn't be at the stars; such a desperado was neither astrologer nor astronomer. It must be at the high gallows, and he was going to be hanged presently. Would the executioner come into possession of his conical-crowned hat and plume of feathers? I counted the feathers again—three white, two green.

While I still lingered over this very improving and intellectual employment, my thoughts insensibly began to wander. The moonlight shining into the room reminded me of a certain moonlight night in England—the night after a picnic party in a Welsh valley. Every incident of the drive homeward, through lovely scenery, which the moonlight made lovelier than ever, came back to my remembrance, though I had never given the picnic a thought for years; though, if I had *tried* to recollect it, I could certainly have recalled little or nothing of that scene long past. Of all the wonderful faculties that help to tell us we are immortal, which speaks the sublime truth more eloquently than memory? Here was I, in a strange house of the most suspicious character, in a situation of uncertainty, and even of peril, which might seem to make the cool exercise of my recollection almost out of the question; nevertheless, remembering, quite involuntarily, places, people, conversations, minute circumstances of every kind, which I had thought forgotten for ever; which I could not possibly have recalled at will, even under the most favourable auspices. And what cause had produced in a moment the whole of this strange, complicated, mysterious effect? Nothing but some rays of moonlight shining in at my bedroom window.

I was still thinking of the picnic—of our merriment on the drive home—of the sentimental young lady who *would* quote *Childe Harold* because it was moonlight. I was absorbed by these past scenes and past amusements, when, in an instant, the thread on which my memories hung snapped asunder; my attention immediately came back to present things more vividly than ever, and I found myself, I neither knew why nor wherefore, looking hard at the picture again.

Looking for what?

Good God! the man had pulled his hat down on his brows!—No! the hat itself was gone! Where was the conical crown? Where the feathers—three white, two green? Not there? In place of the hat and feathers, what dusky object was it that now hid his forehead, his eyes, his shading hand?

Was the bed moving?

I turned on my back and looked up. Was I mad? drunk? dreaming? giddy again? or was the top of the bed really moving down—sinking slowly, regularly, silently, horribly, right down throughout the whole of its length and breadth—right down upon me, as I lay underneath ?

My blood seemed to stand still. A deadly paralysing coldness stole all over me, as I turned my head round on the pillow, and determined to test whether the bed-top was really moving or not, by keeping my eye on the man in the picture.

The next look in that direction was enough. The dull, black, frowsy outline of the valance above me was within an inch of being parallel with his waist. I still looked breathlessly. And steadily, and slowly—very slowly—I saw the figure, and the line of frame below the figure, vanish, as the valance moved down before it.

I am, constitutionally, anything but timid. I have been on more than one occasion in peril of my life, and have not lost my self-possession for an instant; but when the conviction first settled on my mind that the bed-top was really moving, was steadily and continuously sinking down upon me, I looked up shuddering, helpless, panic-stricken, beneath the hideous machinery for murder, which was advancing closer and closer to suffocate me where I lay.

I looked up, motionless, speechless, breathless. The candle, fully spent, went out; but the moonlight still brightened the room. Down and down, without pausing and without sounding, came the bed-top, and still my panic-terror seemed to bind me faster and faster to the mattress on which I lay—down and down it sank, till the dusty odour from the lining of the canopy came stealing into my nostrils.

At that final moment the instinct of self-preservation startled me out of my trance, and I moved at last. There was just room for me to roll myself sideways off the bed. As I dropped noiselessly to the floor, the edge of the murderous canopy touched me on the shoulder.

Without stopping to draw my breath, without wiping the cold sweat from my face, I rose instantly on my knees to watch the bed-top. I was literally spell-bound by it. If I had heard footsteps behind me, I could not have turned round; if a means of escape had been miraculously provided for me, I could not have moved to take advantage of it. The whole life in me was, at that moment, concentrated in my eyes.

It descended—the whole canopy, with the fringe round it, came down—down—close down; so close that there was not room now to squeeze my finger between the bed-top and the bed. I felt at the sides, and discovered that what had appeared to me from beneath to be the ordinary light canopy of a four-post bed, was in reality a thick, broad mattress, the substance of which was concealed by the valance and its fringe. I looked up and saw the four posts rising hideously bare. In the middle of the bed-top was a huge wooden screw that had evidently worked it down through a hole in the ceiling, just as ordinary presses are worked down on the substance selected for compression. The frightful apparatus moved without making the faintest noise. There had been no creaking as it came down; there was now not the faintest sound from the room above. Amid a dead and awful silence I beheld before me—in the nineteenth century, and in the civilized capital of France—such a machine for secret murder by suffocation as might have existed in the worst days of the Inquisition, in the lonely inns among the Hartz Mountains, in the mysterious tribunals of Westphalia! Still, as I looked on it, I could not move, I could hardly breathe, but I began to recover the power of thinking, and in a moment I discovered the murderous conspiracy framed against me in all its horror.

My cup of coffee had been drugged, and drugged too strongly. I had been saved from being smothered by having taken an overdose of some narcotic. How I had chafed and fretted at the fever-fit which had preserved my life by keeping me awake! How recklessly I had confided myself to the two wretches who had led me into this room, determined, for the sake of my winnings, to kill me in my sleep by the surest and most horrible contrivance for secretly accomplishing my destruction! How many men, winners like me, had slept, as I had proposed to sleep, in that bed, and had never been seen or heard of more! I shuddered at the bare idea of it.

But, ere long, all thought was again suspended by the sight of the murderous canopy moving once more. After it had remained on the bed—as nearly as I could guess—about ten minutes, it began to move up again. The villains who worked it from above evidently believed that their purpose was now accomplished. Slowly and silently, as it had descended, that horrible bed-top rose towards its former place. When it reached the upper extremities of the four posts, it reached the ceiling too. Neither hole nor screw could be seen; the bed became in appearance an ordinary bed again—the canopy an ordinary canopy—even to the most suspicious eyes.

Now, for the first time, I was able to move—to rise from my knees—to dress myself in my upper clothing—and to consider of how I should escape. If I betrayed, by the smallest noise, that the attempt to suffocate me had failed, I was certain to be murdered. Had I made any noise already? I listened intently, looking towards the door.

No! no footsteps in the passage outside—no sound of a tread, light or heavy, in the room above—absolute silence everywhere. Besides locking and bolting my door, I had moved an old wooden chest against it, which I had found under the bed. To remove this chest (my blood ran cold as I thought of what its contents *might* be!) without making some disturbance was impossible; and, moreover, to think of escaping through the house, now barred up for the night, was sheer insanity. Only one chance was left me—the window. I stole to it on tiptoe.

My bedroom was on the first floor, above an *entrcsol*, and looked into the back street, which you have sketched in your view. I raised my hand to open the window, knowing that on that action hung, by the merest hair's-breadth, my chance of safety. They keep vigilant watch in a House of Murder. If any part of the frame cracked, if the hinge creaked, I was a lost man! It must have occupied me at least five minutes, reckoning by time—five *hours*, reckoning by suspense—to open that window. I succeeded in doing it silently—in doing it with all the dexterity of a housebreaker—and then looked down into the street. To leap the distance beneath me would be almost certain destruction! Next, I looked round at the sides of the house. Down the left side ran the thick water-pipe which you have drawn—it passed close by the outer edge of the window. The moment I saw the pipe, I knew I was saved. My breath came and went freely for the first time since I had seen the canopy of the bed moving down upon me!

To some men the means of escape which I had discovered might have seemed difficult and dangerous enough—to *me* the prospect of slipping down the pipe into the street did not suggest even a thought of peril. I had always been accustomed, by the practice of gymnastics, to keep up my schoolboy powers as a daring and expert climber; and knew that my head, hands, and feet would serve me faithfully in any hazards of ascent or descent. I had already got one leg over the window-sill, when I remembered the handkerchief filled with money under my pillow. I could well have afforded to leave it behind me, but I was revengefully determined that the miscreants of the gambling-house should miss their plunder as well as their victim. So I went back to the bed and tied the heavy handkerchief at my back by my cravat.

Just as I had made it tight and fixed it in a comfortable place, I thought I heard a sound of breathing outside the door. The chill feeling of horror ran through me again as I listened. No! dead silence still in the passage—I had only heard the night-air blowing softly into the room. The next moment I was on the window-sill—and the next I had a firm grip on the water-pipe with my hands and knees.

I slid down into the street easily and quietly, as I thought I should, and immediately set off at the top of my speed to a branch 'Prefecture' of Police, which I knew was situated in the immediate neighbourhood. A 'Sub-prefect,' and several picked men among his subordinates, happened to be up, maturing, I believe, some scheme for discovering the perpetrator of a mysterious murder which all Paris was talking of just then. When I began my story, in a breathless hurry and in very bad French, I could see that the Sub-prefect suspected me of being a drunken Englishman who had robbed somebody; but he soon altered his opinion as I went on, and before I had anything like concluded, he shoved all the papers before him into a drawer, put on his hat, supplied me with another (for I was bare-headed), ordered a file of soldiers, desired his expert followers to get ready all sorts of tools for breaking open doors and ripping up brick-flooring, and took my arm, in the most friendly and familiar manner possible, to lead me with him out of the house. I will venture to say, that when the Sub-prefect was a little boy, and was taken for the first time to the play, he was not half as much pleased as he was now at the job in prospect for him at the gambling-house!

Away we went through the streets, the Sub-prefect cross-examining and congratulating me in the same breath as we marched at the head of our formidable *posse comitatus.* Sentinels were placed at the back and front of the house the moment we got to it; a tremendous battery of knocks was directed against the door; a light appeared at a window; I was told to conceal myself behind the police—then came more knocks, and a cry of 'Open in the name of the law!' At that terrible summons bolts and locks gave way before an invisible hand, and the moment after the Sub-prefect was in the passage, confronting a waiter half-dressed and ghastly pale. This was the short dialogue which immediately took place:—

'We want to see the Englishman who is sleeping in this house?'

'He went away hours ago.'

'He did no such thing. His friend went away; *he* remained. Show us to his bedroom!'

'I swear to you, Monsieur le Sous-prefect, he is not here! he——.'

'I swear to you, Monsieur le Garçon, he is. He slept here—he didn't find your bed comfortable—he came to us to complain of it—here he is among my men—and here am I ready to look for a flea or two in his bedstead. Renaudin!' (calling to one of the subordinates, and pointing to the waiter) 'collar that man, and tie his hands behind him. Now, then, gentlemen, let us walk upstairs!'

Every man and woman in the house was secured—the 'Old Soldier' the first. Then I identified the bed in which I had slept, and then we went into the room above.

No object that was at all extraordinary appeared in any part of it. The Sub-prefect looked round the place, commanded everybody to be silent, stamped twice on the floor, called for a candle, looked attentively at the spot he had stamped on, and ordered the flooring there to be carefully taken up. This was done in no time. Lights were produced, and we saw a deep raftered cavity between the floor of this room and the ceiling of the room beneath. Through this cavity there ran perpendicularly a sort of case of iron thickly greased; and inside the case appeared the screw, which communicated with the bed-top below. Extra lengths of screw, freshly oiled; levers covered with felt; all the complete upper works of a heavy press—constructed with infernal ingenuity so as to join the fixtures below, and when taken to pieces again to go into the smallest possible compass—were next discovered and pulled out on the floor. After some little difficulty the Sub-prefect succeeded in putting the machinery together, and, leaving his men to work it, descended with me to the bedroom. The smothering canopy was then lowered, but not so noiselessly as I had seen it lowered. When I mentioned this to the Sub-prefect, his answer, simple as it was, had a terrible significance. 'My men,' said he, 'are working down the bed-top for the first time—the men whose money you won were in better practice.'

We left the house in the sole possession of two police agents—every one of the inmates being removed to prison on the spot. The Sub-prefect, after taking down my '*procès-verbal*' in his office, returned with me to my hotel to get my passport. 'Do you think,' I asked, as I gave it to him, 'that any men have really been smothered in that bed, as they tried to smother *me*?'

'I have seen dozens of drowned men laid out at the Morgue,' answered the Sub-prefect, 'in whose pocket-books were found letters, stating that they had committed suicide in the Seine, because they had lost everything at the gaming-table. Do I know how many of those men entered the same gambling-house that *you* entered? won as *you* won? took that bed as *you* took it? slept in it? were smothered in it? and were privately thrown into the river, with a letter of explanation written by the murderers and placed in their pocket-books? No man can say how many or how few have suffered the fate from which you have escaped. The people of the gambling-house kept their bedstead machinery a secret from *us*—even from the police! The dead kept the rest of the secret for them. Good night, or rather good morning, Monsieur Faulkner! Be at my office again at nine o'clock—in the meantime, *au revoir!*'

The rest of my story is soon told. I was examined and re-examined; the gambling-house was strictly searched all through from top to bottom; the prisoners were separately interrogated; and two of the less guilty among them made a confession. *I* discovered that the Old Soldier was the master of the gambling-house—*justice* discovered that he had been drummed out of the army as a vagabond years ago; that he had been guilty of all sorts of villanies since; that he was in possession of stolen property, which the owners identified; and that he, the croupier, another accomplice, and the woman who had made my cup of coffee, were all in the secret of the bedstead. There appeared some reason to doubt whether the inferior persons attached to the house knew anything of the suffocating machinery; and they received the benefit of that doubt, by being treated simply as thieves and vagabonds. As for the Old Soldier and his two head-myrmidons, they went to the galleys; the woman who had drugged my coffee was imprisoned for I forget how many years; the regular attendants at the gambling-house were considered 'suspicious,' and placed under 'surveillance'; and I became, for one whole week (which is a long time), the head 'lion' in Parisian society. My adventure was dramatized by three illustrious playmakers, but never saw theatrical daylight; for the censorship forbade the introduction on the stage of a correct copy of the gambling-house bedstead.

One good result was produced by my adventure, which any censorship must have approved:—it cured me of ever again trying 'Rouge et Noir' as an amusement. The sight of a green cloth, with packs of cards and heaps of money on it, will henceforth be for ever associated in my mind with the sight of a bed-canopy descending to suffocate me in the silence and darkness of the night.

WILLIAM HALE WHITE

('Mark Rutherford')

1831—1913

'THE SWEETNESS OF A MAN'S FRIEND'

'But when he came to himself he said——'

Forty years ago I had been a clerk in a Government office in Whitehall for three years. My father was a small squire owning about 1,500 acres of land in the Midlands, and, as he had only two children, a girl and a boy, he contrived to send me to Harrow, his own school. When I left Harrow I went to Cambridge, and came out well in the Civil Service examination. Soon afterwards I became engaged to Margaret Rushworth, daughter of the rector in the little town of Hemsworth, about five miles from my home, and in 1870 we were married. In addition to my salary I had an allowance of over £100 a year from home, and Margaret had £50 a year of her own. We set up house at Blackheath.

Margaret was not a great reader, although what she read she read slowly and thoroughly. I thought she would 'open out,' as I infelicitously described a liking for literature, but in this way she did not open out. Perhaps it was required of her that she should develop according to the law of her own nature. Providence may have considered it necessary, although probably she was not conscious of the command, that her particular character should be preserved without the interference or imposition of any other. I, on the contrary, lived in books; I worked hard at Cambridge, and I hated dissipation. It was this love of books that was answerable for certain defects in me; one of which was the absence of a sense of proportion. It is curious—Glycine's song of three or four verses in *Zapolya* or a dozen lines from *The Rape of the Lock* were more to me than the news of great events. I should even have thought it better worth while to discover how Shakespeare laced his shoes than to understand the provisions of a revolutionary Reform Bill. Conversation was interesting to me mainly in so far as it turned upon what I had been reading. I was often, no doubt, set down as a prig. I was not a prig, for I was much in earnest. I was however, I admit, an uncomfortable, unpopular acquaintance. The gay, the empty-hearted, empty-headed society joker scoffed at me because I was an easy chance he could not afford to miss of securing laughter at the expense of that stock subject, 'a serious person.'

My peculiar temperament did not fully reveal itself until some time after I was engaged. I then hoped for a happy time with Margaret: when in long evenings we could study Shelley together and discuss the connexion of the story in *The Revolt of Islam*, a problem I had not yet been able to solve. I belonged to a club, called, for no particular reason, the Saturday Club, of a dozen men about the same age as myself and of a somewhat similar disposition, who met together for mutual edification on the second and fifteenth of each month. It looks strange to many people, no doubt, but to me, even now, it is not strange that twelve persons belonging to this commonplace world could quietly seat themselves round a table and begin, without the aid of alcohol, tobacco, or even of coffee, to impart to one another their opinions on subjects which would generally be considered most uninviting. Once I came home with my head full of Milton's prosody. I proceeded immediately to pour out upon Margaret all the results of our debate and, more particularly, my own observations, but as she had never read

Paradise Lost, and knew nothing of the laws of blank verse, I did not go on and was disappointed. She also was sad, and the evening passed as an evening passes in late September when we have not begun fires, and cold rain sets in with the growing darkness. When either the second or fifteenth of the month fell on a Saturday, the hour of meeting was four o'clock. One Saturday we had tried to make out what really happened to the magic boat in *Alastor*. The eddying waters rise 'stair above stair,' and the boat is

> 'Seized by the sway of the ascending stream.'

I was puzzled and eager ; I got home early and could not help trying to explain the difficulty to Margaret ! I read all that part of *Alastor* to her which has to do with the movement of the boat, and I expatiated on it with some eloquence and almost with emotion. I could see she tried to follow me and to make clear to herself the miraculous course of the stream, but she did not succeed, and her irrelevant remarks made me irritable. She asked me who the wanderer was, and what was the object of his voyage. 'O Margaret,' I broke out, and I propped my elbows on the table, my head falling in despondency between my hands, 'O Margaret, I do wish I could find a little more sympathy in you. What a joy it would be for me if you cared for the things for which I care, those which really concern me.' She said nothing and I left the room, but as I went I thought I saw tears in her eyes. I was frightened. I loved her passionately, and I said to myself that perhaps this was the beginning of decay in my love for her. What should I do, what should I be if we became estranged ? I felt that horrible half-insane terror which men feel during an earthquake, when the ground under their feet begins to shake.

That night an old college friend came to supper with us. I had not seen him for two years. His name was Robert Barclay. His father was a clergyman who had been trained theologically in the school of Simeon, and was, consequently, very Low Church. Robert also, who went to Cambridge, was Low Church while he was there, but when he was five-and-twenty there came a great change. He woke up as if from a trance, and began to ask questions, the result of which was that the creed in which he had been educated seemed to have no rock-foundation, but to hang in the air. He went on until he could only say *I do not know*; but it was impossible for him to rest here. He was so constituted that he was compelled to affirm, and, by a process which I cannot now develop, he became a Roman Catholic, conquering, to his own satisfaction, the difficulty of finding for Papal authority a support reaching down to the centre which he could not find in Simeonism. He was content to rest where Newman rested—'there is no help for it: we must either give up the belief in the Church as a divine institution altogether, or we must recognize it in that communion of which the Pope is the head; we must take things as they are; to believe in a Church is to believe in the Pope.'

Barclay was often at my father's house before his conversion, and there he fell in love with Veronica, Margaret's sister, who, with Margaret, was staying with my mother. Veronica also was deeply in love with him, and they were engaged. Slowly he became possessed with a desire to be a priest, with a sure conviction, in fact, that he ought to be one. Veronica by this time was a Roman Catholic, and she was strong enough to urge him to obey what both of them believed to be a divine injunction. What these two went through no mortal can tell: Heaven only knows. I had a glimpse every now and then of a struggle even unto death, of wrestling till the blood forced itself through the pores of the skin.

The difficulty lay not in doing what they were sure was right, but in discovering what the right was.

Sometimes it seemed a clear command that they should give themselves up to one another. There was no hesitation in it. Both of them were ardent, passionate, vividly imaginative. Was it conceivable that such an overwhelming impulse was not of God? The command that Robert should be a priest was nothing like so clear; but, on the other hand, both Veronica and Robert were too well instructed not to be aware that clearness is not decisive as to the authority of a direction, and that the true path may be suggested in a whisper when we are bidden, as if through a speaking trumpet, to take that which leads to destruction. What made the separation especially terrible, both to Veronica and Robert, it is hard to say. Here are a couple of lines from one of Robert's letters to me which may partly explain: 'There is something in this trouble I cannot put into words. It is the complete unfolding, the making real to myself, all that is hidden in that word *Never.*' Is it possible to express by speech a white handkerchief waved from the window of the railway train, or the deserted platform where ten minutes before a certain woman stood, where her image still lingers? There is something in this which is not mere sorrow. It is rather the disclosure of that dread Abyss which underlies the life of man. One consequence of this experience was the purest sincerity. All insincerity, everything unsound, everything which could not stand the severest test, was by this trial crushed out of him. His words uniformly stood for facts. Perhaps it was his sincerity which gave him a power over me such as no other man ever possessed. He could not persuade me to follow him into the Roman Catholic Church, but this was because Margaret held me back. She was the only person who could have enabled me to resist.

Robert was much struck with Margaret's account during supper of the manner in which she helped her poorer neighbours. She did not give them money or clothes or food, nor did she play the district visitor;

but she went into their houses and devoted to one woman an hour in cooking, to another an hour in washing clothes, or cleaning rooms and scrubbing floors. Not only was this real assistance, but it was an opportunity for her to show how work ought to be done. 'I can slip in something now and then,' she said, 'which may do their souls good, and I am sure that it is the word which is spoken casually that is most effective with them. It is useless to talk abstractions or to preach in general terms the heinousness of sin ; but if Bill next door has beaten his wife or drinks and gives her nothing out of his wages, you can enlarge on his bad behaviour with much profit. As to religion as we understand it when we kneel at Holy Communion, it cannot be taught. It requires a heavenly endowment as much as writing great poems. Keeping your hands from picking and stealing is a different matter.'

Margaret went early to bed. Her little girl, six months old, required her attention. We had been silent for a few minutes. Somewhat unexpectedly, without any introduction, Robert spoke.

'Margaret is original, and has real genius. What a blessing it is that she has honoured you with marriage ! Let stupid people say what they will, originality and genius in a wife are amongst the greatest of earthly blessings. But, although amongst the greatest, there is something greater.' His voice shook a little. Genius ! originality ! I had not thought of it before. The boat in *Alastor* crossed my mind, but Robert's power asserted itself, a strength sufficient not only to change an opinion, but to alter entirely the aspect of things, just as in a flash, without argument, Saul perceived that he had been utterly mistaken. Robert revealed the truth of Margaret to me, and the revelation was almost miraculous, so strangely disproportionate were means to the effect.

I went into her room. I opened the door gently, and saw that she and her child were both asleep, but the night-light was burning. I took off my shoes outside and crept noiselessly to the little table by the side of the bed. A bookmarker in a volume of Shelley showed me she had been studying the passages which I had read to her about the boat. I went back to bed, but not to sleep. Next morning, early, I again went into her room. She had been awake, for a page was turned over, but her eyes were closed. Her arm lay upon the coverlet. I knelt down and took her hand, that delicately beautiful hand with its filbert finger-nails—knelt down and kissed it softly. She started a little, sat up, and bent over me, and I felt her lips on my head, her thick hair falling over it and enveloping it. She died ten years ago. The face in the vision which is always before me is a happy face, thank God.

RICHARD GARNETT

1835—1906

ANANDA THE MIRACLE WORKER

THE holy Buddha, Sakhya Muni, on dispatching his apostles to proclaim his religion throughout the peninsula of India, failed not to provide them with salutary precepts for their guidance. He exhorted them to meekness, to compassion, to abstemiousness, to zeal in the promulgation of his doctrine, and added an injunction never before or since prescribed by the founder of any religion—namely, on no account to perform any miracle.

It is further related, that whereas the apostles experienced considerable difficulty in complying with the other instructions of their master, and sometimes actually failed therein, the prohibition to work miracles was never once transgressed by any of them, save only the pious Ananda, the history of whose first year's apostolate is recorded as follows.

Ananda repaired to the kingdom of Magadha, and instructed the inhabitants diligently in the law of Buddha. His doctrine being acceptable, and his speech persuasive, the people hearkened to him willingly, and began to forsake the Brahmins whom they had previously revered as spiritual guides. Perceiving this, Ananda became elated in spirit, and one day he exclaimed:

'How blessed is the apostle who propagates truth by the efficacy of reason and virtuous example, combined with eloquence, rather than error by imposture and devil-mongering, like those miserable Brahmins!'

As he uttered this vainglorious speech, the mountain of his merits was diminished by sixteen yojanas, and virtue and efficacy departed from him, insomuch that when he next addressed the multitude they first mocked, then hooted, and finally pelted him.

When matters had reached this pass, Ananda lifted his eyes and discerned a number of Brahmins of the lower sort, busy about a boy who lay in a fit upon the ground. They had long been applying exorcisms and other approved methods with scant success, when the most sagacious among them suggested:

'Let us render the body of this patient an uncomfortable residence for the demon; peradventure he will then cease to abide therein.'

They were accordingly engaged with branding the sufferer with hot irons, filling his nostrils with smoke, and otherwise to the best of their ability disquieting the intrusive devil. Ananda's first thought was, 'The lad is in a fit'; the second, 'It were a pious deed to deliver him from his tormentors'; the third, 'By good management this may extricate me from my present uncomfortable predicament, and redound to the glory of the most holy Buddha.'

Yielding to this temptation, he strode forward, chased away the Brahmins with an air of authority, and, uplifting his countenance to heaven, recited the appellations of seven devils. No effect ensuing, he repeated seven more, and so continued until, the fit having passed off in the course of nature, the patient's paroxysms ceased, he opened his eyes, and Ananda restored him to his relatives. But the people cried loudly, 'A miracle! a miracle!' and when Ananda resumed his instructions, they gave heed to him, and numbers embraced the religion of Buddha. Whereupon Ananda exulted, and applauded himself for his dexterity and presence of mind, and said to himself:

'Surely the end sanctifies the means.'

As he propounded this heresy, the eminence of his

merits was reduced to the dimensions of a mole-hill, and he ceased to be of account in the eyes of any of the saints, save only of Buddha, whose compassion is inexhaustible.

The fame of his achievement, nevertheless, was bruited about the whole country, and soon reached the ears of the King, who sent for him, and inquired if he had actually expelled the demon.

Ananda replied in the affirmative.

'I am indeed rejoiced,' returned the King, 'as thou now wilt without doubt proceed to heal *my* son, who has lain in a trance for twenty-nine days.'

'Alas! dread sovereign,' modestly returned Ananda, 'how should the merits which barely suffice to effect the cure of a miserable Pariah avail to restore the offspring of an Elephant among Kings?'

'By what process are these merits acquired?' demanded the monarch.

'By the exercise of penance,' responded Ananda, 'in virtue of which the austere devotee quells the winds, allays the waters, expostulates convincingly with tigers, carries the moon in his sleeve, and otherwise performs all acts and deeds appropriate to the character of a peripatetic thaumaturgist.'

'This being so,' answered the King, 'thy inability to heal my son manifestly arises from defect of merit, and defect of merit from defect of penance. I will therefore consign thee to the charge of my Brahmins, that they may aid thee to fill up the measure of that which is lacking.'

Ananda vainly strove to explain that the austerities to which he had referred were entirely of a spiritual and contemplative character. The Brahmins, enchanted to get a heretic into their clutches, immediately seized upon him, and conveyed him to one of their temples. They stripped him, and perceived with astonishment that not one single weal or scar was visible anywhere on his person. 'Horror!' they exclaimed; 'here is a man who expects to go to heaven in a whole skin!' To obviate this breach of etiquette, they laid him upon his face, and flagellated him until the obnoxious soundness of cuticle was entirely removed. They then departed, promising to return next day and operate in a corresponding manner upon the anterior part of his person, after which, they jeeringly assured him, his merits would be in no respect less than those of the saintly Bhagiratha, or of the regal Viswâmitra himself.

Ananda lay half dead upon the floor of the temple, when the sanctuary was illuminated by the apparition of a resplendent Glendoveer, who thus addressed him:

'Well, backsliding disciple, art thou yet convinced of thy folly?'

Ananda relished neither the imputation on his orthodoxy nor that on his wisdom. He replied, notwithstanding, with all meekness:

'Heaven forbid that I should repine at any variety of martyrdom that tends to the propagation of my master's faith.'

'Wilt thou then first be healed, and moreover become the instrument of converting the entire realm of Magadha?'

'How shall this be accomplished?' demanded Ananda.

'By perseverance in the path of deceit and disobedience,' returned the Glendoveer.

Ananda winced, but maintained silence in the expectation of more explicit directions.

'Know,' pursued the spirit, 'that the king's son will revive from his trance at the expiration of the thirtieth day, which takes place at noon to-morrow. Thou hast but to proceed at the fitting period to the couch whereon he is deposited, and, placing thy hand upon his heart, to command him to rise forthwith. His recovery will be ascribed to thy supernatural powers, and the establishment of Buddha's religion will result. Before this it will be needful that I should perform an actual cure upon thy back, which is within the compass of my capacity. I only request thee to take notice, that thou wilt on this occasion be transgressing the precepts of thy master with thine eyes open. It is also meet to apprise thee that thy temporary extrication from thy present difficulties will only involve thee in others still more formidable.'

'An incorporeal Glendoveer is no judge of the feelings of a flayed apostle,' thought Ananda. 'Heal me,' he replied, 'if thou canst, and reserve thy admonitions for a more convenient opportunity.'

'So be it,' returned the Glendoveer; and as he extended his hand over Ananda, the latter's back was clothed anew with skin, and his previous smart simultaneously allayed. The Glendoveer vanished at the same moment, saying, 'When thou hast need of me, pronounce but the incantation, *Gnooh Imdap Inam Mua*,[1] and I will immediately be by thy side.'

The anger and amazement of the Brahmins may be conceived when, on returning equipped with fresh implements of flagellation, they discovered the salubrious condition of their victim. Their scourges would probably have undergone conversion into halters, had they not been accompanied by a royal officer, who took the really triumphant martyr under his protection, and carried him off to the palace. He was speedily conducted to the young prince's couch, whither a vast crowd attended him. The hour of noon not having yet arrived, Ananda discreetly protracted the time by a seasonable discourse on the impossibility of miracles, those only excepted which should be wrought by the professors of the faith of Buddha. He then descended from his pulpit, and precisely as the sun attained the zenith laid his hand upon the bosom of

1 The mystic formula of the Buddhists, read backwards.

the young prince, who instantly revived, and completed a sentence touching the game of dice which had been interrupted by his catalepsy.

The people shouted, the courtiers went into ecstasies. the countenances of the Brahmins assumed an exceedingly sheepish expression. Even the king seemed impressed, and craved to be more particularly instructed in the law of Buddha. In complying with this request, Ananda, who had made marvellous progress in worldly wisdom during the last twenty-four hours, deemed it needless to dilate on the cardinal doctrines of his master, the misery of existence, the need of redemption, the path to felicity, the prohibition to shed blood. He simply stated that the priests of Buddha were bound to perpetual poverty, and that under the new dispensation all ecclesiastical property would accrue to the temporal authorities.

'By the holy cow!' exclaimed the monarch, 'this is something like a religion!'

The words were scarcely out of the royal lips ere the courtiers professed themselves converts. The multitude followed their example. The Brahminical church was promptly disestablished and disendowed, and more injustice was committed in the name of the new and purified religion in one day than the old corrupt one had occasioned in a hundred years.

Ananda had the satisfaction of feeling able to forgive his adversaries, and of valuing himself accordingly; and to complete his felicity, he was received in the palace, and entrusted with the education of the king's son, which he strove to conduct agreeably to the precepts of Buddha. This was a task of some delicacy, as it involved interference with the princely youth's favourite amusement, which had previously consisted in torturing small reptiles.

After a short interval Ananda was again summoned to the monarch's presence. He found his majesty in the company of two most ferocious ruffians, one of whom bore a huge axe, and the other an enormous pair of pincers.

'My chief executioner and my chief tormentor,' said the king.

Ananda expressed his gratification at becoming acquainted with such exalted functionaries.

'Thou must know, most holy man,' resumed the king, 'that need has again arisen for the exercise of fortitude and self-denial on thy part. A powerful enemy has invaded my dominions, and has impiously presumed to discomfit my troops. Well might I feel dismayed, were it not for the consolations of religion; but my trust is in thee, O my spiritual father! It is urgent that thou shouldst accumulate the largest amount of merit with the least delay possible. I am unable to invoke the ministrations of thy old friends the Brahmins to this end, they being, as thou knowest, in disgrace, but I have summoned these trusty and experienced counsellors in their room. I find them not wholly in accord. My chief tormentor, being a man of mild temper and humane disposition, considers that it might at first suffice to employ gentle measures, such, for example, as suspending thee head downwards in the smoke of a wood fire, and filling thy nostrils with red pepper. My chief executioner, taking, peradventure, a too professional view of the subject, deems it best to resort at once to crucifixion or impalement. I would gladly know thy thoughts on the matter.'

Ananda expressed, as well as his terror would suffer him, his entire disapproval of both the courses recommended by the royal advisers.

'Well,' said the king, with an air of resignation, 'if we cannot agree upon either, it follows that we must try both. We will meet for that purpose to-morrow morning at the second hour. Go in peace!'

Ananda went, but not in peace. His alarm would have well-nigh deprived him of his faculties if he had not remembered the promise made him by his former deliverer. On reaching a secluded spot he pronounced the mystic formula, and immediately became aware of the presence, not of a radiant Glendoveer, but of a holy man, whose head was strewn with ashes, and his body anointed with cow-dung.

'Thy occasion,' said the Fakir, 'brooks no delay. Thou must immediately accompany me, and assume the garb of a Jogi.'

Ananda rebelled excessively in his heart, for he had imbibed from the mild and sage Buddha a befitting contempt for these grotesque and cadaverous fanatics. The emergency, however, left him no resource, and he followed his guide to a charnel house, which the latter had selected as his domicile. There, with many lamentations over the smoothness of his hair and the brevity of his nails, the Jogi besprinkled and besmeared Ananda agreeably to his own pattern, and scored him with chalk and ochre until the peaceful apostle of the gentlest of creeds resembled a Bengal tiger. He then hung a chaplet of infants' skulls about his neck, placed the skull of a malefactor in one of his hands, and the thigh-bone of a necromancer in the other, and at nightfall conducted him into the adjacent cemetery, where, seating him on the ashes of a recent funeral pile, he bade him drum upon the skull with the thigh-bone, and repeat after himself the incantations which he began to scream out towards the western part of the firmament. These charms were apparently possessed of singular efficacy, for scarcely were they commenced ere a hideous tempest arose, rain descended in torrents, phosphoric flashes darted across the sky, wolves and hyænas thronged howling from their dens, and gigantic goblins, arising from the earth, extended their fleshless arms towards Ananda, and strove to drag him from his seat. Urged by frantic terror, and the example and exhortations of his companion, he battered, banged, and vociferated, until on the very verge of exhaustion; when, as if by enchantment, the tempest ceased, the spectres disappeared, and joyous shouts and a burst of music announced the occurrence of something auspicious in the adjoining city.

'The hostile king is dead,' said the Jogi; 'and his army has dispersed. This will be attributed to thy incantations. They are coming in quest of thee even now. Farewell until thou again hast need of me.'

The Jogi disappeared, the tramp of a procession became audible, and soon torches glared feebly through the damp, cheerless dawn. The monarch descended from his state elephant, and, prostrating himself before Ananda, exclaimed:

'Inestimable man! why didst thou not disclose that thou wert a Jogi? Never more shall I feel the least apprehension of any of my enemies, so long as thou continuest an inmate of this cemetery.'

A family of jackals were unceremoniously dislodged from a disused sepulchre, which was allotted to Ananda for his future residence. The king permitted no alteration in his costume, and took care that the food doled out to him should have no tendency to impair his sanctity, which speedily gave promise of attaining a very high pitch. His hair had already become as matted and his nails as long as the Jogi could have desired, when he received a visit from another royal messenger. The Rajah, so ran the regal missive, had been suddenly and mysteriously attacked by a dangerous malady, but confidently anticipated relief from Ananda's merits and incantations.

Ananda resumed his thigh-bone and his skull, and ruefully began to thump the latter with the former, in dismal expectation of the things that were to come. But the spell seemed to have lost its potency. Nothing more unearthly than a bat presented itself, and Ananda was beginning to think that he might as well desist when his reflections were diverted by the apparition of a tall and grave personage, wearing a sad-coloured robe, and carrying a long wand, who stood by his side as suddenly as though just risen from the earth.

'The caldron is ready,' said the stranger.

'What caldron ?' demanded Ananda.

'That wherein thou art about to be immersed.'

'I immersed in a caldron ! wherefore ?'

'Thy spells,' returned his interlocutor, 'having hitherto failed to afford his Majesty the slightest relief, and his experience of their efficacy on a former occasion forbidding him to suppose that they can be inoperative, he is naturally led to ascribe to their pernicious influence that aggravation of pain of which he has for some time past unfortunately been sensible. I have confirmed him in this conjecture, esteeming it for the interest of science that his anger should fall upon an impudent impostor like thee rather than on a discreet and learned physician like myself. He has consequently directed the principal caldron to be kept boiling all night, intending to immerse thee therein at daybreak, unless he should in the meantime derive some benefit from thy conjurations.'

'Heavens !' exclaimed Ananda, 'whither shall I fly ?'

'Nowhere beyond this cemetery,' returned the physician, 'inasmuch as it is entirely surrounded by the royal forces.'

'Wherein, then,' demanded the agonized apostle, 'doth the path of safety lie ?'

'In this phial,' answered the physician. 'It contains a subtle poison. Demand to be led before the king. Affirm that thou hast received a sovereign medicine from the hands of benignant spirits. He will drink it and perish, and thou wilt be richly rewarded by his successor.'

'Avaunt, tempter !' cried Ananda, hurling the phial indignantly away. 'I defy thee! and will have recourse to my old deliverer—*Gnooh Imdap Inam Mua!*"

But the charm appeared to fail of its effect. No figure was visible to his gaze, save that of the physician, who seemed to regard him with an expression of pity as he gathered up his robes and melted rather than glided into the encompassing darkness.

Ananda remained, contending with himself. Countless times was he on the point of calling after the physician and imploring him to return with a potion of like properties to the one rejected, but something seemed always to rise in his throat and impede his utterance, until, worn out by agitation, he fell asleep and dreamed this dream.

He thought he stood at the vast and gloomy entrance of Patala.[1] The lugubrious spot wore a holiday appearance; everything seemed to denote a diabolical gala. Swarms of demons of all shapes and sizes beset the portal, contemplating what appeared to be preparations for an illumination. Strings of coloured lamps were in course of disposition in wreaths and festoons by legions of frolicsome imps, chattering, laughing, and swinging by their tails like so many monkeys. The operation was directed from below by superior fiends of great apparent gravity and respectability. These bore wands of office, tipped with yellow flames, wherewith they singed the tails of the imps when such discipline appeared to them to be requisite. Ananda could not refrain from asking the reason of these festive preparations.

'They are in honour,' responded the demon interrogated, 'of the pious Ananda, one of the apostles of the Lord Buddha, whose advent is hourly expected among us with much eagerness and satisfaction.'

The horrified Ananda with much difficulty mustered resolution to inquire on what account the apostle in

1 The Hindoo Pandemonium.

question was necessitated to take up his abode in the infernal regions.

'On account of poisoning,' returned the fiend laconically.

Ananda was about to seek further explanations, when his attention was arrested by a violent altercation between two of the supervising demons.

'Kammuragha, evidently,' croaked one.

'Damburanana, of course,' snarled the other.

'May I,' inquired Ananda of the fiend he had before addressed, 'presume to ask the signification of Kammuragha and Damburanana ?'

'They are two hells,' replied the demon. 'In Kammuragha the occupant is plunged into melted pitch and fed with melted lead. In Damburanana he is plunged into melted lead and fed with melted pitch. My colleagues are debating which is the more appropriate to the demerits of our guest Ananda.'

Ere Ananda had time to digest this announcement a youthful imp descended from above with agility, and, making a profound reverence, presented himself before the disputants.

'Venerable demons,' interposed he, 'might my insignificance venture to suggest that we cannot well testify too much honour for our visitor Ananda, seeing that he is the only apostle of Buddha with whose company we are likely ever to be indulged ? Wherefore I would propose that neither Kammuragha nor Damburanana be assigned for his residence, but that the amenities of all the two hundred and forty-four thousand hells be combined in a new one, constructed especially for his reception.'

The imp having thus spoken, the senior demons were amazed at his precocity, and performed a *pradakshina*, exclaiming, 'Truly thou art a highly superior young devil!' They then departed to prepare the new infernal chamber, agreeably to his recipe.

Ananda awoke, shuddering with terror.

'Why,' he exclaimed, 'why was I ever an apostle? O Buddha! Buddha! how hard are the paths of saintliness! How prone to error are the well-meaning! How huge is the absurdity of spiritual pride!'

'Thou hast discovered that, my son?' said a gentle voice in his vicinity.

He turned and beheld the divine Buddha, radiant with a mild and benignant light. A cloud seemed rolled away from his vision, and he recognized in his master the Glendoveer, the Jogi, and the Physician.

'O holy teacher!' exclaimed he in extreme perturbation, 'whither shall I turn? My sin forbids me to approach thee.'

'Not on account of thy sin art thou forbidden, my son,' returned Buddha, 'but on account of the ridiculous and unsavoury plight to which thy knavery and disobedience have reduced thee. I have now appeared to remind thee that this day all my apostles meet on Mount Vindhya to render an account of their mission, and to inquire whether I am to deliver thine in thy stead, or whether thou art minded to proclaim it thyself.'

'I will render it with my own lips,' resolutely exclaimed Ananda. 'It is meet that I should bear the humiliation of acknowledging my folly.'

'Thou hast said well, my son,' replied Buddha, 'and in return I will permit thee to discard the attire, if such it may be termed, of a Jogi, and to appear in our assembly wearing the yellow robe as beseems my disciple. Nay, I will even infringe my own rule on thy behalf, and perform a not inconsiderable miracle by immediately transporting thee to the summit of Vindhya, where the faithful are already beginning to assemble. Thou wouldst otherwise incur much risk of being torn to pieces by the multitude, who, as the shouts now approaching may instruct thee, are beginning to extirpate my religion at the instigation of the new king, thy hopeful pupil. The old king is dead, poisoned by the Brahmins.'

'O master! master!' exclaimed Ananda, weeping bitterly, 'and is all the work undone, and all by my fault and folly?'

'That which is built on fraud and imposture can by no means endure,' returned Buddha, 'be it the very truth of heaven. Be comforted; thou shalt proclaim my doctrine to better purpose in other lands. Thou hast this time but a sorry account to render of thy stewardship; yet thou mayest truly declare that thou hast obeyed my precept in the letter, if not in the spirit, since none can assert that thou hast ever wrought any miracle.'

FRANCIS BRET HARTE

1839—1902

THE OUTCASTS OF POKER FLAT

As Mr. John Oakhurst, gambler, stepped into the main street of Poker Flat on the morning of the twenty-third of November, 1850, he was conscious of a change in its moral atmosphere since the preceding night. Two or three men, conversing earnestly together, ceased as he approached, and exchanged significant glances. There was a Sabbath lull in the air, which, in a settlement unused to Sabbath influences, looked ominous.

Mr. Oakhurst's calm, handsome face betrayed small concern in these indications. Whether he was conscious of any predisposing cause, was another question. 'I reckon they're after somebody,' he reflected; 'likely it's me.' He returned to his pocket the handkerchief with which he had been whipping away the red dust of Poker Flat from his neat boots, and quietly discharged his mind of any further conjecture.

In point of fact, Poker Flat was 'after somebody.' It had lately suffered the loss of several thousand dollars, two valuable horses, and a prominent citizen. It was experiencing a spasm of virtuous reaction, quite as lawless and ungovernable as any of the acts that had provoked it. A secret committee had determined to rid the town of all improper persons. This was done permanently in regard of two men who were then hanging from the boughs of a sycamore in the gulch, and temporarily in the banishment of certain other objectionable characters. I regret to say that some of these were ladies. It is but due to the sex, however, to state that their impropriety was professional, and it was only in such easily established standards of evil that Poker Flat ventured to sit in judgement.

Mr. Oakhurst was right in supposing that he was included in this category. A few of the committee had urged hanging him as a possible example, and a sure method of reimbursing themselves from his pockets of the sums he had won from them. 'It's agin justice,' said Jim Wheeler, 'to let this yer young man from Roaring Camp—an entire stranger—carry away our money.' But a crude sentiment of equity residing in the breasts of those who had been fortunate enough to win from Mr. Oakhurst overruled this narrower local prejudice.

Mr. Oakhurst received his sentence with philosophic calmness, none the less coolly that he was aware of the hesitation of his judges. He was too much of a gambler not to accept fate. With him life was at best an uncertain game, and he recognized the usual percentage in favour of the dealer.

A body of armed men accompanied the deported wickedness of Poker Flat to the outskirts of the settlement. Besides Mr. Oakhurst, who was known to be a coolly desperate man, and for whose intimidation the armed escort was intended, the expatriated party consisted of a young woman familiarly known as 'The Duchess'; another, who had won the title of 'Mother Shipton'; and 'Uncle Billy,' a suspected sluice-robber and confirmed drunkard. The cavalcade provoked no comments from the spectators, nor was any word uttered by the escort. Only when the gulch which marked the uttermost limit of Poker Flat was reached, the leader spoke briefly and to the point. The exiles were forbidden to return at the peril of their lives.

As the escort disappeared, their pent-up feelings found vent in a few hysterical tears from the Duchess, some bad language from Mother Shipton, and a Parthian volley of expletives from Uncle Billy. The philosophic Oakhurst alone remained silent. He listened calmly to Mother Shipton's desire to cut somebody's heart out, to the repeated statements of the Duchess that she would die in the road, and to the alarming oaths that seemed to be bumped out of Uncle Billy as he rode forward. With the easy good-humour characteristic of his class, he insisted upon exchanging his own riding-horse, 'Five Spot,' for the sorry mule which the Duchess rode. But even this act did not draw the party into any closer sympathy. The young woman readjusted her somewhat draggled plumes with a feeble, faded coquetry; Mother Shipton eyed the possessor of 'Five Spot' with malevolence; and Uncle Billy included the whole party in one sweeping anathema.

The road to Sandy Bar—a camp that, not having as yet experienced the regenerating influences of Poker Flat, consequently seemed to offer some invitation to the emigrants—lay over a steep mountain range. It was distant a day's severe travel. In that advanced season, the party soon passed out of the moist, temperate regions of the foot-hills into the dry, cold, bracing air of the Sierras. The trail was narrow and difficult. At noon the Duchess, rolling out of her saddle upon the ground, declared her intention of going no farther, and the party halted.

The spot was singularly wild and impressive. A wooded amphitheatre, surrounded on three sides by precipitous cliffs of naked granite, sloped gently toward the crest of another precipice that overlooked the valley. It was, undoubtedly, the most suitable spot for a camp, had camping been advisable. But Mr. Oakhurst knew that scarcely half the journey to Sandy Bar was accomplished, and the party were not equipped or provisioned for delay. This fact he pointed out to his companions curtly, with a philosophic commentary on the folly of 'throwing up their hand before the game was played out.' But they were furnished with liquor, which in this emergency stood them in place of food, fuel, rest, and prescience. In spite of his remonstrances, it was not long before they were more or less under its influence. Uncle Billy passed rapidly from a bellicose state into one of stupor, the Duchess became maudlin, and Mother Shipton snored. Mr. Oakhurst alone remained erect, leaning against a rock, calmly surveying them.

Mr. Oakhurst did not drink. It interfered with a profession which required coolness, impassiveness, and presence of mind, and, in his own language, he 'couldn't afford it.' As he gazed at his recumbent fellow-exiles, the loneliness begotten of his pariah-trade, his habits of life, his very vices, for the first time seriously oppressed him. He bestirred himself in dusting his black clothes, washing his hands and face, and other acts characteristic of his studiously neat habits, and for a moment forgot his annoyance. The thought of deserting his weaker and more pitiable companions never perhaps occurred to him. Yet he could not help feeling the want of that excitement which, singularly enough, was most conducive to that calm equanimity for which he was notorious. He looked at the gloomy walls that rose a thousand feet sheer above the circling pines around him; at the sky, ominously clouded; at the valley below, already deepening into shadow. And, doing so, suddenly he heard his own name called.

A horseman slowly ascended the trail. In the fresh, open face of the new-comer Mr. Oakhurst recognized Tom Simson, otherwise known as 'The Innocent' of Sandy Bar. He had met him some months before over a 'little game,' and had, with perfect equanimity, won the entire fortune—amounting to some forty dollars—of that guileless youth. After the game was finished, Mr. Oakhurst drew the youthful speculator behind the door, and thus addressed him: 'Tommy, you're a good little man, but you can't gamble worth a cent. Don't try it over again.' He then handed him his money back, pushed him gently from the room, and so made a devoted slave of Tom Simson.

There was a remembrance of this in his boyish and enthusiastic greeting of Mr. Oakhurst. He had started, he said, to go to Poker Flat to seek his fortune. 'Alone?' No, not exactly alone; in fact (a giggle), he had run away with Piney Woods. Didn't Mr. Oakhurst remember Piney? She that used to wait on the table at the Temperance House? They had been engaged a long time, but old Jake Woods had objected, and so they had run away, and were going to Poker Flat to be married, and here they were. And they were tired out, and how lucky it was they had found a place to camp and company! All this the Innocent delivered rapidly, while Piney, a stout, comely damsel of fifteen, emerged from behind the pine-tree, where she had been blushing unseen, and rode to the side of her lover.

Mr. Oakhurst seldom troubled himself with sentiment, still less with propriety; but he had a vague idea that the situation was not fortunate. He retained, however, his presence of mind sufficiently to kick Uncle Billy, who was about to say something, and Uncle Billy was sober enough to recognize in Mr. Oakhurst's kick a superior power that would not bear trifling. He then endeavoured to dissuade Tom Simson from delaying further, but in vain. He even pointed out the fact that there was no provision, nor means of making a camp. But, unluckily, the Innocent met this objection by assuring the party that he was provided with an extra mule loaded with provisions, and by the discovery of a rude attempt at a log-house near the trail. 'Piney can stay with Mrs. Oakhurst,' said the Innocent, pointing to the Duchess, 'and I can shift for myself.'

Nothing but Mr. Oakhurst's admonishing foot saved Uncle Billy from bursting into a roar of laughter. As it was, he felt compelled to retire up the cañon until he could recover his gravity. There he confided the joke to the tall pine-trees, with many slaps of his leg, contortions of his face, and the usual profanity. But when he returned to the party, he found them seated by a fire—for the air had grown strangely chill and the sky overcast—in apparently amicable conversation. Piney was actually talking in an impulsive, girlish fashion to the Duchess, who was listening with an interest and animation she had not shown for many days. The Innocent was holding forth, apparently with equal effect, to Mr. Oakhurst and Mother Shipton, who was actually relaxing into amiability. 'Is this yer a d—d picnic ?' said Uncle Billy, with inward scorn, as he surveyed the sylvan group, the glancing firelight, and the tethered animals in the foreground. Suddenly an idea mingled with the alcoholic fumes that disturbed his brain. It was apparently of a jocular nature, for he felt impelled to slap his leg again and cram his fist into his mouth.

As the shadows crept slowly up the mountain, a slight breeze rocked the tops of the pine-trees, and moaned through their long and gloomy aisles. The ruined cabin, patched and covered with pine-boughs, was set apart for the ladies. As the lovers parted, they unaffectedly exchanged a kiss, so honest and sincere that it might have been heard above the swaying pines. The frail Duchess and the malevolent Mother Shipton were probably too stunned to remark upon this last evidence of simplicity, and so turned without a word to the hut. The fire was replenished, the men lay down before the door, and in a few minutes were asleep.

Mr. Oakhurst was a light sleeper. Toward morning he awoke benumbed and cold. As he stirred the dying fire, the wind, which was now blowing strongly, brought to his cheek that which caused the blood to leave it,—snow !

He started to his feet with the intention of awakening the sleepers, for there was no time to lose. But turning to where Uncle Billy had been lying, he found him gone. A suspicion leaped to his brain and a curse to his lips.

He ran to the spot where the mules had been tethered; they were no longer there. The tracks were already rapidly disappearing in the snow.

The momentary excitement brought Mr. Oakhurst back to the fire with his usual calm. He did not waken the sleepers. The Innocent slumbered peacefully, with a smile on his good-humoured, freckled face; the virgin Piney slept beside her frailer sisters as sweetly as though attended by celestial guardians, and Mr. Oakhurst, drawing his blanket over his shoulders, stroked his moustaches and waited for the dawn. It came slowly in a whirling mist of snow-flakes, that dazzled and confused the eye. What could be seen of the landscape appeared magically changed. He looked over the valley, and summed up the present and future in two words—'snowed in!'

A careful inventory of the provisions, which, fortunately for the party, had been stored within the hut, and so escaped the felonious fingers of Uncle Billy, disclosed the fact that with care and prudence they might last ten days longer. 'That is,' said Mr. Oakhurst, *sotto voce* to the Innocent, 'if you're willing to board us. If you ain't—and perhaps you'd better not—you can wait till Uncle Billy gets back with provisions.' For some occult reason, Mr. Oakhurst could not bring himself to disclose Uncle Billy's rascality, and so offered the hypothesis that he had wandered from the camp and had accidentally stampeded the animals. He dropped a warning to the Duchess and Mother Shipton, who of course knew the facts of their associate's defection. 'They'll find out the truth about us *all* when they find out anything,' he added, significantly, 'and there's no good frightening them now.'

Tom Simson not only put all his worldly store at the disposal of Mr. Oakhurst, but seemed to enjoy the prospect of their enforced seclusion. 'We'll have a good camp for a week, and then the snow'll melt, and we'll all go back together.' The cheerful gaiety of the young man and Mr. Oakhurst's calm infected the others. The Innocent, with the aid of pine-boughs, extemporized a thatch for the roofless cabin, and the Duchess directed Piney in the rearrangement of the interior with a taste and tact that opened the blue eyes of that provincial maiden to their fullest extent. 'I reckon now you're used to fine things at Poker Flat,' said Piney. The Duchess turned away sharply to conceal something that reddened her cheeks through their professional tint, and Mother Shipton requested Piney not to 'chatter.' But when Mr. Oakhurst returned from a weary search for the trail, he heard the sound of happy laughter echoed from the rocks. He stopped in some alarm, and his thoughts first naturally reverted to the whisky, which he had prudently *cachéd.* 'And yet it don't somehow sound like whisky,' said the gambler. It was not until he caught sight of the blazing fire through the still blinding storm and the group around it, that he settled to the conviction that it was 'square fun.'

Whether Mr. Oakhurst had *cachéd* his cards with the whisky as something debarred the free access of the community, I cannot say. It was certain that, in Mother Shipton's words, he 'didn't say cards once' during that evening. Haply the time was beguiled by an accordion, produced somewhat ostentatiously by Tom Simson from his pack. Notwithstanding some difficulties attending the manipulation of this instrument, Piney Woods managed to pluck several reluctant melodies from its keys, to an accompaniment by the Innocent on a pair of bone castanets. But the crowning festivity of the evening was reached in a rude camp-meeting hymn, which the lovers, joining hands, sang with great earnestness and vociferation. I fear that a certain defiant tone and Covenanter's swing to its chorus, rather than any devotional quality, caused it speedily to infect the others, who at last joined in the refrain :—

'I'm proud to live in the service of the Lord,
And I'm bound to die in His army.'

The pines rocked, the storm eddied and whirled above the miserable group, and the flames of their altar leaped heavenward, as if in token of the vow.

At midnight the storm abated, the rolling clouds parted, and the stars glittered keenly above the sleeping camp. Mr. Oakhurst, whose professional habits had enabled him to live on the smallest possible amount of sleep, in dividing the watch with Tom Simson, somehow managed to take upon himself the greater part of that duty. He excused himself to the Innocent by saying that he had 'often been a week without sleep.' 'Doing what?' asked Tom. 'Poker!' replied Oakhurst, sententiously; 'when a man gets a streak of luck—nigger-luck—he don't get tired. The luck gives in first. Luck,' continued the gambler, reflectively, 'is a mighty queer thing. All you know about it for certain is that it's bound to change. And it's finding out when it's going to change that makes you. We've had a streak of bad luck since we left Poker Flat—you come along, and slap you get into it, too. If you can hold your cards right along you're all right. For,' added the gambler, with cheerful irrelevance—

'"I'm proud to live in the service of the Lord,
And I'm bound to die in His army."'

The third day came, and the sun, looking through the white-curtained valley, saw the outcasts divide their slowly decreasing store of provisions for the morning meal. It was one of the peculiarities of that mountain climate that its rays diffused a kindly warmth over the wintry landscape, as if in regretful commiseration of the past. But it revealed drift on drift of snow piled high around the hut—a hopeless, uncharted, trackless sea of white lying below the rocky shores to which the castaways still clung. Through the marvellously clear air the smoke of the pastoral village of Poker Flat rose miles away. Mother Shipton saw it, and from a remote pinnacle of her rocky fastness, hurled in that direction a final malediction. It was her last vituperative attempt, and perhaps for that reason was invested with a certain degree of sublimity. It did her good, she privately informed the Duchess. ‘Just you go out there and cuss, and see.’ She then set herself to the task of amusing ‘the child,’ as she and the Duchess were pleased to call Piney. Piney was no chicken, but it was a soothing and original theory of the pair thus to account for the fact that she didn't swear and wasn't improper.

When night crept up again through the gorges, the reedy notes of the accordion rose and fell in fitful spasms and long-drawn gasps by the flickering camp-fire. But music failed to fill entirely the aching void left by insufficient food, and a new diversion was proposed by Piney—story-telling. Neither Mr. Oakhurst nor his female companions caring to relate their personal experiences, this plan would have failed, too, but for the Innocent. Some months before he had chanced upon a stray copy of Mr. Pope's ingenious translation of the *Iliad*. He now proposed to narrate the principal incidents of that poem—having thoroughly mastered the argument and fairly forgotten the words—in the current vernacular of Sandy Bar. And so for the rest of that night the Homeric demi-gods again walked the earth. Trojan bully and wily Greek wrestled in the winds, and the great pines in the cañon seemed to bow to the wrath of the son of Peleus. Mr. Oakhurst listened with quiet satisfaction. Most especially was he interested in the fate of ‘Ash-heels,’ as the Innocent persisted in denominating the ‘swift-footed Achilles.’

So with small food and much of Homer and the accordion, a week passed over the heads of the outcasts. The sun again forsook them, and again from leaden skies the snowflakes were sifted over the land. Day by day closer around them drew the snowy circle, until at last they looked from their prison over drifted walls of dazzling white, that towered twenty feet above their heads. It became more and more difficult to replenish their fires, even from the fallen trees beside them, now half hidden in the drifts. And yet no one complained. The lovers turned from the dreary prospect and looked into each other's eyes, and were happy. Mr. Oakhurst settled himself coolly to the losing game before him. The Duchess, more cheerful than she had been, assumed the care of Piney. Only Mother Shipton—once the strongest of the party—seemed to sicken and fade. At midnight on the tenth day she called Oakhurst to her side. 'I'm going,' she said, in a voice of querulous weakness, 'but don't say anything about it. Don't waken the kids. Take the bundle from under my head and open it.' Mr. Oakhurst did so. It contained Mother Shipton's rations for the last week, untouched. 'Give 'em to the child,' she said, pointing to the sleeping Piney. 'You've starved yourself,' said the gambler. 'That's what they call it,' said the woman, querulously, as she lay down again, and, turning her face to the wall, passed quietly away.

The accordion and the bones were put aside that day, and Homer was forgotten. When the body of Mother Shipton had been committed to the snow, Mr. Oakhurst took the Innocent aside, and showed him a pair of snow-shoes, which he had fashioned from the old pack-saddle. 'There's one chance in a hundred to save her yet,' he said, pointing to Piney; 'but it's there,' he added, pointing towards Poker Flat. 'If you can reach there in two days she's safe.' 'And you?' asked Tom Simson. 'I'll stay here,' was the curt reply.

The lovers parted with a long embrace. 'You are not going, too?' said the Duchess, as she saw Mr. Oakhurst apparently waiting to accompany him. 'As far as the cañon,' he replied. He turned suddenly, and kissed the Duchess, leaving her pallid face aflame, and her trembling limbs rigid with amazement.

Night came, but not Mr. Oakhurst. It brought the

storm again and the whirling snow. Then the Duchess, feeding the fire, found that someone had quietly piled beside the hut enough fuel to last a few days longer. The tears rose to her eyes, but she hid them from Piney.

The women slept but little. In the morning, looking into each other's faces, they read their fate. Neither spoke; but Piney, accepting the position of the stronger, drew near and placed her arm around the Duchess's waist. They kept this attitude for the rest of the day. That night the storm reached its greatest fury, and, rending asunder the protecting pines, invaded the very hut.

Toward morning they found themselves unable to feed the fire, which gradually died away. As the embers slowly blackened, the Duchess crept closer to Piney, and broke the silence of many hours: 'Piney, can you pray?' 'No, dear,' said Piney, simply. The Duchess, without knowing exactly why, felt relieved, and, putting her head upon Piney's shoulder, spoke no more. And so reclining, the younger and purer pillowing the head of her soiled sister upon her virgin breast, they fell asleep.

The wind lulled as if it feared to waken them. Feathery drifts of snow, shaken from the long pine-boughs, flew like white-winged birds, and settled about them as they slept. The moon through the rifted clouds looked down upon what had been the camp. But all human stain, all trace of earthly travail, was hidden beneath the spotless mantle mercifully flung from above.

They slept all that day and the next, nor did they waken when voices and footsteps broke the silence of the camp. And when pitying fingers brushed the snow from their wan faces, you could scarcely have told, from the equal peace that dwelt upon them, which was she that had sinned. Even the law of Poker Flat recognized this, and turned away, leaving them still locked in each other's arms.

But at the head of the gulch, on one of the largest pine-trees, they found the deuce of clubs pinned to the bark with a bowie-knife. It bore the following, written in pencil, in a firm hand:

†

BENEATH THIS TREE

LIES THE BODY

OF

JOHN OAKHURST,

WHO STRUCK A STREAK OF BAD LUCK

ON THE 23RD OF NOVEMBER, 1850,

AND

HANDED IN HIS CHECKS

ON THE 7TH DECEMBER, 1850.

†

And pulseless and cold, with a Derringer by his side and a bullet in his heart, though still calm as in life, beneath the snow lay he who was at once the strongest and yet the weakest of the outcasts of Poker Flat.

HOW SANTA CLAUS CAME TO SIMPSON'S BAR

It had been raining in the valley of the Sacramento. The North Fork had overflowed its banks, and Rattlesnake Creek was impassable. The few boulders that had marked the summer ford at Simpson's Crossing were obliterated by a vast sheet of water stretching to the foothills. The up-stage was stopped at Grangers; the last mail had been abandoned in the *tules*, the rider swimming for his life. 'An area,' remarked the *Sierra Avalanche*, with pensive local pride, 'as large as the State of Massachusetts is now under water.'

Nor was the weather any better in the foothills. The mud lay deep on the mountain road ; wagons that neither physical force nor moral objurgation could move from the evil ways into which they had fallen, encumbered the track, and the way to Simpson's Bar was indicated by broken-down teams and hard swearing. And farther on, cut off and inaccessible, rained upon and bedraggled, smitten by high winds and threatened by high water, Simpson's Bar, on the eve of Christmas Day, 1862, clung like a swallow's nest to the rocky entablature and splintered capitals of Table Mountain, and shook in the blast.

As night shut down on the settlement, a few lights gleamed through the mist from the windows of cabins on either side of the highway now crossed and gullied by lawless streams and swept by marauding winds. Happily most of the population were gathered at Thompson's store, clustered round a red-hot stove, at which they silently spat in some accepted sense of social communion that perhaps rendered conversation unnecessary. Indeed, most methods of diversion had long since been exhausted on Simpson's Bar ; high water had suspended the regular occupations on gulch and on river, and a consequent lack of money and whisky had taken the zest from most illegitimate recreation. Even Mr. Hamlin was fain to leave the Bar with fifty dollars in his pocket—the only amount actually realized of the large sums won by him in the successful exercise of his arduous profession. 'Ef I was asked,' he remarked somewhat later,—'ef I was asked to pint out a purty little village where a retired sport as didn't care for money could exercise hisself, frequent and lively, I'd say Simpson's Bar ; but for a young man with a large family depending on his exertions, it don't pay.' As Mr. Hamlin's family consisted mainly of female adults, this remark is quoted rather to show the breadth of his humour than the exact extent of his responsibilities.

Howbeit, the unconscious objects of this satire sat

that evening in the listless apathy begotten of idleness and lack of excitement. Even the sudden splashing of hoofs before the door did not arouse them. Dick Bullen alone paused in the act of scraping out his pipe, and lifted his head, but no other one of the group indicated any interest in, or recognition of, the man who entered.

It was a figure familiar enough to the company, and known in Simpson's Bar as 'The Old Man.' A man of perhaps fifty years; grizzled and scant of hair, but still fresh and youthful of complexion. A face full of ready but not very powerful sympathy, with a chameleon-like aptitude for taking on the shade and colour of contiguous moods and feelings. He had evidently just left some hilarious companions, and did not at first notice the gravity of the group, but clapped the shoulder of the nearest man jocularly, and threw himself into a vacant chair.

'Jest heard the best thing out, boys! Ye know Smiley, over yar—Jim Smiley—funniest man in the Bar? Well, Jim was jest telling the richest yarn about——'

'Smiley's a —— fool,' interrupted a gloomy voice.

'A particular —— skunk,' added another in sepulchral accents.

A silence followed these positive statements. The Old Man glanced quickly around the group. Then his face slowly changed. 'That's so,' he said reflectively, after a pause, 'certingly a sort of a skunk and suthin' of a fool. In course.' He was silent for a moment as in painful contemplation of the unsavouriness and folly of the unpopular Smiley. 'Dismal weather, ain't it?' he added, now fully embarked on the current of prevailing sentiment. 'Mighty rough papers on the boys, and no show for money this season. And to-morrow's Christmas.'

There was a movement among the men at this announcement, but whether of satisfaction or disgust was not plain. 'Yes,' continued the Old Man in the lugubrious tone he had, within the last few moments, unconsciously adopted,—'yes, Christmas, and to-night's Christmas Eve. Ye see, boys, I kinder thought—that is, I sorter had an idee, jest passin' like, you know—that maybe ye'd all like to come over to my house to-night and have a sort of tear round. But I suppose, now, you wouldn't? Don't feel like it, maybe?' he added with anxious sympathy, peering into the faces of his companions.

'Well, I don't know,' responded Tom Flynn with some cheerfulness. 'P'r'aps we may. But how about your wife, Old Man? What does *she* say to it?'

The Old Man hesitated. His conjugal experience had not been a happy one, and the fact was known to Simpson's Bar. His first wife, a delicate, pretty little woman, had suffered keenly and secretly from the jealous suspicions of her husband, until one day he invited the whole Bar to his house to expose her infidelity. On arriving, the party found the shy, *petite* creature quietly engaged in her household duties, and retired abashed and discomfited. But the sensitive woman did not easily recover from the shock of this extraordinary outrage. It was with difficulty she regained her equanimity sufficiently to release her lover from the closet in which he was concealed, and escape with him. She left a boy of three years to comfort her bereaved husband. The Old Man's present wife had been his cook. She was large, loyal, and aggressive.

Before he could reply, Joe Dimmick suggested with great directness that it was the 'Old Man's house,' and that, invoking the Divine Power, if the case were his own, he would invite whom he pleased, even if in so doing he imperilled his salvation. The Powers of Evil, he further remarked, should contend against him vainly. All this delivered with a terseness and vigour lost in this necessary translation.

'In course. Certainly. Thet's it,' said the Old

Man with a sympathetic frown. 'Thar's no trouble about *thet*. It's my own house, built every stick on it myself. Don't you be afeard o' her, boys. She *may* cut up a trifle rough—ez wimmin do—but she'll come round.' Secretly the Old Man trusted to the exaltation of liquor and the power of courageous example to sustain him in such an emergency.

As yet, Dick Bullen, the oracle and leader of Simpson's Bar, had not spoken. He now took his pipe from his lips. 'Old Man, how's that yer Johnny gettin' on? Seems to me he didn't look so peart last time I seed him on the bluff heavin' rocks at Chinamen. Didn't seem to take much interest in it. Thar was a gang of 'em by yar yesterday—drownded out up the river—and I kinder thought o' Johnny, and how he'd miss 'em! Maybe now, we'd be in the way ef he wus sick?'

The father, evidently touched not only by this pathetic picture of Johnny's deprivation, but by the considerate delicacy of the speaker, hastened to assure him that Johnny was better and that a 'little fun might 'liven him up.' Whereupon Dick arose, shook himself, and saying, 'I'm ready. Lead the way, Old Man: here goes,' himself led the way with a leap, a characteristic howl, and darted out into the night. As he passed through the outer room he caught up a blazing brand from the hearth. The action was repeated by the rest of the party, closely following and elbowing each other, and before the astonished proprietor of Thompson's grocery was aware of the intention of his guests, the room was deserted.

The night was pitchy dark. In the first gust of wind their temporary torches were extinguished, and only the red brands dancing and flitting in the gloom like drunken will-o'-the-wisps indicated their whereabouts. Their way led up Pine-Tree Cañon, at the head of which a broad, low, bark-thatched cabin burrowed in the mountain-side. It was the home of the Old Man, and the entrance to the tunnel in which he worked when he worked at all. Here the crowd paused for a moment, out of delicate deference to their host, who came up panting in the rear.

'P'r'aps ye'd better hold on a second out yer, whilst I go in and see that things is all right,' said the Old Man, with an indifference he was far from feeling. The suggestion was graciously accepted, the door opened and closed on the host, and the crowd, leaning their backs against the wall and cowering under the eaves, waited and listened.

For a few moments there was no sound but the dripping of water from the eaves, and the stir and rustle of wrestling boughs above them. Then the men became uneasy, and whispered suggestion and suspicion passed from the one to the other. 'Reckon she's caved in his head the first lick!' 'Decoyed him inter the tunnel and barred him up, likely.' 'Got him down and sittin' on him.' 'Prob'ly biling suthin' to heave on us: stand clear the door, boys!' For just then the latch clicked, the door slowly opened, and a voice said, 'Come in out o' the wet.'

The voice was neither that of the Old Man nor of his wife. It was the voice of a small boy, its weak treble broken by that preternatural hoarseness which only vagabondage and the habit of premature self-assertion can give. It was the face of a small boy that looked up at theirs,—a face that might have been pretty, and even refined, but that it was darkened by evil knowledge from within, and dirt and hard experience from without. He had a blanket around his shoulders, and had evidently just risen from his bed. 'Come in,' he repeated, 'and don't make no noise. The Old Man's in there talking to mar,' he continued, pointing to an adjacent room which seemed to be a kitchen, from which the Old Man's voice came in deprecating accents. 'Let me be,' he added querulously, to Dick Bullen, who had caught him up, blanket and all, and was affecting to toss him into the fire, 'let go o' me, you d—d old fool, d'ye hear ?'

Thus adjured, Dick Bullen lowered Johnny to the ground with a smothered laugh, while the men, entering quietly, ranged themselves around a long table of rough boards which occupied the centre of the room. Johnny then gravely proceeded to a cupboard and brought out several articles, which he deposited on the table. 'Thar's whisky. And crackers. And red herons. And cheese.' He took a bite of the latter on his way to the table. 'And sugar.' He scooped up a mouthful *en route* with a small and very dirty hand. 'And terbacker. Thar's dried appils too on the shelf, but I don't admire 'em. Appils is swellin'. Thar,' he concluded, 'now wade in, and don't be afeard. *I* don't mind the old woman. She don't b'long to *me*. S'long.'

He had stepped to the threshold of a small room, scarcely larger than a closet, partitioned off from the main apartment, and holding in its dim recess a small bed. He stood there a moment looking at the company, his bare feet peeping from the blanket, and nodded.

'Hello, Johnny! You ain't goin' to turn in agin, are ye ?' said Dick.

'Yes, I are,' responded Johnny decidedly.

'Why, wot's up, old fellow ?'

'I'm sick.'

'How sick ?'

'I've got a fevier. And childblains. And roomatiz,' returned Johnny, and vanished within. After a moment's pause, he added in the dark, apparently from under the bed-clothes,—'And biles !'

There was an embarrassing silence. The men looked at each other and at the fire. Even with the appetizing banquet before them, it seemed as if they might again fall into the despondency of Thompson's grocery, when the voice of the Old Man, incautiously lifted, came deprecatingly from the kitchen.

'Certainly! Thet's so. In course they is. A gang o' lazy, drunken loafers, and that ar Dick Bullen's the ornariest of all. Didn't hev no more *sabe* than to come round yar with sickness in the house and no provision. Thet's what I said: "Bullen," sez I, "it's crazy drunk you are, or a fool," sez I, "to think o' such a thing." "Staples," I sez, "be you a man, Staples, and 'spect to raise h—ll under my roof and invalids lyin' round?" But they would come,—they would. Thet's wot you must 'spect o' such trash as lays round the Bar.'

A burst of laughter from the men followed this unfortunate exposure. Whether it was overheard in the kitchen, or whether the Old Man's irate companion had just then exhausted all other modes of expressing her contemptuous indignation, I cannot say, but a back door was suddenly slammed with great violence. A moment later and the Old Man reappeared, haply unconscious of the cause of the late hilarious outburst, and smiled blandly.

'The old woman thought she'd jest run over to Mrs. McFadden's for a sociable call,' he explained, with jaunty indifference, as he took a seat at the board.

Oddly enough it needed this untoward incident to relieve the embarrassment that was beginning to be felt by the party, and their natural audacity returned with their host. I do not propose to record the convivialities of that evening. The inquisitive reader will accept the statement that the conversation was characterized by the same intellectual exaltation, the same cautious reverence, the same fastidious delicacy, the same rhetorical precision, and the same logical and coherent discourse somewhat later in the evening, which distinguish similar gatherings of the masculine sex in more civilized localities and under more favourable auspices. No glasses were broken in the absence of any; no liquor was uselessly spilt on the floor or table in the scarcity of that article.

It was nearly midnight when the festivities were interrupted. 'Hush,' said Dick Bullen, holding up his hand. It was the querulous voice of Johnny from his adjacent closet: 'Oh, dad!'

The Old Man arose hurriedly and disappeared in the closet. Presently he reappeared. 'His rheumatiz is coming on agin bad,' he explained, 'and he wants rubbin'.' He lifted the demijohn of whisky from the table and shook it. It was empty. Dick Bullen put down his tin cup with an embarrassed laugh. So did the others. The Old Man examined their contents and said hopefully, 'I reckon that's enough; he don't need much. You hold on all o' you for a spell, and I'll be back'; and vanished in the closet with an old flannel shirt and the whisky. The door closed but imperfectly, and the following dialogue was distinctly audible:—

'Now, sonny, whar does she ache worst?'

'Sometimes over yar and sometimes under yer; but it's most powerful from yer to yer. Rub yer, dad.'

A silence seemed to indicate a brisk rubbing. Then Johnny:

'Hevin' a good time out yer, dad?'

'Yes, sonny.'

'To-morrer's Chrismiss,—ain't it?'

'Yes, sonny. How does she feel now?'

'Better. Rub a little furder down. Wot's Chrismiss, anyway? Wot's it all about?'

'Oh, it's a day.'

This exhaustive definition was apparently satisfactory, for there was a silent interval of rubbing. Presently Johnny again:

'Mar sez that everywhere else but yer everybody gives things to everybody Chrismiss, and then she jist waded inter you. She sez thar's a man they call Sandy Claws, not a white man, you know, but a kind o' Chinemin, comes down the chimbley night afore

Chrismiss and gives things to chillern,—boys like me. Puts 'em in their butes! Thet's what she tried to play upon me. Easy now, pop, whar are you rubbin' to,—thet's a mile from the place. She jest made that up, didn't she, jest to aggrewate me and you? Don't rub thar. . . . Why, dad!'

In the great quiet that seemed to have fallen upon the house the sigh of the near pines and the drip of leaves without was very distinct. Johnny's voice, too, was lowered as he went on, 'Don't you take on now, fur I'm gettin' all right fast. Wot's the boys doin' out thar?'

The Old Man partly opened the door and peered through. His guests were sitting there sociably enough, but there were a few silver coins and a lean buckskin purse on the table. 'Bettin' on suthin'—some little game or 'nother. They're all right,' he replied to Johnny, and recommenced his rubbing.

'I'd like to take a hand and win some money,' said Johnny reflectively after a pause.

The Old Man glibly repeated what was evidently a familiar formula, that if Johnny would wait until he struck it rich in the tunnel he'd have lots of money, etc., etc.

'Yes,' said Johnny, 'but you don't. And whether you strike it or I win it, it's about the same. It's all luck. But it's mighty cur'o's about Chrismiss—ain't it? Why do they call it Chrismiss?'

Perhaps from some instinctive deference to the overhearing of his guests, or from some vague sense of incongruity, the Old Man's reply was so low as to be inaudible beyond the room.

'Yes,' said Johnny, with some slight abatement of interest, 'I've heerd o' *him* before. Thar, that'll do, dad. I don't ache near so bad as I did. Now wrap me tight in this yer blanket. So. Now,' he added in a muffled whisper, 'sit down yer by me till I go asleep.' To assure himself of obedience, he disengaged one hand from the blanket and, grasping his father's sleeve, again composed himself to rest.

For some moments the Old Man waited patiently. Then the unwonted stillness of the house excited his curiosity, and without moving from the bed he cautiously opened the door with his disengaged hand, and looked into the main room. To his infinite surprise it was dark and deserted. But even then a smouldering log on the hearth broke, and by the upspringing blaze he saw the figure of Dick Bullen sitting by the dying embers.

'Hello!'

Dick started, rose, and came somewhat unsteadily toward him.

'Whar's the boys?' said the Old Man.

'Gone up the cañon on a little *pasear*. They're coming back for me in a minit. I'm waitin' round for 'em. What are you starin' at, Old Man?' he added with a forced laugh; 'do you think I'm drunk?'

The Old Man might have been pardoned the supposition, for Dick's eyes were humid and his face flushed. He loitered and lounged back to the chimney, yawned, shook himself, buttoned up his coat and laughed. 'Liquor ain't so plenty as that, Old Man. Now don't you git up,' he continued, as the Old Man made a movement to release his sleeve from Johnny's hand. 'Don't you mind manners. Sit jest whar you be; I'm goin' in a jiffy. Thar, that's them now.'

There was a low tap at the door. Dick Bullen opened it quickly, nodded 'Good night' to his host, and disappeared. The Old Man would have followed him but for the hand that still unconsciously grasped his sleeve. He could have easily disengaged it; it was small, weak, and emaciated. But perhaps because it *was* small, weak, and emaciated, he changed his mind, and, drawing his chair closer to the bed, rested his head upon it. In this defenceless attitude the potency of his earlier potations surprised him.

The room flickered and faded before his eyes, reappeared, faded again, went out, and left him—asleep.

Meantime Dick Bullen, closing the door, confronted his companions. 'Are you ready?' said Staples. 'Ready,' said Dick; 'what's the time?' 'Past twelve,' was the reply; 'can you make it?—it's nigh on fifty miles, the round trip hither and yon.' 'I reckon,' returned Dick shortly. 'Whar's the mare?' 'Bill and Jack's holdin' her at the crossin'.' 'Let 'em hold on a minit longer,' said Dick.

He turned and re-entered the house softly. By the light of the guttering candle and dying fire he saw that the door of the little room was open. He stepped toward it on tiptoe and looked in. The Old Man had fallen back in his chair, snoring, his helpless feet thrust out in a line with his collapsed shoulders, and his hat pulled over his eyes. Beside him, on a narrow wooden bedstead, lay Johnny, muffled tightly in a blanket that hid all save a strip of forehead and a few curls damp with perspiration. Dick Bullen made a step forward, hesitated, and glanced over his shoulder into the deserted room. Everything was quiet. With a sudden resolution he parted his huge moustaches with both hands and stooped over the sleeping boy. But even as he did so a mischievous blast, lying in wait, swooped down the chimney, rekindled the hearth, and lit up the room with a shameless glow from which Dick fled in bashful terror.

His companions were already waiting for him at the crossing. Two of them were struggling in the darkness with some strange misshapen bulk, which as Dick came nearer took the semblance of a great yellow horse.

It was the mare. She was not a pretty picture. From her Roman nose to her rising haunches, from her arched spine hidden by the stiff *machillas* of a Mexican saddle, to her thick, straight, bony legs, there was not a line of equine grace. In her half-blind but wholly vicious white eyes, in her protruding underlip, in her monstrous colour, there was nothing but ugliness and vice.

'Now then,' said Staples, 'stand cl'ar of her heels, boys, and up with you. Don't miss your first hold of her mane, and mind ye get your off stirrup *quick*. Ready!'

There was a leap, a scrambling struggle, a bound, a wild retreat of the crowd, a circle of flying hoofs, two springless leaps that jarred the earth, a rapid play and jingle of spurs, a plunge, and then the voice of Dick somewhere in the darkness, 'All right!'

'Don't take the lower road back onless you're hard pushed for time! Don't hold her in down hill. We'll be at the ford at five. G'lang! Hoopa! Mula! GO!'

A splash, a spark struck from the ledge in the road, a clatter in the rocky cut beyond, and Dick was gone.

. . . . .

Sing, O Muse, the ride of Richard Bullen! Sing, O Muse, of chivalrous men! the sacred quest, the doughty deeds, the battery of low churls, the fearsome ride and gruesome perils of the Flower of Simpson's Bar! Alack! she is dainty, this Muse! She will have none of this bucking brute and swaggering, ragged rider, and I must fain follow him in prose, afoot!

It was one o'clock, and yet he had only gained Rattlesnake Hill. For in that time Jovita had rehearsed to him all her imperfections and practised all her vices. Thrice had she stumbled. Twice had she thrown up her Roman nose in a straight line with the reins, and, resisting bit and spur, struck out madly across country. Twice had she reared, and, rearing, fallen backward; and twice had the agile Dick, unharmed, regained his seat before she found her vicious legs again. And a mile beyond them, at the foot of a long hill, was Rattlesnake Creek. Dick knew that here was the crucial test of his ability to perform his enterprise, set his teeth grimly, put his knees well into her flanks, and changed his defensive tactics to brisk aggression. Bullied and maddened, Jovita began the descent of the hill. Here the artful Richard pretended to hold her in with ostentatious objurgation and well-feigned cries of alarm. It is unnecessary to add that Jovita instantly ran away. Nor need I state the time made in the descent; it is written in the chronicles of Simpson's Bar. Enough that in another moment, as it seemed to Dick, she was splashing on the overflowed banks of Rattlesnake Creek. As Dick expected, the momentum she had acquired carried her beyond the point of balking, and, holding her well together for a mighty leap, they dashed into the middle of the swiftly flowing current. A few moments of kicking, wading, and swimming, and Dick drew a long breath on the opposite bank.

The road from Rattlesnake Creek to Red Mountain was tolerably level. Either the plunge in Rattlesnake Creek had dampened her baleful fire, or the art which led to it had shown her the superior wickedness of her rider, for Jovita no longer wasted her surplus energy in wanton conceits. Once she bucked, but it was from force of habit; once she shied, but it was from a new, freshly-painted meeting-house at the crossing of the county road. Hollows, ditches, gravelly deposits, patches of freshly-springing grasses, flew from beneath her rattling hoofs. She began to smell unpleasantly, once or twice she coughed slightly, but there was no abatement of her strength or speed. By two o'clock he had passed Red Mountain and begun the descent to the plain. Ten minutes later the driver of the fast Pioneer coach was overtaken and passed by a 'man on a Pinto hoss,'—an event sufficiently notable for remark. At half-past two Dick rose in his stirrups with a great shout. Stars were glittering through the rifted clouds, and beyond him, out of the plain, rose two spires, a flagstaff, and a straggling line of black objects. Dick jingled his spurs and swung his *riata*, Jovita bounded forward, and in another moment they swept into Tuttleville, and drew up before the wooden piazza of 'The Hotel of All Nations.'

What transpired that night at Tuttleville is not strictly a part of this record. Briefly I may state, however, that after Jovita had been handed over to a sleepy ostler, whom she at once kicked into unpleasant consciousness, Dick sallied out with the bar-keeper for a tour of the sleeping town. Lights still gleamed from a few saloons and gambling-houses; but, avoiding these, they stopped before several closed shops, and by persistent tapping and judicious outcry roused the proprietors from their beds, and made them unbar the doors of their magazines and expose their wares. Sometimes they were met by curses, but oftener by interest and some concern in their needs, and the interview was invariably concluded by a drink. It was three o'clock before this pleasantry was given over, and with a small waterproof bag of indiarubber strapped on his shoulders Dick returned to the hotel. But here he was waylaid by Beauty,—Beauty opulent in charms, affluent in dress, persuasive in speech, and Spanish in accent! In vain she repeated the invitation in 'Excelsior,' happily scorned by all Alpine-climbing youth, and rejected by this child of the Sierras,—a rejection softened in this instance by a laugh and his last gold coin. And then he sprang to the saddle and dashed down the lonely street and out into the lonelier plain, where presently the lights, the black line of houses, the spires, and the flagstaff sank into the earth behind him again and were lost in the distance.

The storm had cleared away, the air was brisk and cold, the outlines of adjacent landmarks were distinct, but it was half-past four before Dick reached the meeting-house and the crossing of the county road. To avoid the rising grade he had taken a longer and more circuitous road, in whose viscid mud Jovita sank fetlock deep at every bound. It was a poor preparation for a steady ascent of five miles more; but Jovita, gathering her legs under her, took it with her usual blind, unreasoning fury, and a half-hour later reached the long level that led to Rattlesnake Creek. Another half-hour would bring him to the creek. He threw the reins lightly upon the neck of the mare, chirruped to her, and began to sing.

Suddenly Jovita shied with a bound that would have unseated a less practised rider. Hanging to her rein was a figure that had leaped from the bank, and at the same time from the road before her arose a shadowy horse and rider. 'Throw up your hands,' commanded the second apparition, with an oath.

Dick felt the mare tremble, quiver, and apparently sink under him. He knew what it meant and was prepared.

'Stand aside, Jack Simpson. I know you, you d—d thief! Let me pass, or——'

He did not finish the sentence. Jovita rose straight in the air with a terrific bound, throwing the figure from her bit with a single shake of her vicious head, and charged with deadly malevolence down on the impediment before her. An oath, a pistol-shot, horse and highwayman rolled over in the road, and the next moment Jovita was a hundred yards away. But the good right arm of her rider, shattered by a bullet, dropped helplessly at his side.

Without slacking his speed he shifted the reins to his left hand. But a few moments later he was obliged to halt and tighten the saddle-girths that had slipped in the onset. This in his crippled condition took some time. He had no fear of pursuit, but looking up he saw that the eastern stars were already paling, and that the distant peaks had lost their ghostly whiteness, and now stood out blackly against a lighter sky. Day was upon him. Then completely absorbed in a single idea, he forgot the pain of his wound, and mounting again dashed on toward Rattlesnake Creek. But now Jovita's breath came broken by gasps, Dick reeled in his saddle, and brighter and brighter grew the sky.

Ride, Richard; run, Jovita; linger, O day!

For the last few rods there was a roaring in his ears. Was it exhaustion from loss of blood, or what? He was dazed and giddy as he swept down the hill, and did not recognize his surroundings. Had he taken the wrong road, or was this Rattlesnake Creek?

It was. But the brawling creek he had swam a few hours before had risen, more than doubled its volume, and now rolled a swift and resistless river between him and Rattlesnake Hill. For the first time that night Richard's heart sank within him. The river, the mountain, the quickening east, swam before his eyes. He shut them to recover his self-control. In that brief interval, by some fantastic mental process, the little room at Simpson's Bar and the figures of the sleeping father and son rose upon him. He opened his eyes wildly, cast off his coat, pistol, boots, and saddle, bound his precious pack tightly to his shoulders, grasped the bare flanks of Jovita with his bared knees, and with a shout dashed into the yellow water. A cry rose from the opposite bank as the head of a man and horse struggled for a few moments against the battling current, and then were swept away amidst uprooted trees and whirling driftwood.

. . . . . .

The Old Man started and woke. The fire on the hearth was dead, the candle in the outer room flickering in its socket, and somebody was rapping at the door. He opened it, but fell back with a cry before the dripping, half-naked figure that reeled against the doorpost.

'Dick?'

'Hush! Is he awake yet?'

'No,—but, Dick—— ?'

'Dry up, you old fool! Get me some whisky, *quick!*' The Old Man flew and returned with—an empty bottle! Dick would have sworn, but his strength was not equal to the occasion. He staggered, caught at the handle of the door, and motioned to the Old Man.

'Thar's suthin' in my pack yer for Johnny. Take it off. I can't.'

The Old Man unstrapped the pack, and laid it before the exhausted man.

'Open it, quick!'

He did so with trembling fingers. It contained only a few poor toys,—cheap and barbaric enough, goodness knows, but bright with paint and tinsel. One of them was broken; another, I fear, was irretrievably ruined by water; and on the third—ah me! there was a cruel spot.

'It don't look like much, that's a fact,' said Dick ruefully. . . . 'But it's the best we could do. . . . Take 'em, Old Man, and put 'em in his stocking, and tell him—tell him, you know—hold me, Old Man——' The Old Man caught at his sinking figure. 'Tell him,' said Dick, with a weak little laugh,—'tell him Sandy Claus has come.'

And even so, bedraggled, ragged, unshaven, and unshorn, with one arm hanging helplessly at his side, Santa Claus came to Simpson's Bar and fell fainting on the first threshold. The Christmas dawn came slowly after, touching the remoter peaks with the rosy warmth of ineffable love. And it looked so tenderly on Simpson's Bar that the whole mountain, as if caught in a generous action, blushed to the skies.

CHARLES GRANT

1841–1889

PEPPINIELLO

I

If you have ever sauntered along the Strada del Molo at Naples, you can hardly have failed to notice the *mozzonari* who gather there in greater numbers than in any other part of the city. You frequently catch sight of a single *mozzonare* in other places, it is true—lounging on the steps of a church, it may be, or basking in the hottest corner of a piazza; but here is the great centre of the trade in old cigar ends, and here its 'merchants most do congregate'—as ragged, dirty, and unkempt a set of little beggar-boys as any European city can show. Each has his stock-in-trade spread out before him on the sheet of an old newspaper, and carefully divided into little heaps of eight or nine ends apiece. The lots have been carefully selected according to the quality of the cigars of which they are composed, and cost one soldo each; for the *mozzonari* are almost the only Neapolitan traders who have really fixed prices, and with whom it is useless to bargain, though even they stoop to human weakness in so far as to keep a general heap from which each purchaser is allowed to select a stump.

Perhaps you may wonder who can be found to buy such nasty rubbish. Wait a minute or two, and you will see.

But first fix your eyes on the boy who lounges at the corner of the road leading down to the custom-house and the landing-place. His name is Peppiniello, and he is about twelve years old. Judging from his face you might fancy him older, it wears in its moments of rest so astute and self-reliant an expression; but if you looked at his body you would think him at least a year or two younger, for a scanty diet has checked his growth. Otherwise his limbs are not ill-formed. If you watch him while bathing in the dirty waters of the harbour, you will be amazed at their suppleness and activity, and also at their leanness. He seems to consist of nothing but skin and bone. 'The wonder is,' as an Italian shopkeeper once remarked to me, 'that there should be so much life in so little flesh!' The whole of his skin is of one colour, a deep greyish-brown; there is not blood enough in the veins to lend it the warmer tint that the Venetian painters loved. The upper part of the face is well formed, and the eyes are very bright and intelligent; the mouth, however, is not only too large, but there is a precocious trait about it of something which generally appears to be merely humour, but at times looks unpleasantly like cunning. Still it is, at the worst, a quick, cheerful, not unkindly face, and it would look far better if the hair were not shorn so closely to the head. In dress, Peppiniello does not greatly differ from his companions. His shirt is open before and torn behind; his trousers are so full of holes that you wonder he should think it worth while to put them on at all, particularly in a town where their absence in a boy of his age would attract but little attention. He is wiser than you, however, and he knows that in Naples it is only the children who have parents to care for them that can afford to run about in their shirts. He does not look at the nether article of his dress—at least during the summer months—as a matter either of comfort or decency, but simply as the badge of the social position he is desirous of occupying. In the same light, too, he regards the little round cap, of nearly the same colour as his skin, which seems to be made of some woollen material. I have never been daring enough to examine it closely. It is rarely to be seen upon his head, and its chief practical purpose seems to be to serve as an elbow cushion.

At present Peppiniello looks idle enough. He is stretched at full length upon the ground, watching a game which two other boys are playing with peach-stones, a natural substitute for marbles; but he has a keen eye for business, and makes more money than any of the fraternity. This his comrades attribute to his luck; but it is really the result of a number of small observations. Thus, more than a year and a half ago he noticed that when four or five of them sat in a row, those at the two ends were sure to sell their wares quickest; for if the purchaser is in haste he will buy of the first that he sees, and hurry on; if he is at leisure he will probably inspect all the piles, and, finding them pretty much alike, he will take his tobacco of the last, in order that he may not have to retrace his steps. Some months passed before he made a second discovery, namely, that the spot he now occupies is the best for its purpose in all Naples, because the mechanics who pass along the Strada del Molo are generally anxious to get to or from their work as quickly as may be, while, on the other hand, the boatmen who return from the landing-place have usually finished their task, and have nothing very particular to do. As soon as he had noticed this, he made a point of occupying the corner before any of his comrades were astir, and he has now almost a prescriptive right to it. Some of his success must also be attributed to his good-nature. When his wares are exhausted, or there is no hope of custom, he is always ready to run an errand for the men who are working near. Sometimes he is rewarded by a crust, a slice of cabbage, or a handful of fruit, and more rarely by a centesimo or two; but on such occasions he never asks for anything, and those whom he serves in this way naturally repay him by giving him their own custom and recommending him to their friends. In fact, he is a favourite with most of the men who are employed in the neighbourhood; and this is useful to him in more ways than one.

Among Peppiniello's other observations is this—that during the morning hours it is useless for him to take much trouble in recommending his wares. Those who want old cigar ends will come and buy them; but every one is then too busy to pay attention to his noise and nonsense. Later in the day it will be different—a joke may secure a customer, or a grin and a caper draw a soldo from the pocket of some foreign gentleman, and Peppiniello is as equal to these as to the other requirements of his trade. But there is a time for everything, and at present the most brilliant display of his talents would make no impression on any one but his companions, for whose applause he does not greatly care; so he lies at his ease with the happy conviction that his own stock is the finest in this morning's market.

It consists of eleven piles, and a little heap of foreign cigar ends, which are their possessor's great joy and pride, though he is a little uncertain as to their exact market value. If a sailor of luxurious tastes and reduced means happens to pass, he will probably offer a good price for them; but at present the boy is not anxious to sell, for he knows the unusual display will attract customers for his other wares. This special heap is the result of a daring raid into the Grand Café which he made the other evening, and in which his retreat was covered by a party of good-natured foreigners. When he found himself in safety, and gesticulated his thanks from the middle of the street, they threw him a soldo or two, and one of them, supposing that an infantile craving for the prohibited joys of tobacco was the cause of his boldness, added a cigar which he had only just lighted. There it lies at the top of the sheet of paper. Peppiniello is resolved not to part with it for less than eight centesimi. It must surely be worth ten, he thinks ; but, unfortunately, those who are ready to pay such a price for a cigar usually prefer to buy it in a shop.

But see, a mechanic in his working-dress pauses for a moment, lays down two soldi, sweeps up two piles, which he wraps in a piece of paper, and thrusts them into his pocket as he walks on. The whole transaction has been the work of a few seconds, and has not cost a single word. The next customer is of a very different type : he is a fisherman coming up from the landing-place to fill his morning pipe. He feels the deepest contempt and animosity for the mechanic on account of his calling ; but, at the same time, he has a firm conviction that he belongs to a class which knows how to cheat the devil, and that consequently it is by no means unadvisable for a good, simple, Christian fisherman to take a hint from it in worldly matters. He has, consequently, made up his mind as to which of the *mozzonari* he will patronize long before he reaches the first of them ; but that does not prevent him inspecting all the other papers with a critical, irresolute air. When he reaches Peppiniello, he looks at his wares with a new expression of marked contempt, pauses for half a minute, and then commences to gesticulate. To all his movements Peppiniello only replies by that slight and peculiar toss of the head which every Neapolitan accepts as a final refusal. In fact, they have been having an animated discussion, although not a single word has been spoken ; for the common people of Naples, though ready enough with their tongues, are fond of 'conversing silently' with each other—not exactly as lovers are said to do, but by means of a perfect language of signs. The fisherman has offered, first three, and then four centesimi for a single lot, and then nine centesimi for two. These offers have of course been refused. He knew from the first that they would be, for any *mozzonare* who was observed to increase the size of his piles, or even suspected of selling below the established price, would not only lose caste, but be subjected to constant persecution by his comrades; but then, as a fisherman, he feels he would be outraging every feeling of propriety if he were tô buy any article whatever without at least attempting to cheapen it. It would almost look as if he wished to be taken for a *signore*. At last, with a sigh, he places the exact price of a single pile—which he has all the time been holding ready—upon the paper, and then, with a most innocent expression, he stretches out his hand to the foreign tobacco at the top of the sheet. He knows that is not its price, and he does not want it, as he greatly prefers the Italian tobacco below: he only wishes to show that he is not quite a fool. Peppiniello gently pushes back his hand, draws a line with his own finger between the upper and the lower lots, and points to the latter. He is very careful not to touch the money, as that might lead to an unpleasant discussion with respect to the exact amount. The fisherman now makes as if he intended to resume it, and purchase of the next dealer; but, as he sees Peppiniello is still unmoved, he takes instead the heap on which from the first his heart has been set, seizes the largest cigar-end in the general pile, and moves off slowly till he finds an empty place on the coping on which to seat himself. When he feels quite comfortable, he slowly takes off that peculiar piece of headgear, which young artists and enthusiastic antiquaries delight to call Phrygian, but which to the uninitiated eyes of ordinary mortals rather suggests a cross between an overgrown night-cap and a gouty stocking; from this, after fumbling about in it for a time, he draws a red clay pipe with a cane stem, and a clasp-knife, and begins to prepare for the enjoyment of a morning smoke. If you could get near enough to look into that Phrygian headdress of his, as it lies there beside him, you would probably find that it still contains a hunch of bread, half an onion, an apple, two peaches, a few small fish wrapped up in seaweed, and a picture of San Antonio; for the fisherman's cap is not only his purse and tobacco-pouch, but a general receptacle for miscellaneous articles of his personal property. It is but just to add, however, that the fish he carries in this way is always intended for his own consumption.

II

At ten o'clock, Peppiniello has disposed of all his wares. As the day is hot he feels almost inclined to have a swim in the harbour; but he sees no one near with whom he could safely deposit the eleven soldi which he has made by his morning's work, and, besides, he is hungry, as well he may be, for he has been up since dawn and has eaten nothing yet. Where to get a dinner?—that is the question; for it never even occurs to him that he might spend a part of his hard-earned gains upon common food, though now and then, when the times are good, he will buy a slice of water-melon. He would hardly feel justified in doing even that to-day; so, as he rolls up the foreign tobacco, which he has not sold, in the old newspaper, and places it inside the breast of his shirt, which serves all Neapolitans of his class as a capacious pocket, he revolves in his mind the chances that are open to him. He knows he could have what he wants at once by going to the narrow street near the Porta Capuana, where his father used to live; for there are still several women in the neighbourhood who remember his family, and who would give him a crust of bread, a slice of raw cabbage, or a part of whatever their own dinner happened to be. But he has noticed that the more rarely he comes the warmer his welcome is; and he wishes to leave these friends as a last resource in cases of the utmost need. Though it is not the hour during which strangers are likely to be moving about, it might be worth while to saunter down to Santa Lucia, as there is no saying what a foreigner may not do, and, if he is out, that is the likeliest place to find him. But the children in that district hold together, and look upon him as an intruder on the hunting-grounds that belong by right to them. They will crowd him out of the circle, if possible, spoil his antics, and snatch the soldi out of his very hand. Nay, a few weeks ago, when he stole the purse from the English gentleman, they seemed half-inclined to betray him, instead of covering his retreat. It is true, that, at last, their instinctive hatred of law and the police got the better of their local jealousy, and he made his escape. In half an hour, when he had brought his booty into safety, he returned, and invited the boys who had helped him into a neighbouring *taverna*, where he placed four litres of wine before them. That was the right thing to do, and he did it; nay, as the purse had contained nearly twenty lire—though that he confessed to nobody—he even added a kilo of bread to the repast. Since then he has enjoyed a half-unwilling respect in that quarter. But Peppiniello is not the boy to forget their hesitation, which seems to him the basest of treachery. Besides, their manners disgust him. It is right enough that boys should cut capers, and make grimaces, and beg, and steal; but it is indecent for girls of eleven or twelve to do so. If he has a contempt for anything in the world, it is for those girls and their relations. No; he will not go to Santa Lucia.

So he turns up one of the dark narrow ways that lead away from the Porto, looking wistfully into every *taverna* that he passes. Most of them are empty. In some a single workman is sitting, with a small piece of bread and one glass of wine before him, or half a dozen have clubbed together to buy a loaf and a bottle. Peppiniello knows it is useless to beg of these—they have little enough to stay their own appetites. 'Ah!' thinks he, who, like all his class, is a bitter enemy of the present government—perhaps only because it is the government—'it was different in good King Ferdinand's days, when bread only cost four soldi the kilo, and wine seven centesimi the litre. Then, they say, if a hungry beggar-boy could find a workman at his dinner, he was sure of a crust and a sup; but how can they give anything now, with bread at eight and wine at twelve soldi?' At last he sees what appears to be a well-dressed man, sitting at the further end of the low, dark room. He slips in in a moment, and stands before him making that movement of the forefinger and thumb to the mouth by which Neapolitan beggars express their hunger. The man cuts off a small fragment of his bread and gives it him. Now Peppiniello is near, he can see by the pinched face and bright eyes of the man that he, too, has nothing to spare. He is almost ashamed of having begged of him; but he munches the bread as he goes along. It is such a little piece that it seems only to make him hungrier. He hardly knows what to do; so he sits down on a doorstep to reflect.

He knows an English ship came into port last night. The chance is that some of the sailors are ashore. If he could find them, they would very likely give him something, and he fancies he can guess pretty nearly where they are; but then—to tell the truth—he is afraid. Such sailors, it is true, have never shown him anything but kindness; but who knows what they may do? They are so strong and rough, and have no respect for anything. He looks upon them as he does on the forces of nature, as something entirely capricious, incalculable, and uncontrollable. They threw him a handful of soldi the other day; perhaps to-day they may throw him out of the window. The people say they are not even Christians. Who can tell? Yet surely the Madonna must have power over them too; and he is very hungry. So he rises, and turns once more in the direction of the Porto, murmuring a Paternoster and an Ave, with eyes in the meantime perfectly open to any other chance of provender.

He goes to one, two, three of the houses they are likely to frequent, and convinces himself they are not there. At last he hears them in the front room of the first story of the fourth. It is the very worst house for his purpose that they could have chosen; for the hostess is a very—well, I know no English word which would not be degraded if applied to her. She looks upon all the money in the pockets of her guests upstairs as already her own, and naturally resents any claim upon it, however small. Peppiniello knows her well; but he has not come thus far to be turned back at last by fear of an old woman. He saunters carelessly and yet wearily into the street, and seats himself on the step opposite the door of the *locanda*, leans his head upon his arm, and finally stretches himself at full length. Any passer would fancy him asleep; in fact, he is on the watch. He knows his only chance is to wait till the lower room and, if possible, the kitchen behind it, are empty, and then make a dart for the staircase. He lies there for more than half an hour. At last the cook is sent out to fetch something, as it seems from a distance; for he takes his coat and hat. The hostess stands at a table at the back of the front room, with a tray of grog-glasses before her which are half-full of spirits. In a moment more the scullion comes with a kettle of boiling water, which he pours into the glasses while the hostess stirs them. By some accident a drop or two falls upon her hand; she says nothing, but simply wipes it with a cloth beside her. As soon, however, as the last glass is full, and the scullion has taken two steps away from the table, she gives him such a cuff as sends him flying to the other end of the kitchen, with the scalding water streaming down his legs. Of course, there is a howl. He, at least, is not likely to take much notice of anything at present. The hostess quietly takes up the tray, puts on a bland smile, and mounts the stairs. This is Peppiniello's chance. He lets her ascend three or four steps, and then, with a spring as stealthy as a cat's, he follows her. His bare feet fall noiselessly, and he steals up so close behind her that there is no chance of her seeing him, even if she should turn, which she can hardly do, as the stairs are narrow and she has the tray in her hand. When she reaches the landing, she stops to place her burden on a table, in order that she may open the door; Peppiniello at once springs forward, and enters without being announced, satisfied so far with his success, but by no means certain that he may not have sprung out of the frying-pan into the fire.

Round a table which is strewed with the remnants of what seems to have been a sumptuous though rather coarse meal, six sailors are seated in company not of the most respectable.

Peppiniello knows that boldness is now his only hope, for if the hostess can catch hold of him before he has attracted the men's attention he will certainly fly down the stairs much more quickly than he ascended them. So he advances at once, and with a low bow and a grin makes the gesture that indicates his hunger.

'What does the young devil mean?' asks one of the men in very imperfect Italian.

'He only wants some of the broken bread,' replies a girl, throwing him half a loaf.

Peppiniello springs into the air, catches it halfway,

makes a gesture of the wildest joy, and then, with a face of preternatural gravity, bows his thanks and stands like a soldier on parade. The men are amused, and soon all the bread upon the table is stowed away within his shirt. This gives him a strange appearance, as the slender arms and legs form a striking contrast to the enormous trunk. He at once sees his advantage, and proceeds to contort his face and limbs in a way that makes him appear hardly human. Shouts of laughter follow, and one of the girls hands him a glass of wine. Meanwhile the grog has been placed on the table and the men have lighted their pipes. One pulls out an Italian cigar, but after the first whiff he throws it away with a curse, declaring that it is made of a mixture of rotten cabbage-leaves and india-rubber. Peppiniello seizes it almost before it falls, seats himself in a corner, and begins to puff away with an expression of the most luxurious enjoyment.

'What, you smoke, do you, you little imp of hell? You'd better take the whole lot of them, for I'll be d——d if any human being can smoke them.'

The words are spoken in English, and Peppiniello can hardly believe his eyes when a parcel of cigars comes flying across the room into his lap.

'Ask him if his mother knows he's out,' says one of the men. His companion puts the question into such Italian as he can command. One of the girls repeats it in the Neapolitan dialect, and explains Peppiniello's answer, which is then translated into English for the benefit of the male part of the company.

'I have no mother.'

'His father, then?'

'I have no father.'

'How does he live, then?'

'How I can.'

'Ask him if he'll come aboard with us; and tell him we'll make a man of him.'

'What would my sisters do then?'

'How many sisters has he?'

'Four.'

'How old?'

'One a year older and three younger than I am, and they have nobody in the world to take care of them but me.'

The idea of that little monkey being the father of a family is too comic not to excite a laugh, yet there is something pathetic in it. None of the girls believe the tale; but if questioned by their companions they would all assert a firm conviction of its truth. Nay, one or two of them would probably say they were personally acquainted with all the facts of the case.

'It's all a d——d lie, of course,' says another of the men; 'but it don't matter,' and he throws the boy a two-soldi piece. The other sailors follow his example.

Peppiniello gathers up his riches. He feels that it is time for him to withdraw, but he knows the landlady is waiting below with a stick, and that she purposes first to beat him as unmercifully as she can, then to rob him of all that has been given him, and finally to kick him into the street. He is afraid that even his morning's earnings will go with the rest of his gains. It is not a pleasant prospect. Fortunately for him the girls at the table know all this as well as he does. One of them whispers a word or two to her companion, rises, beckons slightly to the boy, and goes downstairs. He makes a silent bow to the company and slinks after her, but when they reach the lower room she takes him by the hand and leads him to the street-door amid a perfect storm of abuse from the landlady, who, however, does not venture to give any more practical expression to her rage.

'Now run, you little devil, run!'

Peppiniello only pauses for a single moment to raise the girl's hand gently to his lips, and before half a minute is past he has put a dozen corners between himself and the scene of his adventure.

But the girl turns and faces the infuriated hostess. 'What harm has the boy done you?' she says quietly. 'If the gentlemen upstairs had been angry I could understand it, but they were amused. What harm has he done you?'

The hostess is rather cowed by the girl's manner, and she replies in an almost whining tone, 'All that bread he has robbed me of—is that nothing?'

'Why, what can you do with broken bread?'

'Sell it to the poor.'

The girl's form assumes a sudden dignity; she feels that this woman has sunk far below her, and her voice is very low but very biting as she says, 'Donna Estere, you are as hard and wicked as a Piedmontese. If you speak another word I will never enter your house again, but take all my friends over there, and she moves her head slightly in the direction of a rival establishment.

This is a threat that Donna Estere cannot afford to disregard, but she is still too excited to be able to fawn on the girl and flatter her as she will in half an hour's time. So she retires silently into the kitchen, to vent her rage first in abusing and then in beating the scullion.

III

When Peppiniello feels himself well out of the reach of danger, he draws out a piece of bread and eats it greedily as he walks slowly in the direction of his father's old home. He has not gone far before he sees another boy of his own class seated in a doorway and dining off a raw cabbage head and two onions. Peppiniello squats himself down opposite, and by way of beginning a conversation he remarks in a friendly tone that the cabbage doesn't look very fresh. The owner of the maligned vegetable replies that he pulled it that very morning in his uncle's garden, and adds that he is sorry for boys who are obliged to dine off stale bread. This gives rise to an animated discussion, which in about five minutes leads to the exchange of a thick slice of cabbage and half an onion for a piece of bread. Each now feels that he is dining sumptuously, and in order to remove any unpleasant impression that may have been left on his neighbour's mind, he praises the provisions he has just received at least as warmly as he before disparaged them. The stranger then gives a glowing description of his uncle's garden, which, by his account, must certainly be the most remarkable estate ever possessed by a violent and eccentric old gentleman, whose only weakness is a doting fondness for his nephew. Peppiniello has his own doubts as to the existence of that earthly paradise, but he is far too polite to express any. In his turn he relates how his father went to sea a year and a half ago and was, as they thought, lost, and how they mourned for him, and how that very morning his aunt had received a letter stating that he had married a great heiress in Palermo, and was going to return to Naples in a few weeks.

'Ah, won't your stepmother just beat you!' says the stranger, in a tone which implies that he could quite enter into the fun of the operation.

'Ah, but she can't!' replies Peppiniello. 'That's the best of it. She's only one leg; the other's a wooden one, but they say it's stuffed full of good French gold pieces.'

And so, having finished his meal, he proceeds upon his way, pondering upon what to do with the fortune he has so unexpectedly invented for himself. The stranger, as he saunters in the opposite direction, considers the important question whether a ferocious miser of an uncle who can refuse nothing to his single pet, or a stepmother with a wooden leg stuffed with gold pieces, is the more desirable imaginary possession for a little street-boy of limited means.

Peppiniello at last reaches a small tobacco-shop at the corner of a narrow close. 'Good-day, Donna Amalia,' he says as he enters.

'What, Peppiniello! you here again, and dinner's over, and I don't believe there's a bite left in the house.' Her tone is rough, but she turns with the evident intention of searching her larder.

'Thank you; I've eaten to-day. I only want to ask you to take care of this for me till the evening,' and he heaps the bread upon the counter.

'What, ten pieces; you *have* had luck to-day!'

'And here are some cigars. Will you sell them for me? Of course I should not expect the full price.'

It goes rather against Donna Amalia's conscience to refuse any lawful profit that may fall in her way; but she remembers that the boy is an orphan, and that the Virgin has a way of rewarding those who are pitiful to such.

'Well, let me see them. Yes, they are whole. They cost, you know, eight centesimi apiece; that makes fourteen soldi and two centesimi. There it is,' and she pays him the whole sum. She has no doubt in her own mind that she is receiving stolen goods, but no one can identify a cigar, and it is no business of hers, so she asks no questions. Peppiniello puts it together with the rest, and then commits the whole to her care. She counts over the sum with him very carefully, wraps it in a piece of paper, and places it on a shelf in the inside room beside the bread. He has already bidden her good-bye, and is passing out of the shop, when she calls him back.

'You will never be able to eat all that bread while it is fresh.'

'It is quite at your service, Donna Amalia;' but there is something in the eyes that contradicts the tone and the words.

'Nay, boy, I don't want to beg your bread of you; but look here, these three pieces are as good as when they came from the baker's. If you like, I will take them to-day, and give you new bread for them to-morrow.'

'A thousand thanks, but let it be the day after to-morrow.'

'Very well.'

He is really grateful to the rough kind woman, but he does not kiss her hand. That one only does to people of a higher social class, and he does not feel so very much below Donna Amalia.

It is now more than time for the mid-day sleep, so Peppiniello retires into a doorway where the stones are pretty smooth, and there is no danger of the sunshine stealing in to waken him. He does not go to sleep so quickly as usual, perhaps because he has dined better; and as he reviews the events of the morning he comes to the conclusion that it is his duty to go to mass next morning, to return thanks for his deliverance from danger. He has no doubt that it was the Madonna who saved him from Donna Estere, and it never occurs to him that she chose rather a strange messenger. Then he begins to consider on what numbers he had better set in this week's *lotto*. He is rather doubtful of his luck, for he has lost six of the francs he found in the purse in that way. How he wishes he could dream of numbers, but somehow he never does. The priests of course know them all, for they are learned, but they are bound by a vow not to impart their knowledge to any one; yet they say that sometimes a monk will whisper the sacred secret to a friend. Surely they ought to do so, if only to be revenged on the government who has turned them out of their monasteries. Peppiniello resolves to be very polite to all monks in future. If he could read, he would try to get hold of one of those wonderful books which explain things so well you can hardly dream of anything without finding the number it signifies in them. Well, this time he will set upon 32, the number of Donna Estere's house, and upon 12, for there were twelve guests at table. Fate will doubtless give him another number before the time for playing comes round. Pondering these things, he falls asleep.

It is later than usual when he awakens, and he sees with some consternation how low the sun has already sunk. He has missed the best early harvest for old cigar ends, which is at its height at two o'clock, when the gentlemen who have lunched and smoked return to their places of business. He must make haste or he will have nothing for the evening market and miss that too. So he hastens off to the railway station, picking up here and there a bit of merchandise by the way. He is not lucky even there, though a good-natured porter lets him slip into the waiting-room, which is empty for the moment; and on his way to the Porto, which he chooses to take through the narrow streets and not by the most frequented road, he walks slowly, as if in doubt. At last he sits down and counts over his scanty gleanings with a look that says plainly enough, 'They won't do.' So he turns once more away from the Porto, and after climbing two or three streets at rather a rapid pace, he reaches the corner of one in which a poverty-stricken café is situated. Then his whole manner changes; he assumes an indolent but merry air, and begins to sing a Neapolitan song. The threadbare waiter who is sitting at the door hails him with a loud jest, and then asks in a low voice,—'Don't you want any cigar-ends to-day?'

'Well, I hardly know. I have such a large stock, and I sell so few: but let me see them.'

They enter the empty café together, and the treasure is displayed.

'What do you want for them?'

'What will you give—four soldi?'

'Not two for that lot,' says the boy contemptuously.

A discussion of course follows, and Peppiniello finally agrees to give two soldi, but only that he may not lose the waiter's friendship and patronage. The tobacco he still insists is not worth the price.

'And when am I to be paid ?'

'To-night, if I sell enough.'

He resumes his indolent walk and his song, which he continues till he reaches the end of the street, when he quickens his pace and leaves off singing. Both parties are rather ashamed of this transaction. The waiter knows he has been acting meanly, and the boy, who looks upon all cigar-ends as the rightful property of the *mozzonari*, feels he has been put upon. It is only in extreme cases like to-day's that he will submit to this. In fact, this perfectly legitimate purchase, by which he is sure of making a large profit, weighs on his conscience far more heavily than any of his thefts. Hence each is sure of the other's secrecy.

As Peppiniello turns again in the direction of the Porto, he fancies that some misfortune is sure to overtake him shortly, for he feels he has deserved a punishment, and only hopes the avenging powers will lay it on with a light hand. So when he finds a perfect stranger to the whole company of *mozzonari*—a great hulking youth of some fifteen years—has taken possession of his place, he looks upon it as the result of their immediate interposition, but this does not make him feel any the more inclined to bear it patiently. Besides, he knows that if he gives way now his favourite seat is lost for ever. Accordingly he utters an indignant protest, which calls forth a contemptuous answer. An angry altercation follows, in which sufficiently strong language is used on both sides. A boatman passing up from the landing-place soon puts an end to the situation by first pushing the youth to a distance of some yards and then tossing his wares after him. This being done, he passes on, fully satisfied that he has been performing an act of justice, for he knows Peppiniello does usually sit there, and then his opponent is old enough to gain his living in some other way. The sale of old cigar-ends is work that children can do, and so it ought to be left to them.

Peppiniello quietly takes his old seat, from which the new-comer does not venture to expel him by force—he has evidently too powerful allies ; so he crouches down at a distance of a few yards in front of him, and covers him with every term of abuse. Hitherto the language, though strong, has been confined within the wide limits of what the lower-class Neapolitans consider decent, or at least tolerable ; now the vilest and most offensive terms which their unusually expressive dialect furnishes are freely used. At first the boy gives epithet for epithet, but then he falls silent, his eyes dilate, his lips tighten, his right hand is fumbling inside his shirt.

'You son of a priest.'

The words are scarcely uttered, when the boy's knife is unclasped, and, with a spring as sudden and unexpected as a cat's, he has flown at his enemy's throat.

Fortunately for both, a well-dressed man has been silently watching the scene, and with a motion as quick as Peppiniello's he has seized the boy, clasping his body with his right arm and grasping the knife with his left hand. Another moment, and a hearty kick has sent the intruder sprawling upon the stones. The latter gathers up first himself and then his wares, and goes off muttering threats and curses. A single glance at his face, however, is sufficient to show that he will never venture to interfere with Peppiniello again.

'If you had ever seen the inside of a prison, my boy,' says the man whose intervention has just been so opportune, 'you would not run the risk of being sent there for such a foul-mouthed fool as that; nor,' he adds in a voice that none but the child in his arms can hear—'nor for a purse either, even if it did contain twenty lire;' and so he pushes him with apparent roughness, but real gentleness, back into his place.

Peppiniello stretches himself at full length. His face is on the ground and covered by his two arms, his whole body is still quivering, but his protector sees at a glance that it is only with subsiding rage, so he passes on as if nothing particular had happened. When he returns in an hour's time the boy is jesting merrily with his comrades; but his quick eyes catch the approaching form, he draws back into his corner, and whispers with a down-bent head, 'Thank you, Don Antonio.'

Don Antonio, if that is his name, takes no notice; he does not even cast a passing glance at the scene of the late conflict.

IV

At about eight o'clock, Peppiniello resolves to give up business for that evening. It is true the market is at its height, and he has not yet sold more than half his wares, but he will want a new supply to-morrow, and the best time for gathering it has now begun. To-night, too, he must make good use of his time, for he will have to return home earlier than usual, as Donna Amalia goes to bed between eleven and twelve. He turns in the direction of San Carlo, and walks slowly past the small theatres, picking up what he can by the way, till he reaches the garden gate of the palace, over which he throws a two-centesimo piece, with a hardly perceptible motion of his hand, and without turning his head. On each side stands a colossal bronze statue of a man governing an unruly horse. The Emperor Nicholas of Russia sent them as a present to King Ferdinand after his return from Italy, and they were supposed by the Italian Liberals of those days to convey a delicate hint as to what the Autocrat of the North considered the true principles of government. Of all this Peppiniello of course knows nothing; but the stalwart forms have made a deep impression on his imagination, and he has invented this strange way of paying his adoration to them. He does not number them with the saints, still less has he any intention of paying them divine honours. What he attributes to them is great, though by no means unlimited, power, and some such capricious goodwill to himself as the boatmen frequently show. He is not given to analysis, and he sees no contradiction between this worship and the rest of his religious creed; indeed, the bronze statues fill a place that would otherwise be left vacant in his pantheon. He looks upon them as leading strong joyous lives of their own, and caring on the whole very little for human affairs, though he thinks they must be somewhat pleased by sincere devotion. At best they are only good-natured, not good; and so they stand far below the saints, whose whole time is spent in acts of graciousness and pity. But then you cannot call upon the saints to help you in committing what the Church calls a sin, though doubtless they will often save you from its consequences. With respect to the two bronze figures, he has no such scruples, for he is convinced that their moral code is no more stringent than his own. So he called upon them when the children at Santa Lucia seemed inclined to abandon him to the police, and we know how well he got out of that scrape. Nevertheless, he keeps his irreligious faith a profound secret, partly from a fear of ridicule, no doubt, but partly also because he has a shrewd suspicion that the objects of it are more likely to pay attention to his prayers if the number of their worshippers remains strictly limited.

Peppiniello now sets to work in good earnest, and by twelve o'clock he has collected an ample stock-in-trade, paid the waiter the two soldi he owed him, and received his bread and money from Donna Amalia. He now turns homewards. It is a long way, but he only pauses to buy two slices of water-melon at a stall, and these he carries in his hand until he reaches a small open court at the mouth of a cavern, where a number of women are seated to enjoy as much of the freshness of the night as the high walls of the neighbouring houses will allow. He gives a sharp whistle, and immediately a girl hastens towards him. You can see at a glance that she is Peppiniello's sister. Her name is Concetta, and she is about thirteen years old, though a Northerner would probably think her a year and a half older. Her complexion is sallower than her brother's, her eyes are very bright, and her black hair, which is tied in a rough wisp round her head, has been burnt and bleached by exposure till the surface coil is almost brown. With a little care it might be made to look well, but it has never been brushed since her mother's death, and is rarely combed more than once a week. Her dress is decent, but it has been patched in many places with different materials, and she is far dirtier than Peppiniello, to whom custom allows the luxury of sea-bathing. Still there is a great deal of intelligence, some kindness, and not a little care in her look. Yet at times she can break into wild fits of merriment, and dance the tarantella with all the wild passion of a bacchanal. She seldom does that, however, when her brother or, indeed, any male person is present, and to-night she follows him very quietly down a narrow street to a little open place, and there seats herself on a doorstep beside him. She feels quite as strongly as he does that it would be beneath his dignity to take a place among the women and girls at the cavern's mouth.

'The children are asleep?' asks Peppiniello, as he gives his sister a hunch of bread and one of the slices of water-melon.

'Yes; and Donna Lucia has promised to have an eye on them till I come back.'

Peppiniello now gives the girl four soldi for the

household expenses of the morrow, and when he adds eight centesimi to enable them each to buy a piece of water-melon, she knows he has had a prosperous day, for in hard times she and her sisters are obliged to live on a soldo each, and what they can manage to earn or pick up. The bread is a new and pleasant surprise, over which her eyes brighten; to-morrow, housekeeping will be an easy task.

Business being over, the two fall to their suppers with a hearty appetite, while Peppiniello relates all his day's adventures, with the exception of the bargain with the waiter, and his sacrifice to the statues. The manner of both is quite changed; they are mere children chatting together as merrily as if they had never known want or care. When he has finished his tale, he places the money in her hand—all except a single soldo which he has hid away before. She counts it over carefully, and then exclaims joyously, 'Why, you *have* been lucky! With the rest this makes seven lire and a half: only ten soldi more and the month's rent is ready, and to-morrow is only the thirteenth.'

Peppiniello's tone assumes some of its old business weightiness, as he replies, 'Yes, but that must be made up before we spend anything.'

Concetta readily assents to this, and then goes on to propose that, even when their rent is ready, they shall continue to hoard their gains until they have money enough to buy one of the children a nice dress, so that they may be able to send her out of an evening to sell flowers to the ladies and gentlemen in the villa. 'That is the way to make money.' But Peppiniello very decisively rejects the proposal, and the girl, who, like most affectionate women that have not been spoiled by culture, has a habit of obeying even the unreasonable wishes of those whom she loves, gives way at once, and all who know more of Neapolitan life than she does will feel that in this difference her brother is in the right. Still, though she does not sulk or quarrel, she is disappointed by the rejection of her plan, and more silent than usual. She has a great trust, love, and admiration for her brother: they never quarrel, partly perhaps because they are so little together, and, what is more, she never yet had a secret from him. He, as we have seen, is not so open. He never told his sister anything about that purse; but he had several good reasons for this. He does not wish her to know that he steals, for she might imitate his example, and that would be unfeminine. There is no harm in boys doing a great many things that girls must not do, and he would be as much shocked to hear that Concetta had been guilty of a theft as to find her swimming in the waters of the harbour. But he had also another reason for keeping that secret. He knew exactly what he wanted to do with the money. The great terror of his life is that some month he may be unable to pay the rent, and that they will consequently be turned into the street. For himself the discomfort would not be great, as in most weathers he can sleep at least as comfortably on a doorstep as in bed; but he dreads it for the children's, and still more for Concetta's sake. So as soon as the money fell into his hands, he resolved to keep eight lire constantly in store as a resource against cases of the utmost need, and to say nothing about this, in order that neither he nor his sister might be tempted to be less careful in always getting the rent together as early in the month as possible. Nearly three lire were spent on the banquet he had to give to his half-hearted associates. He has still three left to dispose of, but they will go, as six have already gone, to the *lotto*. For that, too. he reserves the soldo, which he daily abstracts from his earnings. It is the only way he knows of investing his savings, but he is afraid of awakening hopes in his sister's mind which a sad experience has shown to be so often fallacious. Yet he has many compunctions of conscience about that soldo, which he tries to quiet by remembering that he allows each of the others the same sum for her daily expenditure. Otherwise he scrupulously shares everything he gains with the rest. If he buys a little fruit, the only way in which he ever spends anything upon himself, he brings them some, or gives them money to do the same. What Concetta and the children can earn or pick up they do as they like with, but though she keeps the family purse, into which all his gains flow, she never thinks of taking a centesimo out of it without his previous consent.

But, by this time, Peppiniello and his sister have finished their supper and are returning to the cavern's mouth. More than twenty families sleep in that gloomy hole, divided from each other by no partition greater than a line drawn upon the floor. The sides of the grotto are damp, and the air close and fetid with a thousand evil odours, though the entrance and the roof are lofty. You can catch no glimpse of the latter at this time of night; there is only one great starless darkness overhead, but below, here and there, a tiny oil flame glimmers before the picture of some saint. There is one burning at the foot of Peppiniello's bed, which occupies the worst place but one, that farthest from the entrance, and when the two reach it, after exchanging a few friendly words with Donna Lucia, one of the occupants of the neighbouring bed, they refill the lamp from a little flask, and then kneel down before a rough print of the Virgin to repeat a Paternoster and an Ave.

The bed itself is large enough not only for the whole family, but also to accommodate a stranger now and then, when, of a stormy night, Peppiniello happens to find some homeless boy shivering on a doorstep that does not shelter him from the rain. Three children are now sleeping quietly enough in it. The eldest of them, who may be nine, has a strong family likeness to Concetta, and so has one of the younger girls, whom you take to be six; but the third, who seems to be of nearly the same age, has quite a different face and figure. She is far more slightly built, has a little rosy mouth and tiny hands and feet. Her skin, though it is bronzed by the sun, is far fairer than that of her bedfellows, and she has fine light brown hair which would be silken if it were kept in proper order. Her name is Mariannina, and she is not in fact one of Peppiniello's sisters. This is her story :—

One night, about a year ago, when the boy was returning home, he saw her sleeping all alone in the portico of a church. If it had been a boy he would have passed on without taking any notice, but that wasn't a proper place for little girls to sleep in, so he wakened her, and asked where her home was, that he might take her there. It was a long way off, she said ; she didn't know where, but a long, long way. At length, in answer to many questions and a good deal of coaxing, she told him she lived alone with her mother, who, as soon as she had had her breakfast, used to give her a hunch of bread, turn her into the street, lock the door, and go to her work, from which she did not return till after dark. But one morning some time ago—Mariannina did not know exactly how long : it seemed a long while—her mother was lazy and would not get up. The child had nothing to eat that day, but in the evening her mother gave her the key of the cupboard where the bread was, and told her where to find some money. Mariannina had a good time of it for several days, as her mother took no notice of her, and would not eat anything ; but when the money was all spent she told her she had no more, and that she must get her breakfast how she could. She went out to play as usual, and a neighbour gave her something to eat. When she came back her mother was talking very loud, but there was no one else in the room, and the child could not understand what she said. She went on in that way for a long time, but at last she made a strange noise and then she was quite still. Afterwards the lamp before the Virgin went out; there had been no oil to replenish it with. Next morning, when Mariannina awoke, her mother was still asleep. When she touched her she was quite cold. At first she had tried to awaken her, but she would not speak nor move, so the child was frightened and ran away. All day she had tried to get as far away as she could. She did not want to go home; she would go with Peppiniello, and she was hungry.

The kindest as well as the wisest thing would of course have been to take the little orphan to the Foundling Hospital, but Peppiniello never thought of that. He was convinced that the Holy Virgin had sent him to take care of this child, and he was not the boy to shrink from such a trust. Concetta was of the same opinion, and from that day to this Mariannina had been a member of the family. She is a quiet child, with soft, caressing ways, and never has those fits of wild merriment into which the others fall; but she has also less cheerfulness to face hard times with, and when the supply of food is very scanty, she is apt to be rather subdued and to look weary. The girls treat her exactly as they do each other, but there is just a shade of extra gentleness in the relation between her and her protector, which may arise from the consciousness that the ties between them have been formed by their own free choice, or perhaps from the belief which both entertain that it was the Blessed Virgin who brought them together.

As soon as Peppiniello and Concetta have finished their prayers they arm themselves with two long sticks. A rusty fork is firmly bound to the end of that which the girl leans against her side of the bed, while her brother's terminates in the blade of an old knife, carefully sharpened. As he creeps into his place, Mariannina puts her hands up to his cheeks and falls asleep again in the midst of the caress. And now the purpose of the strange weapons soon becomes clear, for scarcely has quiet been restored when the floor is literally covered with hundreds of rats. Concetta makes several ineffectual thrusts before Peppiniello moves his arm, but at his first blow he succeeds in wounding one of them, which utters a sharp squeak as it disappears. In a moment all the rest have vanished, and a shrill yet tremulous voice is raised in angry protest from the darkness beyond. At first it utters nothing but vile abuse and frightful curses, but then in a whine it urges that it is a sin to maim and injure the poor creatures. 'They, too, are God's children.'

'Why doesn't He keep them at home, then? While I'm here, they're not going to nibble Mariannina's toes,' replies Peppiniello, but in a tone only just loud enough to catch Concetta's ear, for he respects the age and pities the suffering of the wretched being who has just spoken.

It is Donna Lucia's mother, who, having been found too loathsome to retain her place in the family bed, has been accommodated with a sack of dried maize-leaves in the darkest corner of the cave. As her daughter and son-in-law are abroad at their work all day, their children are too little to be of any use, and she cannot move from her pallet, she has perhaps some reason to be grateful to the natural scavengers she vainly endeavours to protect. Perhaps, too, the last affectionate instincts of a motherly nature have centred themselves on the only living beings that constantly surround her. At length the querulous voice dies away, the stick falls from Peppiniello's hand, and he sinks into a sound sleep.[1]

[1] The incident of the old woman's affection for the rats is borrowed from Renato Fucini's interesting *Napoli a occhio nudo*, p. 67. On his visiting one of the habitations of the poor, some such wretched being as Donna Lucia's mother used the expression employed in the text, in reproving him for frightening the rats away. The Italian words are *Son creature di Dio anche loro*, and the verbal translation would of course be, 'They, too, are God's

V

When Peppiniello wakes he feels instinctively that it is dawn, though as yet no ray of light has penetrated even to the entrance of the cavern; so he awakens Concetta. She is tired, and would willingly sleep another hour or two as she usually does, but in that case she could not go to mass with her brother, so she rouses herself, and they are soon on their way to a neighbouring church.

It is still dusk, the larger stars have not yet faded out of the sky, and the freshness of the morning air is felt even in the narrow streets through which their way leads them. There is a stillness everywhere, and an unusual light on common things, which impress both the children, but chiefly Concetta, who never rises so early except when she goes to mass. And when they pass the portal of the church the blaze of the candles upon the altar, the glow of the polished marble, the rich colours of the hangings, seem to stand in a strange contrast, not only to the quiet twilight outside, but also to all their ordinary surroundings. To you and me the church looks gaudy, a miracle of bad taste, it may be; to them it is a little glimpse of splendour which they feel all the more keenly because it is so

creatures'; but this would quite fail to give the point of the reproof, for the word *creatura* is constantly applied in affectionate excuse for little children, or to urge their claim on the pity of adults. When a poor widow says in begging, *Tengo tre creature,* she means to insist on their inability to care for themselves in any way, and *Sono creature* is the constant plea of the mother whose children have excited the anger of a grown-up person; pretty much as an Englishwoman might say, 'They are too young to know what they are doing, poor things.' In calling the rats *creature di Dio,* therefore, the old woman wished to insist upon their weakness and their ignorance of right and wrong as a claim upon human pity, quite as much as on the fact of their having been created by God; almost as if she had said, 'Spare the poor helpless innocents who have no protector but Him Who made them.'

different from all the sordid circumstances of their daily life. And they are so safe here, too. Dirty as they are, no one rudely forbids their entrance or will push them from the altar step at which they kneel. For this is no great man's palace, but the house of God and the Madonna, and even these outcast children have a right to a place in it.

And so the mass begins, and Peppiniello remembers a number of trifles, and asks forgiveness for them. He thinks about the daily soldo he conceals from his sister, and has half a mind not to do so any more, though he is by no means sure it is a sin, and he thanks God and the Madonna for having taken care of him so often, but particularly yesterday, and prays them still to be good to him and his sisters and Mariannina, and to the girl who so kindly befriended him yesterday. For the rest of his friends and benefactors he prays in a general way and in the usual form; he does not specially think even of Donna Amalia or Don Antonio (though he would pray for both if they asked him), far less of the English sailors; and when he repeats the petition which he has been taught to use with respect to his enemies, I doubt whether any remembrance of Donna Estere comes into his head. When the elevation of the Host is past, and the time has come to remember the dead, Concetta gently presses his hand, and he prays for the souls of his parents and of Mariannina's mother, and for 'all that rest in Christ.' She remembers their old home better, and thinks oftener about it, than he does, and so she is more moved by this part of the service, which he is sometimes apt to forget.

And all his real sins, his lies and thefts, doesn't he repent of them? I am afraid not. Some time ago he took his sisters to see the miracle of San Gennaro, and, when the liquefaction of the blood was long delayed, did not think of all the other spectators who crowded the church, but concluded that it was some personal sin of his that had offended the saint. So he searched his conscience, and remembered that some time before he had refused an old woman a part of his scanty dinner, even though she had begged for it in the Madonna's name, and that he had spoken harshly to Donna Lucia's mother a few days afterwards ; and he resolved to be gentler and kinder to the aged and infirm in future. Then the miracle was wrought, and hitherto he has kept his resolution. But his lies and thefts he did not remember. Nay, when he next prepares himself for confession, they will probably be the last sins that come into his mind. When the priest insists on their wickedness, the boy will be moved, and he will really repent, and make up his mind to give them up altogether, and for a day or two he will persevere ; but then he will begin to consider the matter from a worldly point of view. The priest was doubtless right in what he said. Peppiniello himself can hardly imagine that a saint ever picked anyone's pocket, but then there is no chance of his ever becoming a saint, and *they* know how hard a poor *mozzonare's* life is, and will not judge him too harshly. In some such way he will probably arrive at the conclusion that perfect honesty is a luxury as far beyond his means as the whelks and periwinkles which are heaped upon the itinerant vendor's tray, and whose dainty odours so often vainly excite his appetite.

But now the mass is over, and Peppiniello and Concetta pass out of the church into the golden morning sunshine and there part, each to begin anew the labours and adventures of the day. And here we must leave them for the present.

AMBROSE BIERCE

1842—1913 (?)

A HORSEMAN IN THE SKY

One sunny afternoon in the autumn of the year 1861, a soldier lay in a clump of laurel by the side of a road in Western Virginia. He lay at full length, upon his stomach, his feet resting upon the toes, his head upon the left forearm. His extended right hand loosely grasped his rifle. But for the somewhat methodical disposition of his limbs and a slight rhythmic movement of the cartridge box at the back of his belt, he might have been thought to be dead. He was asleep at his post of duty. But if detected he would be dead shortly afterward, that being the just and legal penalty of his crime.

The clump of laurel in which the criminal lay was in the angle of a road which, after ascending, southward, a steep acclivity to that point, turned sharply to the west, running along the summit for perhaps one hundred yards. There it turned southward again and went zigzagging downward through the forest. At the salient of that second angle was a large flat rock, jutting out from the ridge to the northward, overlooking the deep valley from which the road ascended. The rock capped a high cliff; a stone dropped from its outer edge would have fallen sheer downward one thousand feet to the tops of the pines. The angle where the soldier lay was on another spur of the same cliff. Had he been awake he would have commanded a view, not only of the short arm of the road and the jutting rock but of the entire profile of the cliff below it. It might well have made him giddy to look.

The country was wooded everywhere except at the bottom of the valley to the northward, where there was a small natural meadow, through which flowed a stream scarcely visible from the valley's rim. This open ground looked hardly larger than an ordinary door-yard, but was really several acres in extent. Its green was more vivid than that of the enclosing forest. Away beyond it rose a line of giant cliffs similar to those upon which we are supposed to stand in our survey of the savage scene, and through which the road had somehow made its climb to the summit. The configuration of the valley, indeed, was such that from our point of observation it seemed entirely shut in, and one could not but have wondered how the road which found a way out of it had found a way into it, and whence came and whither went the waters of the stream that parted the meadow two thousand feet below.

No country is so wild and difficult but men will make it a theatre of war; concealed in the forest at the bottom of that military rat-trap, in which half a hundred men in possession of the exits might have starved an army to submission, lay five regiments of Federal infantry. They had marched all the previous day and night and were resting. At nightfall they would take to the road again, climb to the place where their unfaithful sentinel now slept, and, descending the other slope of the ridge, fall upon a camp of the enemy at about midnight. Their hope was to surprise it, for the road led to the rear of it. In case of failure their position would be perilous in the extreme; and fail they surely would should accident or vigilance apprise the enemy of the movement.

The sleeping sentinel in the clump of laurel was a young Virginian named Carter Druse. He was the son of wealthy parents, an only child, and had known such ease and cultivation and high living as wealth and taste were able to command in the mountain country of Western Virginia. His home was but a few miles from where he now lay. One morning he had risen from the breakfast table and said, quietly and gravely: 'Father, a Union regiment has arrived at Grafton. I am going to join it.'

The father lifted his leonine head, looked at the son a moment in silence, and replied: 'Go, Carter, and, whatever may occur, do what you conceive to be your duty. Virginia, to which you are a traitor, must get on without you. Should we both live to the end of the war, we will speak further of the matter. Your mother, as the physician has informed you, is in a most critical condition; at the best she cannot be with us longer than a few weeks, but that time is precious. It would be better not to disturb her.'

So Carter Druse, bowing reverently to his father, who returned the salute with a stately courtesy which masked a breaking heart, left the home of his childhood to go soldiering. By conscience and courage, by deeds of devotion and daring, he soon commended himself to his fellows and his officers; and it was to these qualities and to some knowledge of the country that he owed his selection for his present perilous duty at the extreme outpost. Nevertheless, fatigue had been stronger than resolution, and he had fallen asleep. What good or bad angel came in a dream to rouse him from his state of crime who shall say? Without a movement, without a sound, in the profound silence and the languor of the late afternoon, some invisible messenger of fate touched with unsealing finger the eyes of his consciousness—whispered into the ear of his spirit the mysterious awakening word which no human lips have ever spoken, no human memory ever has recalled. He quietly raised his forehead from his arm and looked between the masking stems of the laurels, instinctively closing his right hand about the stock of his rifle.

His first feeeling was a keen artistic delight. On a colossal pedestal, the cliff, motionless at the extreme edge of the capping rock and sharply outlined against the sky, was an equestrian statue of impressive dignity. The figure of the man sat the figure of the horse, straight and soldierly, but with the repose of a Grecian god carved in the marble which limits the suggestion of activity. The grey costume harmonized with its aerial background; the metal of accoutrement and caparison was softened and subdued by the shadow; the animal's skin had no points of high light. A carbine, strikingly foreshortened, lay across the pommel of the saddle, kept in place by the right hand grasping it at the 'grip'; the left hand, holding the bridle rein, was invisible. In silhouette against the sky, the profile of the horse was cut with the sharpness of a cameo; it looked across the heights of air to the confronting cliffs beyond. The face of the rider, turned slightly to the left, showed only an outline of temple and beard; he was looking downward to the bottom of the valley. Magnified by its lift against the sky and by the soldier's testifying sense of the formidableness of a near enemy, the group appeared of heroic, almost colossal, size.

For an instant Druse had a strange, half-defined feeling that he had slept to the end of the war and was looking upon a noble work of art reared upon that commanding eminence to commemorate the deeds of an heroic past of which he had been an inglorious part. The feeling was dispelled by a slight movement of the group; the horse, without moving its feet, had drawn its body slightly backward from the verge; the man remained immobile as before. Broad awake and keenly alive to the significance of the situation, Druse now brought the butt of his rifle against his cheek by cautiously pushing the barrel forward through the bushes, cocked the piece, and, glancing through the sights, covered a vital spot of the horseman's breast. A touch upon the trigger and all would have been well with Carter Druse. At that instant the horseman turned his head and looked in the direction of his concealed foeman—seemed to look into his very face, into his eyes, into his brave compassionate heart.

Is it, then, so terrible to kill an enemy in war—an enemy who has surprised a secret vital to the safety of one's self and comrades—an enemy more formidable for his knowledge than all his army for its numbers? Carter Druse grew deathly pale; he shook in every limb, turned faint, and saw the statuesque group before him as black figures, rising, falling, moving unsteadily in arcs of circles in a fiery sky. His hand fell away from his weapon, his head slowly dropped until his face rested on the leaves in which he lay. This courageous gentleman and hardy soldier was near swooning from intensity of emotion.

It was not for long; in another moment his face was raised from earth, his hands resumed their places on the rifle, his forefinger sought the trigger; mind, heart, and eyes were clear, conscience and reason sound. He could not hope to capture that enemy; to alarm him would but send him dashing to his camp with his fatal news. The duty of the soldier was plain: the man must be shot dead from ambush—without warning, without a moment's spiritual preparation, with never so much as an unspoken prayer, he must be sent to his account. But no—there is a hope; he may have discovered nothing—perhaps he is but admiring the sublimity of the landscape. If permitted he may turn and ride carelessly away in the direction whence he came. Surely it will be possible to judge at the instant of his withdrawing whether he knows. It may well be that his fixity of attention—Druse turned his head and looked below, through the deeps of air downward, as from the surface to the bottom of a translucent sea. He saw creeping across the green meadow a sinuous line of figures of men and horses—some foolish commander was permitting the soldiers of his escort to water their beasts in the open, in plain view from a hundred summits!

Druse withdrew his eyes from the valley and fixed them again upon the group of man and horse in the sky, and again it was through the sights of his rifle. But this time his aim was at the horse. In his memory, as if they were a divine mandate, rang the words of his father at their parting. 'Whatever may occur, do what you conceive to be your duty.' He was calm now. His teeth were firmly but not rigidly closed; his nerves were as tranquil as a sleeping babe's—not a tremor affected any muscle of his body; his breathing until suspended in the act of taking aim, was regular and slow. Duty had conquered; the spirit had said to the body: 'Peace, be still.' He fired.

At that moment an officer of the Federal force, who, in a spirit of adventure or in quest of knowledge, had left the hidden bivouac in the valley, and, with aimless feet, had made his way to the lower edge of a small open space near the foot of the cliff, was considering what he had to gain by pushing his exploration further. At a distance of a quarter-mile before him, but apparently at a stone's throw, rose from its fringe of pines the gigantic face of rock, towering to so great a height above him that it made him giddy to look up to where its edge cut a sharp, rugged line against the sky. At some distance away to his right it presented a clean, vertical profile against a background of blue sky to a point half of the way down, and of distant hills hardly less blue thence to the tops of the trees at its base. Lifting his eyes to the dizzy altitude of its summit, the officer saw an astonishing sight—a man on horseback riding down into the valley through the air!

Straight upright sat the rider, in military fashion, with a firm seat in the saddle, a strong clutch upon the rein to hold his charger from too impetuous a plunge. From his bare head his long hair streamed upward, waving like a plume. His right hand was concealed in the cloud of the horse's lifted mane. The animal's body was as level as if every hoof stroke encountered the resistant earth. Its motions were those of a wild gallop, but even as the officer looked they ceased, with all the legs thrown sharply forward as in the act of alighting from a leap. But this was a flight!

Filled with amazement and terror by this apparition of a horseman in the sky—half believing himself the chosen scribe of some new Apocalypse, the officer was overcome by the intensity of his emotions; his legs failed him and he fell. Almost at the same instant he heard a crashing sound in the trees—a sound that died without an echo, and all was still.

The officer rose to his feet, trembling. The familiar sensation of an abraded shin recalled his dazed faculties. Pulling himself together, he ran rapidly obliquely away from the cliff to a point a half-mile from its foot; thereabout he expected to find his man; and thereabout he naturally failed. In the fleeting instant of his vision his imagination had been so wrought upon by the apparent grace and ease and intention of the marvellous performance that it did not occur to him that the line of march of aerial cavalry is directed downward, and that he could find the objects of his search at the very foot of the cliff. A half-hour later he returned to camp.

This officer was a wise man; he knew better than to tell an incredible truth. He said nothing of what he had seen. But when the commander asked him if in his scout he had learned anything of advantage to the expedition, he answered:

'Yes, sir; there is no road leading down into this valley from the southward.'

The commander, knowing better, smiled.

After firing his shot Private Carter Druse reloaded his rifle and resumed his watch. Ten minutes had hardly passed when a Federal sergeant crept cautiously to him on hands and knees. Druse neither turned his head nor looked at him, but lay without motion or sign of recognition.

'Did you fire?' the sergeant whispered.

'Yes.'

'At what?'

'A horse. It was standing on yonder rock—pretty far out. You see it is no longer there. It went over the cliff.'

The man's face was white, but he showed no other sign of emotion. Having answered, he turned away his face and said no more. The sergeant did not understand.

'See here, Druse,' he said, after a moment's silence, 'it's no use making a mystery. I order you to report. Was there anybody on the horse?'

'Yes.'

'Who?'

'My father.'

The sergeant rose to his feet and walked away. 'Good God!' he said.

HENRY JAMES

1843–1916

OWEN WINGRAVE

I

'UPON my honour you must be off your head!' cried Spencer Coyle, as the young man, with a white face, stood there panting a little and repeating 'Really, I've quite decided,' and 'I assure you I've thought it all out.' They were both pale, but Owen Wingrave smiled in a manner exasperating to his interlocutor, who however still discriminated sufficiently to see that his grimace (it was like an irrelevant leer) was the result of extreme and conceivable nervousness.

'It was certainly a mistake to have gone so far; but that is exactly why I feel I mustn't go further,' poor Owen said, waiting mechanically, almost humbly (he wished not to swagger, and indeed he had nothing to swagger about) and carrying through the window to the stupid opposite houses the dry glitter of his eyes.

'I'm unspeakably disgusted. You've made me dreadfully ill,' Mr. Coyle went on, looking thoroughly upset.

'I'm very sorry. It was the fear of the effect on you that kept me from speaking sooner.'

'You should have spoken three months ago. Don't you know your mind from one day to the other?'

The young man for a moment said nothing. Then he replied with a little tremor: 'You're very angry with me, and I expected it. I'm awfully obliged to you for all you've done for me. I'll do anything else for you in return, but I can't do that. Everyone else will let me have it, of course. I'm prepared for it—I'm prepared for everything. That's what has taken the time: to be sure I was prepared. I think it's your displeasure I feel most and regret most. But little by little you'll get over it.'

'*You'll* get over it rather faster, I suppose!' Spencer Coyle satirically exclaimed. He was quite as agitated as his young friend, and they were evidently in no condition to prolong an encounter in which they each drew blood. Mr. Coyle was a professional 'coach'; he prepared young men for the army, taking only three or four at a time, to whom he applied the irresistible stimulus of which the possession was both his secret and his fortune. He had not a great establishment; he would have said himself that it was not a wholesale business. Neither his system, his health, nor his temper could have accommodated itself to numbers; so he weighed and measured his pupils and turned away more applicants than he passed. He was an artist in his line, caring only for picked subjects and capable of sacrifices almost passionate for the individual. He liked ardent young men (there were kinds of capacity to which he was indifferent) and he had taken a particular fancy to Owen Wingrave. This young man's facility really fascinated him. His candidates usually did wonders, and he might have sent up a multitude. He was a person of exactly the stature of the great Napoleon, with a certain flicker of genius in his light blue eye: it had been said of him that he looked like a pianist. The tone of his favourite pupil now expressed, without intention indeed, a superior wisdom which irritated him. He had not especially suffered before from Wingrave's high opinion of himself, which had seemed justified by remarkable parts; but to-day it struck him as intolerable. He cut short the discussion, declining absolutely to regard their relations as terminated, and remarked to his pupil that he had better go off somewhere (down to Eastbourne, say; the sea would bring him round) and take a few days to find his feet and come to his senses. He could afford the time, he was so well up: when Spencer Coyle remembered how well up he was he could have boxed his ears. The tall, athletic young man was not physically a subject for simplified reasoning; but there was a troubled gentleness in his handsome face, the index of compunction mixed with pertinacity, which signified that if it could have done any good he would have turned both cheeks. He evidently didn't pretend that his wisdom was superior; he only presented it as his own. It was his own career after all that was in question. He couldn't refuse to go through the form of trying Eastbourne or at least of holding his tongue, though there was that in his manner which implied that if he should do so it would be really to give Mr. Coyle a chance to recuperate. He didn't feel a bit overworked, but there was nothing more natural than that with their tremendous pressure Mr. Coyle should be. Mr. Coyle's own intellect would derive an advantage from his pupil's holiday. Mr. Coyle saw what he meant, but he controlled himself; he only demanded, as his right, a truce of three days. Owen Wingrave granted it, though as fostering sad illusions this went visibly against his conscience; but before they separated the famous crammer remarked:

'All the same I feel as if I ought to see someone. I think you mentioned to me that your aunt had come to town?'

'Oh yes; she's in Baker Street. Do go and see her,' the boy said comfortingly.

Mr. Coyle looked at him an instant. 'Have you broached this folly to her?'

'Not yet—to no one. I thought it right to speak to you first.'

'Oh, what you "think right"!' cried Spencer

Coyle, outraged by his young friend's standards. He added that he would probably call on Miss Wingrave; after which the recreant youth got out of the house.

Owen Wingrave didn't however start punctually for Eastbourne; he only directed his steps to Kensington Gardens, from which Mr. Coyle's desirable residence (he was terribly expensive and had a big house) was not far removed. The famous coach 'put up' his pupils, and Owen had mentioned to the butler that he would be back to dinner. The spring day was warm to his young blood, and he had a book in his pocket which, when he had passed into the gardens and, after a short stroll, dropped into a chair, he took out with the slow, soft sigh that finally ushers in a pleasure postponed. He stretched his long legs and began to read it; it was a volume of Goethe's poems. He had been for days in a state of the highest tension, and now that the cord had snapped the relief was proportionate; only it was characteristic of him that this deliverance should take the form of an intellectual pleasure. If he had thrown up the probability of a magnificent career it was not to dawdle along Bond Street nor parade his indifference in the window of a club. At any rate he had in a few moments forgotten everything—the tremendous pressure, Mr. Coyle's disappointment, and even his formidable aunt in Baker Street. If these watchers had overtaken him, there would surely have been some excuse for their exasperation. There was no doubt he was perverse, for his very choice of a pastime only showed how he had got up his German.

'What the devil's the matter with him, do *you* know?' Spencer Coyle asked that afternoon of young Lechmere, who had never before observed the head of the establishment to set a fellow such an example of bad language. Young Lechmere was not only Wingrave's fellow-pupil, he was supposed to be his intimate, indeed quite his best friend, and had unconsciously performed for Mr. Coyle the office of making the promise of his great gifts more vivid by contrast. He was short and sturdy and as a general thing uninspired, and Mr. Coyle, who found no amusement in believing in him, had never thought him less exciting than as he stared now out of a face from which you could never guess whether he had caught an idea. Young Lechmere concealed such achievements as if they had been youthful indiscretions. At any rate he could evidently conceive no reason why it should be thought there was anything more than usual the matter with the companion of his studies; so Mr. Coyle had to continue:

'He declines to go up. He chucks the whole thing!'

The first thing that struck young Lechmere in the case was the freshness it had imparted to the governor's vocabulary.

'He doesn't want to go to Sandhurst?'

'He doesn't want to go anywhere. He gives up the army altogether. He objects,' said Mr. Coyle, in a tone that made young Lechmere almost hold his breath, 'to the military profession.'

'Why, it has been the profession of all his family!'

'Their profession? It has been their religion! Do you know Miss Wingrave?'

'Oh, yes. Isn't she awful?' young Lechmere candidly ejaculated.

His instructor demurred.

'She's formidable, if you mean that, and it's right she should be; because somehow in her very person, good maiden lady as she is, she represents the might, she represents the traditions and the exploits of the British army. She represents the expansive property of the English name. I think his family can be trusted to come down on him, but every influence should be set in motion. I want to know what yours is. Can *you* do anything in the matter?'

'I can try a couple of rounds with him,' said young Lechmere reflectively. 'But he knows a fearful lot. He has the most extraordinary ideas.'

'Then he has told you some of them—he has taken you into his confidence?'

'I've heard him jaw by the yard,' smiled the honest youth. 'He has told me he despises it.'

'What *is* it he despises? I can't make out.'

The most consecutive of Mr. Coyle's nurslings considered a moment, as if he were conscious of a responsibility.

'Why, I think, military glory. He says we take the wrong view of it.'

'He oughtn't to talk to *you* that way. It's corrupting the youth of Athens. It's sowing sedition.'

'Oh, I'm all right!' said young Lechmere. 'And he never told me he meant to chuck it. I always thought he meant to see it through, simply because he had to. He'll argue on any side you like. It's a tremendous pity—I'm sure he'd have a big career.'

'Tell him so, then; plead with him; struggle with him—for God's sake.'

'I'll do what I can—I'll tell him it's a regular shame.'

'Yes, strike *that* note—insist on the disgrace of it.'

The young man gave Mr. Coyle a more perceptive glance. 'I'm sure he wouldn't do anything dishonourable'.

'Well—it won't look right. He must be made to feel *that*—work it up. Give him a comrade's point of view—that of a brother-in-arms.'

'That's what I thought we were going to be!' young Lechmere mused romantically, much uplifted by the nature of the mission imposed on him. 'He's an awfully good sort.'

'No one will think so if he backs out!' said Spencer Coyle.

'They mustn't say it to *me*!' his pupil rejoined with a flush.

Mr. Coyle hesitated a moment, noting his tone and aware that in the perversity of things, though this young man was a born soldier, no excitement would ever attach to *his* alternatives save perhaps on the part of the nice girl to whom at an early day he was sure to be placidly united. 'Do you like him very much—do you believe in him?'

Young Lechmere's life in these days was spent in answering terrible questions; but he had never been subjected to so queer an interrogation as this. 'Believe in him? Rather!'

'Then *save* him!'

The poor boy was puzzled, as if it were forced upon him by this intensity that there was more in such an appeal than could appear on the surface; and he doubtless felt that he was only entering into a complex situation when after another moment, with his hands in his pockets, he replied hopefully but not pompously: 'I daresay I can bring him round!'

II

Before seeing young Lechmere Mr. Coyle had determined to telegraph an inquiry to Miss Wingrave. He had prepaid the answer, which, being promptly put into his hand, brought the interview we have just related to a close. He immediately drove off to Baker Street, where the lady had said she awaited him, and five minutes after he got there, as he sat with Owen Wingrave's remarkable aunt, he repeated over several times, in his angry sadness and with the infallibility of his experience: 'He's so intelligent—he's so intelligent!' He had declared it had been a luxury to put such a fellow through.

'Of course he's intelligent, what else could he be?

We've never, that I know of, had but *one* idiot in the family!' said Jane Wingrave. This was an allusion that Mr. Coyle could understand, and it brought home to him another of the reasons for the disappointment, the humiliation, as it were, of the good people at Paramore, at the same time that it gave an example of the conscientious coarseness he had on former occasions observed in his interlocutress. Poor Philip Wingrave, her late brother's eldest son, was literally imbecile and banished from view; deformed, unsocial, irretrievable, he had been relegated to a private asylum and had become among the friends of the family only a little hushed lugubrious legend. All the hopes of the house, picturesque Paramore, now unintermittently old Sir Philip's rather melancholy home (his infirmities would keep him there to the last), were therefore collected on the second boy's head, which nature, as if in compunction for her previous botch, had, in addition to making it strikingly handsome, filled with marked originalities and talents. These two had been the only children of the old man's only son, who, like so many of his ancestors, had given up a gallant young life to the service of his country. Owen Wingrave the elder had received his death-cut, in close-quarters, from an Afghan sabre; the blow had come crashing across his skull. His wife, at that time in India, was about to give birth to her third child; and when the event took place, in darkness and anguish, the baby came lifeless into the world and the mother sank under the multiplication of her woes. The second of the little boys in England, who was at Paramore with his grandfather, became the peculiar charge of his aunt, the only unmarried one, and during the interesting Sunday that, by urgent invitation, Spencer Coyle, busy as he was, had, after consenting to put Owen through, spent under that roof, the celebrated crammer received a vivid impression of the influence exerted at least in intention by

Miss Wingrave. Indeed the picture of this short visit remained with the observant little man a curious one—the vision of an impoverished Jacobean house, shabby and remarkably 'creepy,' but full of character still and full of felicity as a setting for the distinguished figure of the peaceful old soldier. Sir Philip Wingrave, a relic rather than a celebrity, was a small brown, erect octogenarian, with smouldering eyes and a studied courtesy. He liked to do the diminished honours of his house, but even when with a shaky hand he lighted a bedroom candle for a deprecating guest it was impossible not to feel that beneath the surface he was a merciless old warrior. The eye of the imagination could glance back into his crowded Eastern past—back at episodes in which his scrupulous forms would only have made him more terrible.

Mr. Coyle remembered also two other figures—a faded inoffensive Mrs. Julian, domesticated there by a system of frequent visits as the widow of an officer and a particular friend of Miss Wingrave, and a remarkably clever little girl of eighteen, who was this lady's daughter and who struck the speculative visitor as already formed for other relations. She was very impertinent to Owen, and in the course of a long walk that he had taken with the young man and the effect of which, in much talk, had been to clinch his high opinion of him, he had learned (for Owen chattered confidentially) that Mrs. Julian was the sister of a very gallant gentleman, Captain Hume-Walker, of the Artillery, who had fallen in the Indian Mutiny and between whom and Miss Wingrave (it had been that lady's one known concession) a passage of some delicacy, taking a tragic turn, was believed to have been enacted. They had been engaged to be married, but she had given way to the jealousy of her nature—had broken with him and sent him off to his fate, which had been horrible. A passionate sense of having wronged him, a hard eternal remorse had thereupon taken possession of her, and when his poor sister, linked also to a soldier, had by a still heavier blow been left almost without resources, she had devoted herself charitably to a long expiation. She had sought comfort in taking Mrs. Julian to live much of the time at Paramore, where she became an unremunerated though not uncriticized housekeeper, and Spencer Coyle suspected that it was a part of this comfort that she could at her leisure trample on her. The impression of Jane Wingrave was not the faintest he had gathered on that intensifying Sunday—an occasion singularly tinged for him with the sense of bereavement and mourning and memory, of names never mentioned, of the far-away plaint of widows and the echoes of battles and bad news. It was all military indeed, and Mr. Coyle was made to shudder a little at the profession of which he helped to open the door to harmless young men. Miss Wingrave moreover might have made such a bad conscience worse—so cold and clear a good one looked at him out of her hard, fine eyes and trumpeted in her sonorous voice.

She was a high, distinguished person; angular but not awkward, with a large forehead and abundant black hair, arranged like that of a woman conceiving perhaps excusably of her head as 'noble,' and irregularly streaked to-day with white. If however she represented for Spencer Coyle the genius of a military race, it was not that she had the step of a grenadier or the vocabulary of a camp-follower; it was only that such sympathies were vividly implied in the general fact to which her very presence and each of her actions and glances and tones were a constant and direct allusion—the paramount valour of her family. If she was military, it was because she sprang from a military house and because she wouldn't for the world have been anything but what the Wingraves had been. She was almost vulgar about her ancestors and if one had been tempted to quarrel with her, one would have found a fair pretext in her defective sense of proportion. This temptation however said nothing to Spencer Coyle, for whom as a strong character revealing itself in colour and sound she was a spectacle and who was glad to regard her as a force exerted on his own side. He wished her nephew had more of her narrowness instead of being almost cursed with the tendency to look at things in their relations. He wondered why when she came up to town she always resorted to Baker Street for lodgings. He had never known nor heard of Baker Street as a residence—he associated it only with bazaars and photographers. He divined in her a rigid indifference to everything that was not the passion of her life. Nothing really mattered to her but that, and she would have occupied apartments in Whitechapel if they had been a feature in her tactics. She had received her visitor in a large cold, faded room, furnished with slippery seats and decorated with alabaster vases and wax-flowers. The only little personal comfort for which she appeared to have looked out was a fat catalogue of the Army and Navy Stores, which reposed on a vast, desolate table-cover of false blue. Her clear forehead—it was like a porcelain slate, a receptacle for addresses and sums—had flushed when her nephew's crammer told her the extraordinary news; but he saw she was fortunately more angry than frightened. She had essentially, she would always have, too little imagination for fear, and the healthy habit moreover of facing everything had taught her that the occasion usually found her a quantity to reckon with. Mr. Coyle saw that her only fear at present could have been that of not being able to prevent her nephew from being absurd and that to such an apprehension as this she was in fact inaccessible. Practically too she was not troubled by surprise; she recognized none of the futile, none of the subtle sentiments. If Philip had for an hour made a fool of himself she was angry; disconcerted as she would have been on learning that he had confessed to debts or fallen in love with a low girl. But there remained in any annoyance the saving fact that no one could make a fool of *her*.

'I don't know when I've taken such an interest in a young man—I think I never have, since I began to handle them,' Mr. Coyle said. 'I like him, I believe in him—it's been a delight to see how he was going.'

'Oh, I know how they go!' Miss Wingrave threw back her head with a familiar briskness, as if a rapid procession of the generations had flashed before her, rattling their scabbards and spurs. Spencer Coyle recognized the intimation that she had nothing to learn from anybody about the natural carriage of a Wingrave, and he even felt convicted by her next words of being, in her eyes, with the troubled story of his check, his weak complaint of his pupil, rather a poor creature. 'If you like him,' she exclaimed, 'for mercy's sake keep him quiet!'

Mr. Coyle began to explain to her that this was less easy than she appeared to imagine; but he perceived that she understood very little of what he said. The more he insisted that the boy had a kind of intellectual independence, the more this struck her as a conclusive proof that her nephew was a Wingrave and a soldier. It was not till he mentioned to her that Owen had spoken of the profession of arms as of something that would be 'beneath' him, it was not till her attention was arrested by this intenser light on the complexity of the problem that Miss Wingrave broke out after a moment's stupefied reflection: 'Send him to see me immediately!'

'That's exactly what I wanted to ask your leave to do. But I wanted also to prepare you for the worst, to make you understand that he strikes me as really obstinate and to suggest to you that the most powerful arguments at your command—especially if you should be able to put your hand on some intensely practical one—will be none too effective.'

'I think I've got a powerful argument.' Miss Wingrave looked very hard at her visitor. He didn't know in the least what it was, but he begged her to put it forward without delay. He promised that their young man should come to Baker Street that evening, mentioning however that he had already urged him to spend without delay a couple of days at Eastbourne. This led Jane Wingrave to inquire with surprise what virtue there might be in *that* expensive remedy, and to reply with decision when Mr. Coyle had said 'The virtue of a little rest, a little change, a little relief to overwrought nerves,' 'Ah, don't coddle him—he's costing us a great deal of money! I'll talk to him and I'll take him down to Paramore; then I'll send him back to you straightened out.'

Spencer Coyle hailed this pledge superficially with satisfaction, but before he quitted Miss Wingrave he became conscious that he had really taken on a new anxiety—a restlessness that made him say to himself, groaning inwardly: 'Oh, she *is* a grenadier at bottom, and she'll have no tact. I don't know what her powerful argument is; I'm only afraid she'll be stupid and make him worse. The old man's better—*he's* capable of tact, though he's not quite an extinct volcano. Owen will probably put him in a rage. In short the difficulty is that the boy's the best of them.'

Spencer Coyle felt afresh that evening at dinner that the boy was the best of them. Young Wingrave (who, he was pleased to observe, had not yet proceeded to the seaside) appeared at the repast as usual, looking inevitably a little self-conscious, but not too original for Bayswater. He talked very naturally to Mrs. Coyle, who had thought him from the first the most beautiful young man they had ever received; so that the person most ill at ease was poor Lechmere, who took great trouble, as if from the deepest delicacy, not to meet the eye of his misguided mate. Spencer Coyle however paid the penalty of his own profundity in feeling more and more worried; he could so easily see that there were all sorts of things in his young friend that the people of Paramore wouldn't understand. He began even already to react against the notion of his being harassed—to reflect that after all he had a right to his ideas—to remember that he was of a substance too fine to be in fairness roughly used. It was in this way that the ardent little crammer, with his whimsical perceptions and complicated sympathies, was generally condemned not to settle down comfortably either into his displeasures or into his enthusiasms. His love of the real truth never gave him a chance to enjoy them. He mentioned to Wingrave after dinner the propriety of an immediate visit to Baker Street, and the young man, looking 'queer,' as he thought—that is smiling again with the exaggerated glory he had shown in their recent interview—went off to face the ordeal. Spencer Coyle noted that he was scared—he was afraid of his aunt; but somehow this didn't strike him as a sign of pusillanimity. *He* should have been scared, he was well aware, in the poor boy's place, and the sight of his pupil marching up to the battery in spite of his terrors was a positive suggestion of the temperament of the soldier. Many a plucky youth would have shirked this particular peril.

'He *has* got ideas!' young Lechmere broke out to his instructor after his comrade had quitted the house. He was evidently bewildered and agitated—he had an emotion to work off. He had before dinner gone straight at his friend, as Mr. Coyle had requested, and had elicited from him that his scruples were founded on an overwhelming conviction of the stupidity—the 'crass barbarism' he called it—of war. His great complaint was that people hadn't invented anything cleverer, and he was determined to show, the only way he could, that *he* wasn't such an ass.

'And he thinks all the great generals ought to have been shot, and that Napoleon Bonaparte in particular, the greatest, was a criminal, a monster for whom language has no adequate name!' Mr. Coyle rejoined, completing young Lechmere's picture. 'He favoured you, I see, with exactly the same pearls of wisdom that he produced for me. But I want to know what *you* said.'

'I said they were awful rot!' Young Lechmere spoke with emphasis, and he was slightly surprised to hear Mr. Coyle laugh incongruously at this just declaration and then after a moment continue:

'It's all very curious—I daresay there's something in it. But it's a pity!'

'He told me when it was that the question began to strike him in that light. Four or five years ago, when he did a lot of reading about all the great swells and their campaigns—Hannibal and Julius Cæsar, Marlborough and Frederick and Bonaparte. He *has* done a lot of reading, and he says it opened his eyes. He says that a wave of disgust rolled over him. He talked about the "immeasurable misery" of wars, and asked me why nations don't tear to pieces the governments, the rulers that go in for them. He hates poor old Bonaparte worst of all.'

'Well, poor old Bonaparte *was* a brute. He was a frightful ruffian, Mr. Coyle unexpectedly declared. 'But I suppose you didn't admit that.'

'Oh, I daresay he was objectionable, and I'm very glad we laid him on his back. But the point I made to Wingrave was that his own behaviour would excite no end of remark.' Young Lechmere hesitated an instant, then he added: 'I told him he must be prepared for the worst.'

'Of course he asked you what you meant by the "worst,"' said Spencer Coyle.

'Yes, he asked me that, and do you know what I said? I said people would say that his conscientious scruples and his wave of disgust are only a pretext. Then he asked "A pretext for what?"'

'Ah, he rather had you there!' Mr. Coyle exclaimed with a little laugh that was mystifying to his pupil.

'Not a bit—for I told him.'

'What did you tell him?'

Once more, for a few seconds, with his conscious eyes in his instructor's, the young man hung fire.

'Why, what we spoke of a few hours ago. The appearance he'd present of not having——' The honest youth faltered a moment, then brought it out: 'The military temperament, don't you know? But do you know what he said to that?' young Lechmere went on.

'Damn the military temperament!' the crammer promptly replied.

Young Lechmere stared. Mr. Coyle's tone left him uncertain if he were attributing the phrase to Wingrave or uttering his own opinion, but he exclaimed:

'Those were exactly his words!'

'He doesn't care,' said Mr. Coyle.

'Perhaps not. But it isn't fair for him to abuse *us* fellows. I told him it's the finest temperament in the world, and that there's nothing so splendid as pluck and heroism.'

'Ah! there you had *him*.'

'I told him it was unworthy of him to abuse a gallant, a magnificent profession. I told him there's no type so fine as that of the soldier doing his duty.'

'That's essentially *your* type, my dear boy.' Young Lechmere blushed; he couldn't make out (and the danger was naturally unexpected to him) whether at that moment he didn't exist mainly for the recreation of his friend. But he was partly reassured by the genial way this friend continued, laying a hand on his shoulder: 'Keep *at* him that way! we may do something. I'm extremely obliged to you.' Another doubt however remained unassuaged—a doubt which led him to exclaim to Mr. Coyle before they dropped the painful subject:

'He *doesn't* care! But it's awfully odd he shouldn't!'

'So it is, but remember what you said this afternoon—I mean about your not advising people to make insinuations to *you.*'

'I believe I should knock a fellow down!' said young Lechmere. Mr. Coyle had got up; the conversation had taken place while they sat together after Mrs. Coyle's withdrawal from the dinner-table and the head of the establishment administered to his disciple, on principles that were a part of his thoroughness, a glass of excellent claret. The disciple, also on his feet, lingered an instant, not for another 'go,' as he would have called it, at the decanter, but to wipe his microscopic moustache with prolonged and unusual care. His companion saw he had something to bring out which required a final effort, and waited for him an instant with a hand on the knob of the door. Then as young Lechmere approached him, Spencer Coyle grew conscious of an unwonted intensity in the round and ingenuous face. The boy was nervous, but he tried to behave like a man of the world. 'Of course, it's between ourselves,' he stammered, 'and I wouldn't breathe such a word to any one who wasn't interested in poor Wingrave as you are. But do you think he funks it?'

Mr. Coyle looked at him so hard for an instant that he was visibly frightened at what he had said.

'Funks it! Funks what?'

'Why, what we're talking about—the service.' Young Lechmere gave a little gulp and added with a *naïveté* almost pathetic to Spencer Coyle: 'The dangers, you know!'

'Do you mean he's thinking of his skin?'

Young Lechmere's eyes expanded appealingly, and what his instructor saw in his pink face—he even thought he saw a tear—was the dread of a disappointment shocking in the degree in which the loyalty of admiration had been great.

'Is he—is he *afraid* ?' repeated the honest lad, with a quaver of suspense.

'Dear no!' said Spencer Coyle, turning his back.

Young Lechmere felt a little snubbed and even a little ashamed; but he felt still more relieved.

III

Less than a week after this Spencer Coyle received a note from Miss Wingrave, who had immediately quitted London with her nephew. She proposed that he should come down to Paramore for the following Sunday—Owen was really so tiresome. On the spot, in that house of examples and memories and in combination with her poor dear father, who was 'dreadfully annoyed,' it might be worth their while to make a last stand. Mr. Coyle read between the lines of this letter that the party at Paramore had got over a good deal of ground since Miss Wingrave, in Baker Street, had treated his despair as superficial. She was not an insinuating woman, but she went so far as to put the question on the ground of his conferring a particular favour on an afflicted family; and she expressed the pleasure it would give them if he should be accompanied by Mrs. Coyle, for whom she inclosed a separate invitation. She mentioned that she was also writing, subject to Mr. Coyle's approval, to young Lechmere. She thought such a nice manly boy might do her wretched nephew some good. The celebrated crammer determined to embrace this opportunity; and now it was the case not so much that he was angry as that he was anxious. As he directed his answer to Miss Wingrave's letter he caught himself smiling at the thought that at bottom he was going to defend his young friend rather than to attack him. He said to his wife, who was a fair, fresh, slow woman—a person of much more presence than himself—that she had better take Miss Wingrave at her word: it was such an extraordinary, such a fascinating specimen of an old English home. This last allusion was amicably sarcastic—he had already accused the good lady more than once of being in love with Owen Wingrave. She admitted that she was, she even gloried in her passion; which shows that the subject, between them, was treated in a liberal spirit. She carried out the joke by accepting the invitation with eagerness. Young Lechmere was delighted to do the same; his instructor had good-naturedly taken the view that the little break would freshen him up for his last spurt.

It was the fact that the occupants of Paramore did indeed take their trouble hard that struck Spencer Coyle after he had been an hour or two in that fine old house. This very short second visit, beginning on the Saturday evening, was to constitute the strangest episode of his life. As soon as he found himself in private with his wife—they had retired to dress for dinner—they called each other's attention with effusion and almost with alarm to the sinister gloom that was stamped on the place. The house was admirable with its old grey front which came forward in wings so as to form three sides of a square, but Mrs. Coyle made no scruple to declare that if she had known in advance the sort of impression she was going to receive she would never have put her foot in it. She characterized it as 'uncanny,' she accused her husband of not having warned her properly. He had mentioned to her in advance certain facts, but while she almost feverishly dressed she had innumerable questions to ask. He hadn't told her about the girl, the extraordinary girl, Miss Julian—that is, he hadn't told her that this young lady, who in plain terms was a mere dependent, would be in effect, and as a consequence of the way she carried herself, the most important person in the house. Mrs. Coyle was already prepared to announce that she hated Miss Julian's affectations. Her husband, above all, hadn't told her that they should find their young charge looking five years older.

'I couldn't imagine that,' said Mr. Coyle, 'nor that the character of the crisis here would be quite so perceptible. But I suggested to Miss Wingrave the other day that they should press her nephew in real earnest, and she has taken me at my word. They've cut off his supplies—they're trying to starve him out. That's not what I meant—but indeed I don't quite *know* to-day what I meant. Owen feels the pressure, but he won't yield.' The strange thing was that, now that he was there, the versatile little coach felt still more that his own spirit had been caught up by a wave of reaction. If he was there it was because he was on poor Owen's side. His whole impression, his whole apprehension, had on the spot become much deeper. There was something in the dear boy's very resistance that began to charm him. When his wife, in the intimacy of the conference I have mentioned, threw off the mask and commended even with extravagance the stand his pupil had taken (he was too good to be a horrid soldier and it was noble of him to suffer for his convictions—wasn't he as upright as a young hero, even though as pale as a Christian martyr?) the good lady only expressed the sympathy which, under cover of regarding his young friend as a rare exception, he had already recognized in his own soul.

For, half an hour ago, after they had had superficial tea in the brown old hall of the house, his young friend had proposed to him, before going to dress, to take a turn outside, and had even, on the terrace, as they walked together to one of the far ends of it, passed his hand entreatingly into his companion's arm, permitting himself thus a familiarity unusual between pupil and master and calculated to show that he had guessed whom he could most depend on to be kind to him. Spencer Coyle, on his own side, had guessed something, so that he was not surprised at the boy's having a particular confidence to make. He had felt on arriving that each member of the party had wished to get hold of him first, and he knew that at that moment Jane Wingrave was peering through the ancient blur of one of the windows (the house had been modernized so little that the thick dim panes were three centuries old) to see if her nephew looked as if he were poisoning the visitor's mind. Mr. Coyle lost no time therefore in reminding the youth (and he took care to laugh as he did so) that he had not come down to Paramore to be corrupted. He had come down to make, face to face, a last appeal to him—he hoped it wouldn't be utterly vain. Owen smiled sadly as they went, asking him if he thought he had the general air of a fellow who was going to knock under.

'I think you look strange—I think you look ill,' Spencer Coyle said very honestly. They had paused at the end of the terrace.

'I've had to exercise a great power of resistance, and it rather takes it out of one.'

'Ah, my dear boy, I wish your great power—for you evidently possess it—were exerted in a better cause!'

Owen Wingrave smiled down at his small instructor. 'I don't believe that!' Then he added, to explain why: 'Isn't what you want, if you're so good as to think well of my character, to see me exert *most* power, in whatever direction? Well, *this* is the way I exert most.' Owen Wingrave went on to relate that he had had some terrible hours with his grandfather, who had denounced him in a way to make one's hair stand up on one's head. He had expected them not to like it, not a bit, but he had had no idea they would make such a row. His aunt was different, but she was equally insulting. Oh, they had made him feel they were ashamed of him; they accused him of putting a public dishonour on their name. He was the only one who had ever backed out—he was the first for three hundred years. Every one had known he was to go up, and now every one would know he was a young hypocrite who suddenly pretended to have scruples. They talked of his scruples as you wouldn't talk of a cannibal's god. His grandfather had called him outrageous names. 'He called me—he called me——' Here the young man faltered, his voice failed him. He looked as haggard as was possible to a young man in such magnificent health.

'I probably know!' said Spencer Coyle, with a nervous laugh.

Owen Wingrave's clouded eyes, as if they were following the far-off consequences of things, rested for an instant on a distant object. Then they met his companion's and for another moment sounded them deeply. 'It isn't true. No, it isn't. It's not *that*!'

'I don't suppose it is! But what *do* you propose instead of it?'

'Instead of what?'

'Instead of the stupid solution of war. If you take that away you should suggest at least a substitute.'

'That's for the people in charge, for governments and cabinets,' said Owen Wingrave. '*They*'ll arrive soon enough at a substitute, in the particular case, if they're made to understand that they'll be hung if they don't find one. Make it a capital crime—that'll quicken the wits of ministers!' His eyes brightened as he spoke, and he looked assured and exalted. Mr. Coyle gave a sigh of perplexed resignation—it was a monomania. He fancied after this for a moment that Owen was going to ask him if he too thought he was a coward; but he was relieved to observe that he either didn't suspect him of it or shrank uncomfortably from putting the question to the test. Spencer Coyle wished to show confidence, but somehow a direct assurance that he didn't doubt of his courage appeared too gross a compliment—it would be like saying he didn't doubt of his honesty. The difficulty was presently averted by Owen's continuing: 'My grandfather can't break the entail, but I shall have nothing but this place, which, as you know, is small and, with the way rents are going, has quite ceased to yield an income. He has some money—not much, but such as it is he cuts me off. My aunt does the same—she has let me know her intentions. She was to have left me her six hundred a year. It was all settled; but now what's settled is that I don't get a penny of it if I give up the army. I must add in fairness that I have from my mother three hundred a year of my own. And I tell you the simple truth when I say that I don't care a rap for the loss of the money.' The young man drew a long, slow breath, like a creature in pain; then he subjoined: '*That's* not what worries me!'

'What are you going to do?' asked Spencer Coyle.

'I don't know; perhaps nothing. Nothing great, at all events. Only something peaceful!'

Owen gave a weary smile, as if, worried as he was, he could yet appreciate the humorous effect of such a declaration from a Wingrave; but what it suggested to his companion, who looked up at him with a sense that he was after all not a Wingrave for nothing and had a military steadiness under fire, was the exasperation that such a programme, uttered in such a way and striking them as the last word of the inglorious, might well have engendered on the part of his grandfather and his aunt. 'Perhaps nothing'—when he might carry on the great tradition! Yes, he wasn't weak, and he was interesting; but there *was* a point of view from which he was provoking. 'What *is* it then that worries you?' Mr. Coyle demanded.

'Oh, the house—the very air and feeling of it. There are strange voices in it that seem to mutter at me—to say dreadful things as I pass. I mean the general consciousness and responsibility of what I'm doing. Of course it hasn't been easy for me—not a bit. I assure you I don't enjoy it.' With a light in them that was like a longing for justice Owen again bent his eyes on those of the little coach; then he pursued: 'I've started up all the old ghosts. The very portraits glower at me on the walls. There's one of my great-great-grandfather (the one the extraordinary story you know is about—the old fellow who hangs on the second landing of the big staircase) that fairly stirs on the canvas—just heaves a little—when I come near it. I have to go up and down stairs—it's rather awkward! It's what my aunt calls the family circle. It's all constituted here, it's a kind of indestructible presence, it stretches away into the past, and when I came back with her the other day Miss Wingrave told me I wouldn't have the impudence to stand in the midst of it and say such things. I *had* to say them to my grandfather; but now that I've said them it seems to me that the question's ended. I want to go away—I don't care if I never come back again.'

'Oh, you *are* a soldier; you must fight it out!' Mr. Coyle laughed.

The young man seemed discouraged at his levity, but as they turned round, strolling back in the direction from which they had come, he himself smiled faintly after an instant and replied:

'Ah, we're tainted—all!'

They walked in silence part of the way to the old portico; then Spencer Coyle, stopping short after having assured himself that he was at a sufficient distance from the house not to be heard, suddenly put the question: 'What does Miss Julian say?'

'Miss Julian?' Owen had perceptibly coloured.

'I'm sure *she* hasn't concealed her opinion.'

'Oh, it's the opinion of the family-circle, for she's a member of it, of course. And then she has her own as well.'

'Her own opinion?'

'Her own family-circle.'

'Do you mean her mother—that patient lady?'

'I mean more particularly her father, who fell in battle. And her grandfather, and *his* father, and her uncles and great-uncles—they all fell in battle.'

'Hasn't the sacrifice of so many lives been sufficient? Why should she sacrifice *you*?'

'Oh, she *hates* me!' Owen declared, as they resumed their walk.

'Ah, the hatred of pretty girls for fine young men!' exclaimed Spencer Coyle.

He didn't believe in it, but his wife did, it appeared, perfectly, when he mentioned this conversation while, in the fashion that has been described, the visitors dressed for dinner. Mrs. Coyle had already discovered that nothing could have been nastier than Miss Julian's manner to the disgraced youth during the half-hour the party had spent in the hall; and it was this lady's judgement that one must have had no eyes in one's head not to see that she was already trying outrageously to flirt with young Lechmere. It was a pity they had brought that silly boy: he was down in the hall with her at that moment. Spencer Coyle's version was different; he thought there were finer elements involved. The girl's footing in the house was inexplicable on any ground save that of her being predestined to Miss Wingrave's nephew. As the niece of Miss Wingrave's own unhappy intended she had been dedicated early by this lady to the office of healing by a union with Owen the tragic breach that had separated their elders; and if in reply to this it was to be said that a girl of spirit couldn't enjoy in such a matter having her duty cut out for her, Owen's enlightened friend was ready with the argument that a young person in Miss Julian's position would never be such a fool as really to quarrel with a capital chance. She was familiar at Paramore and she felt safe; therefore she might trust herself to the amusement of pretending that she had her option. But it was all innocent coquetry. She had a curious charm, and it was vain to pretend that the heir of that house wouldn't seem good enough to a girl, clever as she might be, of eighteen. Mrs. Coyle reminded her husband that the poor young man was precisely now *not* of that house: this problem was among the questions that exercised their wits after the two men had taken the turn on the terrace. Spencer Coyle told his wife that Owen was afraid of the portrait of his great-great-grandfather. He would show it to her, since she hadn't noticed it, on their way downstairs.

'Why of his great-great-grandfather more than of any of the others?'

'Oh, because he's the most formidable. He's the one who's sometimes seen.'

'Seen where?' Mrs. Coyle had turned round with a jerk.

'In the room he was found dead in—the White Room they've always called it.'

'Do you mean to say the house has a *ghost*?' Mrs. Coyle almost shrieked. 'You brought me here without telling me?'

'Didn't I mention it after my other visit?'

'Not a word. You only talked about Miss Wingrave.'

'Oh, I was full of the story—you have simply forgotten.'

'Then you should have reminded me!'

'If I had thought of it I would have held my peace, for you wouldn't have come.'

'I wish, indeed, I hadn't!' cried Mrs. Coyle. 'What *is* the story?'

'Oh, a deed of violence that took place here ages ago. I think it was in George the First's time. Colonel Wingrave, one of their ancestors, struck in a fit of passion one of his children, a lad just growing up, a blow on the head of which the unhappy child died. The matter was hushed up for the hour—some other explanation was put about. The poor boy was laid out in one of those rooms on the other side of the house, and amid strange smothered rumours the funeral was hurried on. The next morning, when the household assembled, Colonel Wingrave was missing; he was looked for vainly, and at last it occurred to some one that he might perhaps be in the room from which his child had been carried to burial. The seeker knocked without an answer—then opened the door. Colonel Wingrave lay dead on the floor, in his clothes, as if he had reeled and fallen back, without a wound, without a mark, without anything in his appearance to indicate that he had either struggled or suffered. He was a strong, sound man—there was nothing to account for such a catastrophe. He is supposed to have gone to the room during the night, just before going to bed, in some fit of compunction or some fascination of dread. It was only after this that the truth about the boy came out. But no one ever sleeps in the room.'

Mrs. Coyle had fairly turned pale. 'I hope not! Thank heaven they haven't put *us* there!'

'We're at a comfortable distance; but I've seen the gruesome chamber.'

'Do you mean you've been *in* it?'

'For a few moments. They're rather proud of it and my young friend showed it to me when I was here before.'

Mrs. Coyle stared. 'And what is it like?'

'Simply like an empty, dull, old-fashioned bedroom, rather big, with the things of the "period" in it. It's panelled from floor to ceiling, and the panels evidently, years and years ago, were painted white. But the paint has darkened with time and there are three or four quaint little ancient "samplers," framed and glazed, hung on the walls.'

Mrs. Coyle looked round with a shudder. 'I'm glad there are no samplers here! I never heard anything so jumpy! Come down to dinner.'

On the staircase as they went down her husband showed her the portrait of Colonel Wingrave—rather a vigorous representation, for the place and period, of a gentleman with a hard, handsome face, in a red coat and a peruke. Mrs. Coyle declared that his descendant Sir Philip was wonderfully like him; and her husband could fancy, though he kept it to himself, that if one should have the courage to walk about the old corridors of Paramore at night one might meet a figure that resembled him roaming, with the restlessness of a ghost, hand in hand with the figure of a tall boy. As he proceeded to the drawing-room with his wife he found himself suddenly wishing that he had made more of a point of his pupil's going to Eastbourne. The evening however seemed to have taken upon itself to dissipate any such whimsical forebodings, for the grimness of the family-circle, as Spencer Coyle had preconceived its composition, was mitigated by an infusion of the 'neighbourhood.' The company at dinner was recruited by two cheerful couples—one of them the vicar and his wife—and by a silent young man who had come down to fish. This was a relief to Mr. Coyle, who had begun to wonder what was after all expected of him and why he had been such a fool as to come, and who now felt that for the first hours at least the situation would not have directly to be dealt with. Indeed he found, as he had found before, sufficient occupation for his ingenuity in reading the various symptoms of which the picture before him was an expression. He should probably have an irritating day on the morrow: he foresaw the difficulty of the long decorous Sunday and how dry Jane Wingrave's ideas, elicited in a strenuous conference, would taste. She and her father would make him feel that they depended upon him for the impossible, and if they should try to associate him with a merely stupid policy he might end by telling them what he thought of it—an accident not required to make his visit a sensible mistake. The old man's actual design was evidently to let their friends see in it a positive mark of their being all right. The presence of the great London coach was tantamount to a profession of faith in the results of the impending examination. It had clearly been obtained from Owen, rather to Spencer Coyle's surprise, that he would do nothing to interfere with the apparent harmony. He let the allusions to his hard work pass, and, holding his tongue about his affairs, talked to the ladies as amicably as if he had not been 'cut off.' When Spencer Coyle looked at him once or twice across the table, catching his eye, which showed an indefinable passion, he saw a puzzling pathos in his laughing face: one couldn't resist a pang for a young lamb so visibly marked for sacrifice. 'Hang him—what a pity he's such a fighter!' he privately sighed, with a want of logic that was only superficial.

This idea however would have absorbed him more if so much of his attention had not been given to Kate Julian, who, now that he had her well before him, struck him as a remarkable and even as a possibly fascinating young woman. The fascination resided not in any extraordinary prettiness, for if she was handsome, with her long Eastern eyes, her magnificent hair and her general unabashed originality, he had seen complexions rosier and features that pleased him more: it resided in a strange impression that she gave of being exactly the sort of person whom, in her position, common considerations, those of prudence and perhaps even a little those of decorum, would have enjoined on her not to be. She was what was vulgarly termed a dependent—penniless, patronized, tolerated; but something in her aspect and manner signified that if her situation was inferior, her spirit, to make up for it, was above precautions or submissions. It was not in the least that she was aggressive, she was too indifferent for that; it was only as if, having nothing either to gain or to lose, she could afford to do as she liked. It occurred to Spencer Coyle that she might really have had more at stake than her imagination appeared to take account of; whatever it was at any rate he had never seen a young woman at less pains to be on the safe side. He wondered inevitably how the peace was kept between Jane Wingrave and such an inmate as this; but those questions of course were unfathomable deeps. Perhaps Kate Julian lorded it even over her protectress. The other time he was at Paramore he had received an impression that, with Sir Philip beside her, the girl could fight with her back to the wall. She amused Sir Philip, she charmed him, and he liked people who weren't afraid; between him and his daughter moreover there was no doubt which was the higher in command. Miss Wingrave took many things for granted, and most of all the rigour of discipline and the fate of the vanquished and the captive.

But between their clever boy and so original a companion of his childhood what odd relation would have grown up? It couldn't be indifference, and yet on the part of happy, handsome, youthful creatures it was still less likely to be aversion. They weren't Paul and Virginia, but they must have had their common summer and their idyll: no nice girl could have disliked such a nice fellow for anything but not liking *her*, and no nice fellow could have resisted such propinquity. Mr. Coyle remembered indeed that Mrs. Julian had spoken to him as if the propinquity had been by no means constant, owing to her daughter's absences at school, to say nothing of Owen's; her visits to a few friends who were so kind as to 'take her' from time to time; her sojourns in London—so difficult to manage, but still managed by God's help—for 'advantages,' for drawing and singing, especially drawing or rather painting, in oils, in which she had had immense success. But the good lady had also mentioned that the young people were quite brother and sister, which *was* a little, after all, like Paul and Virginia. Mrs. Coyle had been right, and it was apparent that Virginia was doing her best to make the time pass agreeably for young Lechmere. There was no such whirl of conversation as to render it an effort for Mr. Coyle to reflect on these things, for the tone of the occasion, thanks principally to the other guests, was not disposed to stray—it tended to the repetition of anecdote and the discussion of rents, topics that huddled together like uneasy animals. He could judge how intensely his hosts wished the evening to pass off as if nothing had happened; and this gave him the measure of their private resentment. Before dinner was over he found himself fidgety about his second pupil. Young Lechmere, since he began to cram, had done all that might have been expected of him; but this couldn't blind his instructor to a present perception of his being in moments of relaxation as innocent as a babe. Mr. Coyle had considered that the amusements of Paramore would probably give him a fillip, and the poor fellow's manner testified to the soundness of the forecast. The fillip had been unmistakably administered; it had come in the form of a revelation. The light on young Lechmere's brow announced with a candour that was almost an appeal for compassion, or at least a deprecation of ridicule, that he had never seen anything like Miss Julian.

IV

In the drawing-room after dinner the girl found an occasion to approach Spencer Coyle. She stood before him a moment, smiling while she opened and shut her fan, and then she said abruptly, raising her strange eyes: 'I know what you've come for, but it isn't any use.'

'I've come to look after *you* a little. Isn't *that* any use?'

'It's very kind. But I'm not the question of the hour. You won't do anything with Owen.'

Spencer Coyle hesitated a moment. 'What will *you* do with his young friend?'

She stared, looked round her.

'Mr. Lechmere? Oh, poor little lad! We've been talking about Owen. He admires him so.'

'So do I. I should tell you that.'

'So do we all. That's why we're in such despair.'

'Personally then you'd *like* him to be a soldier?' Spencer Coyle inquired.

'I've quite set my heart on it. I adore the army and I'm awfully fond of my old playmate,' said Miss Julian.

Her interlocutor remembered the young man's own different version of her attitude; but he judged it loyal not to challenge the girl.

'It's not conceivable that your own playmate shouldn't be fond of you. He must therefore wish to please you; and I don't see why—between you—you don't set the matter right.'

'Wish to please me!' Miss Julian exclaimed. 'I'm sorry to say he shows no such desire. He thinks me an impudent wretch. I've told him what I think of *him*, and he simply hates me.'

'But you think so highly! You just told me you admire him.'

'His talents, his possibilities, yes; even his appearance, if I may allude to such a matter. But I don't admire his present behaviour.'

'Have you had the question out with him?' Spencer Coyle asked.

'Oh, yes, I've ventured to be frank—the occasion seemed to excuse it. He couldn't like what I said.'

'What did you say?'

Miss Julian, thinking a moment, opened and shut her fan again.

'Why, that such conduct isn't that of a gentleman!'

After she had spoken her eyes met Spencer Coyle's, who looked into their charming depths.

'Do you want then so much to send him off to be killed?'

'How odd for *you* to ask that—in such a way!' she replied with a laugh. 'I don't understand your position: I thought your line was to *make* soldiers!'

'You should take my little joke. But, as regards Owen Wingrave, there's no "making" needed,' Mr. Coyle added. 'To my sense'—the little crammer paused a moment, as if with a consciousness of responsibility for his paradox—'to my sense he *is*, in a high sense of the term, a fighting man.'

'Ah, let him prove it!' the girl exclaimed, turning away.

Spencer Coyle let her go; there was something in her tone that annoyed and even a little shocked him. There had evidently been a violent passage between these young people, and the reflection that such a matter was after all none of his business only made him more sore. It was indeed a military house, and she was at any rate a person who placed her ideal of manhood (young persons doubtless always had their ideals of manhood) in the type of the belted warrior. It was a taste like another; but, even a quarter of an hour later, finding himself near young Lechmere, in whom this type was embodied, Spencer Coyle was still so ruffled that he addressed the innocent lad with a certain magisterial dryness. 'You're not to sit up late, you know. That's not what I brought you down for.' The dinner-guests were taking leave and the bedroom candles twinkled in a monitory row. Young Lechmere however was too agreeably agitated to be accessible to a snub: he had a happy preoccupation which almost engendered a grin.

'I'm only too eager for bedtime. Do you know there's an awfully jolly room?'

'Surely they haven't put you there?'

'No indeed: no one has passed a night in it for ages. But that's exactly what I want to do—it would be tremendous fun.'

'And have you been trying to get Miss Julian's permission?'

'Oh, *she* can't give leave, she says. But she believes in it, and she maintains that no man dare.'

'No man *shall!* A man in your critical position in particular must have a quiet night,' said Spencer Coyle.

Young Lechmere gave a disappointed but reasonable sigh.

'Oh, all right. But mayn't I sit up for a little go at Wingrave? I haven't had any yet.'

Mr. Coyle looked at his watch.

'You may smoke *one* cigarette.'

He felt a hand on his shoulder, and he turned round to see his wife tilting candle-grease upon his coat. The ladies were going to bed and it was Sir Philip's inveterate hour; but Mrs. Coyle confided to her husband that after the dreadful things he had told her she positively declined to be left alone, for no matter how short an interval, in any part of the house. He promised to follow her in three minutes, and after the orthodox handshakes the ladies rustled away. The forms were kept up at Paramore as bravely as if the old house had no present heartache. The only one of which Spencer Coyle noticed the omission was some salutation to himself from Kate Julian. She gave him neither a word nor a glance, but he saw her look hard at Owen Wingrave. Her mother, timid and pitying, was apparently the only person from whom this young man caught an inclination of the head. Miss Wingrave marshalled the three ladies—her little procession of twinkling tapers—up the wide oaken stairs and past the watching portrait of her ill-fated ancestor. Sir Philip's servant appeared and offered his arm to the old man, who turned a perpendicular back on poor Owen when the boy made a vague movement to anticipate this office. Spencer Coyle learned afterwards that before Owen had forfeited favour it had always, when he was at home, been his privilege at bedtime to conduct his grandfather ceremoniously to rest. Sir Philip's habits were contemptuously different now. His apartments were on the lower floor, and he shuffled stiffly off to them with his valet's help, after fixing for a moment significantly on the most responsible of his visitors the thick red ray, like the glow of stirred embers, that always made his eyes conflict oddly with his mild manners. They seemed to say to Spencer Coyle, 'We'll let the young scoundrel have it to-morrow!' One might have gathered from them that the young scoundrel, who had now strode to the other end of the hall, had at least forged a cheque. Mr. Coyle watched him an instant, saw him drop nervously into a chair and then with a restless movement get up. The same movement brought him back to where his late instructor stood addressing a last injunction to young Lechmere.

'I'm going to bed and I should like you particularly to conform to what I said to you a short time ago.

Smoke a single cigarette with your friend here and then go to your room. You'll have me down on you if I hear of your having, during the night, tried any preposterous games.' Young Lechmere, looking down with his hands in his pockets, said nothing—he only poked at the corner of a rug with his toe; so that Spencer Coyle, dissatisfied with so tacit a pledge, presently went on, to Owen: 'I must request you, Wingrave, not to keep this sensitive subject sitting up—and indeed to put him to bed and turn his key in the door.' As Owen stared an instant, apparently not understanding the motive of so much solicitude, he added: 'Lechmere has a morbid curiosity about one of your legends—of your historic rooms. Nip it in the bud.'

'Oh, the legend's rather good, but I'm afraid the room's an awful sell!' Owen laughed.

'You know you don't *believe* that, my boy!' young Lechmere exclaimed.

'I don't think he does,' said Mr. Coyle, noticing Owen's mottled flush.

'He wouldn't try a night there himself!' young Lechmere pursued.

'I know who told you that,' rejoined Owen, lighting a cigarette in an embarrassed way at the candle, without offering one to either of his companions.

'Well, what if she did?' asked the younger of these gentlemen, rather red. 'Do you want them *all* yourself?' he continued facetiously, fumbling in the cigarette box.

Owen Wingrave only smoked quietly; then he exclaimed:

'Yes—what if she did? But she doesn't know,' he added.

'She doesn't know what?'

'She doesn't know anything!—I'll tuck him in!' Owen went on gaily to Mr. Coyle, who saw that his presence, now that a certain note had been struck, made the young men uncomfortable. He was curious, but there was a kind of discretion, with his pupils, that he had always pretended to practise; a discretion that however didn't prevent him as he took his way upstairs from recommending them not to be donkeys.

At the top of the staircase, to his surprise, he met Miss Julian, who was apparently going down again. She had not begun to undress, nor was she perceptibly disconcerted at seeing him. She nevertheless in a manner slightly at variance with the rigour with which she had overlooked him ten minutes before, dropped the words: 'I'm going down to look for something. I've lost a jewel.'

'A jewel?'

'A rather good turquoise, out of my locket. As it's the only ornament I have the honour to possess——!' And she passed down.

'Shall I go with you and help you?' asked Spencer Coyle.

The girl paused a few steps below him, looking back with her Oriental eyes.

'Don't I hear voices in the hall?'

'Those remarkable young men are there.'

'*They'll* help me.' And Kate Julian descended. Spencer Coyle was tempted to follow her, but remembering his standard of tact he rejoined his wife in their apartment. He delayed however to go to bed, and though he went into his dressing-room, he couldn't bring himself even to take off his coat. He pretended for half an hour to read a novel; after which, quietly, or perhaps I should say agitatedly, he passed from the dressing-room into the corridor. He followed this passage to the door of the room which he knew to have been assigned to young Lechmere and was comforted to see that it was closed. Half an hour earlier he had seen it standing open; therefore he could take for granted that the bewildered boy had come to bed. It was of this he had wished to assure himself, and having done so he was on the point of retreating. But at the same instant he heard a sound in the room—the occupant was doing, at the window, something which showed him that he might knock without the reproach of waking his pupil up. Young Lechmere came in fact to the door in his shirt and trousers. He admitted his visitor in some surprise, and when the door was closed again Spencer Coyle said:

'I don't want to make your life a burden to you, but I had it on my conscience to see for myself that you're not exposed to undue excitement.'

'Oh, there's plenty of that!' said the ingenuous youth. 'Miss Julian came down again.'

'To look for a turquoise?'

'So she said.'

'Did she find it?'

'I don't know. I came up. I left her with poor Wingrave.'

'Quite the right thing,' said Spencer Coyle.

'I don't know,' young Lechmere repeated uneasily. 'I left them quarrelling.'

'What about?'

'I don't understand. They're a quaint pair!'

Spencer Coyle hesitated. He had, fundamentally, principles and scruples, but what he had in particular just now was a curiosity, or rather, to recognize it for what it was, a sympathy, which brushed them away.

'Does it strike you that *she's* down on him?' he permitted himself to inquire.

'Rather!—when she tells him he lies!'

'What do you mean?'

'Why, before *me*. It made me leave them; it was getting too hot. I stupidly brought up the question of the haunted room again, and said how sorry I was that I had had to promise you not to try my luck with it.'

'You can't pry about in that gross way in other

people's houses—you can't take such liberties, you know!' Mr Coyle interjected.

'I'm all right—see how good I am. I don't want to go *near* the place!' said young Lechmere, confidingly. 'Miss Julian said to me "Oh, I daresay *you'd* risk it, but"—and she turned and laughed at poor Owen—"that's more than we can expect of a gentleman who has taken *his* extraordinary line." I could see that something had already passed between them on the subject—some teasing or challenging of hers. It may have been only chaff, but his chucking the profession had evidently brought up the question of his pluck.'

'And what did Owen say?'

'Nothing at first; but presently he brought out very quietly: "I spent all last night in the confounded place." We both stared and cried out at this and I asked him what he had seen there. He said he had seen nothing, and Miss Julian replied that he ought to tell his story better than that—he ought to make something good of it. "It's not a story—it's a simple fact," said he; on which she jeered at him and wanted to know why, if he had done it, he hadn't told her in the morning, since he knew what she thought of him. "I know, but I don't care," said Wingrave. This made her angry, and she asked him quite seriously whether he would care if he should know she believed him to be trying to deceive us.'

'Ah, what a brute!' cried Spencer Coyle.

'She's a most extraordinary girl—I don't know what she's up to.'

'Extraordinary indeed—to be romping and bandying words at that hour of the night with fast young men!'

Young Lechmere reflected a moment. 'I mean because I think she likes him.'

Spencer Coyle was so struck with this unwonted symptom of subtlety that he flashed out: 'And do you think he likes *her*?'

But his interlocutor only replied with a puzzled sigh and a plaintive 'I don't know—I give it up!—I'm sure he *did* see something or hear something,' young Lechmere added.

'In that ridiculous place? What makes you sure?'

'I don't know—he looks as if he had. He behaves as if he had.'

'Why then shouldn't he mention it?'

Young Lechmere thought a moment. 'Perhaps it's too gruesome!'

Spencer Coyle gave a laugh. 'Aren't you glad then *you're* not in it?'

'Uncommonly!'

'Go to bed, you goose,' said Spencer Coyle, with another laugh. 'But before you go tell me what he said when she told him he was trying to deceive you.'

'"Take me there yourself, then, and lock me in!"'

'And *did* she take him?'

'I don't know—I came up.'

Spencer Coyle exchanged a long look with his pupil.

'I don't think they're in the hall now. Where's Owen's own room?'

'I haven't the least idea.'

Mr. Coyle was perplexed; he was in equal ignorance, and he couldn't go about trying doors. He bade young Lechmere sink to slumber, and came out into the passage. He asked himself if he should be able to find his way to the room Owen had formerly shown him, remembering that in common with many of the others it had its ancient name painted upon it. But the corridors of Paramore were intricate; moreover some of the servants would still be up, and he didn't wish to have the appearance of roaming over the house. He went back to his own quarters, where Mrs. Coyle soon perceived that his inability to rest had not subsided. As she confessed for her own part, in the dreadful place, to an increased sense of 'creepiness,' they spent the early part of the night in conversation, so that a portion of their vigil was inevitably beguiled by her husband's account of his colloquy with little Lechmere and by their exchange of opinions upon it. Toward two o'clock Mrs. Coyle became so nervous about their persecuted young friend, and so possessed by the fear that that wicked girl had availed herself of his invitation to put him to an abominable test, that she begged her husband to go and look into the matter at whatever cost to his own equilibrium. But Spencer Coyle, perversely, had ended, as the perfect stillness of the night settled upon them, by charming himself into a tremulous acquiescence in Owen's readiness to face a formidable ordeal—an ordeal the more formidable to an excited imagination as the poor boy now knew from the experience of the previous night how resolute an effort he should have to make. 'I hope he *is* there,' he said to his wife: 'it puts them all so in the wrong!' At any rate he couldn't take upon himself to explore a house he knew so little. He was inconsequent—he didn't prepare for bed. He sat in the dressing-room with his light and his novel, waiting to find himself nodding. At last however Mrs. Coyle turned over and ceased to talk, and at last he too fell asleep in his chair. How long he slept he only knew afterwards by computation; what he knew to begin with was that he had started up, in confusion, with the sense of a sudden appalling sound. His sense cleared itself quickly, helped doubtless by a confirmatory cry of horror from his wife's room. But he gave no heed to his wife; he had already bounded into the passage. There the sound was repeated—it was the 'Help! help!' of a woman in agonized terror. It came from a distant quarter of the house, but the quarter was sufficiently indicated.

Spencer Coyle rushed straight before him, with the sound of opening doors and alarmed voices in his ears and the faintness of the early dawn in his eyes. At a turn of one of the passages he came upon the white figure of a girl in a swoon on a bench, and in the vividness of the revelation he read as he went that Kate Julian, stricken in her pride too late with a chill of compunction for what she had mockingly done, had, after coming to release the victim of her derision, reeled away, overwhelmed, from the catastrophe that was her work—the catastrophe that the next moment he found himself aghast at on the threshold of an open door. Owen Wingrave, dressed as he had last seen him, lay dead on the spot on which his ancestor had been found. He looked like a young soldier on a battle-field.

FOUR MEETINGS

I SAW her only four times, but I remember them vividly; she made an impression upon me. I thought her very pretty and very interesting—a charming specimen of a type. I am very sorry to hear of her death; and yet, when I think of it, why should I be sorry? The last time I saw her she was certainly not—— But I will describe all our meetings in order.

I

The first one took place in the country, at a little tea-party, one snowy night. It must have been some seventeen years ago. My friend Latouche, going to spend Christmas with his mother, had persuaded me to go with him, and the good lady had given in our honour the entertainment of which I speak. To me it was really entertaining; I had never been in the depths of New England at that season. It had been snowing all day and the drifts were knee-high. I wondered how the ladies had made their way to the house; but I perceived that at Grimwinter a conversazione offering the attraction of two gentlemen from New York was felt to be worth an effort.

Mrs. Latouche in the course of the evening asked me if I 'didn't want to' show the photographs to some of the young ladies. The photographs were in a couple of great portfolios, and had been brought home by her son, who, like myself, was lately returned from Europe. I looked round and was struck with the fact that most of the young ladies were provided with an object of interest more absorbing than the most vivid sun-picture. But there was a person standing alone near the mantel-shelf, and looking round the room with a small, gentle smile which seemed at odds, somehow, with her isolation. I looked at her a moment, and then said, 'I should like to show them to that young lady.'

'Oh yes,' said Mrs. Latouche, 'she is just the person. She doesn't care for flirting; I will speak to her.'

I rejoined that if she did not care for flirting, she was, perhaps, not just the person; but Mrs. Latouche had already gone to propose the photographs to her.

'She's delighted,' she said, coming back. 'She is just the person, so quiet and so bright.' And then she told me the young lady was, by name, Miss Caroline Spencer, and with this she introduced me.

Miss Caroline Spencer was not exactly a beauty, but she was a charming little figure. She must have been close upon thirty, but she was made almost like a little girl, and she had the complexion of a child. She had a very pretty head, and her hair was arranged as nearly as possible like the hair of a Greek bust, though indeed it was to be doubted if she had ever seen a Greek bust. She was 'artistic,' I suspected, so far as Grimwinter allowed such tendencies. She had a soft, surprised eye, and thin lips, with very pretty teeth. Round her neck she wore what ladies call, I believe, a 'ruche,' fastened with a very small pin in pink coral, and in her hand she carried a fan made of plaited straw and adorned with pink ribbon. She wore a scanty black silk dress. She spoke with a kind of soft precision, showing her white teeth between her narrow but tender-looking lips, and she seemed extremely pleased, even a little fluttered, at the prospect of my demonstrations. These went forward very smoothly, after I had moved the portfolios out of their corner and placed a couple of chairs near a lamp. The photographs were usually things I knew—large views of Switzerland, Italy, and Spain, landscapes, copies of famous buildings, pictures and statues. I said what I could about them, and my companion, looking at them as I held them up, sat perfectly still, with her straw fan raised to her underlip. Occasionally, as I laid one of the pictures down, she said very softly, 'Have you seen that place?' I usually answered that I had seen it several times (I had been a great traveller), and then I felt that she looked at me askance for a moment with her pretty eyes. I had asked her at the outset whether she had been to Europe; to this she answered, 'No, no, no,' in a little quick, confidential whisper. But after that, though she never took her eyes off the pictures, she said so little that I was afraid she was bored. Accordingly, after we had finished one portfolio, I offered, if she desired it, to desist. I felt that she was not bored, but her reticence puzzled me and I wished to make her speak. I turned round to look at her, and saw that there was a faint flush in each of her cheeks. She was waving her little fan to and fro. Instead of looking at me she fixed her eyes upon the other portfolio, which was leaning against the table.

'Won't you show me that?' she asked, with a little tremor in her voice. I could almost have believed she was agitated.

'With pleasure,' I answered, 'if you are not tired.'

'No, I am not tired,' she affirmed. 'I like it—I love it.'

And as I took up the other portfolio she laid her hand upon it, rubbing it softly.

'And have you been here too?' she asked.

On my opening the portfolio it appeared that I had been there. One of the first photographs was a large view of the Castle of Chillon, on the Lake of Geneva.

'Here,' I said, 'I have been many a time. Is it not beautiful?' And I pointed to the perfect reflection of the rugged rocks and pointed towers in the clear, still water. She did not say, 'Oh, enchanting!' and push it away to see the next picture. She looked awhile, and then she asked if it was not where Bonivard, about whom Byron wrote, was confined. I assented, and tried to quote some of Byron's verses, but in this attempt I succeeded imperfectly.

She fanned herself a moment and then repeated the lines correctly, in a soft, flat, and yet agreeable voice. By the time she had finished, she was blushing. I complimented her and told her she was perfectly equipped for visiting Switzerland and Italy. She looked at me askance again, to see whether I was serious, and I added, that if she wished to recognize Byron's descriptions she must go abroad speedily; Europe was getting sadly dis-Byronised.

'How soon must I go?' she asked.

'Oh, I will give you ten years.'

'I think I can go within ten years,' she answered very soberly.

'Well,' I said, 'you will enjoy it immensely; you will find it very charming.' And just then I came upon a photograph of some nook in a foreign city which I had been very fond of, and which recalled tender memories. I discoursed (as I suppose) with a certain eloquence; my companion sat listening, breathless.

'Have you been *very* long in foreign lands?' she asked, some time after I had ceased.

'Many years,' I said.

'And have you travelled everywhere?'

'I have travelled a great deal. I am very fond of it; and, happily, I have been able.'

Again she gave me her sidelong gaze. 'And do you know the foreign languages?'

'After a fashion.'

'Is it hard to speak them?'

'I don't believe you would find it hard,' I gallantly responded.

'Oh, I shouldn't want to speak—I should only want to listen,' she said. Then, after a pause, she added—'They say the French theatre is so beautiful.'

'It is the best in the world.'

'Did you go there very often?'

'When I was first in Paris I went every night.'

'Every night!' And she opened her clear eyes very wide. 'That to me is—' and she hesitated a moment—'is very wonderful.' A few minutes later she asked—'Which country do you prefer?'

'There is one country I prefer to all others. I think you would do the same.'

She looked at me a moment, and then she said softly—'Italy?'

'Italy,' I answered softly, too; and for a moment we looked at each other. She looked as pretty as if, instead of showing her photographs, I had been making love to her. To increase the analogy, she glanced away, blushing. There was a silence, which she broke at last by saying—

'That is the place, which—in particular—I thought of going to.'

'Oh, that's the place—that's the place!' I said.

She looked at two or three photographs in silence. 'They say it is not so dear.'

'As some other countries? Yes, that is not the least of its charms.'

'But it is all very dear, is it not?'

'Europe, you mean?'

'Going there and travelling. That has been the trouble. I have very little money. I give lessons,' said Miss Spencer.

'Of course one must have money,' I said, 'but one can manage with a moderate amount.'

'I think I should manage. I have laid something by, and I am always adding a little to it. It's all for that.' She paused a moment, and then went on with a kind of suppressed eagerness, as if telling me the story were a rare, but a possibly impure, satisfaction. 'But it has not been only the money; it has been everything. Everything has been against it. I have waited and waited. It has been a mere castle in the air. I am almost afraid to talk about it. Two or three times it has been a little nearer, and then I have talked about it and it has melted away. I have talked about it too much,' she said, hypocritically; for I saw that such talking was now a small tremulous ecstasy. 'There is a lady who is a great friend of mine; she doesn't want to go; I always talk to her about it. I tire her dreadfully. She told me once she didn't know what would become of me. I should go crazy if I did not go to Europe, and I should certainly go crazy if I did.'

'Well,' I said, 'you have not gone yet and nevertheless you are not crazy.'

She looked at me a moment, and said—'I'm not so sure. I don't think of anything else. I am always thinking of it. It prevents me from thinking of things that are nearer home—things that I ought to attend to That is a kind of craziness.'

'The cure for it is to go,' I said.

'I have a faith that I shall go. I have a cousin in Europe!' she announced.

We turned over some more photographs, and I asked her if she had always lived at Grimwinter.

'Oh, no, sir,' said Miss Spencer. 'I have spent twenty-three months in Boston.'

I answered, jocosely, that in that case foreign lands would probably prove a disappointment to her; but I quite failed to alarm her.

'I know more about them than you might think,' she said, with her shy, neat little smile. 'I mean by reading; I have read a great deal. I have not only read Byron; I have read histories and guide-books. I know I shall like it!'

'I understand your case,' I rejoined. 'You have the native American passion—the passion for the picturesque. With us, I think, it is primordial—antecedent to experience. Experience comes and only shows us something we have dreamt of.'

'I think that is very true,' said Caroline Spencer. 'I have dreamt of everything; I shall know it all!'

'I am afraid you have wasted a great deal of time.'

'Oh yes, that has been my great wickedness.'

The people about us had begun to scatter; they were taking their leave. She got up and put out her hand to me, timidly, but with a peculiar brightness in her eyes.

'I am going back there,' I said, as I shook hands with her. 'I shall look out for you.'

'I will tell you,' she answered, 'if I am disappointed.'

And she went away, looking delicately agitated and moving her little straw fan.

II

A few months after this I returned to Europe, and some three years elapsed. I had been living in Paris, and, toward the end of October, I went from that city to Havre, to meet my sister and her husband, who had written me that they were about to arrive there. On reaching Havre I found that the steamer was already in; I was nearly two hours late. I repaired directly to the hotel, where my relatives were already established. My sister had gone to bed, exhausted and disabled by her voyage; she was a sadly incompetent sailor, and her sufferings on this occasion had been extreme. She wished, for the moment, for undisturbed rest, and was unable to see me more than five minutes; so it was agreed that we should remain at Havre until the next day. My brother-in-law, who was anxious about his wife, was unwilling to leave her room; but she insisted upon his going out with me to take a walk and recover his land-legs. The early autumn day was warm and charming, and our stroll through the bright-coloured, busy streets of the old French sea-port was sufficiently entertaining. We walked along the sunny, noisy quays and then turned into a wide, pleasant street which lay half in sun and half in shade—a French provincial street, that looked like an old water-colour drawing: tall, grey, steep-roofed, red-gabled, many-storied houses; green shutters on windows and old scroll-work above them; flower-pots in balconies and white-capped women in door-ways. We walked in the shade; all this stretched away on the sunny side of the street and made a picture. We looked at it as we passed along; then, suddenly, my brother-in-law stopped—pressing my arm and staring. I followed his gaze and saw that we had paused just before coming to a café, where, under an awning, several tables and chairs were disposed upon the pavement. The windows were open behind; half-a-dozen plants in tubs were ranged beside the door; the pavement was besprinkled with clean bran. It was a nice little, quiet, old-fashioned café; inside, in the comparative dusk, I saw a stout, handsome woman, with pink ribbons in her cap, perched up with a mirror behind her back, smiling at some one who was out of sight. All this, however, I perceived afterwards; what I first observed was a lady sitting alone, outside, at one of the little marble-topped tables. My brother-in-law had stopped to look at her. There was something on the little table, but she was leaning back quietly, with her hands folded, looking down the street, away from us. I saw her only in something less than profile; nevertheless, I instantly felt that I had seen her before.

'The little lady of the steamer!' exclaimed my brother-in-law.

'Was she on your steamer?' I asked.

'From morning till night. She was never sick. She used to sit perpetually at the side of the vessel with her hands crossed that way, looking at the eastward-horizon.'

'Are you going to speak to her?'

'I don't know her. I never made acquaintance with her. I was too seedy. But I used to watch her and—I don't know why—to be interested in her. She's a dear little Yankee woman. I have an idea she is a school-mistress taking a holiday—for which her scholars have made up a purse.'

She turned her face a little more into profile, looking at the steep, grey house-fronts opposite to her. Then I said—'I shall speak to her myself.'

'I wouldn't; she is very shy,' said my brother-in-law.

'My dear fellow, I know her. I once showed her photographs at a tea-party.'

And I went up to her. She turned and looked at me, and I saw she was in fact Miss Caroline Spencer. But she was not so quick to recognize me; she looked startled. I pushed a chair to the table and sat down.

'Well,' I said, 'I hope you are not disappointed!'

She stared, blushing a little; then she gave a small jump which betrayed recognition.

'It was you who showed me the photographs—at Grimwinter!'

'Yes, it was I. This happens very charmingly, for I feel as if it were for me to give you a formal reception here—an official welcome. I talked to you so much about Europe.'

'You didn't say too much. I am so happy!' she softly exclaimed.

Very happy she looked. There was no sign of her being older; she was as gravely, decently, demurely pretty as before. If she had seemed before a thin-stemmed, mild-hued flower of Puritanism, it may be imagined whether in her present situation this delicate bloom was less apparent. Beside her an old gentleman was drinking absinthe; behind her the *dame de comptoir* in the pink ribbons was calling 'Alcibiade! Alcibiade!' to the long-aproned waiter. I explained to Miss Spencer that my companion had lately been her ship-mate, and my brother-in-law came up and was introduced to her. But she looked at him as if she had never seen him before, and I remembered that he had told me that her eyes were always fixed upon the eastward horizon. She had evidently not noticed him, and, still timidly smiling, she made no attempt whatever to pretend that she had. I stayed with her at the café door, and he went back to the hotel and to his wife. I said to Miss Spencer that this meeting of ours in the first hour of her landing was really very strange, but that I was delighted to be there and receive her first impressions.

'Oh, I can't tell you,' she said; 'I feel as if I were in a dream. I have been sitting here for an hour, and I don't want to move. Everything is so picturesque. I don't know whether the coffee has intoxicated me; it's so delicious.'

'Really,' said I, 'if you are so pleased with this poor prosaic Havre, you will have no admiration left for better things. Don't spend all your admiration the first day; remember it's your intellectual letter of credit. Remember all the beautiful places and things that are waiting for you; remember that lovely Italy!'

'I'm not afraid of running short,' she said gaily, still looking at the opposite houses. 'I could sit here all day, saying to myself that here I am at last. It's so dark, and old, and different.'

'By the way,' I inquired, 'how come you to be sitting here? Have you not gone to one of the inns?' For I was half amused, half alarmed at the good conscience with which this delicately pretty woman had stationed herself in conspicuous isolation on the edge of the side-walk.

'My cousin brought me here,' she answered. 'You know I told you I had a cousin in Europe. He met me at the steamer this morning.'

'It was hardly worth his while to meet you if he was to desert you so soon.'

'Oh, he has only left me for half an hour,' said Miss Spencer. 'He has gone to get my money.'

'Where is your money?'

She gave a little laugh. 'It makes me feel very fine to tell you! It is in some circular notes.'

'And where are your circular notes?'

'In my cousin's pocket.'

This statement was very serenely uttered, but—I can hardly say why—it gave me a sensible chill. At the moment I should have been utterly unable to give the reason of this sensation, for I knew nothing of Miss Spencer's cousin. Since he was her cousin, the presumption was in his favour. But I felt suddenly uncomfortable at the thought that, half an hour after her landing, her scanty funds should have passed into his hands.

'Is he to travel with you?' I asked.

'Only as far as Paris. He is an art-student in Paris. I wrote to him that I was coming, but I never expected him to come off to the ship. I supposed he would only just meet me at the train in Paris. It is very kind of him. But he *is* very kind—and very bright.'

I instantly became conscious of an extreme curiosity to see this bright cousin who was an art-student.

'He is gone to the banker's?' I asked.

'Yes, to the banker's. He took me to an hotel—such a queer, quaint, delicious little place, with a court in the middle, and a gallery all round, and a lovely landlady, in such a beautifully fluted cap, and such a perfectly fitting dress! After a while we came out to walk to the banker's, for I haven't got any French money. But I was very dizzy from the motion of the vessel, and I thought I had better sit down. He found this place for me here, and he went off to the banker's himself. I am to wait here till he comes back.'

It may seem very fantastic, but it passed through my mind that he would never come back. I settled myself in my chair beside Miss Spencer and determined to await the event. She was extremely observant; there was something touching in it. She noticed everything that the movement of the street brought before us—the peculiarities of costume, the shapes of vehicles, the big Norman horses, the fat priests, the shaven poodles. We talked of these things, and there was something charming in her freshness of perception and the way her book-nourished fancy recognized and welcomed everything.

'And when your cousin comes back what are you going to do?' I asked.

She hesitated a moment. 'We don't quite know.'

'When do you go to Paris? If you go by the four o'clock train I may have the pleasure of making the journey with you.'

'I don't think we shall do that. My cousin thinks I had better stay here a few days.'

'Oh!' said I; and for five minutes said nothing

more. I was wondering what her cousin was, in vulgar parlance, 'up to.' I looked up and down the street, but saw nothing that looked like a bright American art-student. At last I took the liberty of observing that Havre was hardly a place to choose as one of the æsthetic stations of a European tour. It was a place of convenience, nothing more; a place of transit, through which transit should be rapid. I recommended her to go to Paris by the afternoon train, and meanwhile to amuse herself by driving to the ancient fortress at the mouth of the harbour—that picturesque, circular structure which bore the name of Francis the First and looked like a small castle of St. Angelo. (It has lately been demolished.)

She listened with much interest; then for a moment she looked grave.

'My cousin told me that when he returned he should have something particular to say to me, and that we could do nothing or decide nothing until I should have heard it. But I will make him tell me quickly, and then we will go to the ancient fortress. There is no hurry to get to Paris; there is plenty of time.'

She smiled with her softly severe little lips as she spoke those last words. But I, looking at her with a purpose, saw just a tiny gleam of apprehension in her eye.

'Don't tell me,' I said, 'that this wretched man is going to give you bad news!'

'I suspect it is a little bad, but I don't believe it is very bad. At any rate, I must listen to it.'

I looked at her again an instant. 'You didn't come to Europe to listen,' I said. 'You came to see!' But now I was sure her cousin would come back; since he had something disagreeable to say to her, he certainly would turn up. We sat a while longer, and I asked her about her plans of travel. She had them on her fingers' ends, and she told over the names with a kind of solemn distinctness: from Paris to Dijon and to Avignon, from Avignon to Marseilles and the Cornice road; thence to Genoa, to Spezia, to Pisa, to Florence, to Rome. It apparently had never occurred to her that there could be the least incommodity in her travelling alone; and since she was unprovided with a companion I of course scrupulously abstained from disturbing her sense of security.

At last her cousin came back. I saw him turn towards us out of a side-street, and from the moment my eyes rested upon him I felt that this was the bright American art-student. He wore a slouch hat and a rusty black velvet jacket, such as I had often encountered in the Rue Bonaparte. His shirt-collar revealed a large section of a throat which, at a distance, was not strikingly statuesque. He was tall and lean; he had red hair and freckles. So much I had time to observe while he approached the café, staring at me with natural surprise from under his umbrageous coiffure. When he came up to us I immediately introduced myself to him as an old acquaintance of Miss Spencer. He looked at me hard with a pair of little red eyes, then he made me a solemn bow in the French fashion, with his sombrero.

'You were not on the ship?' he said.

'No, I was not on the ship. I have been in Europe these three years.'

He bowed once more, solemnly, and motioned me to be seated again. I sat down, but it was only for the purpose of observing him an instant—I saw it was time I should return to my sister. Miss Spencer's cousin was a queer fellow. Nature had not shaped him for a Raphaelesque or Byronic attire, and his velvet doublet and naked throat were not in harmony with his facial attributes. His hair was cropped close to his head; his ears were large and ill-adjusted to the same. He had a lackadaisical carriage and a sentimental droop which were peculiarly at variance with his keen, strange-coloured eyes. Perhaps I was prejudiced, but I thought his eyes treacherous. He said nothing for some time; he leaned his hands on his cane and looked up and down the street. Then at last, slowly lifting his cane and pointing with it, 'That's a very nice bit,' he remarked, softly. He had his head on one side, and his little eyes were half closed. I followed the direction of his stick; the object it indicated was a red cloth hung out of an old window. 'Nice bit of colour,' he continued; and without moving his head he transferred his half-closed gaze to me. 'Composes well,' he pursued. 'Make a nice thing.' He spoke in a hard, vulgar voice.

'I see you have a great deal of eye,' I replied. 'Your cousin tells me you are studying art.' He looked at me in the same way without answering, and I went on with deliberate urbanity—'I suppose you are at the studio of one of those great men.'

Still he looked at me, and then he said softly—'Gérôme.'

'Do you like it?' I asked.

'Do you understand French?' he said.

'Some kinds,' I answered.

He kept his little eyes on me; then he said—'J'adore la peinture!'

'Oh, I understand that kind!' I rejoined. Miss Spencer laid her hand upon her cousin's arm with a little pleased and fluttered movement; it was delightful to be among people who were on such easy terms with foreign tongues. I got up to take leave, and asked Miss Spencer where, in Paris, I might have the honour of waiting upon her. To what hotel would she go?

She turned to her cousin inquiringly and he honoured me again with his little languid leer. 'Do you know the Hôtel des Princes?'

'I know where it is.'

'I shall take her there.'

'I congratulate you,' I said to Caroline Spencer. 'I believe it is the best inn in the world; and in case I should still have a moment to call upon you here, where are you lodged?'

'Oh, it's such a pretty name,' said Miss Spencer, gleefully. 'À la Belle Normande.'

As I left them her cousin gave me a great flourish with his picturesque hat.

III

My sister, as it proved, was not sufficiently restored to leave Havre by the afternoon train; so that, as the autumn dusk began to fall, I found myself at liberty to call at the sign of the Fair Norman. I must confess that I had spent much of the interval in wondering what the disagreeable thing was that my charming friend's disagreeable cousin had been telling her. The 'Belle Normande' was a modest inn in a shady by-street, where it gave me satisfaction to think Miss Spencer must have encountered local colour in abundance. There was a crooked little court, where much of the hospitality of the house was carried on; there was a staircase climbing to bedrooms on the outer side of the wall; there was a small trickling fountain with a stucco statuette in the midst of it; there was a little boy in a white cap and apron cleaning copper vessels at a conspicuous kitchen door; there was a chattering landlady, neatly laced, arranging apricots and grapes into an artistic pyramid upon a pink plate. I looked about, and on a green bench outside of an open door labelled *Salle à Manger*, I perceived Caroline Spencer. No sooner had I looked at her than I saw that something had happened since the morning. She was leaning back on her bench, her hands were clasped in her lap, and her eyes were fixed upon the landlady, at the other side of the court, manipulating her apricots.

But I saw she was not thinking of apricots. She was staring absently, thoughtfully; as I came near her I perceived that she had been crying. I sat down on the bench beside her before she saw me; then, when she had done so, she simply turned round, without surprise, and rested her sad eyes upon me. Something very bad indeed had happened; she was completely changed.

I immediately charged her with it. 'Your cousin has been giving you bad news; you are in great distress.'

For a moment she said nothing, and I supposed that she was afraid to speak, lest her tears should come back. But presently I perceived that in the short time that had elapsed since my leaving her in the morning she had shed them all, and that she was now softly stoical—intensely composed.

'My poor cousin is in distress,' she said at last. 'His news was bad.' Then, after a brief hesitation— 'He was in terrible want of money.'

'In want of yours, you mean?'

'Of any that he could get—honestly. Mine was the only money.'

'And he has taken yours?'

She hesitated again a moment, but her glance, meanwhile, was pleading. 'I gave him what I had.'

I have always remembered the accent of those words as the most angelic bit of human utterance I had ever listened to; but then, almost with a sense of personal outrage, I jumped up. 'Good heavens!' I said, 'do you call that getting it honestly?'

I had gone too far; she blushed deeply. 'We will not speak of it,' she said.

'We *must* speak of it,' I answered, sitting down again. 'I am your friend; it seems to me you need one. What is the matter with your cousin?'

'He is in debt.'

'No doubt! But what is the special fitness of your paying his debts?'

'He has told me all his story; I am very sorry for him.'

'So am I! But I hope he will give you back your money.'

'Certainly he will; as soon as he can.'

'When will that be?'

'When he has finished his great picture.'

'My dear young lady, confound his great picture! Where is this desperate cousin?'

She certainly hesitated now. Then—'At his dinner,' she answered.

I turned about and looked through the open door into the *salle à manger*. There, alone at the end of a long table, I perceived the object of Miss Spencer's compassion—the bright young art-student. He was dining too attentively to notice me at first; but in the act of setting down a well-emptied wine-glass he caught sight of my observant attitude. He paused in his repast, and, with his head on one side and his meagre jaws slowly moving, fixedly returned my gaze. Then the landlady came lightly brushing by with her pyramid of apricots.

'And that nice little plate of fruit is for him?' I exclaimed.

Miss Spencer glanced at it tenderly. 'They do that so prettily!' she murmured.

I felt helpless and irritated. 'Come now, really,' I said; 'do you approve of that long strong fellow accepting your funds?' She looked away from me; I was evidently giving her pain. The case was hopeless; the long strong fellow had 'interested' her.

'Excuse me if I speak of him so unceremoniously,' I said. 'But you are really too generous, and he is not quite delicate enough. He made his debts himself—he ought to pay them himself.'

'He has been foolish,' she answered; 'I know that. He has told me everything. We had a long talk this morning; the poor fellow threw himself upon my charity. He has signed notes to a large amount.'

'The more fool he!'

'He is in extreme distress; and it is not only himself. It is his poor wife.'

'Ah, he has a poor wife?'

'I didn't know it—but he confessed everything. He married two years since, secretly.'

'Why secretly?'

Caroline Spencer glanced about her, as if she feared listeners. Then softly, in a little impressive tone—'She was a Countess!'

'Are you very sure of that?'

'She has written me a most beautiful letter.'

'Asking you for money, eh?'

'Asking me for confidence and sympathy,' said Miss Spencer. 'She has been disinherited by her father. My cousin told me the story and she tells it in her own way, in the letter. It is like an old romance. Her father opposed the marriage, and when he discovered that she had secretly disobeyed him he cruelly cast her off. It is really most romantic. They are the oldest family in Provence.'

I looked and listened, in wonder. It really seemed that the poor woman was enjoying the 'romance' of having a discarded Countess-cousin, out of Provence, so deeply as almost to lose the sense of what the forfeiture of her money meant for her.

'My dear young lady,' I said, 'you don't want to be ruined for picturesqueness' sake?'

'I shall not be ruined. I shall come back before long to stay with them. The Countess insists upon that.'

'Come back! You are going home, then?'

She sat for a moment with her eyes lowered, then with an heroic suppression of a faint tremor of the voice—'I have no money for travelling!' she answered.

'You gave it *all* up?'

'I have kept enough to take me home.'

I gave an angry groan, and at this juncture Miss Spencer's cousin, the fortunate possessor of her sacred savings and of the hand of the Provençal Countess, emerged from the little dining-room. He stood on the threshold for an instant, removing the stone from a plump apricot which he had brought away from the table; then he put the apricot into his mouth, and while he let it sojourn there, gratefully, stood looking at us, with his long legs apart and his hands dropped into the pockets of his velvet jacket. My companion got up, giving him a thin glance which I caught in its passage, and which expressed a strange commixture of resignation and fascination—a sort of perverted exaltation. Ugly, vulgar, pretentious, dishonest as I thought the creature, he had appealed successfully to her eager and tender imagination. I was deeply disgusted, but I had no warrant to interfere, and at any rate I felt that it would be vain.

The young man waved his hand with a pictorial gesture. 'Nice old court,' he observed. 'Nice mellow old place. Good tone in that brick. Nice crooked old stair-case.'

Decidedly, I couldn't stand it; without responding I gave my hand to Caroline Spencer. She looked at me an instant with her little white face and expanded eyes, and as she showed her pretty teeth I suppose she meant to smile.

'Don't be sorry for me,' she said; 'I am very sure I shall see something of this dear old Europe yet.'

I told her that I would not bid her good-bye—I should find a moment to come back the next morning. Her cousin, who had put on his sombrero again, flourished it off at me by way of a bow—upon which I took my departure.

The next morning I came back to the inn, where I met in the court the landlady, more loosely laced than in the evening. On my asking for Miss Spencer—'*Partie*, monsieur,' said the hostess. 'She went away last night at ten o'clock, with her—her—not her husband, eh ?—in fine her *Monsieur*. They went down to the American ship.' I turned away ; the poor girl had been about thirteen hours in Europe.

IV

I myself, more fortunate, was there some five years longer. During this period I lost my friend Latouche, who died of a malarious fever during a tour in the Levant. One of the first things I did on my return was to go up to Grimwinter to pay a consolatory visit to his poor mother. I found her in deep affliction, and I sat with her the whole of the morning that followed my arrival (I had come in late at night), listening to her tearful descant and singing the praises of my friend. We talked of nothing else, and our conversation terminated only with the arrival of a quick little woman who drove herself up to the door in a 'carry-all,' and whom I saw toss the reins upon the horse's back with the briskness of a startled sleeper throwing back the bed-clothes. She jumped out of the carry-all and she jumped into the room. She proved to be the minister's wife and the great town-gossip, and she had evidently, in the latter capacity, a choice morsel to communicate. I was as sure of this as I was that poor Mrs. Latouche was not absolutely too bereaved to listen to her. It seemed to me discreet to retire ; I said I believed I would go and take a walk before dinner. 'And, by the way,' I added, 'if you will tell me where my old friend Miss Spencer lives I will walk to her house.'

The minister's wife immediately responded. Miss Spencer lived in the fourth house beyond the Baptist church ; the Baptist church was the one on the right, with that queer green thing over the door ; they called it a portico, but it looked more like an old-fashioned bedstead.

'Yes, do go and see poor Caroline,' said Mrs. Latouche. 'It will refresh her to see a strange face.'

'I should think she had had enough of strange faces!' cried the minister's wife.

'I mean, to see a visitor,' said Mrs. Latouche, amending her phrase.

'I should think she had had enough of visitors!' her companion rejoined. 'But *you* don't mean to stay ten years,' she added glancing at me.

'Has she a visitor of that sort?' I enquired, perplexed.

'You will see the sort!' said the minister's wife. 'She's easily seen; she generally sits in the front yard. Only take care what you say to her, and be very sure you are polite.'

'Ah, she is so sensitive?'

The minister's wife jumped up and dropped me a curtsey—a most ironical curtsey.

'That's what she is, if you please. She's a Countess!'

And pronouncing this word with the most scathing accent, the little woman seemed fairly to laugh in the Countess's face. I stood a moment, staring, wondering, remembering.

'Oh, I shall be very polite!' I cried; and, grasping my hat and stick, I went on my way.

I found Miss Spencer's residence without difficulty. The Baptist church was easily identified, and the small dwelling near it, of a rusty white, with a large central chimney stack and a Virginia creeper, seemed naturally and properly the abode of a frugal old maid with a taste for the picturesque. As I approached I slackened my pace, for I had heard that some one was always sitting in the front yard, and I wished to reconnoitre. I looked cautiously over the low white fence which separated the small garden-space from the unpaved street; but I descried nothing in the shape of a Countess. A small straight path led up to the crooked door-step, and on either side of it was a little grass-plot, fringed with currant-bushes. In the middle of the grass, on either side, was a large quince-tree, full of antiquity and contortions, and beneath one of the quince-trees were placed a small table and a couple of chairs. On the table lay a piece of unfinished embroidery and two or three books in bright-coloured paper covers. I went in at the gate and paused half-way along the path, scanning the place for some farther token of its occupant, before whom—I could hardly have said why—I hesitated abruptly to present myself. Then I saw that the poor little house was very shabby. I felt a sudden doubt of my right to intrude; for curiosity had been my motive, and curiosity here seemed singularly indelicate. While I hesitated, a figure appeared in the open door-way and stood there looking at me. I immediately recognized Caroline Spencer, but she looked at me as if she had never seen me before. Gently, but gravely and timidly, I advanced to the door-step, and then I said, with an attempt at friendly badinage—

'I waited for you over there to come back, but you never came.'

'Waited where, sir?' she asked softly, and her light-coloured eyes expanded more than before.

She was much older; she looked tired and wasted.

'Well,' I said, 'I waited at Havre.'

She stared; then she recognized me. She smiled and blushed and clasped her two hands together. 'I remember you now,' she said. 'I remember that day.' But she stood there, neither coming out nor asking me to come in. She was embarrassed.

I, too, felt a little awkward. I poked my stick into the path. 'I kept looking out for you, year after year,' I said.

'You mean in Europe?' murmured Miss Spencer.

'In Europe, of course! Here, apparently, you are easy enough to find.'

She leaned her hand against the unpainted door-post, and her head fell a little to one side. She looked at me for a moment without speaking, and I thought I recognized the expression that one sees in women's eyes when tears are rising. Suddenly she stepped out upon the cracked slab of stone before the threshold and closed the door behind her. Then she began to smile intently, and I saw that her teeth were as pretty as ever. But there had been tears too.

'Have you been there ever since?' she asked, almost in a whisper.

'Until three weeks ago. And you—you never came back?'

Still looking at me with her fixed smile, she put her hand behind her and opened the door again. 'I am not very polite,' she said. 'Won't you come in?'

'I am afraid I incommode you.'

'Oh no!' she answered, smiling more than ever. And she pushed back the door, with a sign that I should enter.

I went in, following her. She led the way to a small room on the left of the narrow hall, which I supposed to be her parlour, though it was at the back of the house, and we passed the closed door of another apartment which apparently enjoyed a view of the quince-trees. This one looked out upon a small wood-shed and two clucking hens. But I thought it very pretty, until I saw that its elegance was of the most frugal kind; after which, presently, I thought it prettier still, for I had never seen faded chintz and old mezzotint engravings, framed in varnished autumn leaves, disposed in so graceful a fashion. Miss Spencer sat down on a very small portion of the sofa, with her hands tightly clasped in her lap. She looked ten years older, and it would have sounded very perverse now to speak of her as pretty. But I thought her so; or at least I thought her touching. She was peculiarly agitated. I tried to appear not to notice it; but suddenly, in the most inconsequent fashion—it was an irresistible memory of our little friendship at Havre —I said to her—'I do incommode you. You are distressed.'

She raised her two hands to her face, and for a moment kept it buried in them. Then, taking them away——'It's because you remind me . . .' she said.

'I remind you, you mean, of that miserable day at Havre?'

She shook her head. 'It was not miserable. It was delightful.'

'I never was so shocked as when, on going back to your inn the next morning, I found you had set sail again.'

She was silent a moment; and then she said—— 'Please let us not speak of that.'

'Did you come straight back here?' I asked.

'I was back here just thirty days after I had gone away.'

'And here you have remained ever since?'

'Oh yes!' she said gently.

'When are you going to Europe again?'

This question seemed brutal; but there was something that irritated me in the softness of her resignation, and I wished to extort from her some expression of impatience.

She fixed her eyes for a moment on a small sun-spot on the carpet; then she got up and lowered the window-blind a little, to obliterate it. Presently, in the same mild voice, answering my question, she said—'Never!'

'I hope your cousin repaid you your money.'

'I don't care for it now,' she said, looking away from me.

'You don't care for your money?'

'For going to Europe.'

'Do you mean that you would not go if you could?'

'I can't—I can't,' said Caroline Spencer. 'It is all over; I never think of it.'

'He never repaid you, then!' I exclaimed.

'Please—please,' she began.

But she stopped; she was looking toward the door. There had been a rustling and a sound of steps in the hall.

I also looked toward the door, which was open, and now admitted another person—a lady who paused just within the threshold. Behind her came a young man. The lady looked at me with a good deal of fixedness—long enough for my glance to receive a vivid impression of herself. Then she turned to Caroline Spencer, and, with a smile and a strong foreign accent——

'Excuse my interruption!' she said. 'I knew not you had company—the gentleman came in so quietly.'

With this, she directed her eyes toward me again.

She was very strange; yet my first feeling was that I had seen her before. Then I perceived that I had only seen ladies who were very much like her. But I had seen them very far away from Grimwinter, and it was an odd sensation to be seeing her here. Whither was it the sight of her seemed to transport me? To some dusky landing before a shabby Parisian *quatrième*—to an open door revealing a greasy ante-chamber, and to Madame leaning over the banisters while she holds a faded dressing-gown together and bawls down to the portress to bring up her coffee. Miss Spencer's visitor was a very large woman, of middle age, with a plump, dead-white face and hair drawn back *à la chinoise.* She had a small, penetrating eye, and what is called in French an agreeable smile. She wore an old pink cashmere dressing-gown, covered with white embroideries, and, like the figure in my momentary vision, she was holding it together in front with a bare and rounded arm and a plump and deeply-dimpled hand.

'It is only to spick about my *café*,' she said to Miss

Spencer with her agreeable smile. 'I should like it served in the garden under the leetle tree.'

The young man behind her had now stepped into the room, and he also stood looking at me. He was a pretty-faced little fellow, with an air of provincial foppishness—a tiny Adonis of Grimwater. He had a small, pointed nose, a small, pointed chin, and, as I observed, the most diminutive feet. He looked at me foolishly, with his mouth open.

'You shall have your coffee,' said Miss Spencer, who had a faint red spot in each of her cheeks.

'It is well!' said the lady in the dressing-gown. 'Find your bouk,' she added, turning to the young man.

He looked vaguely round the room. 'My grammar, d'ye mean?' he asked, with a helpless intonation.

But the large lady was looking at me curiously, and gathering in her dressing-gown with her white arm.

'Find your bouk, my friend,' she repeated.

'My poetry, d'ye mean?' said the young man, also gazing at me again.

'Never mind your bouk,' said his companion. 'To-day we will talk. We will make some conversation. But we must not interrupt. Come,' and she turned away. 'Under the leetle tree,' she added, for the benefit of Miss Spencer.

Then she gave me a sort of salutation, and a 'Monsieur!'—with which she swept away again, followed by the young man.

Caroline Spencer stood there with her eyes fixed upon the ground.

'Who is that?' I asked.

'The Countess, my cousin."

'And who is the young man?'

'Her pupil, Mr. Mixter.'

This description of the relation between the two persons who had just left the room made me break into a little laugh. Miss Spencer looked at me gravely.

'She gives French lessons; she has lost her fortune.'

'I see,' I said. 'She is determined to be a burden to no one. That is very proper.'

Miss Spencer looked down on the ground again. 'I must go and get the coffee,' she said.

'Has the lady many pupils?' I asked.

'She has only Mr. Mixter. She gives all her time to him.'

At this I could not laugh, though I smelt provocation. Miss Spencer was too grave. 'He pays very well,' she presently added, with simplicity. 'He is very rich. He is very kind. He takes the Countess to drive.' And she was turning away.

'You are going for the Countess's coffee?' I said.

'If you will excuse me for a few moments.'

'Is there no one else to do it?'

She looked at me with the softest serenity. 'I keep no servants.'

'Can she not wait upon herself?'

'She is not used to that.'

'I see,' said I, as gently as possible. 'But before you go, tell me this: who is this lady?'

'I told you about her before—that day. She is the wife of my cousin, whom you saw.'

'The lady who was disowned by her family in consequence of her marriage?'

'Yes; they have never seen her again. They have cast her off.'

'And where is her husband?'

'He is dead.'

'And where is your money?'

The poor girl flinched, there was something too methodical in my questions. 'I don't know,' she said wearily.

But I continued a moment. 'On her husband's death this lady came over here?'

'Yes, she arrived one day.'

'How long ago?'

'Two years.'

'She has been here ever since?'

'Every moment.'

'How does she like it?'

'Not at all.'

'And how do *you* like it?'

Miss Spencer laid her face in her two hands an instant, as she had done ten minutes before. Then, quickly, she went to get the Countess's coffee.

I remained alone in the little parlour; I wanted to see more—to learn more. At the end of five minutes the young man whom Miss Spencer had described as the Countess's pupil came in. He stood looking at me for a moment with parted lips. I saw he was a very rudimentary young man.

'She wants to know if you won't come out there?' he observed at last.

'Who wants to know?'

'The Countess. That French lady.'

'She has asked you to bring me?'

'Yes, sir,' said the young man feebly, looking at my six feet of stature.

I went out with him, and we found the Countess sitting under one of the little quince-trees in front of the house. She was drawing a needle through the piece of embroidery which she had taken from the small table. She pointed graciously to the chair beside her and I seated myself. Mr. Mixter glanced about him, and then sat down in the grass at her feet. He gazed upward, looking with parted lips from the Countess to me.

'I am sure you speak French,' said the Countess, fixing her brilliant little eyes upon me.

'I do, madam, after a fashion,' I answered, in the lady's own tongue.

'*Voilà!*' she cried most expressively. 'I knew it so soon as I looked at you. You have been in my poor dear country.'

'A long time.'

'You know Paris?'

'Thoroughly, madam.' And with a certain conscious purpose I let my eyes meet her own.

She presently, hereupon, moved her own and glanced down at Mr. Mixter. 'What are we talking about?' she demanded of her attentive pupil.

He pulled his knees up, plucked at the grass with his hand, stared, blushed a little. 'You are talking French,' said Mr. Mixter.

'*La belle découverte!*' said the Countess. 'Here are ten months,' she explained to me, 'that I am giving him lessons. Don't put yourself out not to say he's a fool; he won't understand you.'

'I hope your other pupils are more gratifying,' I remarked.

'I have no others. They don't know what French is in this place; they don't want to know. You may therefore imagine the pleasure it is to me to meet a person who speaks it like yourself.' I replied that my own pleasure was not less, and she went on drawing her stitches through her embroidery, with her little finger curled out. Every few moments she put her eyes close to her work, near-sightedly. I thought her a very disagreeable person; she was coarse, affected, dishonest, and no more a Countess than I was a caliph. 'Talk to me of Paris,' she went on. 'The very name of it gives me an emotion! How long since you were there?'

'Two months ago.'

'Happy man! Tell me something about it. What were they doing? Oh, for an hour of the boulevard!'

'They were doing about what they are always doing—amusing themselves a good deal.'

'At the theatres, eh?' sighed the Countess. 'At the *cafés-concerts*—at the little tables in front of the doors? *Quelle existence!* You know I am a Parisienne, monsieur,' she added, '—to my finger-tips.'

'Miss Spencer was mistaken, then,' I ventured to rejoin, 'in telling me that you are a Provençale.'

She stared a moment, then she put her nose to her embroidery, which had a dingy, desultory aspect. 'Ah, I am a Provençale by birth; but I am a Parisienne by inclination.'

'And by experience, I suppose?' I said.

She questioned me a moment with her hard little eyes. 'Oh, experience! I could talk of experience if I wished. I never expected, for example, that experience had *this* in store for me.' And she pointed with her bare elbow, and with a jerk of her head, at everything that surrounded her—at the little white house, the quince-tree, the rickety paling, even at Mr. Mixter.

'You are in exile!' I said smiling.

'You may imagine what it is! These two years that I have been here I have passed hours—hours! One gets used to things, and sometimes I think I have got used to this. But there are some things that are always beginning over again. For example, my coffee.'

'Do you always have coffee at this hour?' I inquired.

She tossed back her head and measured me.

'At what hour would you prefer me to have it? I must have my little cup after breakfast.'

'Ah, you breakfast at this hour?'

'At mid-day—*comme cela se fait*. Here they breakfast at a quarter past seven! That "quarter past" is charming!'

'But you were telling me about your coffee,' I observed, sympathetically.

'My *cousine* can't believe in it: she can't understand it. She's an excellent girl; but that little cup of black coffee, with a drop of cognac, served at this hour—they exceed her comprehension. So I have to break the ice every day, and it takes the coffee the time you see to arrive. And when it arrives, monsieur! If I don't offer you any of it you must not take it ill. It will be because I know you have drunk it on the boulevard.'

I resented extremely this scornful treatment of poor Caroline Spencer's humble hospitality; but I said nothing, in order to say nothing uncivil. I only looked on Mr. Mixter, who had clasped his arms round his knees and was watching my companion's demonstrative graces in solemn fascination. She presently saw that I was observing him; she glanced at me with a little bold explanatory smile. 'You know, he adores me,' she murmured, putting her nose into her tapestry again. I expressed the promptest credence, and she went on. 'He dreams of becoming my lover! Yes, it's his dream. He has read a French novel; it took him six months. But ever since that he has thought himself the hero, and me the heroine!'

Mr. Mixter had evidently not an idea that he was being talked about; he was too preoccupied with the ecstasy of contemplation. At this moment Caroline Spencer came out of the house, bearing a coffee-pot on a little tray. I noticed that on her way from the door to the table she gave me a single quick, vaguely appealing glance. I wondered what it signified; I felt that it signified a sort of half-frightened longing to know what, as a man of the world who had been in France, I thought of the Countess. It made me extremely uncomfortable. I could not tell her that the Countess was very possibly the runaway wife of a little hairdresser. I tried suddenly, on the contrary, to show a high consideration for her. But I got up; I couldn't stay longer. It vexed me to see Caroline Spencer standing there like a waiting-maid.

'You expect to remain some time at Grimwinter?' I said to the Countess.

She gave a terrible shrug.

'Who knows? Perhaps for years. When one is in misery! . . . *Chère belle*,' she added, turning to Miss Spencer, 'you have forgotten the cognac!'

I detained Caroline Spencer as, after looking a moment in silence at the little table, she was turning away to procure this missing delicacy. I silently gave her my hand in farewell. She looked very tired, but there was a strange hint of prospective patience in her severely mild little face. I thought she was rather glad I was going. Mr. Mixter had risen to his feet and was pouring out the Countess's coffee. As I went back past the Baptist church I reflected that poor Miss Spencer had been right in her presentiment that she should still see something of that dear old Europe.

ROBERT LOUIS STEVENSON

1850—1894

THE SIRE DE MALÉTROIT'S DOOR

Denis de Beaulieu was not yet two-and-twenty, but he counted himself a grown man, and a very accomplished cavalier into the bargain. Lads were early formed in that rough, warfaring epoch; and when one has been in a pitched battle and a dozen raids, has killed one's man in an honourable fashion, and knows a thing or two of strategy and mankind, a certain swagger in the gait is surely to be pardoned. He had put up his horse with due care, and supped with due deliberation; and then, in a very agreeable frame of mind, went out to pay a visit in the grey of the evening. It was not a very wise proceeding on the young man's part. He would have done better to remain beside the fire or go decently to bed. For the town was full of the troops of Burgundy and England under a mixed command; and though Denis was there on safe-conduct, his safe-conduct was like to serve him little on a chance encounter.

It was September 1429; the weather had fallen sharp; a flighty piping wind, laden with showers, beat about the township; and the dead leaves ran riot along the streets. Here and there a window was already lighted up; and the noise of men-at-arms making merry over supper within came forth in fits and was swallowed up and carried away by the wind. The night fell swiftly; the flag of England, fluttering on the spire-top, grew ever fainter and fainter against the flying clouds—a black speck like a swallow in the tumultuous, leaden chaos of the sky. As the night fell the wind rose, and began to hoot under archways and roar amid the tree-tops in the valley below the town.

Denis de Beaulieu walked fast and was soon knocking at his friend's door; but though he promised himself to stay only a little while and make an early return, his welcome was so pleasant, and he found so much to delay him, that it was already long past midnight before he said good-bye upon the threshold. The wind had fallen again in the meanwhile; the night was as black as the grave; not a star, nor a glimmer of moonshine, slipped through the canopy of cloud. Denis was ill-acquainted with the intricate lanes of Château Landon; even by daylight he had found some trouble in picking his way; and in this absolute darkness he soon lost it altogether. He was certain of one thing only—to keep mounting the hill; for his friend's house lay at the lower end, or tail, of Château Landon, while the inn was up at the head, under the great church spire. With this clue to go upon he stumbled and groped forward, now breathing more freely in open places where there was a good slice of sky overhead, now feeling along the wall in stifling closes. It is an eerie and mysterious position to be thus submerged in opaque blackness in an almost unknown town. The silence is terrifying in its possibilities. The touch of cold window bars to the exploring hand startles the man like the touch of a toad; the inequalities of the pavement shake his heart into his mouth; a piece of denser darkness threatens an ambuscade or a chasm in the pathway; and where the air is brighter, the houses put on strange and bewildering appearances, as if to lead him farther from his way. For Denis, who had to regain his inn without attracting notice, there was real danger as well as mere discomfort in the walk; and he went warily and boldly at once, and at every corner paused to make an observation.

He had been for some time threading a lane so

narrow that he could touch a wall with either hand, when it began to open out and go sharply downward. Plainly this lay no longer in the direction of his inn; but the hope of a little more light tempted him forward to reconnoitre. The lane ended in a terrace with a bartizan wall, which gave an outlook between high houses, as out of an embrasure, into the valley lying dark and formless several hundred feet below. Denis looked down, and could discern a few tree-tops waving and a single speck of brightness where the river ran across a weir. The weather was clearing up, and the sky had lightened, so as to show the outline of the heavier clouds and the dark margin of the hills. By the uncertain glimmer, the house on his left hand should be a place of some pretensions; it was surmounted by several pinnacles and turret-tops; the round stern of a chapel, with a fringe of flying buttresses, projected boldly from the main block; and the door was sheltered under a deep porch carved with figures and overhung by two long gargoyles. The windows of the chapel gleamed through their intricate tracery with a light as of many tapers, and threw out the buttresses and the peaked roof in a more intense blackness against the sky. It was plainly the hôtel of some great family of the neighbourhood; and as it reminded Denis of a town house of his own at Bourges, he stood for some time gazing up at it and mentally gauging the skill of the architects and the consideration of the two families.

There seemed to be no issue to the terrace but the lane by which he had reached it; he could only retrace his steps, but he had gained some notion of his whereabouts, and hoped by this means to hit the main thoroughfare and speedily regain the inn. He was reckoning without that chapter of accidents which was to make this night memorable above all others in his career; for he had not gone back above a hundred yards before he saw a light coming to meet him, and heard loud voices speaking together in the echoing narrows of the lane. It was a party of men-at-arms going the night round with torches. Denis assured himself that they had all been making free with the wine-bowl, and were in no mood to be particular about safe-conducts or the niceties of chivalrous war. It was as like as not that they would kill him like a dog and leave him where he fell. The situation was inspiriting but nervous. Their own torches would conceal him from sight, he reflected ; and he hoped that they would drown the noise of his footsteps with their own empty voices. If he were but fleet and silent, he might evade their notice altogether.

Unfortunately, as he turned to beat a retreat, his foot rolled upon a pebble ; he fell against the wall with an ejaculation, and his sword rang loudly on the stones. Two or three voices demanded who went there—some in French, some in English ; but Denis made no reply, and ran the faster down the lane. Once upon the terrace, he paused to look back. They still kept calling after him, and just then began to double the pace in pursuit, with a considerable clank of armour, and great tossing of the torchlight to and fro in the narrow jaws of the passage.

Denis cast a look around and darted into the porch. There he might escape observation, or—if that were too much to expect—was in a capital posture whether for parley or defence. So thinking, he drew his sword and tried to set his back against the door. To his surprise, it yielded behind his weight; and though he turned in a moment, continued to swing back on oiled and noiseless hinges, until it stood wide open on a black interior. When things fall out opportunely for the person concerned, he is not apt to be critical about the how or why, his own immediate personal convenience seeming a sufficient reason for the strangest oddities and revolutions in our sublunary things ; and so Denis, without a moment's hesitation, stepped within and partly closed the door behind him to conceal his place of refuge. Nothing was further from his thoughts than to close it altogether; but for some inexplicable reason—perhaps by a spring or a weight—the ponderous mass of oak whipped itself out of his fingers and clanked to, with a formidable rumble and a noise like the falling of an automatic bar.

The round, at that very moment, debouched upon the terrace and proceeded to summon him with shouts and curses. He heard them ferreting in the dark corners; and the stock of a lance even rattled along the outer surface of the door behind which he stood; but these gentlemen were in too high a humour to be long delayed, and soon made off down a corkscrew pathway which had escaped Denis's observation, and passed out of sight and hearing along the battlements of the town.

Denis breathed again. He gave them a few minutes' grace for fear of accidents, and then groped about for some means of opening the door and slipping forth again. The inner surface was quite smooth, not a handle, not a moulding, not a projection of any sort. He got his finger-nails round the edges and pulled, but the mass was immovable. He shook it, it was as firm as a rock. Denis de Beaulieu frowned and gave vent to a little noiseless whistle. What ailed the door? he wondered. Why was it open? How came it to shut so easily and so effectually after him? There was something obscure and underhand about all this that was little to the young man's fancy. It looked like a snare; and yet who could suppose a snare in such a quiet by-street and in a house of so prosperous and even noble an exterior? And yet—snare or no snare, intentionally or unintentionally—here he was, prettily trapped; and for the life of him he could see no way out of it again. The darkness began to weigh upon him. He gave ear; all was silent without, but within and close by he seemed to catch a faint sighing, a faint sobbing rustle, a little stealthy creak—as though many persons were at his side, holding themselves quite still, and governing even their respiration with the extreme of slyness. The idea went to his vitals with a shock, and he faced about suddenly as if to defend his life. Then, for the first time, he became aware of a light about the level of his eyes and at some distance in the interior of the house—a vertical thread of light, widening towards the bottom, such as might escape between two wings of arras over a doorway. To see anything was a relief to Denis ; it was like a piece of solid ground to a man labouring in a morass ; his mind seized upon it with avidity ; and he stood staring at it and trying to piece together some logical conception of his surroundings. Plainly there was a flight of steps ascending from his own level to that of this illuminated doorway ; and indeed he thought he could make out another thread of light, as fine as a needle and as faint as phosphorescence, which might very well be reflected along the polished wood of a handrail. Since he had begun to suspect that he was not alone, his heart had continued to beat with smothering violence, and an intolerable desire for action of any sort had possessed itself of his spirit. He was in deadly peril, he believed. What could be more natural than to mount the staircase, lift the curtain, and confront his difficulty at once ? At least he would be dealing with something tangible ; at least he would be no longer in the dark. He stepped slowly forward with outstretched hands, until his foot struck the bottom step ; then he rapidly scaled the stairs, stood for a moment to compose his expression, lifted the arras and went in.

He found himself in a large apartment of polished stone. There were three doors ; one on each of three sides ; all similarly curtained with tapestry. The fourth side was occupied by two large windows and a great stone chimney-piece, carved with the arms of the Malétroits. Denis recognized the bearings, and was gratified to find himself in such good hands. The room was strongly illuminated; but it contained little furniture except a heavy table and a chair or two, the hearth was innocent of fire, and the pavement was but sparsely strewn with rushes clearly many days old.

On a high chair beside the chimney, and directly facing Denis as he entered, sat a little old gentleman in a fur tippet. He sat with his legs crossed and his hands folded, and a cup of spiced wine stood by his elbow on a bracket on the wall. His countenance had a strongly masculine cast; not properly human, but such as we see in the bull, the goat, or the domestic boar; something equivocal and wheedling, something greedy, brutal, and dangerous. The upper lip was inordinately full, as though swollen by a blow or a toothache; and the smile, the peaked eyebrows, and the small, strong eyes were quaintly and almost comically evil in expression. Beautiful white hair hung straight all round his head, like a saint's, and fell in a single curl upon the tippet. His beard and moustache were the pink of venerable sweetness. Age, probably in consequence of inordinate precautions, had left no mark upon his hands; and the Malétroit hand was famous. It would be difficult to imagine anything at once so fleshy and so delicate in design; the taper, sensual fingers were like those of one of Leonardo's women; the fork of the thumb made a dimpled protuberance when closed; the nails were perfectly shaped, and of a dead, surprising whiteness. It rendered his aspect tenfold more redoubtable, that a man with hands like these should keep them devoutly folded in his lap like a virgin martyr—that a man with so intense and startling an expression of face should sit patiently on his seat and contemplate people with an unwinking stare, like a god, or a god's statue. His quiescence seemed ironical and treacherous, it fitted so poorly with his looks.

Such was Alain, Sire de Malétroit.

Denis and he looked silently at each other for a second or two.

'Pray step in,' said the Sire de Malétroit. 'I have been expecting you all the evening.'

He had not risen, but he accompanied his words with a smile, and a slight but courteous inclination of the head. Partly from the smile, partly from the strange musical murmur with which the Sire prefaced his observation, Denis felt a strong shudder of disgust go through his marrow. And what with disgust and honest confusion of mind, he could scarcely get words together in reply.

'I fear,' he said, 'that this is a double accident. I am not the person you suppose me. It seems you were looking for a visit; but for my part, nothing was further from my thoughts—nothing could be more contrary to my wishes—than this intrusion.'

'Well, well,' replied the old gentleman indulgently, 'here you are, which is the main point. Seat yourself, my friend, and put yourself entirely at your ease. We shall arrange our little affairs presently.'

Denis perceived that the matter was still complicated with some misconception, and he hastened to continue his explanations.

'Your door . . .' he began.

'About my door?' asked the other, raising his peaked eyebrows. 'A little piece of ingenuity.' And he shrugged his shoulders. 'A hospitable fancy! By your own account, you were not desirous of making my acquaintance. We old people look for such reluctance now and then; and when it touches our honour, we cast about until we find some way of overcoming it. You arrive uninvited, but believe me, very welcome.'

'You persist in error, sir,' said Denis. 'There can be no question between you and me. I am a stranger in this country-side. My name is Denis, damoiseau de Beaulieu. If you see me in your house, it is only——'

'My young friend,' interrupted the other, 'you will permit me to have my own ideas on that subject. They probably differ from yours at the present moment,' he added with a leer, 'but time will show which of us is in the right.'

Denis was convinced he had to do with a lunatic. He seated himself with a shrug, content to wait the upshot; and a pause ensued, during which he thought he could distinguish a hurried gabbling as of prayer from behind the arras immediately opposite him. Sometimes there seemed to be but one person engaged, sometimes two; and the vehemence of the voice, low as it was, seemed to indicate either great haste or an agony of spirit. It occurred to him that this piece of tapestry covered the entrance to the chapel he had noticed from without.

The old gentleman meanwhile surveyed Denis from head to foot with a smile, and from time to time emitted little noises like a bird or a mouse, which seemed to indicate a high degree of satisfaction. This state of matters became rapidly insupportable; and Denis, to put an end to it, remarked politely that the wind had gone down.

The old gentleman fell into a fit of silent laughter, so prolonged and violent that he became quite red in the face. Denis got upon his feet at once, and put on his hat with a flourish.

'Sir,' he said, 'if you are in your wits, you have affronted me grossly. If you are out of them, I flatter myself I can find better employment for my brains than to talk with lunatics. My conscience is clear; you have made a fool of me from the first moment; you have refused to hear my explanations; and now there is no power under God will make me stay here any longer; and if I cannot make my way out in a more decent fashion, I will hack your door in pieces with my sword."

The Sire de Malétroit raised his right hand and

wagged it at Denis with the fore and little fingers extended.

'My dear nephew,' he said, 'sit down.'

'Nephew!' retorted Denis, 'you lie in your throat'; and he snapped his fingers in his face.

'Sit down, you rogue!' cried the old gentleman, in a sudden, harsh voice, like the barking of a dog. 'Do you fancy,' he went on, 'that when I had made my little contrivance for the door I had stopped short with that? If you prefer to be bound hand and foot till your bones ache, rise and try to go away. If you choose to remain a free young buck, agreeably conversing with an old gentleman—why, sit where you are in peace, and God be with you.'

'Do you mean I am a prisoner?' demanded Denis.

'I state the facts,' replied the other. 'I would rather leave the conclusion to yourself.'

Denis sat down again. Externally he managed to keep pretty calm; but within, he was now boiling with anger, now chilled with apprehension. He no longer felt convinced that he was dealing with a madman. And if the old gentleman was sane, what, in God's name, had he to look for? What absurd or tragical adventure had befallen him? What countenance was he to assume?

While he was thus unpleasantly reflecting, the arras that overhung the chapel door was raised, and a tall priest in his robes came forth and, giving a long, keen stare at Denis, said something in an undertone to Sire de Malétroit.

'She is in a better frame of spirit?' asked the latter.

'She is more resigned, messire,' replied the priest.

'Now the Lord help her, she is hard to please!' sneered the old gentleman. 'A likely stripling—not ill-born—and of her own choosing, too? Why, what more would the jade have?'

'The situation is not usual for a young damsel,' said the other, 'and somewhat trying to her blushes.'

'She should have thought of that before she began the dance? It was none of my choosing, God knows that: but since she is in it, by our Lady, she shall carry it to the end.' And then addressing Denis, 'Monsieur de Beaulieu,' he asked, 'may I present you to my niece? She has been waiting your arrival, I may say, with even greater impatience than myself.'

Denis had resigned himself with a good grace—all he desired was to know the worst of it as speedily as possible; so he rose at once, and bowed in acquiescence. The Sire de Malétroit followed his example and limped, with the assistance of the chaplain's arm, towards the chapel door. The priest pulled aside the arras, and all three entered. The building had considerable architectural pretensions. A light groining sprang from six stout columns, and hung down in two rich pendants from the centre of the vault. The place terminated behind the altar in a round end, embossed and honeycombed with a superfluity of ornament in relief, and pierced by many little windows shaped like stars, trefoils, or wheels. These windows were imperfectly glazed, so that the night air circulated freely in the chapel. The tapers, of which there must have been half a hundred burning on the altar, were unmercifully blown about; and the light went through many different phases of brilliancy and semi-eclipse. On the steps in front of the altar knelt a young girl richly attired as a bride. A chill settled over Denis as he observed her costume; he fought with desperate energy against the conclusion that was being thrust upon his mind; it could not—it should not—be as he feared.

'Blanche,' said the Sire, in his most flute-like tones, 'I have brought a friend to see you, my little girl; turn round and give him your pretty hand. It is good to be devout; but it is necessary to be polite, my niece.'

The girl rose to her feet and turned towards the newcomers. She moved all of a piece; and shame and exhaustion were expressed in every line of her fresh young body; and she held her head down and kept her eyes upon the pavement, as she came slowly forward. In the course of her advance, her eyes fell upon Denis de Beaulieu's feet—feet of which he was justly vain, be it remarked, and wore in the most elegant accoutrement even while travelling. She paused—started, as if his yellow boots had conveyed some shocking meaning—and glanced suddenly up into the wearer's countenance. Their eyes met; shame gave place to horror and terror in her looks; the blood left her lips; with a piercing scream she covered her face with her hands and sank upon the chapel floor.

'That is not the man!' she cried. 'My uncle; that is not the man!'

The Sire de Malétroit chirped agreeably. 'Of course not,' he said, 'I expected as much. It was so unfortunate you could not remember his name.'

'Indeed,' she cried, 'indeed, I have never seen this person till this moment—I have never so much as set eyes upon him—I never wish to see him again. Sir,' she said, turning to Denis, 'if you are a gentleman, you will bear me out. Have I ever seen you—have you ever seen me—before this accursed hour?'

'To speak for myself, I have never had that pleasure,' answered the young man. 'This is the first time, messire, that I have met with your engaging niece.'

The old gentleman shrugged his shoulders.

'I am distressed to hear it,' he said. 'But it is never too late to begin. I had little more acquaintance with my own late lady ere I married her; which proves,' he added with a grimace, 'that these impromptu marriages may often produce an excellent understanding in the long-run. As the bridegroom is to have a voice in the matter, I will give him two hours to make up for lost time before we proceed with the ceremony.' And he turned towards the door, followed by the clergyman.

The girl was on her feet in a moment. 'My uncle,

you cannot be in earnest,' she said. 'I declare before God I will stab myself rather than be forced on that young man. The heart rises at it; God forbids such marriages; you dishonour your white hair. Oh, my uncle, pity me! There is not a woman in all the world but would prefer death to such a nuptial. Is it possible,' she added, faltering—'is it possible that you do not believe me—that you still think this'—and she pointed at Denis with a tremor of anger and contempt—'that you still think *this* to be the man?'

'Frankly,' said the old gentleman, pausing on the threshold, 'I do. But let me explain to you once for all, Blanche de Malétroit, my way of thinking about this affair. When you took it into your head to dishonour my family and the name that I have borne, in peace and war, for more than threescore years, you forfeited, not only the right to question my designs, but that of looking me in the face. If your father had been alive, he would have spat on you and turned you out of doors. His was the hand of iron. You may bless your God you have only to deal with the hand of velvet, mademoiselle. It was my duty to get you married without delay. Out of pure goodwill, I have tried to find your own gallant for you. And I believe I have succeeded. But before God and all the holy angels, Blanche de Malétroit, if I have not, I care not one jack-straw. So let me recommend you to be polite to our young friend; for upon my word, your next groom may be less appetizing.'

And with that he went out, with the chaplain at his heels; and the arras fell behind the pair.

The girl turned upon Denis with flashing eyes.

'And what, sir,' she demanded, 'may be the meaning of all this?'

'God knows,' returned Denis gloomily. 'I am a prisoner in this house, which seems full of mad people. More I know not; and nothing do I understand.'

'And pray how came you here?' she asked.

He told her as briefly as he could. 'For the rest,' he added, 'perhaps you will follow my example, and tell me the answer to all these riddles, and what, in God's name, is like to be the end of it.'

She stood silent for a little, and he could see her lips tremble and her tearless eyes burn with a feverish lustre. Then she pressed her forehead in both hands.

'Alas, how my head aches!' she said wearily—'to say nothing of my poor heart! But it is due to you to know my story, unmaidenly as it must seem. I am called Blanche de Malétroit: I have been without father or mother for—oh! for as long as I can recollect, and indeed I have been most unhappy all my life. Three months ago a young captain began to stand near me every day in church. I could see that I pleased him; I am much to blame, but I was so glad that any one should love me; and when he passed me a letter, I took it home with me and read it with great pleasure. Since that time he has written many. He was so anxious to speak with me, poor fellow! and kept asking me to leave the door open some evening that we might have two words upon the stair. For he knew how much my uncle trusted me.' She gave something like a sob at that, and it was a moment before she could go on. 'My uncle is a hard man, but he is very shrewd,' she said at last. 'He has performed many feats in war, and was a great person at court, and much trusted by Queen Isabeau in old days. How he came to suspect me I cannot tell; but it is hard to keep anything from his knowledge; and this morning, as we came from mass, he took my hand in his, forced it open, and read my little billet, walking by my side all the while. When he had finished, he gave it back to me with great politeness. It contained another request to have the door left open; and this has been the ruin of us all. My uncle kept me strictly in my room until evening, and then ordered me to dress myself as you see me—

a hard mockery for a young girl; do you not think so? I suppose, when he could not prevail with me to tell him the young captain's name, he must have laid a trap for him: into which, alas! you have fallen in the anger of God. I looked for much confusion; for how could I tell whether he was willing to take me for his wife on these sharp terms? He might have been trifling with me from the first; or I might have made myself too cheap in his eyes. But truly I had not looked for such a shameful punishment as this! I could not think that God would let a girl be so disgraced before a young man. And now I have told you all; and I can scarcely hope that you will not despise me.'

Denis made her a respectful inclination.

'Madam,' he said, 'you have honoured me by your confidence. It remains for me to prove that I am not unworthy of the honour. Is Messire de Malétroit at hand?'

'I believe he is writing in the salle without,' she answered.

'May I lead you thither, madam?' asked Denis, offering his hand with his most courtly bearing.

She accepted it; and the pair passed out of the chapel, Blanche in a very drooping and shamefast condition, but Denis strutting and ruffling in the consciousness of a mission, and the boyish certainty of accomplishing it with honour.

The Sire de Malétroit rose to meet them with an ironical obeisance.

'Sir,' said Denis, with the grandest possible air, 'I believe I am to have some say in the matter of this marriage; and let me tell you at once, I will be no party to forcing the inclination of this young lady. Had it been freely offered to me, I should have been proud to accept her hand, for I perceive she is as good as she is beautiful; but as things are, I have now the honour, messire, of refusing.'

Blanche looked at him with gratitude in her eyes;

but the old gentleman only smiled and smiled, until his smile grew positively sickening to Denis.

'I am afraid,' he said, 'Monsieur de Beaulieu, that you do not perfectly understand the choice I have to offer you. Follow me, I beseech you, to this window.' And he led the way to one of the large windows which stood open on the night. 'You observe,' he went on, 'there is an iron ring in the upper masonry, and reeved through that a very efficacious rope. Now, mark my words: if you should find your disinclination to my niece's person insurmountable, I shall have you hanged out of this window before sunrise. I shall only proceed to such an extremity with the greatest regret, you may believe me. For it is not at all your death that I desire, but my niece's establishment in life. At the same time, it must come to that if you prove obstinate. Your family, Monsieur de Beaulieu, is very well in its way; but if you sprang from Charlemagne, you should not refuse the hand of a Malétroit with impunity—not if she had been as common as the Paris road—not if she were as hideous as the gargoyle over my door. Neither my niece nor you, nor my own private feelings, move me at all in this matter. The honour of my house has been compromised; I believe you to be the guilty person; at least you are now in the secret; and you can hardly wonder if I request you to wipe out the stain. If you will not, your blood be on your own head! It will be no great satisfaction to me to have your interesting relics kicking their heels in the breeze below my windows; but half a loaf is better than no bread, and if I cannot cure the dishonour, I shall at least stop the scandal.'

There was a pause.

'I believe there are other ways of settling such imbroglios among gentlemen,' said Denis. 'You wear a sword, and I hear you have used it with distinction.'

The Sire de Malétroit made a signal to the chaplain, who crossed the room with long silent strides and raised the arras over the third of the three doors. It was only a moment before he let it fall again ; but Denis had time to see a dusky passage full of armed men.

'When I was a little younger, I should have been delighted to honour you, Monsieur de Beaulieu,' said Sire Alain ; 'but I am now too old. Faithful retainers are the sinews of age, and I must employ the strength I have. This is one of the hardest things to swallow as a man grows up in years ; but with a little patience, even this becomes habitual. You and the lady seem to prefer the salle for what remains of your two hours ; and as I have no desire to cross your preference, I shall resign it to your use with all the pleasure in the world. No haste !' he added, holding up his hand, as he saw a dangerous look come into Denis de Beaulieu's face. 'If your mind revolts against hanging, it will be time enough two hours hence to throw yourself out of the window or upon the pikes of my retainers. Two hours of life are always two hours. A great many things may turn up in even as little a while as that. And, besides, if I understand her appearance, my niece has still something to say to you. You will not disfigure your last hours by a want of politeness to a lady ?'

Denis looked at Blanche, and she made him an imploring gesture.

It is likely that the old gentleman was hugely pleased at this symptom of an understanding ; for he smiled on both, and added sweetly : 'If you will give me your word of honour, Monsieur de Beaulieu, to await my return at the end of the two hours before attempting anything desperate, I shall withdraw my retainers, and let you speak in greater privacy with mademoiselle.'

Denis again glanced at the girl, who seemed to beseech him to agree.

'I give you my word of honour,' he said.

Messire de Malétroit bowed, and proceeded to limp about the apartment, clearing his throat the while with that odd musical chirp which had already grown so irritating in the ears of Denis de Beaulieu. He first possessed himself of some papers which lay upon the table; then he went to the mouth of the passage and appeared to give an order to the men behind the arras; and lastly, he hobbled out through the door by which Denis had come in, turning upon the threshold to address a last smiling bow to the young couple, and followed by the chaplain with a hand-lamp.

No sooner were they alone than Blanche advanced towards Denis with her hands extended. Her face was flushed and excited, and her eyes shone with tears.

'You shall not die!' she cried, 'you shall marry me after all.'

'You seem to think, madam,' replied Denis, 'that I stand much in fear of death.'

'Oh no, no,' she said, 'I see you are no poltroon. It is for my own sake—I could not bear to have you slain for such a scruple.'

'I am afraid,' returned Denis, 'that you underrate the difficulty, madam. What you may be too generous to refuse, I may be too proud to accept. In a moment of noble feeling towards me, you forgot what you perhaps owe to others.'

He had the decency to keep his eyes upon the floor as he said this, and after he had finished, so as not to spy upon her confusion. She stood silent for a moment, then walked suddenly away, and falling on her uncle's chair, fairly burst out sobbing. Denis was in the acme of embarrassment. He looked round, as if to seek for inspiration, and seeing a stool, plumped down upon it for something to do. There he sat, playing with the guard of his rapier, and wishing himself dead a thousand times over, and buried in the nastiest kitchen-heap in France. His eyes wandered round the apartment, but found nothing to arrest them. There were such wide spaces between the furniture, the light fell so baldly and cheerlessly over all, the dark outside air looked in so coldly through the windows, that he thought he had never seen a church so vast, nor a tomb so melancholy. The regular sobs of Blanche de Malétroit measured out the time like the ticking of a clock. He read the device upon the shield over and over again, until his eyes became obscured; he stared into shadowy corners until he imagined they were swarming with horrible animals; and every now and again he awoke with a start, to remember that his last two hours were running, and death was on the march.

Oftener and oftener, as the time went on, did his glance settle on the girl herself. Her face was bowed forward and covered with her hands, and she was shaken at intervals by the convulsive hiccup of grief. Even thus she was not an unpleasant object to dwell upon, so plump and yet so fine, with a warm brown skin, and the most beautiful hair, Denis thought, in the whole world of womankind. Her hands were like her uncle's; but they were more in place at the end of her young arms, and looked infinitely soft and caressing. He remembered how her blue eyes had shone upon him, full of anger, pity, and innocence. And the more he dwelt on her perfections, the uglier death looked, and the more deeply was he smitten with penitence at her continued tears. Now he felt that no man could have the courage to leave a world which contained so beautiful a creature; and now he would have given forty minutes of his last hour to unsay this cruel speech.

Suddenly a hoarse and ragged peal of cockcrow rose to their ears from the dark valley below the windows. And this shattering noise in the silence of all around was like a light in a dark place, and shook them both out of their reflections.

'Alas, can I do nothing to help you?' she said, looking up.

'Madam,' replied Denis, with a fine irrelevancy,

'if I have said anything to wound you, believe me, it was for your own sake and not for mine.'

She thanked him with a tearful look.

'I feel your position cruelly,' he went on. 'The world has been bitter hard on you. Your uncle is a disgrace to mankind. Believe me, madam, there is no young gentleman in all France but would be glad of my opportunity, to die in doing you a momentary service.'

'I know already that you can be very brave and generous,' she answered. 'What I *want* to know is whether I can serve you—now or afterwards,' she added, with a quaver.

'Most certainly,' he answered with a smile. 'Let me sit beside you as if I were a friend, instead of a foolish intruder; try to forget how awkwardly we are placed to one another; make my last moments go pleasantly; and you will do me the chief service possible.'

'You are very gallant,' she added, with a yet deeper sadness . . . 'very gallant . . . and it somehow pains me. But draw nearer, if you please; and if you find anything to say to me, you will at least make certain of a very friendly listener. Ah! Monsieur de Beaulieu,' she broke forth—'ah! Monsieur de Beaulieu, how can I look you in the face?' And she fell to weeping again with a renewed effusion.

'Madam,' said Denis, taking her hand in both of his, 'reflect on the little time I have before me, and the great bitterness into which I am cast by the sight of your distress. Spare me, in my last moments, the spectacle of what I cannot cure even with the sacrifice of my life.'

'I am very selfish,' answered Blanche. 'I will be braver, Monsieur de Beaulieu, for your sake. But think if I can do you no kindness in the future—if you have no friends to whom I could carry your adieux. Charge me as heavily as you can; every burden will lighten, by so little, the invaluable gratitude I owe you. Put it in my power to do something more for you than weep.'

'My mother is married again, and has a young family to care for. My brother Guichard will inherit my fiefs; and if I am not in error, that will content him amply for my death. Life is a little vapour that passeth away, as we are told by those in holy orders. When a man is in a fair way and sees all life open in front of him, he seems to himself to make a very important figure in the world. His horse whinnies to him; the trumpets blow and the girls look out of window as he rides into town before his company; he receives many assurances of trust and regard—sometimes by express in a letter—sometimes face to face, with persons of great consequence falling on his neck. It is not wonderful if his head is turned for a time. But once he is dead, were he as brave as Hercules or as wise as Solomon, he is soon forgotten. It is not ten years since my father fell, with many other knights around him, in a very fierce encounter, and I do not think that any one of them, nor so much as the name of the fight, is now remembered. No, no, madam, the nearer you come to it, you see that death is a dark and dusty corner, where a man gets into his tomb and has the door shut after him till the Judgement Day. I have few friends just now, and once I am dead I shall have none.'

'Ah, Monsieur de Beaulieu!' she exclaimed, 'you forget Blanche de Malétroit.'

'You have a sweet nature, madam, and you are pleased to estimate a little service far beyond its worth.'

'It is not that,' she answered. 'You mistake me if you think I am so easily touched by my own concerns. I say so, because you are the noblest man I have ever met; because I recognize in you a spirit that would have made even a common person famous in the land.'

'And yet here I die in a mousetrap—with no more noise about it than my own squeaking,' answered he.

A look of pain crossed her face, and she was silent for a little while. Then a light came into her eyes, and with a smile she spoke again.

'I cannot have my champion think meanly of himself. Any one who gives his life for another will be met in Paradise by all the heralds and angels of the Lord God. And you have no such cause to hang your head. For . . . Pray, do you think me beautiful?' she asked, with a deep flush.

'Indeed, madam, I do,' he said.

'I am glad of that,' she answered heartily. 'Do you think there are many men in France who have been asked in marriage by a beautiful maiden—with her own lips—and who have refused her to her face? I know you men would half despise such a triumph; but believe me, we women know more of what is precious in love. There is nothing that should set a person higher in his own esteem; and we women would prize nothing more dearly.'

'You are very good,' he said; 'but you cannot make me forget that I was asked in pity and not for love.'

'I am not so sure of that,' she replied, holding down her head. 'Hear me to an end, Monsieur de Beaulieu. I know how you must despise me; I feel you are right to do so; I am too poor a creature to occupy one thought of your mind, although, alas! you must die for me this morning. But when I asked you to marry me, indeed, and indeed, it was because I respected and admired you, and loved you with my whole soul, from the very moment that you took my part against my uncle. If you had seen yourself, and how noble you looked, you would pity rather than despise me. And now,' she went on, hurriedly checking him with her hand, 'although I have laid aside all reserve and told you so much, remember that I know your sentiments towards me already. I would not, believe me, being nobly born, weary you with importunities into consent. I too have a pride of my own: and I declare before the holy mother of God, if you should now go back from your word already given, I would no more marry you than I would marry my uncle's groom.'

Denis smiled a little bitterly.

'It is a small love,' he said, 'that shies at a little pride.'

She made no answer, although she probably had her own thoughts.

'Come hither to the window,' he said, with a sigh. 'Here is the dawn.'

And indeed the dawn was already beginning. The hollow of the sky was full of essential daylight, colourless and clean; and the valley underneath was flooded with a grey reflection. A few thin vapours clung in the coves of the forest or lay along the winding course of the river. The scene disengaged a surprising effect of stillness, which was hardly interrupted when the cocks began once more to crow among the steadings. Perhaps the same fellow who had made so horrid a clangour in the darkness not half an hour before, now sent up the merriest cheer to greet the coming day. A little wind went bustling and eddying among the treetops underneath the windows. And still the daylight kept flooding insensibly out of the east, which was soon to grow incandescent and cast up that red-hot cannonball, the rising sun.

Denis looked out over all this with a bit of a shiver. He had taken her hand and retained it in his almost unconsciously.

'Has the day begun already?' she said; and then, illogically enough: 'the night has been so long! Alas! what shall we say to my uncle when he returns?'

'What you will,' said Denis, and he pressed her fingers in his.

She was silent.

'Blanche,' he said, with a swift, uncertain, passionate utterance, 'you have seen whether I fear death. You must know well enough that I would as gladly leap out of that window into the empty air as lay a finger on you without your free and full consent. But if you care for me at all, do not let me lose my life in a misapprehension; for I love you better than the whole world; and though I will die for you blithely, it would be like all the joys of Paradise to live on and spend my life in your service.'

As he stopped speaking, a bell began to ring loudly in the interior of the house; and a clatter of armour in the corridor showed that the retainers were returning to their post, and the two hours were at an end.

'After all that you have heard?' she whispered, leaning towards him with her lips and eyes.

'I have heard nothing,' he replied.

'The captain's name was Florimond de Champdivers,' she said in his ear.

'I did not hear it,' he answered, taking her supple body in his arms, and covered her wet face with kisses.

A melodious chirping was audible behind, followed by a beautiful chuckle, and the voice of Messire de Malétroit wished his new nephew a good morning.

OSCAR WILDE

1856—1900

THE BIRTHDAY OF THE INFANTA

It was the birthday of the Infanta. She was just twelve years of age, and the sun was shining brightly in the gardens of the palace.

Although she was a real Princess and the Infanta of Spain, she had only one birthday every year, just like the children of quite poor people, so it was naturally a matter of great importance to the whole country that she should have a really fine day for the occasion. And a really fine day it certainly was. The tall striped tulips stood straight up upon their stalks, like long rows of soldiers, and looked defiantly across the grass at the roses, and said: 'We are quite as splendid as you are now.' The purple butterflies fluttered about with gold dust on their wings, visiting each flower in turn; the little lizards crept out of the crevices of the wall, and lay basking in the white glare; and the pomegranates split and cracked with the heat, and showed their bleeding red hearts. Even the pale yellow lemons, that hung in such profusion from the mouldering trellis and along the dim arcades, seemed to have caught a richer colour from the wonderful sunlight, and the magnolia trees opened their great globe-like blossoms of folded ivory, and filled the air with a sweet heavy perfume.

The little Princess herself walked up and down the terrace with her companions, and played at hide and seek round the stone vases and the old moss-grown statues. On ordinary days she was only allowed to play with children of her own rank, so she had always to play alone, but her birthday was an exception, and the King had given orders that she was to invite any of her young friends whom she liked to come and amuse themselves with her. There was a stately grace about these slim Spanish children as they glided about, the boys with their large-plumed hats and short fluttering cloaks, the girls holding up the trains of their long brocaded gowns, and shielding the sun from their eyes with huge fans of black and silver. But the Infanta was the most graceful of all, and the most tastefully attired, after the somewhat cumbrous fashion of the day. Her robe was of grey satin, the skirt and the wide puffed sleeves heavily embroidered with silver, and the stiff corset studded with rows of fine pearls. Two tiny slippers with big pink rosettes peeped out beneath her dress as she walked. Pink and pearl was her great gauze fan, and in her hair, which like an aureole of faded gold stood out stiffly round her pale little face, she had a beautiful white rose.

From a window in the palace the sad melancholy King watched them. Behind him stood his brother, Don Pedro of Aragon, whom he hated, and his confessor, the Grand Inquisitor of Granada, sat by his side. Sadder even than usual was the King, for as he looked at the Infanta bowing with childish gravity to the assembling courtiers, or laughing behind her fan at the grim Duchess of Albuquerque who always accompanied her, he thought of the young Queen, her mother, who but a short time before—so it seemed to him—had come from the gay country of France, and had withered away in the sombre splendour of the Spanish court, dying just six months after the birth of her child, and before she had seen the almonds blossom twice in the orchard, or plucked the second year's fruit from the old gnarled fig-tree that stood in the centre of the now grass-grown courtyard. So great had been his love for her that he had not suffered even the grave to hide her from him. She had been embalmed by a Moorish physician, who in return for this service had been granted his life, which for heresy and suspicion of magical practices had been already forfeited, men said, to the Holy Office, and her body was still lying on its tapestried bier in the black marble chapel of the Palace, just as the monks had borne her in on that windy March day nearly twelve years before. Once every month the King, wrapped in a dark cloak and with a muffled lantern in his hand, went in and knelt by her side calling out, '*Mi reina! Mi reina!*' and sometimes breaking through the formal etiquette that in Spain governs every separate action of life, and sets limits even to the sorrow of a King, he would clutch at the pale jewelled hands in a wild agony of grief, and try to wake by his mad kisses the cold painted face.

To-day he seemed to see her again, as he had seen her first at the Castle of Fontainebleau, when he was but fifteen years of age, and she still younger. They had been formally betrothed on that occasion by the Papal Nuncio in the presence of the French King and all the Court, and he had returned to the Escurial bearing with him a little ringlet of yellow hair, and the memory of two childish lips bending down to kiss his hand as he stepped into his carriage. Later on had followed the marriage, hastily performed at Burgos, a small town on the frontier between the two countries, and the grand public entry into Madrid with the customary celebration of high mass at the Church of La Atocha, and a more than usually solemn *auto-da-fé*, in which nearly three hundred heretics, amongst whom were many Englishmen, had been delivered over to the secular arm to be burned.

Certainly he had loved her madly, and to the ruin, many thought, of his country, then at war with England for the possession of the empire of the New World. He had hardly ever permitted her to be out of his sight; for her, he had forgotten, or seemed to have forgotten, all grave affairs of State; and, with that terrible blindness that passion brings upon its servants, he had failed to notice that the elaborate ceremonies by which he sought to please her did but aggravate the strange malady from which she suffered. When she died he was, for a time, like one bereft of reason. Indeed, there is no doubt but that he would have formally abdicated and retired to the great Trappist monastery at Granada, of which he was already titular Prior, had he not been afraid to leave the little Infanta at the mercy of his brother, whose cruelty, even in Spain, was notorious, and who was suspected by many of having caused the Queen's death by means of a pair of poisoned gloves that he had presented to her on the occasion of her visiting his castle in Aragon. Even after the expiration of the three years of public mourning that he had ordained throughout his whole dominions by royal edict, he would never suffer his ministers to speak about any new alliance, and when the Emperor himself sent to him, and offered him the hand of the lovely Archduchess of Bohemia, his niece, in marriage, he bade the ambassadors tell their master that the King of Spain was already wedded to Sorrow, and that though she was but a barren bride, he loved her better than Beauty; an answer that cost his crown the rich provinces of the Netherlands, which soon after, at the Emperor's instigation, revolted against him under the leadership of some fanatics of the Reformed Church.

His whole married life, with its fierce, fiery-coloured joys and the terrible agony of its sudden ending, seemed to come back to him to-day as he watched the Infanta playing on the terrace. She had all the Queen's pretty petulance of manner, the same wilful way of tossing her head, the same proud curved beautiful mouth, the same wonderful smile—*vrai sourire de France* indeed—as she glanced up now and then at the window, or stretched out her little hand for the stately Spanish gentlemen to kiss. But the shrill laughter of the children grated on his ears, and the bright pitiless sunlight mocked his sorrow, and a dull odour of strange spices, spices such as embalmers use, seemed to taint—or was it fancy ?—the clear morning air. He buried his face in his hands, and when the Infanta looked up again the curtains had been drawn, and the King had retired.

She made a little *moue* of disappointment, and shrugged her shoulders. Surely he might have stayed with her on her birthday. What did the stupid State-affairs matter ? Or had he gone to that gloomy chapel where the candles were always burning, and where she was never allowed to enter ? How silly of him, when the sun was shining so brightly, and everybody was so happy ! Besides, he would miss the sham bull-fight for which the trumpet was already sounding, to say nothing of the puppet-show and the other wonderful things. Her uncle and the Grand Inquisitor were much more sensible. They had come out on the terrace, and paid her nice compliments. So she tossed her pretty head, and taking Don Pedro by the hand, she walked slowly down the steps towards a long pavilion of purple silk that had been erected at the end of the garden, the other children following in strict order of precedence, those who had the longest names going first.

A procession of noble boys, fantastically dressed as *toreadors*, came out to meet her, and the young Count of Tierra-Nueva, a wonderfully handsome lad of about fourteen years of age, uncovering his head with all the grace of a born hidalgo and grandee of Spain, led her solemnly in to a little gilt and ivory chair that was placed on a raised dais above the arena. The children grouped themselves all round, fluttering their big fans and whispering to each other, and Don Pedro and the Grand Inquisitor stood laughing at the entrance.

Even the Duchess—the Camerera-Mayor as she was called—a thin, hard-featured woman with a yellow ruff, did not look quite so bad-tempered as usual, and something like a chill smile flitted across her wrinkled face and twitched her thin bloodless lips.

It certainly was a marvellous bull-fight, and much nicer, the Infanta thought, than the real bull-fight that she had been brought to see at Seville, on the occasion of the visit of the Duke of Parma to her father. Some of the boys pranced about on richly-caparisoned hobby-horses brandishing long javelins with gay streamers of bright ribands attached to them; others went on foot waving their scarlet cloaks before the bull, and vaulting lightly over the barrier when he charged them; and as for the bull himself, he was just like a live bull, though he was only made of wicker-work and stretched hide, and sometimes insisted on running round the arena on his hind legs, which no live bull ever dreams of doing. He made a splendid fight of it too, and the children got so excited that they stood up upon the benches, and waved their lace handkerchiefs and cried out: *Bravo toro! Bravo toro!* just as sensibly as if they had been grown-up people. At last, however, after a prolonged combat, during which several of the hobby-horses were gored through and through, and their riders dismounted, the young Count of Tierra-Nueva brought the bull to his knees, and having obtained permission from the Infanta to give the *coup de grâce*, he plunged his wooden sword into the neck of the animal with such violence that the head came right off, and disclosed the laughing face of little Monsieur de Lorraine, the son of the French Ambassador at Madrid.

The arena was then cleared amidst much applause, and the dead hobby-horses dragged solemnly away by two Moorish pages in yellow and black liveries, and after a short interlude, during which a French posture-master performed upon the tight-rope, some Italian puppets appeared in the semi-classical tragedy of *Sophonisba* on the stage of a small theatre that had been built up for the purpose. They acted so well, and their gestures were so extremely natural, that at the close of the play the eyes of the Infanta were quite dim with tears. Indeed, some of the children really cried, and had to be comforted with sweetmeats, and the Grand Inquisitor himself was so affected that he could not help saying to Don Pedro that it seemed to him intolerable that things made simply out of wood and coloured wax, and worked mechanically by wires, should be so unhappy and meet with such terrible misfortunes.

An African juggler followed, who brought in a large flat basket covered with a red cloth, and having placed it in the centre of the arena, he took from his turban a curious reed pipe, and blew through it. In a few moments the cloth began to move, and as the pipe grew shriller and shriller two green and gold snakes put out their strange wedge-shaped heads and rose slowly up, swaying to and fro with the music as a plant sways in the water. The children, however, were rather frightened at their spotted hoods and quick darting tongues, and were much more pleased when the juggler made a tiny orange-tree grow out of the sand and bear pretty white blossoms and clusters of real fruit; and when he took the fan of the little daughter of the Marquess de Las-Torres, and changed it into a blue bird that flew all around the pavilion and sang, their delight and amusement knew no bounds. The solemn minuet, too, performed by the dancing boys from the church of Nuestra Senora Del Pilar, was charming. The Infanta had never before seen this wonderful ceremony which takes place every year at Maytime in front of the high altar of the Virgin, and in her honour; and indeed none of the royal family of Spain had entered the great cathedral of Saragossa since a mad priest, supposed by many to have been in the pay of Elizabeth of England, had tried to administer a poisoned wafer to the Prince of the Asturias. So she had known only by hearsay of 'Our Lady's Dance,' as it was called, and it certainly was a beautiful sight. The boys wore old-fashioned court dresses of white velvet, and their curious three-cornered hats were fringed with silver and surmounted with huge plumes of ostrich feathers, the dazzling whiteness of their costumes, as they moved about in the sunlight, being still more accentuated by their swarthy faces and long black hair. Everybody was fascinated by the grave dignity with which they moved through the intricate figures of the dance, and by the elaborate grace of their slow gestures and stately bows; and when they had finished their performance and doffed their great plumed hats to the Infanta, she acknowledged their reverence with much courtesy, and made a vow that she would send a large wax candle to the shrine of Our Lady of Pilar in return for the pleasure that she had given her.

A troop of handsome Egyptians—as the gipsies were termed in those days—then advanced into the arena, and sitting down cross-legs, in a circle, began to play softly upon their zithers, moving their bodies to the tune, and humming, almost below their breath, a low dreamy air. When they caught sight of Don Pedro they scowled at him, and some of them looked terrified, for only a few weeks before he had had two of their tribe hanged for sorcery in the market-place at Seville, but the pretty Infanta charmed them as she leaned back peeping over her fan with her great blue eyes, and they felt sure that one so lovely as she was could never be cruel to anybody. So they played on very gently and just touching the chords of the zithers with their long pointed nails, and their heads began to nod as though they were falling asleep. Suddenly, with a cry so shrill that all the children were startled and Don Pedro's hand clutched at the agate pommel of his dagger, they leapt to their feet and whirled madly round the enclosure beating their tambourines, and chaunting some wild love-song in their strange guttural language. Then at another signal they all flung themselves again to the ground and lay there quite still, the dull strumming of the zithers being the only sound that broke the silence. After that they had done this several times, they disappeared for a moment and came back leading a brown shaggy bear by a chain, and carrying on their shoulders some little Barbary apes. The bear stood upon his head with the utmost gravity, and the wizened apes played all kinds of amusing tricks with two gipsy boys who seemed to be their masters, and fought with tiny swords, and fired off guns, and went through a regular soldiers' drill just like the King's own bodyguard. In fact the gipsies were a great success.

But the funniest part of the whole morning's entertainment was undoubtedly the dancing of the little Dwarf. When he stumbled into the arena, waddling on his crooked legs and wagging his huge misshapen head from side to side, the children went off into a loud shout of delight, and the Infanta herself laughed so much that the Camerera was obliged to remind her that although there were many precedents in Spain for a King's daughter weeping before her equals, there were none for a Princess of the blood royal making so merry before those who were her inferiors in birth. The Dwarf, however, was really quite irresistible, and even at the Spanish Court, always noted for its cultivated passion for the horrible, so fantastic a little monster had never been seen. It was his first appearance, too. He had been discovered only the day before, running wild through the forest, by two of the nobles who happened to have been hunting in a remote part of the great cork-wood that surrounded the town, and had been carried off by them to the Palace as a surprise for the Infanta; his father, who was a poor charcoal-burner, being but too well pleased to get rid of so ugly and useless a child. Perhaps the most amusing thing about him was his complete unconsciousness of his own grotesque appearance. Indeed he seemed quite happy and full of the highest spirits. When the children laughed, he laughed as freely and as joyously as any of them, and at the close of each dance he made them each the funniest of bows, smiling and nodding at them just as if he was really one of themselves, and not a little misshapen thing that Nature, in some humorous mood, had fashioned for others to mock at. As for the Infanta, she absolutely fascinated him. He could not keep his eyes off her, and seemed to dance for her alone, and when at the close of the performance, remembering how she had seen the great ladies of the Court throw bouquets to Caffarelli, the famous Italian treble, whom the Pope had sent from his own chapel to Madrid that he might cure the King's melancholy by the sweetness of his voice, she took out of her hair the beautiful white rose, and partly for a jest and partly to tease the Camerera, threw it to him across the arena with her sweetest smile, he took the whole matter quite seriously, and, pressing the flower to his rough coarse lips, he put his hand upon his heart, and sank on one knee before her, grinning from ear to ear, and with his little bright eyes sparkling with pleasure.

This so upset the gravity of the Infanta that she kept on laughing long after the little Dwarf had run out of the arena, and expressed a desire to her uncle that the dance should be immediately repeated. The Camerera, however, on the plea that the sun was too hot, decided that it would be better that her Highness should return without delay to the Palace, where a wonderful feast had been already prepared for her, including a real birthday cake with her own initials worked all over it in painted sugar and a lovely silver flag waving from the top. The Infanta accordingly rose up with much dignity, and having given orders that the little Dwarf was to dance again for her after the hour of siesta, and conveyed her thanks to the young Count of Tierra-Nueva for his charming reception, she went back to her apartments, the children following in the same order in which they had entered.

Now when the little Dwarf heard that he was to dance a second time before the Infanta, and by her own express command, he was so proud that he ran out into the garden, kissing the white rose in an absurd ecstasy of pleasure, and making the most uncouth and clumsy gestures of delight.

The Flowers were quite indignant at his daring to intrude into their beautiful home, and when they saw him capering up and down the walks, and waving his arms above his head in such a ridiculous manner, they could not restrain their feelings any longer.

'He is really far too ugly to be allowed to play in any place where we are,' cried the Tulips.

'He should drink poppy-juice, and go to sleep for a thousand years,' said the great scarlet Lilies, and they grew quite hot and angry.

'He is a perfect horror!' screamed the Cactus. 'Why, he is twisted and stumpy, and his head is completely out of proportion with his legs. Really he makes me feel prickly all over, and if he comes near me I will sting him with my thorns.'

'And he has actually got one of my best blooms,' exclaimed the White Rose-Tree. 'I gave it to the Infanta this morning myself, as a birthday present, and he has stolen it from her.' And she called out: 'Thief, thief, thief!' at the top of her voice.

Even the red Geraniums, who did not usually give themselves airs, and were known to have a great many poor relations themselves, curled up in disgust when they saw him, and when the Violets meekly remarked that though he was certainly extremely plain, still he could not help it, they retorted with a good deal of justice that that was his chief defect, and that there was no reason why one should admire a person because he was incurable; and, indeed, some of the Violets themselves felt that the ugliness of the little Dwarf was almost ostentatious, and that he would have shown much better taste if he had looked sad, or at least pensive, instead of jumping about merrily, and throwing himself into such grotesque and silly attitudes.

As for the old Sundial, who was an extremely remarkable individual, and had once told the time of day to no less a person than the Emperor Charles V himself, he was so taken aback by the little Dwarf's appearance, that he almost forgot to mark two whole minutes with his long shadowy finger, and could not help saying to the great milk-white Peacock, who was sunning herself on the balustrade, that every one knew that the children of Kings were Kings, and that the children of charcoal-burners were charcoal-burners, and that it was absurd to pretend that it wasn't so; a statement with which the Peacock entirely agreed, and indeed screamed out, 'Certainly, certainly,' in such a loud, harsh voice, that the gold-fish who lived in the basin of the cool splashing fountain put their heads out of the water, and asked the huge stone Tritons what on earth was the matter.

But somehow the Birds liked him. They had seen him often in the forest, dancing about like an elf after the eddying leaves, or crouched up in the hollow of some old oak-tree, sharing his nuts with the squirrels. They did not mind his being ugly, a bit. Why, even the nightingale herself, who sang so sweetly in the orange groves at night that sometimes the Moon leaned down to listen, was not much to look at after all; and, besides, he had been kind to them, and during that terribly bitter winter, when there were no berries on the trees, and the ground was as hard as iron, and the wolves had come down to the very gates of the city to look for food, he had never once forgotten them, but had always given them crumbs out of his little hunch of black bread, and divided with them whatever poor breakfast he had.

So they flew round and round him, just touching his cheek with their wings as they passed, and chattered to each other, and the little Dwarf was so pleased that he could not help showing them the beautiful white rose, and telling them that the Infanta herself had given it to him because she loved him.

They did not understand a single word of what he was saying, but that made no matter, for they put their heads on one side, and looked wise, which is quite as good as understanding a thing, and very much easier.

The Lizards also took an immense fancy to him, and when he grew tired of running about and flung himself down on the grass to rest, they played and romped all over him, and tried to amuse him in the best way they could. 'Every one cannot be as beautiful as a lizard,' they cried; 'that would be too much to expect. And, though it sounds absurd to say so, he is really not so ugly after all, provided, of course, that one shuts one's eyes, and does not look at him.' The Lizards were extremely philosophical by nature, and often sat thinking for hours and hours together, when there was nothing else to do, or when the weather was too rainy for them to go out.

The Flowers, however, were excessively annoyed at their behaviour, and at the behaviour of the birds. 'It only shows,' they said, 'what a vulgarizing effect this incessant rushing and flying about has. Well-bred people always stay exactly in the same place, as we do. No one ever saw us hopping up and down the walks, or galloping madly through the grass after dragon-flies. When we do want change of air, we send for the gardener, and he carries us to another bed. This is dignified, and as it should be. But birds and lizards have no sense of repose, and indeed birds have not even a permanent address. They are mere vagrants like the gipsies, and should be treated in exactly the same manner.' So they put their noses in the air, and looked very haughty, and were quite delighted when after some time they saw the little Dwarf scramble up from the grass, and make his way across the terrace to the palace.

'He should certainly be kept indoors for the rest of his natural life,' they said. 'Look at his hunched back, and his crooked legs,' and they began to titter.

But the little Dwarf knew nothing of all this. He liked the birds and the lizards immensely, and thought that the flowers were the most marvellous things in the whole world, except of course the Infanta, but then she had given him the beautiful white rose, and she loved him, and that made a great difference. How he wished that he had gone back with her! She would have put him on her right hand, and smiled at him, and he would have never left her side, but would have made her his playmate, and taught her all kinds of delightful tricks. For though he had never been in a palace before, he knew a great many wonderful things. He could make little cages out of rushes for the grass-hoppers to sing in, and fashion the long-jointed bamboo into the pipe that Pan loves to hear. He knew the cry of every bird, and could call the starlings from the tree-top, or the heron from the mere. He knew the trail of every animal, and could track the hare by its delicate footprints, and the boar by the trampled leaves. All the wild-dances he knew, the mad dance in red raiment with the autumn, the light dance in blue sandals over the corn, the dance with white snow-wreaths in winter, and the blossom-dance through the orchards in spring. He knew where the wood-pigeons built their nests, and once when a fowler had snared the parent birds, he had brought up the young ones himself, and had built a little dovecot for them in the cleft of a pollard elm. They were quite tame, and used to feed out of his hands every morning. She would like them, and the rabbits that scurried about in the long fern, and the jays with their steely feathers and black bills, and the hedgehogs that could curl themselves up into prickly balls, and the great wise tortoises that crawled slowly about, shaking their heads and nibbling at the young leaves. Yes, she must certainly come to the forest and play with him. He would give her his own little bed, and would watch outside the window till dawn, to see that the wild horned cattle did not harm her, nor the gaunt wolves creep too near the hut. And at dawn he would tap at the shutters and wake her, and they would go out and dance together all the day long. It was really not a bit lonely in the forest. Sometimes a Bishop rode through on his white mule, reading out of a painted book. Sometimes in their green velvet caps, and their jerkins of tanned deerskin, the falconers passed by with hooded hawks on their wrists. At vintage-time came the grape-treaders, with purple hands and feet, wreathed with glossy ivy and carrying dripping skins of wine ; and the charcoal-burners sat round their huge braziers at night, watching the dry logs charring slowly in the fire, and roasting chestnuts in the ashes, and the robbers came out of their caves and made merry with them. Once, too, he had seen a beautiful procession winding up the long, dusty road to Toledo. The monks went in front singing sweetly, and carrying bright banners and crosses of gold, and then, in silver armour, with matchlocks and pikes, came the soldiers, and in their midst walked three barefooted men, in strange yellow dresses painted all over with wonderful figures, and carrying lighted candles in their hands. Certainly there was a great deal to look at in the forest, and when she was tired he would find a soft bank of moss for her, or carry her in his arms, for he was very strong, though he knew that he was not tall. He would make her a necklace of red bryony berries, that would be quite as pretty as the white berries that she wore on her dress, and when she was tired of them she could throw them away, and he would find her others. He would bring her acorn-cups and dew-drenched anemones, and tiny glow-worms to be stars in the pale gold of her hair.

But where was she ? He asked the white rose, and it made him no answer. The whole palace seemed asleep, and even where the shutters had not been closed, heavy curtains had been drawn across the windows to keep out the glare. He wandered all round looking for some place through which he might gain an entrance, and at last he caught sight of a little private door that was lying open. He slipped through, and found himself in a splendid hall, far more splendid, he feared, than the forest, there was so much more gilding everywhere, and even the floor was made of great coloured stones, fitted together into a sort of geometrical pattern. But the little Infanta was not there, only some wonderful white statues that looked down on him from their jasper pedestals, with sad blank eyes and strangely smiling lips.

At the end of the hall hung a richly embroidered curtain of black velvet, powdered with suns and stars, the King's favourite devices, and broidered on the colour he loved best. Perhaps she was hiding behind that ? He would try, at any rate.

So he stole quietly across, and drew it aside. No ; there was only another room, though a prettier room, he thought, than the one he had just left. The walls were hung with a many-figured green arras of needle-wrought tapestry representing a hunt, the work of some Flemish artists who had spent more than seven years in its composition. It had once been the chamber of *Jean le Fou*, as he was called, that mad King who was so enamoured of the chase that he had often tried in his delirium to mount the huge rearing horses, and to drag down the stag on which the great hounds were leaping, sounding his hunting-horn, and stabbing with his dagger at the pale, flying deer. It was now used as the council-room, and on the centre table were lying the red portfolios of the ministers, stamped with the gold tulips of Spain, and with the arms and emblems of the house of Hapsburg.

The little Dwarf looked in wonder all round him, and was half-afraid to go on. The strange silent horsemen that galloped so swiftly through the long glades without making any noise, seemed to him like those terrible phantoms of whom he had heard the charcoal-burners speaking—the Comprachos, who hunt only at night, and if they meet a man, turn him into a hind, and chase him. But he thought of the pretty Infanta, and took courage. He wanted to find her alone, and to tell her that he too loved her. Perhaps she was in the room beyond.

He ran across the soft Moorish carpets, and opened the door. No ! She was not here either. The room was quite empty.

It was a throne-room, used for the reception of foreign ambassadors, when the King, which of late had not been often, consented to give them a personal audience ; the same room in which, many years before, envoys had appeared from England to make arrangements for the marriage of their Queen, then one of the Catholic sovereigns of Europe, with the Emperor's eldest son. The hangings were of gilt Cordovan leather, and a heavy gilt chandelier with branches for three hundred wax lights hung down from the black and white ceiling. Underneath a great canopy of gold cloth, on which the lions and towers of Castile were broidered in seed pearls, stood the throne itself, covered with a rich pall of black velvet studded with silver tulips and elaborately fringed with silver and pearls. On the second step of the throne was placed the kneeling-stool of the Infanta, with its cushion of cloth of silver tissue, and below that again, and beyond the limit of the canopy, stood the chair for the Papal Nuncio, who alone had the right to be seated in the King's presence on the occasion of any public ceremonial, and whose Cardinal's hat, with its tangled scarlet tassels, lay on a purple *tabouret* in front. On the wall, facing the throne, hung a life-sized portrait of Charles V in hunting-dress, with a great mastiff by his side; and a picture of Philip II receiving the homage of the Netherlands occupied the centre of the other wall. Between the windows stood a black ebony cabinet, inlaid with plates of ivory, on which the figures from Holbein's Dance of Death had been graved—by the hand, some said, of that famous master himself.

But the little Dwarf cared nothing for all this magnificence. He would not have given his rose for all the pearls on the canopy, nor one white petal of his rose for the throne itself. What he wanted was to see the Infanta before she went down to the pavilion, and to ask her to come away with him when he had finished his dance. Here, in the Palace, the air was close and heavy, but in the forest the wind blew free, and the sunlight, with wandering hands of gold, moved the tremulous leaves aside. There were flowers, too, in the forest, not so splendid, perhaps, as the flowers in the garden, but more sweetly scented for all that; hyacinths in early spring that flooded with waving purple the cool glens, and grassy knolls; yellow primroses that nestled in little clumps round the gnarled roots of the oak-trees; bright celandine, and blue speedwell, and irises lilac and gold. There were grey catkins on the hazels, and the foxgloves drooped with the white of their dappled bee-haunted cells. The chestnut had its spires of white stars, and the hawthorn its pallid moons of beauty. Yes: surely she would come if he could only find her! She would come with him to the fair forest, and all day long he would dance for her delight. A smile lit up his eyes at the thought, and he passed into the next room.

Of all the rooms this was the brightest and the most

beautiful. The walls were covered with a pink-flowered Lucca damask, patterned with birds and dotted with dainty blossoms of silver; the furniture was of massive silver, festooned with florid wreaths and swinging Cupids; in front of the two large fire-places stood great screens broidered with parrots and peacocks; and the floor, which was of sea-green onyx, seemed to stretch far away into the distance. Nor was he alone. Standing under the shadow of the door-way, at the extreme end of the room, he saw a little figure watching him. His heart trembled, a cry of joy broke from his lips, and he moved out into the sunlight. As he did so, the figure moved out also, and he saw it plainly.

The Infanta! It was a monster, the most grotesque monster he had ever beheld. Not properly shaped, as all other people were, but hunchbacked, and crooked-limbed, with huge lolling head and mane of black hair. The little Dwarf frowned, and the monster frowned also. He laughed, and it laughed with him, and held its hands to its sides, just as he himself was doing. He made it a mocking bow, and it returned him a low reverence. He went towards it, and it came to meet him, copying each step that he made, and stopping when he stopped himself. He shouted with amusement, and ran forward, and reached out his hand, and the hand of the monster touched his, and it was as cold as ice. He grew afraid, and moved his hand across, and the monster's hand followed it quickly. He tried to press on, but something smooth and hard stopped him. The face of the monster was now close to his own, and seemed full of terror. He brushed his hair off his eyes. It imitated him. He struck at it, and it returned blow for blow. He loathed it, and it made hideous faces at him. He drew back, and it retreated.

What is it? He thought for a moment, and looked round at the rest of the room. It was strange, but everything seemed to have its double in this invisible wall of clear water. Yes, picture for picture was repeated, and couch for couch. The sleeping Faun that lay in the alcove by the doorway had its twin brother that slumbered, and the silver Venus that stood in the sunlight held out her arms to a Venus as lovely as herself.

Was it Echo? He had called to her once in the valley, and she had answered him word for word. Could she mock the eye, as she mocked the voice? Could she make a mimic world just like the real world? Could the shadows of things have colour and life and movement? Could it be that——?

He started, and taking from his breast the beautiful white rose, he turned round, and kissed it. The monster had a rose of its own, petal for petal the same! It kissed it with like kisses, and pressed it to its heart with horrible gestures.

When the truth dawned upon him, he gave a wild cry of despair, and fell sobbing to the ground. So it was he who was misshapen and hunchbacked, foul to look at and grotesque. He himself was the monster, and it was at him that all the children had been laughing, and the little Princess who he had thought loved him—she too had been merely mocking at his ugliness, and making merry over his twisted limbs. Why had they not left him in the forest, where there was no mirror to tell him how loathsome he was? Why had his father not killed him, rather than sell him to his shame? The hot tears poured down his cheeks, and he tore the white rose to pieces. The sprawling monster did the same, and scattered the faint petals in the air. It grovelled on the ground, and, when he looked at it, it watched him with a face drawn with pain. He crept away, lest he should see it, and covered his eyes with his hands. He crawled, like some wounded thing, into the shadow, and lay there moaning.

And at that moment the Infanta herself came in with her companions through the open window, and when they saw the ugly little dwarf lying on the ground and beating the floor with his clenched hands, in the most fantastic and exaggerated manner, they went off into shouts of happy laughter, and stood all round him and watched him.

'His dancing was funny,' said the Infanta; 'but his acting is funnier still. Indeed he is almost as good as the puppets, only of course not quite so natural.' And she fluttered her big fan, and applauded.

But the little Dwarf never looked up, and his sobs grew fainter and fainter, and suddenly he gave a curious gasp, and clutched his side. And then he fell back again, and lay quite still.

'That is capital,' said the Infanta, after a pause; 'but now you must dance for me.'

'Yes,' cried all the children, 'you must get up and dance, for you are as clever as the Barbary apes, and much more ridiculous.'

But the little Dwarf made no answer.

And the Infanta stamped her foot, and called out to her uncle, who was walking on the terrace with the Chamberlain, reading some despatches that had just arrived from Mexico, where the Holy Office had recently been established. 'My funny little dwarf is sulking,' she cried, 'you must wake him up, and tell him to dance for me.'

They smiled at each other, and sauntered in, and Don Pedro stooped down, and slapped the Dwarf on the cheek with his embroidered glove. 'You must dance,' he said, '*petit monstre.* You must dance. The Infanta of Spain and the Indies wishes to be amused.'

But the little Dwarf never moved.

'A whipping-master should be sent for,' said Don Pedro wearily, and he went back to the terrace. But the Chamberlain looked grave, and he knelt beside the little Dwarf, and put his hand upon his heart. And after a few moments he shrugged his shoulders, and rose up, and having made a low bow to the Infanta, he said—

'*Mi bella Princesa*, your funny little Dwarf will never dance again. It is a pity, for he is so ugly that he might have made the King smile.'

'But why will he not dance again?' asked the Infanta, laughing.

'Because his heart is broken,' answered the Chamberlain.

And the Infanta frowned, and her dainty rose-leaf lips curled in pretty disdain. 'For the future let those who come to play with me have no hearts,' she cried, and she ran out into the garden.

GEORGE GISSING

1857—1903

A POOR GENTLEMAN

IT was in the drawing-room, after dinner. Mrs. Charman, the large and kindly hostess, sank into a chair beside her little friend Mrs. Loring, and sighed a question.

'How do you like Mr. Tymperley ?'

'Very nice. Just a little peculiar.'

'Oh, he *is* peculiar ! Quite original. I wanted to tell you about him before we went down, but there wasn't time. Such a very old friend of ours. My dear husband and he were at school together—Harrovians. The sweetest, the most affectionate character ! Too good for this world, I'm afraid; he takes everything so seriously. I shall never forget his grief at my poor husband's death.—I'm telling Mrs. Loring about Mr. Tymperley, Ada.'

She addressed her married daughter, a quiet young woman who reproduced Mrs. Charman's good-natured countenance, with something more of intelligence, the reflective serenity of a higher type.

'I'm sorry to see him looking so far from well,' remarked Mrs. Weare, in reply.

'He never had any colour, you know, and his life . . . But I must tell you,' she resumed to Mrs. Loring. 'He's a bachelor, in comfortable circumstances, and—would you believe it ?—he lives quite alone in one of the distressing parts of London. Where is it, Ada ?'

'A poor street in Islington.'

'Yes. There he lives, I'm afraid in shocking lodgings—it must be *so* unhealthy—just to become acquainted with the life of poor people, and be helpful to them. Isn't it heroic? He seems to have given up his whole life to it. One never meets him anywhere; I think ours is the only house where he's seen. A noble life! He never talks about it. I'm sure you would never have suspected such a thing from his conversation at dinner?'

'Not for a moment,' answered Mrs. Loring, astonished. 'He wasn't very gossipy—I gathered that his chief interests were fretwork and foreign politics.'

Mrs. Weare laughed. 'The very man! When I was a little girl he used to make all sorts of pretty things for me with his fret-saw; and when I grew old enough, he instructed me in the Balance of Power. It's possible, mamma, that he writes leading articles. We should never hear of it.'

'My dear, anything is possible with Mr. Tymperley. And such a change, this, after his country life. He had a beautiful little house near ours, in Berkshire. I really can't help thinking that my husband's death caused him to leave it. He was so attached to Mr. Charman! When my husband died, and we left Berkshire, we altogether lost sight of him—oh, for a couple of years. Then I met him by chance in London. Ada thinks there must have been some sentimental trouble.'

'Dear mamma,' interposed the daughter, 'it was you, not I, who suggested that.'

'Was it? Well, perhaps it was. One can't help seeing that he has gone through something. Of course it may be only pity for the poor souls he gives his life to. A wonderful man!'

When masculine voices sounded at the drawing-room door, Mrs. Loring looked curiously for the eccentric gentleman. He entered last of all. A man of more than middle-height, but much bowed in the shoulders; thin, ungraceful, with an irresolute step and a shy demeanour; his pale-grey eyes, very soft in expression, looked timidly this way and that from beneath brows nervously bent, and a self-obliterating smile wavered upon his lips. His hair had begun to thin and to turn grey, but he had a heavy moustache, which would better have sorted with sterner lineaments. As he walked—or sidled—into the room, his hands kept shutting and opening, with rather ludicrous effect. Something which was not exactly shabbiness, but a lack of lustre, of finish, singled him among the group of men; looking closer, one saw that his black suit belonged to a fashion some years old. His linen was irreproachable, but he wore no sort of jewellery, one little black stud showing on his front, and, at the cuffs, solitaires of the same simple description.

He drifted into a corner, and there would have sat alone, seemingly at peace, had not Mrs. Weare presently moved to a seat beside him.

'I hope you won't be staying in town through August, Mr. Tymperley?'

'No!—Oh no!—Oh no, I think not!'

'But you seem uncertain. Do forgive me if I say that I'm sure you need a change. Really, you know, you are *not* looking quite the thing. Now, can't I persuade you to join us at Lucerne? My husband would be so pleased—delighted to talk with you about the state of Europe. Give us a fortnight—do!'

'My dear Mrs. Weare, you are kindness itself! I am deeply grateful. I can't easily express my sense of your most friendly thoughtfulness. But, the truth is, I am half engaged to other friends. Indeed, I think I may almost say that I have practically . . . yes, indeed, it amounts to that.'

He spoke in a thinly fluting voice, with a preciseness of enunciation akin to the more feebly clerical, and with smiles which became almost lachrymose in their expressiveness as he dropped from phrase to phrase of embarrassed circumlocution. And his long bony hands writhed together till the knuckles were white.

'Well, so long as you *are* going away. I'm so afraid

lest your conscientiousness should go too far. You won't benefit anybody, you know, by making yourself ill.'

'Obviously not!—Ha, ha!—I assure you that fact is patent to me. Health is a primary consideration. Nothing more detrimental to one's usefulness than an impaired . . . Oh, to be sure, to be sure!'

'There's the strain upon your sympathies. That must affect one's health, quite apart from an unhealthy atmosphere.'

'But Islington is not unhealthy, my dear Mrs. Weare! Believe me, the air has often quite a tonic quality. We are so high, you must remember. If only we could subdue in some degree the noxious exhalations of domestic and industrial chimneys!—Oh, I assure you, Islington has every natural feature of salubrity.'

Before the close of the evening there was a little music, which Mr. Tymperley seemed much to enjoy. He let his head fall back, and stared upwards; remaining rapt in that posture for some moments after the music ceased, and at length recovering himself with a sigh.

When he left the house he donned an overcoat considerably too thick for the season, and bestowed in the pockets his patent-leather shoes. His hat was a hard felt, high in the crown. He grasped an ill-folded umbrella, and set forth at a brisk walk, as if for the neighbouring station. But the railway was not his goal, nor yet the omnibus. Through the ambrosial night he walked and walked, at the steady pace of one accustomed to pedestrian exercise: from Notting Hill Gate to the Marble Arch; from the Marble Arch to New Oxford Street; thence by Theobald's Road to Pentonville, and up, and up, until he attained the heights of his own salubrious quarter. Long after midnight he entered a narrow byway, which the pale moon showed to be decent, though not inviting. He admitted himself with a latchkey to a little house which smelt of glue, lit a candle-end which he found in his pocket, and ascended two flights of stairs to a back bedroom, its size eight feet by seven and a half. A few minutes more, and he lay sound asleep.

Waking at eight o'clock—he knew the time by a bell that clanged in the neighbourhood—Mr. Tymperley clad himself with nervous haste. On opening his door, he found lying outside a tray, with the materials of a breakfast reduced to its lowest terms: half a pint of milk, bread, butter. At nine o'clock he went downstairs, tapped civilly at the door of the front parlour, and by an untuned voice was bidden enter. The room was occupied by an oldish man and a girl, addressing themselves to the day's work of plain bookbinding.

'Good morning to you, sir,' said Mr. Tymperley, bending his head. 'Good morning, Miss Suggs. Bright! Sunny! How it cheers one!'

He stood rubbing his hands, as one might on a morning of sharp frost. The bookbinder, with a dry nod for greeting, forthwith set Mr. Tymperley a task, to which that gentleman zealously applied himself. He was learning the elementary processes of the art. He worked with patience, and some show of natural aptitude, all through the working hours of the day.

To this pass had things come with Mr. Tymperley, a gentleman of Berkshire, once living in comfort and modest dignity on the fruit of sound investments. Schooled at Harrow, a graduate of Cambridge, he had meditated the choice of a profession until it seemed, on the whole, too late to profess anything at all; and, as there was no need of such exertion, he settled himself to a life of innocent idleness, hard by the country-house of his wealthy and influential friend, Mr. Charman. Softly the years flowed by. His thoughts turned once or twice to marriage, but a profound diffidence withheld him from the initial step; in the end, he knew himself born for bachelorhood, and with that estate was content. Well for him had he seen as clearly the delusiveness of other temptations! In an evil moment he listened to Mr. Charman, whose familiar talk was of speculation, of companies, of shining percentages. Not on his own account was Mr. Tymperley lured: he had enough and to spare; but he thought of his sister, married to an unsuccessful provincial barrister, and of her six children, whom it would be pleasant to help, like the opulent uncle of fiction, at their entering upon the world. In Mr. Charman he put blind faith, with the result that one morning he found himself shivering on the edge of ruin; the touch of confirmatory news, and over he went.

No one was aware of it but Mr. Charman himself, and he, a few days later, lay sick unto death. Mr. Charman's own estate suffered inappreciably from what to his friend meant sheer disaster. And Mr. Tymperley breathed not a word to the widow; spoke not a word to any one at all, except the lawyer, who quietly wound up his affairs, and the sister whose children must needs go without avuncular aid. During the absence of his friendly neighbours after Mr. Charman's death, he quietly disappeared.

The poor gentleman was then close upon forty years old. There remained to him a capital which he durst not expend: invested, it bore him an income upon which a labourer could scarce have subsisted. The only possible place of residence—because the only sure place of hiding—was London, and to London Mr. Tymperley betook himself. Not at once did he learn the art of combating starvation with minim resources. During his initiatory trials he was once brought so low, by hunger and humiliation, that he swallowed something of his pride, and wrote to a certain acquaintance, asking counsel and indirect help. But only a man in Mr. Tymperley's position learns how vain is well-meaning advice, and how impotent is social influence. Had he begged for money, he would have received, no doubt, a cheque, with words of compassion; but Mr. Tymperley could never bring himself to that.

He tried to make profit of his former amusement, fretwork, and to a certain extent succeeded, earning in six months half a sovereign. But the prospect of adding one pound a year to his starveling dividends did not greatly exhilarate him.

All this time he was of course living in absolute solitude. Poverty is the great secluder—unless one belongs to the rank which is born to it; a sensitive man who no longer finds himself on equal terms with his natural associates, shrinks into loneliness, and learns with some surprise how very willing people are to forget his existence. London is a wilderness abounding in anchorites—voluntary or constrained. As he wandered about the streets and parks, or killed time in museums and galleries (where nothing had to be paid), Mr. Tymperley often recognized brethren in seclusion; he understood the furtive glance which met his own, he read the peaked visage, marked with understanding sympathy the shabby-genteel apparel. No interchange of confidences between these lurking mortals; they would like to speak, but pride holds them aloof; each goes on his silent and unfriended way, until, by good luck, he finds himself in hospital or workhouse, when at length the tongue is loosed, and the sore heart pours forth its reproach of the world.

Strange knowledge comes to a man in this position. He learns wondrous economies, and will feel a sort of pride in his ultimate discovery of how little money is needed to support life. In his old days Mr. Tymperley would have laid it down as an axiom that 'one' cannot live on less than such-and-such an income; he found that 'a man' can live on a few coppers a day. He became aware of the prices of things to eat, and was taught the relative virtues of nutriment. Perforce a vegetarian, he found that a vegetable diet was good for his health, and delivered to himself many a scornful speech on the habits of the carnivorous multitude. He of necessity abjured alcohols, and straightway longed to utter his testimony on a teetotal platform. These were his satisfactions. They compensate astonishingly for the loss of many kinds of self-esteem.

But it happened one day that, as he was in the act of drawing his poor little quarterly salvage at the Bank of England, a lady saw him and knew him. It was Mr. Charman's widow.

'Why, Mr. Tymperley, what *has* become of you all this time? Why have I never heard from you? Is it true, as some one told me, that you have been living abroad?'

So utterly was he disconcerted, that in a mechanical way he echoed the lady's last word: 'Abroad.'

'But why didn't you write to us?' pursued Mrs. Charman, leaving him no time to say more. 'How very unkind! Why did you go away without a word? My daughter says that we must have unconsciously offended you in some way. Do explain! Surely there can't have been anything——'

'My dear Mrs. Charman, it is I alone who am to blame. I . . . the explanation is difficult; it involves a multiplicity of detail. I beg you to interpret my unjustifiable behaviour as—as pure idiosyncrasy.'

'Oh, you must come and see me. You know that Ada's married? Yes, nearly a year ago. How glad she will be to see you again. So often she has spoken of you. When can you dine? To-morrow?'

'With pleasure—with great pleasure.'

'Delightful!'

She gave her address, and they parted.

Now, a proof that Mr. Tymperley had never lost all hope of restitution to his native world lay in the fact of his having carefully preserved an evening-suit, with the appropriate patent-leather shoes. Many a time had he been sorely tempted to sell these seeming superfluities; more than once, towards the end of his pinched quarter, the suit had been pledged for a few shillings; but to part with the supreme symbol of respectability would have meant despair—a state of mind alien to Mr. Tymperley's passive fortitude. His jewellery, even watch and chain, had long since gone: such gauds are not indispensable to a gentleman's outfit. He now congratulated himself on his prudence, for the meeting with Mrs. Charman had delighted as much as it embarrassed him, and the prospect of an evening in society made his heart glow. He hastened home; he examined his garb of ceremony with anxious care, and found no glaring defect in it. A shirt, a collar, a necktie must needs be purchased; happily he had the means. But how explain himself? Could he confess his place of abode, his startling poverty? To do so would be to make an appeal to the compassion of his old friends, and from that he shrank in horror. A gentleman will not, if it can possibly be avoided, reveal circumstances likely to cause pain. Must he, then, tell or imply a falsehood? The whole truth involved a reproach of Mrs. Charman's husband—a thought he could not bear.

The next evening found him still worrying over this dilemma. He reached Mrs. Charman's house without having come to any decision. In the drawing-room three persons awaited him: the hostess, with her daughter and son-in-law, Mr. and Mrs. Weare. The cordiality of his reception moved him all but to tears; overcome by many emotions, he lost his head. He talked at random; and the result was so strange a piece of fiction, that no sooner had he evolved it than he stood aghast at himself.

It came in reply to the natural question where he was residing.

'At present'—he smiled fatuously—'I inhabit a bed-sitting-room in a little street up at Islington.'

Dead silence followed. Eyes of wonder were fixed upon him. But for those eyes, who knows what confession Mr. Tymperley might have made? As it was . . .

'I said, Mrs. Charman, that I had to confess to an eccentricity. I hope it won't shock you. To be brief, I have devoted my poor energies to social work. I live among the poor, and as one of them, to obtain knowledge that cannot otherwise be procured.'

'Oh, how noble!' exclaimed the hostess.

The poor gentleman's conscience smote him terribly. He could say no more. To spare his delicacy, his friends turned the conversation. Then or afterwards, it never occurred to them to doubt the truth of what he had said. Mrs. Charman had seen him transacting business at the Bank of England, a place not suggestive of poverty; and he had always passed for a man somewhat original in his views and ways. Thus was Mr. Tymperley committed to a singular piece of deception, a fraud which could not easily be discovered, and which injured only its perpetrator.

Since then about a year had elapsed. Mr. Tymperley had seen his friends perhaps half a dozen times, his enjoyment of their society pathetically intense, but troubled by any slightest allusion to his mode of life. It had come to be understood that he made it a matter of principle to hide his light under a bushel, so he seldom had to take a new step in positive falsehood. Of course he regretted ceaselessly the original deceit, for Mrs. Charman, a wealthy woman, might very well have assisted him to some not undignified mode of earning his living. As it was, he had hit upon the idea of making himself a bookbinder, a craft somewhat to his taste. For some months he had lodged in the bookbinder's house; one day courage came to him, and he entered into a compact with his landlord, whereby he was to pay for instruction by a certain period of unremunerated work after he became proficient. That stage was now approaching. On the whole, he felt much happier than in the time of brooding idleness.

He looked forward to the day when he would have a little more money in his pocket, and no longer dread the last fortnight of each quarter, with its supperless nights.

Mrs. Weare's invitation to Lucerne cost him pangs. Lucerne ! Surely it was in some former state of existence that he had taken delightful holidays as a matter of course. He thought of the many lovely places he knew, and so many dream-landscapes ; the London streets made them infinitely remote, utterly unreal. His three years of gloom and hardship were longer than all the life of placid contentment that came before. Lucerne ! A man of more vigorous temper would have been maddened at the thought ; but Mr. Tymperley nursed it all day long, his emotions only expressing themselves in a little sigh or a sadly wistful smile.

Having dined so well yesterday, he felt it his duty to expend less than usual on to-day's meals. About eight o'clock in the evening, after a meditative stroll in the air which he had so praised, he entered the shop where he was wont to make his modest purchases. A fat woman behind the counter nodded familiarly to him, with a grin at another customer. Mr. Tymperley bowed, as was his courteous habit.

'Oblige me,' he said, 'with one new-laid egg and a small, crisp lettuce.'

'Only one to-night, eh ?' said the woman.

'Thank you, only one,' he replied, as if speaking in a drawing-room. 'Forgive me if I express a hope that it will be, in the strict sense of the word, new-laid. The last, I fancy, had got into that box by some oversight—pardonable in the press of business.'

'They're always the same,' said the fat shopkeeper. 'We don't make no mistakes of that kind.'

'Ah ! Forgive me ! Perhaps I imagined——'

Egg and lettuce were carefully deposited in a little handbag he carried, and he returned home. An hour later, when his meal was finished, and he sat on a straight-backed chair meditating in the twilight, a rap sounded at his door, and a letter was handed to him. So rarely did a letter arrive for Mr. Tymperley that his hand shook as he examined the envelope. On opening it, the first thing he saw was a cheque. This excited him still more; he unfolded the written sheet with agitation. It came from Mrs. Weare, who wrote thus:

'MY DEAR MR. TYMPERLEY,—After our talk last evening, I could not help thinking of you and your beautiful life of self-sacrifice. I contrasted the lot of these poor people with my own, which, one cannot but feel, is so undeservedly blest and so rich in enjoyments. As a result of these thoughts, I feel impelled to send you a little contribution to your good work—a sort of thank-offering at the moment of setting off for a happy holiday. Divide the money, please, among two or three of your most deserving pensioners; or, if you see fit, give it all to one. I cling to the hope that we may see you at Lucerne.—With very kind regards.'

The cheque was for five pounds. Mr. Tymperley held it up by the window, and gazed at it. By his present standards of value five pounds seemed a very large sum. Think of what one could do with it! His boots—which had been twice repaired—would not decently serve him much longer. His trousers were in the last stage of presentability. The hat he wore (how carefully tended!) was the same in which he had come to London three years ago. He stood in need, verily, of a new equipment from head to foot; and in Islington five pounds would more than cover the whole expense. When, pray, was he likely to have such a sum at his free disposal?

He sighed deeply, and stared about him in the dusk.

The cheque was crossed. For the first time in his life Mr. Tymperley perceived that the crossing of a cheque may occasion its recipient a great deal of trouble. How was he to get it changed? He knew his landlord for a suspicious curmudgeon, and refusal of the favour, with such a look as Mr. Suggs knew how to give, would be a sore humiliation; besides, it was very doubtful whether Mr. Suggs could make any use of the cheque himself. To whom else could he apply? Literally, to no one in London.

'Well, the first thing to do was to answer Mrs. Weare's letter. He lit his lamp and sat down at the crazy little deal table; but his pen dipped several times into the ink before he found himself able to write.

'Dear Mrs. Weare,'—

Then, so long a pause that he seemed to be falling asleep. With a jerk, he bent again to his task.

'With sincere gratitude I acknowledge the receipt of your most kind and generous donation. The money . . .'

(Again his hand lay idle for several minutes.)

'shall be used as you wish, and I will render to you a detailed account of the benefits conferred by it.'

Never had he found composition so difficult. He felt that he was expressing himself wretchedly; a clog was on his brain. It cost him an exertion of physical strength to conclude the letter. When it was done, he went out, purchased a stamp at a tobacconist's shop, and dropped the envelope into the post.

Little slumber had Mr. Tymperley that night. On lying down, he began to wonder where he should find the poor people worthy of sharing in this benefaction. Of course he had no acquaintance with the class of persons of whom Mrs. Weare was thinking. In a sense, all the families round about were poor, but—he asked himself—had poverty the same meaning for them as for him? Was there a man or woman in this grimy street who, compared with himself, had any right to be called poor at all? An educated man forced to live among the lower classes arrives at many interesting conclusions with regard to them; one conclusion long since fixed in Mr. Tymperley's mind was that the 'suffering' of those classes is very much exaggerated by outsiders using a criterion quite inapplicable. He saw around him a world of coarse jollity, of contented labour, and of brutal apathy. It seemed to him more than probable that the only person in this street conscious of poverty, and suffering under it, was himself.

From nightmarish dozing, he started with a vivid thought, a recollection which seemed to pierce his brain. To whom did he owe his fall from comfort and self-respect, and all his long miseries? To Mrs. Weare's father. And, from this point of view, might the cheque for five pounds be considered as mere restitution? Might it not strictly be applicable to his own necessities?

Another little gap of semi-consciousness led to another strange reflection. What if Mrs. Weare (a sensible woman) suspected, or even had discovered, the truth about him? What if she secretly *meant* the money for his own use?

Earliest daylight made this suggestion look very insubstantial; on the other hand, it strengthened his memory of Mr. Charman's virtual indebtedness to him. He jumped out of bed to reach the cheque, and for an hour lay with it in his hand. Then he rose and dressed mechanically.

After the day's work he rambled in a street of large shops. A bootmaker's arrested him; he stood before the window for a long time, turning over and over in his pocket a sovereign—no small fraction of the ready coin which had to support him until dividend day. Then he crossed the threshold.

Never did man use less discretion in the purchase of a pair of boots. His business was transacted in a dream; he spoke without hearing what he said; he stared at objects without perceiving them. The result was that not till he had got home, with his easy old footgear under his arm, did he become aware that the new boots pinched him most horribly. They creaked too: heavens! how they creaked! But doubtless all new boots had these faults; he had forgotten; it was so long since he had bought a pair. The fact was, he felt dreadfully tired, utterly worn out. After munching a mouthful of supper he crept into bed.

All night long he warred with his new boots. Footsore, he limped about the streets of a spectral city, where at every corner some one seemed to lie in ambush for him, and each time the lurking enemy proved to be no other than Mrs. Weare, who gazed at him with scornful eyes and let him totter by. The creaking of the boots was an articulate voice, which ever and anon screamed at him a terrible name. He shrank and shivered and groaned; but on he went, for in his hand he held a crossed cheque, which he was bidden to get changed, and no one would change it. What a night!

When he woke his brain was heavy as lead; but his meditations were very lucid. Pray, what did he mean by that insane outlay of money, which he could not possibly afford, on a new (and detestable) pair of boots? The old would have lasted, at all events, till winter began. What was in his mind when he entered the shop? Did he intend . . . ? Merciful powers!

Mr. Tymperley was not much of a psychologist. But all at once he saw with awful perspicacity the moral crisis through which he had been living. And it taught him one more truth on the subject of poverty.

Immediately after his breakfast he went downstairs and tapped at the door of Mr. Suggs' sitting-room.

'What is it?' asked the bookbinder, who was eating his fourth large rasher, and spoke with his mouth full.

'Sir, I beg leave of absence for an hour or two this morning. Business of some moment demands my attention.'

Mr. Suggs answered, with the grace natural to his

order, 'I s'pose you can do as you like. I don't pay you nothing.'

The other bowed and withdrew.

Two days later he again penned a letter to Mrs. Weare. It ran thus:

'The money which you so kindly sent, and which I have already acknowledged, has now been distributed. To ensure a proper use of it, I handed the cheque, with clear instructions, to a clergyman in this neighbourhood, who has been so good as to jot down, on the sheet enclosed, a memorandum of his beneficiaries, which I trust will be satisfactory and gratifying to you.

'But why, you will ask, did I have recourse to a clergyman. Why did I not use my own experience, and give myself the pleasure of helping poor souls in whom I have a personal interest—I who have devoted my life to this mission of mercy?

'The answer is brief and plain. I have lied to you.

'I am *not* living in this place of my free will. I am *not* devoting myself to works of charity. I am—no, no, I was—merely a poor gentleman, who, on a certain day, found that he had wasted his substance in a foolish speculation, and who, ashamed to take his friends into his confidence, fled to a life of miserable obscurity. You see that I have added disgrace to misfortune. I will not tell you how very near I came to something still worse.

'I have been serving an apprenticeship to a certain handicraft which will, I doubt not, enable me so to supplement my own scanty resources that I shall be in better circumstances than hitherto. I entreat you to forgive me, if you can, and henceforth to forget

Yours unworthily,

'S. V. TYMPERLEY.'

HENRY HARLAND

1861—1905

THE HOUSE OF EULALIE

It was a pretty little house, in very charming country—in an untravelled corner of Normandy, near the sea; a country of orchards and colza-fields, of soft green meadows where cattle browsed, and of deep elm-shaded lanes.

One was rather surprised to see this little house just here, for all the other houses in the neighbourhood were rude farm-houses or labourers' cottages; and this was a coquettish little chalet, white-walled, with slim French windows, and balconies of twisted iron-work, and Venetian blinds: a gay little pleasure-house, standing in a bright little garden, among rose-bushes, and parterres of geraniums, and smooth stretches of greensward. Beyond the garden there was an orchard—rows and couples of old gnarled apple-trees, bending towards one another like fantastic figures arrested in the middle of a dance. Then, turning round, you looked over feathery colza-fields and yellow corn-fields, a mile away, to the sea, and to a winding perspective of white cliffs, which the sea bathed in transparent greens and purples, luminous shadows of its own nameless hues.

A board attached to the wall confirmed, in roughly-painted characters, the information I had had from an agent in Dieppe. The house was to let; and I had driven out—a drive of two long hours—to inspect it. Now I stood on the doorstep and rang the bell. It was a big bell, hung in the porch, with a pendent handle of bronze, wrought in the semblance of a rope and tassel. Its voice would carry far on that still country air.

It carried, at any rate, as far as a low thatched farm-house, a hundred yards down the road. Presently a man and a woman came out of the farm-house, gazed for an instant in my direction, and then moved towards me: an old brown man, an old grey woman, the man in corduroys, the woman wearing a neat white cotton cap and a blue apron, both moving with the burdened gait of peasants.

'You are Monsieur and Madame Leroux?' I asked, when we had accomplished our preliminary good-days; and I explained that I had come from the agent in Dieppe to look over their house. For the rest, they must have been expecting me; the agent had said that he would let them know.

But, to my perplexity, this business-like announcement seemed somehow to embarrass them; even, I might have thought, to agitate, to distress them. They lifted up their worn old faces, and eyed me anxiously. They exchanged anxious glances with each other. The woman clasped her hands, nervously working her fingers. The man hesitated and stammered a little, before he was able to repeat vaguely, 'You have come to look over the house, Monsieur?'

'Surely,' I said, 'the agent has written to you? I understood from him that you would expect me at this hour to-day.'

'Oh yes,' the man admitted, 'we were expecting you.' But he made no motion to advance matters. He exchanged another anxious glance with his wife. She gave her head a sort of helpless nod, and looked down.

'You see, Monsieur,' the man began, as if he were about to elucidate the situation, 'you see——' But then he faltered, frowning at the air, as one at a loss for words.

'The house is already let, perhaps?' suggested I.

'No, the house is not let,' said he.

'You had better go and fetch the key,' his wife said at last, in a dreary way, still looking down.

He trudged heavily back to the farm-house. While he was gone we stood by the door in silence, the woman always nervously working the fingers of her clasped hands. I tried, indeed, to make a little conversation: I ventured something about the excellence of the site, the beauty of the view. She replied with a murmur of assent, civilly but wearily; and I did not feel encouraged to persist.

By-and-by her husband rejoined us, with the key; and they began silently to lead me through the house.

There were two pretty drawing-rooms on the ground floor, a pretty dining-room, and a delightful kitchen, with a broad hearth of polished red bricks, a tiled chimney, and shining copper pots and pans. The drawing-rooms and the dining-room were pleasantly furnished in a light French fashion, and their windows opened to the sun and to the fragrance and greenery of the garden. I expressed a good deal of admiration; whereupon, little by little, the manner of my conductors changed. From constrained, depressed, it became responsive; even, in the end, effusive. They met my exclamations with smiles, my inquiries with voluble eager answers. But it remained an agitated manner, the manner of people who were shaken by an emotion. Their old hands trembled as they opened the doors for me or drew up the blinds; their voices trembled. There was something painful in their very smiles, as if these were but momentary ripples on the surface of a trouble.

'Ah,' I said to myself, 'they are hard-pressed for money. They have put their whole capital into this house, very likely. They are excited by the prospect of securing a tenant.'

'Now, if you please, Monsieur, we will go upstairs, and see the bedrooms,' the old man said.

The bedrooms were airy, cheerful rooms, gaily papered, with chintz curtains and the usual French bedroom furniture. One of them exhibited signs of being actually lived in; there were things about it, personal things, a woman's things. It was the last room we visited, a front room, looking off to the sea. There were combs and brushes on the toilet-table; there were pens, an inkstand, and a portfolio on the writing-desk; there were books in the bookcase. Framed photographs stood on the mantelpiece. In the closet dresses were suspended, and shoes and slippers were primly ranged on the floor. The bed was covered with a counterpane of blue silk; a crucifix hung on the wall above it; beside it there was a *prie-dieu*, with a little porcelain holy-water vase.

'Oh,' I exclaimed, turning to Monsieur and Madame Leroux, 'this room is occupied?'

Madame Leroux did not appear to hear me. Her eyes were fixed in a dull stare before her, her lips were parted slightly. She looked tired, as if she would be glad when our tour through the house was finished. Monsieur Leroux threw his hand up towards the ceiling in an odd gesture, and said, 'No, the room is not occupied at present.'

We went back downstairs, and concluded an agreement. I was to take the house for the summer. Madame Leroux would cook for me. Monsieur Leroux would drive into Dieppe on Wednesday to fetch me and my luggage out.

. . . . .

On Wednesday we had been driving for something like half an hour without speaking, when all at once Leroux said to me, 'That room, Monsieur, the room you thought was occupied——'

'Yes?' I questioned, as he paused.

'I have a proposition to make,' said he. He spoke, as it seemed to me, half shyly, half doggedly, gazing the while at the ears of his horse.

'What is it?' I asked.

'If you will leave that room as it is, with the things in it, we will make a reduction in the rent. If you will let us keep it as it is?' he repeated, with a curious pleading intensity. 'You are alone. The house will be big enough for you without that room, will it not, Monsieur?'

Of course, I consented at once. If they wished to keep the room as it was, they were to do so, by all means.

'Thank you, thank you very much. My wife will be grateful to you,' he said.

For a little while longer we drove on without speaking. Presently, 'You are our first tenant. We have never let the house before,' he volunteered.

'Ah? Have you had it long?' I asked.

'I built it. I built it, five, six, years ago,' said he. Then, after a pause, he added, 'I built it for my daughter.'

His voice sank, as he said this. But one felt that it was only the beginning of something he wished to say. I invited him to continue by an interested 'Oh?'

'You see what we are, my wife and I,' he broke out suddenly. 'We are rough people, we are peasants. But my daughter, sir'—he put his hand on my knee, and looked earnestly into my face—'my daughter was as fine as satin, as fine as lace.'

He turned back to his horse, and again drove for a minute or two in silence. At last, always with his eyes on the horse's ears, 'There was not a lady in this country finer than my daughter,' he went on, speaking rapidly, in a thick voice, almost as if to himself. 'She was beautiful, she had the sweetest character, she had the best education. She was educated at the convent, in Rouen, at the Sacré Cœur. Six years—from twelve to eighteen—she studied at the convent. She knew English, sir—your language. She took prizes for history. And the piano! Nobody living can touch the piano as my daughter could. Well,' he demanded abruptly, with a kind of fierceness, 'was a rough farm-house good enough for her?' He answered his own question. 'No, Monsieur. You would not soil fine lace by putting it in a dirty box. My daughter was finer than lace. Her hands were softer than Lyons velvet. And oh,' he cried, 'the sweet smell they had, her hands! It was good to smell her hands. I used to kiss them and smell them, as you would smell a rose.' His voice died away at the reminiscence, and there was another interval of silence. By-and-by he began again, 'I had plenty of money. I was the richest farmer of this neighbourhood. I sent to Rouen for the best architect they have there. Monsieur Clermont, the best architect of Rouen, laureate of the Fine Arts School of Paris, he built that house for my daughter; he built it and furnished it, to make it fit for a countess, so that when she came home for good from the convent she should have a home worthy of her. Look at this, Monsieur. Would the grandest palace in the world be too good for her?'

He had drawn a worn red leather case from his pocket, and taken out a small photograph, which he handed to me. It was the portrait of a girl, a delicate-looking girl, of about seventeen. Her face was pretty, with the irregular prettiness not uncommon in France, and very sweet and gentle. The old man almost held his breath while I was examining the photograph. 'Est-elle gentille? Est-elle belle, Monsieur?' he besought me, with a very hunger for sympathy, as I returned it. One answered, of course, what one could, as best one could. He, with shaking fingers, replaced the photograph in its case. 'Here, Monsieur,' he said, extracting from an opposite compartment a little white card. It was the usual French memorial of mourning: an engraving of the Cross and Dove, under which was printed: 'Eulalie-Joséphine-Marie Leroux. Born the 16th May, 1874. Died the 12th August, 1892. Pray for her.'

'The good God knows what He does. I built that house for my daughter, and when it was built the good God took her away. We were mad with grief, my wife and I; but that could not save her. Perhaps we are still mad with grief,' the poor old man said simply. 'We can think of nothing else. We never wish to speak of anything else. We could not live in the house—her house, without her. We never thought to let it. I built that house for my daughter, I furnished it for her, and when it was ready for her—she died. Was it not hard, Monsieur? How could I let the house to strangers? But lately I have had losses. I am compelled to let it, to pay my debts. I would not let it to everybody. You are an Englishman. Well, if I did not like you, I would not let it to you for a million English pounds. But I am glad I have let it to you. You will respect her memory. And you will allow us to keep that room—her room. We shall be able to keep it as it was, with her things in it. Yes, that room which you thought was occupied—that was my daughter's room.'

Madame Leroux was waiting for us in the garden of the chalet. She looked anxiously up at her husband as we arrived. He nodded his head, and called out, 'It's all right. Monsieur agrees.'

The old woman took my hands, wringing them hysterically almost. 'Ah, Monsieur, you are very good,' she said. She raised her eyes to mine. But I could not look into her eyes. There was a sorrow in them, an awfulness, a sacredness of sorrow, which, I felt, it would be like sacrilege for me to look at.

. . . .

We became good friends, the Leroux and I, during the three months I passed as their tenant. Madame, indeed, did for me and looked after me with a zeal that was almost maternal. Both of them, as the old man had said, loved above all things to talk of their daughter, and I hope I was never loath to listen. Their passion, their grief, their constant thought of her, appealed to me as very beautiful, as well as very touching. And something like a pale spirit of the girl seemed gently, sweetly, always to be present in the house, the house that Love had built for her, not guessing that Death would come, as soon as it was finished, and call her away. 'Oh, but it is a joy, Monsieur, that you have left us her room,' the old couple were never tired of repeating. One day Madame took me up into the room, and showed me Eulalie's pretty dresses, her trinkets, her books, the handsomely bound books that she had won as prizes at the convent. And on another day she showed me some of Eulalie's letters, asking me if she hadn't a beautiful handwriting, if the letters were not beautifully expressed. She showed me photographs of the girl at all ages; a lock of her hair; her baby clothes; the priest's certificate of her first communion; the bishop's certificate of her confirmation. And she showed me letters from the good sisters of the Sacred Heart, at Rouen, telling of Eulalie's progress in her studies, praising her conduct and her character. 'Oh, to think that she is gone, that she is gone!' the old woman wailed, in a kind of helpless incomprehension, incredulity, of loss. Then, in a moment, she murmured, with what submissiveness she could, 'Le bon Dieu sait ce qu'il fait,' crossing herself.

On the 12th of August, the anniversary of her death, I went with them to the parish church, where a mass was said for the repose of Eulalie's soul. And the kind old curé afterwards came round, and pressed their hands, and spoke words of comfort to them.

. . . . .

In September I left them, returning to Dieppe. One afternoon I chanced to meet that same old curé in the high street there. We stopped and spoke together—naturally, of the Leroux, of what excellent people they were, of how they grieved for their daughter. 'Their love was more than love. They adored the child, they idolized her. I have never witnessed such affection,' the curé told me. 'When she died, I seriously feared they would lose their reason. They were dazed, they were beside themselves; for a long while they were quite as if mad. But God is merciful. They have learnt to live with their affliction.'

'It is very beautiful,' said I, 'the way they have sanctified her memory, the way they worship it. You know, of course, they keep her room, with her things in it, exactly as she left it. That seems to me very beautiful.'

'Her room?' questioned the curé, looking vague. 'What room?'

'Oh, didn't you know?' I wondered. 'Her bedroom in the chalet. They keep it as she left it, with all her things about, her books, her dresses.'

'I don't think I follow you,' the curé said. 'She never had a bedroom in the chalet.'

'Oh, I beg your pardon. One of the front rooms on the first floor was her room,' I informed him.

But he shook his head. 'There is some mistake. She never lived in the chalet. She died in the old house. The chalet was only just finished when she died. The workmen were hardly out of it.'

'No,' I said, 'it is you who must be mistaken; you must forget. I am quite sure. The Leroux have spoken of it to me times without number.'

'But, my dear sir,' the curé insisted, 'I am not merely sure; I know. I attended the girl in her last agony. She died in the farm-house. They had not moved into the chalet. The chalet was being furnished. The last pieces of furniture were taken in the very day before her death. The chalet was never lived in. You are the only person who has ever lived in the chalet. I assure you of the fact.'

'Well,' I said, 'that is very strange, that is very strange indeed.' And for a minute I was bewildered,

I did not know what to think. But only for a minute. Suddenly I cried out, ' Oh, I see—I see. I understand.'

I saw, I understood. Suddenly I saw the pious, the beautiful deception that these poor stricken souls had sought to practise on themselves ; the beautiful, the fond illusion they had created for themselves. They had built the house for their daughter, and she had died just when it was ready for her. But they could not bear—they could not bear—to think that not for one little week even, not even for one poor little day or hour, had she lived in the house, enjoyed the house. That was the uttermost farthing of their sorrow, which they could not pay. They could not acknowledge it to their own stricken hearts. So, piously, reverently—with closed eyes, as it were, that they might not know what they were doing—they had carried the dead girl's things to the room they had meant for her, they had arranged them there, they had said, ' This was her room ; this *was* her room.' They would not admit to themselves, they would not let themselves stop to think, that she had never, even for one poor night, slept in it, enjoyed it. They told a beautiful pious falsehood to themselves. It was a beautiful pious game of ' make-believe,' which, like children, they could play together. And—the curé had said it : God is merciful. In the end they had been enabled to confuse their beautiful falsehood with reality, and to find comfort in it ; they had been enabled to forget that their 'make-believe' was a 'make-believe,' and to mistake it for a beautiful comforting truth. The uttermost farthing of their sorrow, which they could not pay, was not exacted. They were suffered to keep it ; and it became their treasure, precious to them as fine gold.

Falsehood—truth ? Nay, I think there are illusions that are not falsehoods—that are Truth's own smiles of pity for us.

WILLIAM SYDNEY PORTER
('O. HENRY')

1867—1910

THE GIFT OF THE MAGI

One dollar and eighty-seven cents. That was all. And sixty cents of it was in pennies. Pennies saved one and two at a time by bulldozing the grocer and the vegetable man and the butcher until one's cheeks burned with the silent imputation of parsimony that such close dealing implied. Three times Della counted it. One dollar and eighty-seven cents. And the next day would be Christmas.

There was clearly nothing left to do but flop down on the shabby little couch and howl. So Della did it. Which instigates the moral reflection that life is made up of sobs, sniffles, and smiles, with sniffles predominating.

While the mistress of the home is gradually subsiding from the first stage to the second, take a look at the home. A furnished flat at $8 per week. It did not exactly beggar description, but it certainly had that word on the look-out for the mendicancy squad.

In the vestibule below was a letter-box into which no letter would go, and an electric button from which no mortal finger could coax a ring. Also appertaining thereunto was a card bearing the name 'Mr. James Dillingham Young.

The 'Dillingham' had been flung to the breeze during a former period of prosperity when its possessor was being paid $30 per week. Now, when the income was shrunk to $20, the letters of 'Dillingham' looked blurred, as though they were thinking seriously of contracting to a modest and unassuming D. But whenever Mr. James Dillingham Young came home and reached his flat above he was called 'Jim' and greatly hugged by Mrs. James Dillingham Young, already introduced to you as Della. Which is all very good.

Della finished her cry and attended to her cheeks with the powder rag. She stood by the window and looked out dully at a grey cat walking a grey fence in a grey backyard. To-morrow would be Christmas Day, and she had only $1.87 with which to buy Jim a present. She had been saving every penny she could for months, with this result. Twenty dollars a week doesn't go far. Expenses had been greater than she had calculated. They always are. Only $1.87 to buy a present for Jim. Her Jim. Many a happy hour she had spent planning for something nice for him. Something fine and rare and sterling—something just a little bit near to being worthy of the honour of being owned by Jim.

There was a pier-glass between the windows of the room. Perhaps you have seen a pier-glass in an $8 flat. A very thin and very agile person may, by observing his reflection in a rapid sequence of longitudinal strips, obtain a fairly accurate conception of his looks. Della, being slender, had mastered the art.

Suddenly she whirled from the window and stood before the glass. Her eyes were shining brilliantly, but her face had lost its colour within twenty seconds. Rapidly she pulled down her hair and let it fall to its full length.

Now, there were two possessions of the James Dillingham Youngs in which they both took a mighty pride. One was Jim's gold watch that had been his father's and his grandfather's. The other was Della's hair. Had the Queen of Sheba lived in the flat across the airshaft, Della would have let her hair hang out of the window some day to dry just to depreciate Her

Majesty's jewels and gifts. Had King Solomon been the janitor, with all his treasures piled up in the basement, Jim would have pulled out his watch every time he passed, just to see him pluck at his beard from envy.

So now Della's beautiful hair fell about her, rippling and shining like a cascade of brown waters. It reached below her knee and made itself almost a garment for her. And then she did it up again nervously and quickly. Once she faltered for a minute and stood still while a tear or two splashed on the worn red carpet.

On went her old brown jacket; on went her old brown hat. With a whirl of skirts and with the brilliant sparkle still in her eyes, she fluttered out of the door and down the stairs to the street.

Where she stopped the sign read: 'Mme Sofronie. Hair Goods of All Kinds.' One flight up Della ran, and collected herself, panting. Madame, large, too white, chilly, hardly looked the 'Sofronie.'

'Will you buy my hair?' asked Della.

'I buy hair,' said Madame. 'Take yer hat off and let's have a sight at the looks of it.'

Down rippled the brown cascade.

'Twenty dollars,' said Madame, lifting the mass with a practised hand.

'Give it to me quick,' said Della.

Oh, and the next two hours tripped by on rosy wings. Forget the hashed metaphor. She was ransacking the stores for Jim's present.

She found it at last. It surely had been made for Jim and no one else. There was no other like it in any of the stores, and she had turned all of them inside out. It was a platinum fob chain simple and chaste in design, properly proclaiming its value by substance alone and not by meretricious ornamentation—as all good things should do. It was even worthy of The Watch. As soon as she saw it she knew that it must be Jim's. It was like him. Quietness and value—the description applied to both. Twenty-one dollars they took from her for it, and she hurried home with the 87 cents. With that chain on his watch Jim might be properly anxious about the time in any company. Grand as the watch was, he sometimes looked at it on the sly on account of the old leather strap that he used in place of a chain.

When Della reached home her intoxication gave way a little to prudence and reason. She got out her curling irons and lighted the gas and went to work repairing the ravages made by generosity added to love. Which is always a tremendous task, dear friends —a mammoth task.

Within forty minutes her head was covered with tiny, close-lying curls that made her look wonderfully like a truant schoolboy. She looked at her reflection in the mirror long, carefully, and critically.

'If Jim doesn't kill me,' she said to herself, 'before he takes a second look at me, he'll say I look like a Coney Island chorus girl. But what could I do—oh! what could I do with a dollar and eighty-seven cents?'

At 7 o'clock the coffee was made and the frying-pan was on the back of the stove hot and ready to cook the chops.

Jim was never late. Della doubled the fob chain in her hand and sat on the corner of the table near the door that he always entered. Then she heard his step on the stair away down on the first flight, and she turned white for just a moment. She had a habit of saying little silent prayers about the simplest everyday things, and now she whispered: 'Please, God, make him think I am still pretty.'

The door opened and Jim stepped in and closed it. He looked thin and very serious. Poor fellow, he was only twenty-two—and to be burdened with a family! He needed a new overcoat and he was without gloves.

Jim stepped inside the door, as immovable as a setter at the scent of quail. His eyes were fixed upon Della, and there was an expression in them that she could not read, and it terrified her. It was not anger, nor surprise, nor disapproval, nor horror, nor any of the sentiments that she had been prepared for. He simply stared at her fixedly with that peculiar expression on his face.

Della wriggled off the table and went for him.

'Jim, darling,' she cried, 'don't look at me that way. I had my hair cut off and sold it because I couldn't have lived through Christmas without giving you a present. It'll grow out again—you won't mind, will you? I just had to do it. My hair grows awfully fast. Say "Merry Christmas!" Jim, and let's be happy. You don't know what a nice—what a beautiful, nice gift I've got for you.'

'You've cut off your hair?' asked Jim, laboriously, as if he had not arrived at that patent fact yet, even after the hardest mental labour.

'Cut it off and sold it,' said Della. 'Don't you like me just as well, anyhow? I'm me without my hair, ain't I?'

Jim looked about the room curiously.

'You say your hair is gone?' he said, with an air almost of idiocy.

'You needn't look for it,' said Della. 'It's sold, I tell you—sold and gone, too. It's Christmas Eve, boy. Be good to me, for it went for you. Maybe the hairs of my head were numbered,' she went on with a sudden serious sweetness, 'but nobody could ever count my love for you. Shall I put the chops on, Jim?'

Out of his trance Jim seemed quickly to wake. He enfolded his Della. For ten seconds let us regard with discreet scrutiny some inconsequential object in the other direction. Eight dollars a week or a million a year—what is the difference? A mathematician or a wit would give you the wrong answer. The magi brought valuable gifts, but that was not among them. This dark assertion will be illuminated later on.

Jim drew a package from his overcoat pocket and threw it upon the table.

'Don't make any mistake, Dell,' he said, 'about me. I don't think there's anything in the way of a haircut or a shave or a shampoo that could make me like my girl any less. But if you'll unwrap that package you may see why you had me going a while at first.'

White fingers and nimble tore at the string and paper. And then an ecstatic scream of joy; and then, alas! a quick feminine change to hysterical tears and wails, necessitating the immediate employment of all the comforting powers of the lord of the flat.

For there lay The Combs—the set of combs, side and back, that Della had worshipped for long in a Broadway window. Beautiful combs, pure tortoise-shell, with jewelled rims—just the shade to wear in the beautiful vanished hair. They were expensive combs, she knew, and her heart had simply craved and yearned over them without the least hope of possession. And now, they were hers, but the tresses that should have adorned the coveted adornments were gone.

But she hugged them to her bosom, and at length she was able to look up with dim eyes and a smile and say: 'My hair grows so fast, Jim!'

And then Della leaped up like a little singed cat and cried, 'Oh, oh!'

Jim had not yet seen his beautiful present. She held it out to him eagerly upon her open palm. The dull precious metal seemed to flash with a reflection of her bright and ardent spirit.

'Isn't it a dandy, Jim? I hunted all over town to find it. You'll have to look at the time a hundred times a day now. Give me your watch. I want to see how it looks on it.'

Instead of obeying, Jim tumbled down on the couch and put his hands under the back of his head and smiled.

'Dell,' said he, 'let's put our Christmas presents

away and keep 'em a while. They're too nice to use just at present. I sold the watch to get the money to buy your combs. And now suppose you put the chops on.'

The magi, as you know, were wise men—wonderfully wise men—who brought gifts to the Babe in the manger. They invented the art of giving Christmas presents. Being wise, their gifts were no doubt wise ones, possibly bearing the privilege of exchange in case of duplication. And here I have lamely related to you the uneventful chronicle of two foolish children in a flat who most unwisely sacrificed for each other the greatest treasures of their house. But in a last word to the wise of these days let it be said that of all who give gifts these two were the wisest. Of all who give and receive gifts, such as they are wisest. Everywhere they are wisest. They are the magi.

A MUNICIPAL REPORT

The cities are full of pride,
  Challenging each to each—
This from her mountainside,
  That from her burthened beach.

R. KIPLING.

Fancy a novel about Chicago or Buffalo, let us say, or Nashville, Tennessee! There are just three big cities in the United States that are "story cities"—New York, of course, New Orleans, and, best of the lot, San Francisco.—FRANK NORRIS.

EAST is East, and West is San Francisco, according to Californians. Californians are a race of people; they are not merely inhabitants of a State. They are the Southerners of the West. Now, Chicagoans are no less loyal to their city; but when you ask them why, they stammer and speak of lake fish and the new Odd Fellows Building. But Californians go into detail.

Of course they have, in the climate, an argument that is good for half an hour while you are thinking of your coal bills and heavy underwear. But as soon as they come to mistake your silence for conviction, madness comes upon them, and they picture the city of the Golden Gate as the Bagdad of the New World. So far, as a matter of opinion, no refutation is necessary. But, dear cousins all (from Adam and Eve descended), it is a rash one who will lay his finger on the map and say: 'In this town there can be no romance—what could happen here?' Yes, it is a bold and a rash deed to challenge in one sentence history, romance, and Rand and McNally.

> NASHVILLE.—A city, port of delivery, and the capital of the State of Tennessee, is on the Cumberland River and on the N.C. & St. L. and the L. & N. railroads. This city is regarded as the most important educational centre in the South.

I stepped off the train at 8 P.M. Having searched the thesaurus in vain for adjectives, I must, as a substitution, hie me to comparison in the form of a recipe.

Take of London fog 30 parts; malaria 10 parts; gas leaks 20 parts; dewdrops gathered in a brick yard at sunrise, 25 parts; odour of honeysuckle 15 parts. Mix.

The mixture will give you an approximate conception of a Nashville drizzle. It is not so fragrant as a moth-ball nor as thick as pea-soup; but 'tis enough—'twill serve.

I went to the hotel in a tumbril. It required strong self-suppression for me to keep from climbing to the top of it and giving an imitation of Sidney Carton. The vehicle was drawn by beasts of a bygone era and driven by something dark and emancipated.

I was sleepy and tired, so when I got to the hotel I hurriedly paid it the fifty cents it demanded (with approximate laggniappe, I assure you). I knew its habits; and I did not want to hear it prate about its old 'marster' or anything that happened 'befo' de wah.'

The hotel was one of the kind described as 'renovated.' That means $20,000 worth of new marble pillars, tiling, electric lights and brass cuspidors in the lobby, and a new L. & N. time table and a lithograph of Lookout Mountain in each one of the great rooms above. The management was without reproach, the attention full of exquisite Southern courtesy, the service as slow as the progress of a snail and as good-humoured as Rip Van Winkle. The food was worth travelling a thousand miles for. There is no other hotel in the world where you can get such chicken livers *en brochette.*

At dinner I asked a negro waiter if there was anything doing in town. He pondered gravely for a minute, and then replied: 'Well, boss, I don't really reckon there's anything at all doin' after sundown.'

Sundown had been accomplished; it had been drowned in the drizzle long before. So that spectacle was denied me. But I went forth upon the streets in the drizzle to see what might be there.

> It is built on undulating grounds; and the streets are lighted by electricity at a cost of $32,470 per annum.

As I left the hotel there was a race riot. Down upon me charged a company of freedmen, or Arabs, or Zulus, armed with—no, I saw with relief that they were not rifles, but whips. And I saw dimly a caravan of black, clumsy vehicles; and at the reassuring shouts, 'Kyar you anywhere in the town, boss, fuh fifty cents,' I reasoned that I was merely a 'fare' instead of a victim.

I walked through long streets, all leading uphill. I wondered how those streets ever came down again. Perhaps they didn't until they were 'graded.' On a few of the 'main streets' I saw lights in stores here and there; saw street cars go by conveying worthy burghers hither and yon; saw people pass engaged in the art of conversation, and heard a burst of semi-lively laughter issuing from a soda-water and ice-cream parlour. The streets other than 'main' seemed to have enticed upon their borders houses consecrated to peace and domesticity. In many of them lights shone behind discreetly drawn window shades; in a few pianos tinkled orderly and irreproachable music. There was, indeed, little 'doing.' I wished I had come before sundown. So I returned to my hotel.

> In November, 1864, the Confederate General Hood advanced against Nashville, where he shut up a National force under General Thomas. The latter then sallied forth and defeated the Confederates in a terrible conflict.

All my life I have heard of, admired, and witnessed the fine marksmanship of the South in its peaceful conflicts in the tobacco-chewing regions. But in my hotel a surprise awaited me. There were twelve bright, new, imposing, capacious brass cuspidors in the great lobby, tall enough to be called urns and so wide-mouthed that the crack pitcher of a lady baseball team should have been able to throw a ball into one of them at five paces distant. But, although a terrible battle had raged and was still raging, the enemy had not suffered. Bright, new, imposing, capacious, untouched, they stood. But shades of Jefferson Brick! the tile floor—the beautiful tile floor! I could not avoid thinking of the battle of Nashville, and trying to draw, as is my foolish habit, some deductions about hereditary marksmanship.

Here I first saw Major (by misplaced courtesy) Wentworth Caswell. I knew him for a type the moment my eyes suffered from the sight of him. A rat has no geographical habitat. My old friend,

A. Tennyson, said, as he so well said almost everything:

> 'Prophet, curse me the babbling lip,
> And curse me the British vermin, the rat.'

Let us regard the word 'British' as interchangeable *ad lib.* A rat is a rat.

This man was hunting about the hotel lobby like a starved dog that had forgotten where he had buried a bone. He had a face of great acreage, red, pulpy, and with a kind of sleepy massiveness like that of Buddha. He possessed one single virtue—he was very smoothly shaven. The mark of the beast is not indelible upon a man until he goes about with a stubble. I think that if he had not used his razor that day I would have repulsed his advances, and the criminal calendar of the world would have been spared the addition of one murder.

I happened to be standing within five feet of a cuspidor when Major Caswell opened fire upon it. I had been observant enough to perceive that the attacking force was using Gatlings instead of squirrel rifles; so I side-stepped so promptly that the major seized the opportunity to apologize to a noncombatant. He had the blabbing lip. In four minutes he had become my friend and had dragged me to the bar.

I desire to interpolate here that I am a Southerner. But I am not one by profession or trade. I eschew the string tie, the slouch hat, the Prince Albert, the number of bales of cotton destroyed by Sherman, and plug chewing. When the orchestra plays Dixie I do not cheer. I slide a little lower on the leather-cornered seat and, well, order another Wurzburger and wish that Longstreet had—but what's the use?

Major Caswell banged the bar with his fist, and the first gun at Fort Sumter re-echoed. When he fired the last one at Appomattox I began to hope. But then he began on family trees, and demonstrated that Adam was only a third cousin of a collateral branch of the Caswell family. Genealogy disposed of, he took up, to my distaste, his private family matters. He spoke of his wife, traced her descent back to Eve, and profanely denied any possible rumour that she may have had relations in the land of Nod.

By this time I began to suspect that he was trying to obscure by noise the fact that he had ordered the drinks, on the chance that I would be bewildered into paying for them. But when they were down he crashed a silver dollar loudly upon the bar. Then, of course, another serving was obligatory. And when I had paid for that I took leave of him brusquely; for I wanted no more of him. But before I had obtained my release he had prated loudly of an income that his wife received, and showed a handful of silver money.

When I got my key at the desk the clerk said to me courteously: 'If that man Caswell has annoyed you, and if you would like to make a complaint, we will have him ejected. He is a nuisance, a loafer, and without any known means of support, although he seems to have some money most the time. But we don't seem to be able to hit upon any means of throwing him out legally.'

'Why, no,' said I, after some reflection; 'I don't see my way clear to making a complaint. But I would like to place myself on record as asserting that I do not care for his company. Your town,' I continued, 'seems to be a quiet one. What manner of entertainment, adventure, or excitement have you to offer to the stranger within your gates?'

'Well, sir,' said the clerk, 'there will be a show here next Thursday. It is—I'll look it up and have the announcement sent up to your room with the ice water. Good night.'

After I went up to my room I looked out of the window. It was only about ten o'clock, but I looked upon a silent town. The drizzle continued, spangled with dim lights, as far apart as currants in a cake sold at the Ladies' Exchange.

'A quiet place,' I said to myself, as my first shoe struck the ceiling of the occupant of the room beneath mine. 'Nothing of the life here that gives colour and variety to the cities in the East and West. Just a good, ordinary, humdrum business town.'

> Nashville occupies a foremost place among the manufacturing centres of the country. It is the fifth boot and shoe market in the United States, the largest candy and cracker manufacturing city in the South, and does an enormous wholesale drygoods, grocery, and drug business.

I must tell you how I came to be in Nashville, and assure you the digression brings as much tedium to me as it does to you. I was travelling elsewhere on my own business, but I had a commission from a Northern literary magazine to stop over there and establish a personal connection between the publication and one of its contributors, Azalea Adair.

Adair (there was no clue to the personality except the handwriting) had sent in some essays (lost art!) and poems that had made the editors swear approvingly over their one o'clock luncheon. So they had commissioned me to round up said Adair and corner by contract his or her output at two cents a word before some other publisher offered her ten or twenty.

At nine o'clock the next morning, after my chicken livers *en brochette* (try them if you can find that hotel), I strayed out into the drizzle, which was still on for an unlimited run. At the first corner I came upon Uncle Cæsar. He was a stalwart negro, older than the pyramids, with grey wool and a face that reminded me of Brutus, and a second afterwards of the late King Cettiwayo. He wore the most remarkable coat that I ever had seen or expect to see. It reached to his ankles and had once been a Confederate grey in colours.

But rain and sun and age had so variegated it that Joseph's coat, beside it, would have faded to a pale monochrome. I must linger with that coat, for it has to do with the story—the story that is so long in coming, because you can hardly expect anything to happen at Nashville.

Once it must have been the military coat of an officer. The cape of it had vanished, but all adown its front it had been frogged and tasselled magnificently. But now the frogs and tassels were gone. In their stead had been patiently stitched (I surmised by some surviving 'black mammy') new frogs made of cunningly twisted common hempen twine. This twine was frayed and dishevelled. It must have been added to the coat as a substitute for vanished splendours, with tasteless but painstaking devotion, for it followed faithfully the curves of the long-missing frogs. And, to complete the comedy and pathos of the garment, all its buttons were gone save one. The second button from the top alone remained. The coat was fastened by other twine strings tied through the button-holes and other holes rudely pierced in the opposite side. There was never such a weird garment so fantastically bedecked and of so many mottled hues. The lone button was the size of a half-dollar, made of yellow horn and sewed on with coarse twine.

This negro stood by a carriage so old that Ham himself might have started a hack line with it after he left the ark with the two animals hitched to it. As I approached he threw open the door, drew out a leather duster, waved it without using it, and said in deep, rumbling tones:

'Step right in, suh ; ain't a speck of dust in it—jus' got back from a funeral, suh.'

I inferred that on such gala occasions carriages were given an extra cleaning. I looked up and down the street and perceived that there was little choice among the vehicles for hire that lined the kerb. I looked in my memorandum book for the address of Azalea Adair.

'I want to go to 861 Jessamine Street,' I said, and was about to step into the hack. But for an instant the thick, long, gorilla-like arm of the old negro barred me. On his massive and saturnine face a look of sudden suspicion and enmity flashed for a moment. Then, with quickly-returning conviction, he asked blandishingly: 'What are you gwine there for, boss?'

'What is that to you?' I asked, a little sharply.

'Nothin', suh, jus' nothin'. Only it's a lonesome kind of part of town and few folks ever has business out there. Step right in. The seats is clean—jes' got back from a funeral, suh.'

A mile and a half it must have been to our journey's end. I could hear nothing but the fearful rattle of the ancient hack over the uneven brick paving; I could smell nothing but the drizzle, now further flavoured with coal smoke and something like a mixture of tar and oleander blossoms. All I could see through the streaming windows were two rows of dim houses.

> The city has an area of 10 square miles; 181 miles of streets, of which 137 miles are paved; a system of waterworks that cost $2,000,000, with 77 miles of mains.

Eight-sixty-one Jessamine Street was a decayed mansion. Thirty yards back from the street it stood, outmerged in a splendid grove of trees and untrimmed shrubbery. A row of box bushes overflowed and almost hid the paling fence from sight; the gate was kept closed by a rope noose that encircled the gate-post and the first paling of the gate. But when you got inside you saw that 861 was a shell, a shadow, a ghost of former grandeur and excellence. But in the story, I have not yet got inside.

When the hack had ceased from rattling and the weary quadrupeds came to a rest I handed my jehu his fifty cents with an additional quarter, feeling a glow of conscious generosity as I did so. He refused it.

'It's two dollars, suh,' he said.

'How's that?' I asked. 'I plainly heard you call out at the hotel: "Fifty cents to any part of the town."'

'It's two dollars, suh,' he repeated obstinately. 'It's a long ways from the hotel.'

'It is within the city limits and well within them,' I argued. 'Don't think that you have picked up a greenhorn Yankee. Do you see those hills over there?' I went on, pointing toward the east (I could not see them, myself, for the drizzle); 'well, I was born and raised on their other side. You old fool nigger, can't you tell people from other people when you see 'em?'

The grim face of King Cettiwayo softened. 'Is you from the South, suh? I reckon it was them shoes of yourn fooled me. There is somethin' sharp in the toes for a Southern gen'l'man to wear.'

'Then the charge is fifty cents, I suppose?' said I inexorably.

His former expression, a mingling of cupidity and hostility, returned, remained ten seconds, and vanished.

'Boss,' he said, 'fifty cents is right; but I *needs* two dollars, suh; I'm *obleeged* to have two dollars. I ain't *demandin'* it now, suh; after I knows whar you's from; I'm jus' sayin' that I *has* to have two dollars to-night, and business is mighty po'.'

Peace and confidence settled upon his heavy features. He had been luckier than he had hoped. Instead of having picked up a greenhorn, ignorant of rates, he had come upon an inheritance.

'You confounded old rascal,' I said, reaching down into my pocket, 'you ought to be turned over to the police.'

For the first time I saw him smile. He knew; *he knew;* HE KNEW.

I gave him two one-dollar bills. As I handed them over I noticed that one of them had seen parlous times. Its upper right-hand corner was missing, and it had been torn through in the middle, but joined again. A strip of blue tissue paper, pasted over the split, preserved its negotiability.

Enough of the African bandit for the present: I left him happy, lifted the rope and opened the creaky gate.

The house, as I said, was a shell. A paint brush had not touched it in twenty years. I could not see why a strong wind should not have bowled it over like a house of cards until I looked again at the trees that hugged it close—the trees that saw the battle of Nashville and still drew their protecting branches around it against storm and enemy and cold.

Azalea Adair, fifty years old, white-haired, a descendant of the cavaliers, as thin and frail as the house she lived in, robed in the cheapest and cleanest dress I ever saw, with an air as simple as a queen's, received me.

The reception-room seemed a mile square, because there was nothing in it except some rows of books, on unpainted white-pine bookshelves, a cracked marble-top table, a rag rug, a hairless horsehair sofa, and two or three chairs. Yes, there was a picture on the wall, a coloured crayon drawing of a cluster of pansies. I looked around for the portrait of Andrew Jackson and the pine-cone hanging basket, but they were not there.

Azalea Adair and I had conversation, a little of which will be repeated to you. She was a product of the old South, gently nurtured in the sheltered life. Her learning was not broad, but was deep and of splendid originality in its somewhat narrow scope. She had been educated at home, and her knowledge of the world was derived from inference and by inspiration. Of such is the precious, small group of essayists made. While she talked to me I kept brushing my fingers, trying, unconsciously, to rid them guiltily of the absent dust from the half-calf backs of Lamb, Chaucer, Hazlitt, Marcus Aurelius, Montaigne, and Hood. She was exquisite, she was a valuable discovery. Nearly everybody nowadays knows too much—oh, so much too much—of real life.

I could perceive clearly that Azalea Adair was very poor. A house and a dress she had, not much else, I fancied. So, divided between my duty to the magazine and my loyalty to the poets and essayists who fought Thomas in the valley of the Cumberland, I listened to her voice, which was like a harpsichord's, and found that I could not speak of contracts. In the presence of the nine Muses and the three Graces one hesitated to lower the topic to two cents. There would have to be another colloquy after I had regained my commercialism. But I spoke of my mission, and three o'clock of the next afternoon was set for the discussion of the business proposition.

'Your town,' I said, as I began to make ready to depart (which is the time for smooth generalities), 'seems to be a quiet, sedate place. A home town, I should say, where few things out of the ordinary ever happen.'

> It carries on an extensive trade in stoves and hollow ware with the West and South, and its flouring mills have a daily capacity of more than 2,000 barrels.

Azalea Adair seemed to reflect.

'I have never thought of it that way,' she said, with a kind of sincere intensity that seemed to belong to her. 'Isn't it in the still, quiet places that things do happen? I fancy that when God began to create the earth on the first Monday morning one could have leaned out one's windows and heard the drop of mud splashing from His trowel as He built up the everlasting hills. What did the noisiest project in the world—I mean the building of the tower of Babel—result in finally? A page and a half of Esperanto in the *North American Review*.'

'Of course,' said I platitudinously, 'human nature is the same everywhere; but there is more colour—er—more drama and movement and—er—romance in some cities than in others.'

'On the surface,' said Azalea Adair. 'I have travelled many times around the world in a golden airship wafted on two wings—print and dreams. I have seen (on one of my imaginary tours) the Sultan of Turkey bowstring with his own hands one of his wives who had uncovered her face in public. I have seen a man in Nashville tear up his theatre tickets because his wife was going out with her face covered—with rice powder. In San Francisco's Chinatown I saw the slave girl Sing Yee dipped slowly, inch by inch, in boiling almond oil to make her swear she would never see her American lover again. She gave in when the boiling oil had reached three inches above her knee. At a euchre party in East Nashville the other night I saw Kitty Morgan cut dead by seven of her schoolmates and lifelong friends because she had married a house painter. The boiling oil was sizzling as high as her heart; but I wish you could have seen the fine little smile that she carried from table to table. Oh, yes, it is a humdrum town. Just a few miles of red-brick houses and mud and stores and lumber yards.'

Some one knocked hollowly at the back of the house. Azalea Adair breathed a soft apology and went to investigate the sound. She came back in three minutes with brightened eyes, a faint flush on her cheeks, and ten years lifted from her shoulders.

'You must have a cup of tea before you go,' she said, 'and a sugar cake.'

She reached and shook a little iron bell. In shuffled a small negro girl about twelve, barefoot, not very tidy, glowering at me with thumb in mouth and bulging eyes.

Azalea Adair opened a tiny, worn purse and drew out

a dollar bill, a dollar bill with the upper right-hand corner missing, torn in two pieces and pasted together again with a strip of blue tissue paper. It was one of the bills I had given the piratical negro—there was no doubt of it.

'Go up to Mr. Baker's store on the corner, Impy,' she said, handing the girl the dollar bill, 'and get me a quarter of a pound of tea—the kind he always sends me—and ten cents worth of sugar cakes. Now hurry. The supply of tea in the house happens to be exhausted,' she explained to me.

Impy left by the back way. Before the scrape of her hard, bare feet had died away on the back porch, a wild shriek—I was sure it was hers—filled the hollow house. Then the deep, gruff tones of an angry man's voice mingled with the girl's further squeals and unintelligible words.

Azalea Adair rose without surprise or emotion and disappeared. For two minutes I heard the hoarse rumble of the man's voice ; then something like an oath and a light scuffle, and she returned calmly to her chair.

'This is a roomy house,' she said, 'and I have a tenant for part of it. I am sorry to have to rescind my invitation to tea. It was impossible to get the kind I always use at the store. Perhaps to-morrow Mr. Baker will be able to supply me.'

I was sure that Impy had not had time to leave the house. I inquired concerning street-car lines and took my leave. After I was well on my way I remembered that I had not learned Azalea Adair's name. But to-morrow would do.

That same day I started in on the course of iniquity that this uneventful city forced upon me. I was in the town only two days, but in that time I managed to lie shamelessly by telegraph, and to be an accomplice—after the fact, if that is the correct legal term—to a murder.

As I rounded the corner nearest my hotel the Afrite

coachman of the polychromatic, nonpareil coat seized me, swung open the dungeony door of his peripatetic sarcophagus, flirted his feather duster and began his ritual: 'Step right in, boss. Carriage is clean—jus' got back from a funeral. Fifty cents to any——'

And then he knew me and grinned broadly. ''Scuse me, boss; you is de gen'l'man what rid out with me dis mawnin'. Thank you kindly, suh.'

'I am going out to 861 again to-morrow afternoon at three,' said I, 'and if you will be here, I'll let you drive me. So you know Miss Adair?' I concluded, thinking of my dollar bill.

'I belonged to her father, Judge Adair, suh,' he replied.

'I judge that she is pretty poor,' I said. 'She hasn't much money to speak of, has she?'

For an instant I looked again at the fierce countenance of King Cettiwayo, and then he changed back to an extortionate old negro hack driver.

'She a'n't gwine to starve, suh,' he said slowly. 'She has reso'ces, suh; she has reso'ces.'

'I shall pay you fifty cents for the trip,' said I.

'Dat is puffeckly correct, suh,' he answered humbly. 'I jus' *had* to have dat two dollars dis mawnin', boss.'

I went to the hotel and lied by electricity. I wired the magazine: 'A. Adair holds out for eight cents a word.'

The answer that came back was: 'Give it to her quick, you duffer.'

Just before dinner 'Major' Wentworth Caswell bore down upon me with the greetings of a long-lost friend. I have seen few men whom I have so instantaneously hated, and of whom it was so difficult to be rid. I was standing at the bar when he invaded me; therefore I could not wave the white ribbon in his face. I would have paid gladly for the drinks, hoping, thereby, to escape another; but he was one of those despicable, roaring, advertising bibbers who must have brass bands and fireworks attend upon every cent that they waste in their follies.

With an air of producing millions he drew two one-dollar bills from a pocket and dashed one of them upon the bar. I looked once more at the dollar bill with the upper right-hand corner missing, torn through the middle, and patched with a strip of blue tissue paper. It was my dollar bill again. It could have been no other.

I went up to my room. The drizzle and the monotony of a dreary, eventless Southern town had made me tired and listless. I remember that just before I went to bed I mentally disposed of the mysterious dollar bill (which might have formed the clue to a tremendously fine detective story of San Francisco) by saying to myself sleepily: 'Seems as if a lot of people here own stock in the Hack-Driver's Trust. Pays dividends promptly, too. Wonder if——' Then I fell asleep.

King Cettiwayo was at his post the next day, and rattled my bones over the stones out to 861. He was to wait and rattle me back again when I was ready.

Azalea Adair looked paler and cleaner and frailer than she had looked the day before. After she had signed the contract at eight cents per word she grew still paler and began to slip out of her chair. Without much trouble I managed to get her up on the antediluvian horsehair sofa and then I ran out to the sidewalk and yelled to the coffee-coloured Pirate to bring a doctor. With a wisdom that I had not suspected in him, he abandoned his team and struck off up the street afoot, realizing the value of speed. In ten minutes he returned with a grave, grey-haired, and capable man of medicine. In a few words (worth much less than eight cents each) I explained to him my presence in the hollow house of mystery. He bowed with stately understanding, and turned to the old negro.

'Uncle Cæsar,' he said calmly, 'run up to my house and ask Miss Lucy to give you a cream pitcher full of fresh milk and half a tumbler of port wine. And hurry back. Don't drive—run. I want you to get back sometime this week.'

It occurred to me that Dr. Merriman also felt a distrust as to the speeding powers of the land-pirate's steeds. After Uncle Cæsar was gone, lumberingly, but swiftly, up the street, the doctor looked me over with great politeness and as much careful calculation until he had decided that I might do.

'It is only a case of insufficient nutrition,' he said. 'In other words, the result of poverty, pride, and starvation. Mrs. Caswell has many devoted friends who would be glad to aid her, but she will accept nothing except from that old negro, Uncle Cæsar, who was once owned by her family.'

'Mrs. Caswell!' said I, in surprise. And then I looked at the contract and saw that she had signed it 'Azalea Adair Caswell.'

'I thought she was Miss Adair,' I said.

'Married to a drunken, worthless loafer, sir,' said the doctor. 'It is said that he robs her even of the small sums that her old servant contributes toward her support.'

When the milk and wine had been brought, the doctor soon revived Azalea Adair. She sat up and talked of the beauty of the autumn leaves that were then in season, and their height of colour. She referred lightly to her fainting seizure as the outcome of an old palpitation of the heart. Impy fanned her as she lay on the sofa. The doctor was due elsewhere, and I followed him to the door. I told him that it was within my power and intentions to make a reasonable advance of money to Azalea Adair on future contributions to the magazine, and he seemed pleased.

'By the way,' he said, 'perhaps you would like to know that you have had royalty for a coachman. Old Cæsar's grandfather was a king in Congo. Cæsar himself has royal ways, as you may have observed.'

As the doctor was moving off I heard Uncle Cæsar's voice inside ; 'Did he git bofe of dem two dollars from you, Mis' Zalea ?'

'Yes, Cæsar,' I heard Azalea Adair answer weakly. And then I went in and concluded business negotiations with our contributor. I assumed the responsibility of advancing fifty dollars, putting it as a necessary formality in binding our bargain. And then Uncle Cæsar drove me back to the hotel.

Here ends all of the story as far as I can testify as a witness. The rest must be only bare statements of facts.

At about six o'clock I went out for a stroll. Uncle Cæsar was at his corner. He threw open the door of his carriage, flourished his duster and began his depressing formula: 'Step right in, suh. Fifty cents to anywhere in the city—hack's puffickly clean, suh—jus' got back from a funeral——'

And then he recognized me. I think his eyesight was getting bad. His coat had taken on a few more faded shades of colour, the twine strings were more frayed and ragged, the last remaining button—the button of yellow horn—was gone. A motley descendant of kings was Uncle Cæsar!

About two hours later I saw an excited crowd besieging the front of a drug store. In a desert where nothing happens this was manna ; so I edged my way inside. On an extemporized couch of empty boxes and chairs was stretched the mortal corporeality of Major Wentworth Caswell. A doctor was testing him for the immortal ingredient. His decision was that it was conspicuous by its absence.

The erstwhile Major had been found dead on a dark street and brought by curious and ennuied citizens to the drug store. The late human being had been engaged in terrific battle—the details showed that. Loafer and reprobate though he had been, he had been also a warrior. But he had lost. His hands were yet clenched so tightly that his fingers would not be opened. The gentle citizens who had known him, stood about and searched their vocabularies to find some good words, if it were possible, to speak of him. One kind-looking man said, after much thought: 'When "Cas" was about fo'teen he was one of the best spellers in school.'

While I stood there the fingers of the right hand of 'the man that was,' which hung down the side of a white pine box, relaxed, and dropped something at my feet. I covered it with one foot quietly, and a little later on I picked it up and pocketed it. I reasoned that in his last struggle his hand must have seized that object unwittingly and held it in a death grip.

At the hotel that night the main topic of conversation, with the possible exception of politics and prohibition, was the demise of Major Caswell. I heard one man say to a group of listeners:

'In my opinion, gentlemen, Caswell was murdered by some of these no-account niggers for his money. He had fifty dollars this afternoon which he showed to several gentlemen in the hotel. When he was found the money was not on his person.'

I left the city the next morning at nine, and as the train was crossing the bridge over the Cumberland River I took out of my pocket a yellow horn overcoat button the size of a fifty-cent piece, with frayed ends of coarse twine hanging from it, and cast it out of the window into the slow, muddy waters below.

I wonder what's doing in Buffalo!

MADAME BO-PEEP, OF THE RANCHES

'AUNT Ellen,' said Octavia cheerfully, as she threw her black kid gloves carefully at the dignified Persian cat on the window-seat, 'I'm a pauper.'

'You are so extreme in your statements, Octavia, dear,' said Aunt Ellen mildly, looking up from her paper. 'If you find yourself temporarily in need of some small change for bonbons, you will find my purse in the drawer of the writing-desk.'

Octavia Beaupree removed her hat and seated herself on a footstool near her aunt's chair, clasping her hands about her knees. Her slim and flexible figure, clad in a modish mourning costume, accommodated itself easily and gracefully to the trying position. Her bright and youthful face, with its pair of sparkling, life-enamoured eyes, tried to compose itself to the seriousness that the occasion seemed to demand.

'You good auntie, it isn't a case of bonbons; it is abject, staring, unpicturesque poverty, with ready-made clothes, gasolined gloves, and probably one o'clock dinners all waiting with the traditional wolf at the door. I've just come from my lawyer, auntie, and, "Please, ma'am, I ain't got nothink 't all. Flowers, lady? Buttonhole, gentleman? Pencils, sir, three for five, to help a poor widow"? Do I do it nicely, auntie, or, as a bread-winning accomplishment, were my lessons in elocution entirely wasted?'

'Do be serious, my dear,' said Aunt Ellen, letting her paper fall to the floor, 'long enough to tell me what you mean. Colonel Beaupree's estate——'

'Colonel Beaupree's estate,' interrupted Octavia, emphasizing her words with appropriate dramatic gestures, 'is of Spanish castellar architecture. Colonel Beaupree's resources are—wind. Colonel Beaupree's stocks are—water. Colonel Beaupree's income is—all in. The statement lacks the legal technicalities to which I have been listening for an hour, but that is what it means when translated.'

'Octavia!' Aunt Ellen was now visibly possessed by consternation. 'I can hardly believe it. And it was the impression that he was worth a million. And the De Peysters themselves introduced him!'

Octavia rippled out a laugh, and then became properly grave.

'*De mortuis nil*, auntie—not even the rest of it. The dear old colonel—what a gold brick he was, after all! I paid for my bargain fairly—I'm all here, am I not?—items: eyes, fingers, toes, youth, old family, unquestionable position in society as called for in the contract—no wild-cat stock here.' Octavia picked up the morning paper from the floor. 'But I'm not going to "squeal"—isn't that what they call it when you rail at Fortune because you've lost the game?' She turned the pages of the paper calmly. '"Stock market"—no use for that. "Society's doings"—that's done. Here is my page—the wish column. A Van Dresser could not be said to "want" for anything, of course. "Chambermaids, cooks, canvassers, stenographers——"'

'Dear,' said Aunt Ellen, with a little tremor in her voice, 'please do not talk in that way. Even if your affairs are in so unfortunate a condition, there is my three thousand——'

Octavia sprang up lithely, and deposited a smart kiss on the delicate cheek of the prim little elderly maid.

'Blessed auntie, your three thousand is just sufficient to insure your Hyson to be free from willow leaves and keep the Persian in sterilized cream. I know I'd be welcome, but I prefer to strike bottom like Beelzebub rather than hang around like the Peri listening to the music from the side entrance. I'm going to earn my own living. There's nothing else to do. I'm a—Oh, oh, oh!—I had forgotten. There's one thing saved from the wreck. It's a corral—no, a ranch in—let me see—Texas; an asset, dear old Mr. Bannister called it. How pleased he was to show me something he could describe as unencumbered! I've a description of it among those stupid papers he made me bring away with me from his office. I'll try to find it.'

Octavia found her shopping-bag, and drew from it a long envelope filled with typewritten documents.

'A ranch in Texas,' sighed Aunt Ellen. 'It sounds

to me more like a liability than an asset. Those are the places where the centipedes are found, and cowboys, and fandangos.'

'"The Rancho de las Sombras,"' read Octavia from a sheet of violently purple typewriting, '"is situated one hundred and ten miles south-east of San Antonio, and thirty-eight miles from its nearest railroad station, Nopal, on the I. and G.N. Ranch consists of 7,680 acres of well-watered land, with title conferred by State patents, and twenty-two sections, or 14,080 acres, partly under yearly running lease and partly bought under State's twenty-year-purchase act. Eight thousand graded merino sheep, with the necessary equipment of horses, vehicles, and general ranch paraphernalia. Ranch-house built of brick, with six rooms comfortably furnished according to the requirements of the climate. All within a strong barbed-wire fence.

'"The present ranch manager seems to be competent and reliable, and is rapidly placing upon a paying basis a business that, in other hands, had been allowed to suffer from neglect and misconduct.

'"This property was secured by Colonel Beaupree in a deal with a Western irrigation syndicate, and the title to it seems to be perfect. With careful management and the natural increase of land values, it ought to be made the foundation for a comfortable fortune for its owner."'

When Octavia ceased reading, Aunt Ellen uttered something as near a sniff as her breeding permitted.

'The prospectus,' she said, with uncompromising metropolitan suspicion, 'doesn't mention the centipedes, or the Indians. And you never did like mutton, Octavia. I don't see what advantage you can derive from this—desert.'

But Octavia was in a trance. Her eyes were steadily regarding something quite beyond their focus. Her lips were parted, and her face was lighted by the kindling furor of the explorer, the ardent, stirring disquiet of the adventurer. Suddenly she clasped her hands together exultantly.

'The problem solves itself, auntie,' she cried. 'I'm going to that ranch. I'm going to live on it. I'm going to learn to like mutton, and even concede the good qualities of centipedes—at a respectful distance. It's just what I need. It's a new life that comes when my old one is just ending. It's a release, auntie; it isn't a narrowing. Think of the gallops over those leagues of prairies, with the wind tugging at the roots of your hair, the coming close to the earth and learning over again the stories of the growing grass and the little wild flowers without names! Glorious is what it will be. Shall I be a shepherdess with a Watteau hat, and a crook to keep the bad wolves from the lambs, or a typical Western ranch girl, with short hair, like the pictures of her in the Sunday papers? I think the latter. And they'll have my picture, too, with the wild-cats I've slain, single-handed, hanging from my saddle horn. "From the Four Hundred to the Flocks" is the way they'll headline it, and they'll print photographs of the old Van Dresser mansion and the church where I was married. They won't have my picture, but they'll get an artist to draw it. It'll be wild and woolly, and I'll grow my own wool.'

'Octavia!' Aunt Ellen condensed into the one word all the protests she was unable to utter.

'Don't say a word, auntie. I'm going. I'll see the sky at night fit down on the world like a big butter-dish cover, and I'll make friends again with the stars that I haven't had a chat with since I was a wee child. I wish to go. I'm tired of all this. I'm glad I haven't any money. I could bless Colonel Beaupree for that ranch, and forgive him for all his bubbles. What if the life will be rough and lonely! I—I deserve it. I shut my heart to everything except that miserable ambition. I—oh, I wish to go away, and forget—forget!'

Octavia swerved suddenly to her knees, laid her

flushed face in her aunt's lap, and shook with turbulent sobs.

Aunt Ellen bent over her, and smoothed the coppery-brown hair.

'I didn't know,' she said, gently; 'I didn't know—that. Who was it, dear?'

. . . . .

When Mrs. Octavia Beaupree, née Van Dresser, stepped from the train at Nopal, her manner lost, for the moment, some of that easy certitude which had always marked her movements. The town was of recent establishment, and seemed to have been hastily constructed of undressed lumber and flapping canvas. The element that had congregated about the station, though not offensively demonstrative, was clearly composed of citizens accustomed to and prepared for rude alarms.

Octavia stood on the platform, against the telegraph office, and attempted to choose by intuition, from the swaggering, straggling string of loungers, the manager of the Rancho de las Sombras, who had been instructed by Mr. Bannister to meet her there. That tall, serious-looking, elderly man in the blue flannel shirt and white tie she thought must be he. But, no; he passed by, removing his gaze from the lady as hers rested on him, according to the Southern custom. The manager, she thought, with some impatience at being kept waiting, should have no difficulty in selecting her. Young women wearing the most recent thing in ash-coloured travelling-suits were not so plentiful in Nopal!

Thus keeping a speculative watch on all persons of possible managerial aspect, Octavia, with a catching breath and a start of surprise, suddenly became aware of Teddy Westlake hurrying along the platform in the direction of the train—of Teddy Westlake or his sun-browned ghost in cheviot, boots, and leather-girdled hat—Theodore Westlake, Jr., amateur polo (almost) champion, all-round butterfly and cumberer of the soil;

but a broader, surer, more emphasized and determined Teddy than the one she had known a year ago when last she saw him.

He perceived Octavia at almost the same time, deflected his course, and steered for her in his old, straightforward way. Something like awe came upon her as the strangeness of his metamorphosis was brought into closer range; the rich, red-brown of his complexion brought out so vividly his straw-coloured moustache and steel-grey eyes. He seemed more grown-up, and, somehow, farther away. But, when he spoke, the old, boyish Teddy came back again. They had been friends from childhood.

'Why, 'Tave!' he exclaimed, unable to reduce his perplexity to coherence. 'How—what—when—where?'

'Train,' said Octavia; 'necessity; ten minutes ago; home. Your complexion's gone, Teddy. Now, how—what—when—where?'

'I'm working down here,' said Teddy. He cast side glances about the station as one does who tries to combine politeness with duty.

'You didn't notice on the train,' he asked, 'an old lady with grey curls and a poodle, who occupied two seats with her bundles and quarrelled with the conductor, did you?'

'I think not,' answered Octavia, reflecting. 'And you haven't, by any chance, noticed a big, grey-moustached man in a blue shirt and six-shooters, with little flakes of merino wool sticking in his hair, have you?'

'Lots of 'em,' said Teddy, with symptoms of mental delirium under the strain. 'Do you happen to know any such individual?'

'No; the description is imaginary. Is your interest in the old lady whom you describe a personal one?'

'Never saw her in my life. She's painted entirely from fancy. She owns a little piece of property where

I earn my bread and butter—the Rancho de las Sombras. I drove up to meet her according to arrangement with her lawyer.'

Octavia leaned against the wall of the telegraph office. Was this possible? And didn't he know?

'Are you the manager of that ranch?' she asked weakly.

'I am,' said Teddy, with pride.

'I am Mrs. Beaupree,' said Octavia faintly; 'but my hair never would curl, and I was polite to the conductor.'

For a moment that strange, grown-up look came back and removed Teddy miles away from her.

'I hope you'll excuse me,' he said, rather awkwardly. 'You see, I've been down here in the chaparral a year. I hadn't heard. Give me your checks, please, and I'll have your traps loaded into the wagon. José will follow with them. We travel ahead in the buckboard.'

Seated by Teddy in a feather-weight buckboard, behind a pair of wild, cream-coloured Spanish ponies, Octavia abandoned all thought for the exhilaration of the present. They swept out of the little town and down the level road toward the south. Soon the road dwindled and disappeared, and they struck across a world carpeted with an endless reach of curly mesquite grass. The wheels made no sound. The tireless ponies bounded ahead at an unbroken gallop. The temperate wind, made fragrant by thousands of acres of blue and yellow wild flowers, roared gloriously in their ears. The motion was aerial, ecstatic, with a thrilling sense of perpetuity in its effect. Octavia sat silent, possessed by a feeling of elemental, sensual bliss. Teddy seemed to be wrestling with some internal problem.

'I'm going to call you madama,' he announced as the result of his labours. 'That is what the Mexicans will call you—they're nearly all Mexicans on the ranch, you know. That seems to be about the proper thing.'

'Very well, Mr. Westlake,' said Octavia primly.

'Oh, now,' said Teddy, in some consternation, 'that's carrying the thing too far, isn't it?'

'Don't worry me with your beastly etiquette. I'm just beginning to live. Don't remind me of anything artificial. If only this air could be bottled! This much alone is worth coming for. Oh, look! there goes a deer!'

'Jack-rabbit,' said Teddy, without turning his head.

'Could I—might I drive?' suggested Octavia, panting, with rose-tinted cheeks and the eye of an eager child.

'On one condition. Could I—might I smoke?'

'For ever!' cried Octavia, taking the lines with solemn joy. 'How shall I know which way to drive?'

'Keep her sou' by sou'east, and all sail set. You see that black speck on the horizon under that lowermost Gulf cloud? That's a group of live-oaks and a landmark. Steer half-way between that and the little hill to the left. I'll recite you the whole code of driving rules for the Texas prairies: keep the reins from under the horse's feet, and swear at 'em frequent.'

'I'm too happy to swear, Ted. Oh, why do people buy yachts or travel in palace-cars, when a buckboard and a pair of plugs and a spring morning like this can satisfy all desire?'

'Now, I'll ask you,' protested Teddy, who was futilely striking match after match on the dashboard, 'not to call those denizens of the air plugs. They can kick out a hundred miles between daylight and dark.' At last he succeeded in snatching a light for his cigar from the flame held in the hollow of his hands.

'Room!' said Octavia intensely. 'That's what produces the effect. I know now what I've wanted—scope—range—room!'

'Smoking-room,' said Teddy unsentimentally. 'I love to smoke in a buckboard. The wind blows the smoke into you and out again. It saves exertion.'

The two fell so naturally into their old-time good-fellowship that it was only by degrees that a sense of the strangeness of the new relations between them came to be felt.

'Madama,' said Teddy wonderingly, 'however did you get it into your head to cut the crowd and come down here ? Is it a fad now among the upper classes to trot off to sheep ranches instead of to Newport ?'

'I was broke, Teddy,' said Octavia sweetly, with her interest centred upon steering safely between a Spanish dagger plant and a clump of chaparral; 'I haven't a thing in the world but this ranch—not even any other home to go to.'

'Come, now,' said Teddy anxiously but incredulously, 'you don't mean it ?'

'When my husband,' said Octavia, with a shy slurring of the word, 'died three months ago I thought I had a reasonable amount of the world's goods. His lawyer exploded that theory in a sixty-minute fully illustrated lecture. I took to the sheep as a last resort. Do you happen to know of any fashionable caprice among the gilded youth of Manhattan that induces them to abandon polo and club windows to become managers of sheep ranches ?'

'It's easily explained in my case,' responded Teddy, promptly. 'I had to go to work. I couldn't have earned my board in New York, so I chummed a while with old Sandford, one of the syndicate that owned the ranch before Colonel Beaupree bought it, and got a place down here. I wasn't manager at first. I jogged around on ponies and studied the business in detail, until I got all the points in my head. I saw where it was losing and what the remedies were, and then Sandford put me in charge. I get a hundred dollars a month, and I earn it.'

'Poor Teddy !' said Octavia, with a smile.

'You needn't. I like it. I save half my wages, and I'm as hard as a water plug. It beats polo.'

'Will it furnish bread and tea and jam for another outcast from civilization ?'

'The spring shearing,' said the manager, 'just cleaned up a deficit in last year's business. Wastefulness and inattention have been the rule heretofore. The autumn clip will leave a small profit over all expenses. Next year there will be jam.'

When, about four o'clock in the afternoon, the ponies rounded a gentle, brush-covered hill, and then swooped, like a double cream-coloured cyclone, upon the Rancho de las Sombras, Octavia gave a little cry of delight. A lordly grove of magnificent live-oaks cast an area of grateful, cool shade, whence the ranch had drawn its name, 'de las Sombras'—of the shadows. The house, of red brick, one story, ran low and long beneath the trees. Through its middle, dividing its six rooms in half, extended a broad, arched passage-way, picturesque with flowering cactus and hanging red earthern jars. A 'gallery,' low and broad, encircled the building. Vines climbed about it, and the adjacent ground was, for a space, covered with transplanted grass and shrubs. A little lake, long and narrow, glimmered in the sun at the rear. Further away stood the shacks of the Mexican workers, the corrals, wool sheds, and shearing pens. To the right lay the low hills, splattered with dark patches of chaparral: to the left the unbounded green prairie blending against the blue heavens.

'It's a home, Teddy,' said Octavia breathlessly; 'that's what it is—it's a home.'

'Not so bad for a sheep ranch,' admitted Teddy, with excusable pride. 'I've been tinkering on it at odd times.'

A Mexican youth sprang from somewhere in the grass, and took charge of the creams. The mistress and the manager entered the house.

'Here's Mrs. MacIntyre,' said Teddy, as a placid, neat, elderly lady came out upon the gallery to meet them. 'Mrs. Mac, here's the boss. Very likely she will be wanting a hunk of bacon and a dish of beans after her drive.'

Mrs. MacIntyre, the housekeeper, as much a fixture on the place as the lake or the live-oaks, received the imputation of the ranch's resources of refreshment with mild indignation, and was about to give it utterance when Octavia spoke.

'Oh, Mrs. MacIntyre, don't apologize for Teddy. Yes, I call him Teddy. So does every one whom he hasn't duped into taking him seriously. You see, we used to cut paper dolls and play jackstraws together ages ago. No one minds what he says.'

'No,' said Teddy, 'no one minds what he says, just so he doesn't do it again.'

Octavia cast one of those subtle, sidelong glances toward him from beneath her lowered eyelids—a glance that Teddy used to describe as an upper-cut. But there was nothing in his ingenuous, weather-tanned face to warrant a suspicion that he was making an allusion—nothing. Beyond a doubt, thought Octavia, he had forgotten.

'Mr. Westlake likes his fun,' said Mrs. MacIntyre, as she conducted Octavia to her rooms. 'But,' she added loyally, 'people around here usually pay attention to what he says when he talks in earnest. I don't know what would have become of this place without him.'

Two rooms at the east end of the house had been arranged for the occupancy of the ranch's mistress. When she entered them a slight dismay seized her at their bare appearance and the scantiness of their furniture; but she quickly reflected that the climate was a semi-tropical one, and was moved to appreciation of the well-conceived efforts to conform to it. The sashes had already been removed from the big windows, and white curtains waved in the Gulf breeze that streamed through the wide jalousies. The bare floor was amply strewn with cool rugs; the chairs were inviting, deep, dreamy willows; the walls were papered with a light, cheerful olive. One whole side of her sitting-room was covered with books on smooth, unpainted pine shelves. She flew to these at once. Before her was a well-selected library. She caught glimpses of titles of volumes of fiction and travel not yet seasoned from the dampness of the press.

Presently, recollecting that she was now in a wilderness given over to mutton, centipedes, and privations, the incongruity of these luxuries struck her, and, with intuitive feminine suspicion, she began turning to the fly-leaves of volume after volume. Upon each one was inscribed in fluent characters the name of Theodore Westlake, Jr.

Octavia, fatigued by her long journey, retired early that night. Lying upon her white, cool bed, she rested deliciously, but sleep coquetted long with her. She listened to faint noises whose strangeness kept her faculties on the alert—the fractious yelping of the coyotes, the ceaseless, low symphony of the wind, the distant booming of the frogs about the lake, the lamentation of a concertina in the Mexicans' quarters. There were many conflicting feelings in her heart—thankfulness and rebellion, peace and disquietude, loneliness and a sense of protecting care, happiness and an old, haunting pain.

She did what any other woman would have done—sought relief in a wholesome tide of unreasonable tears, and her last words, murmured to herself before slumber, capitulating, came softly to woo her, were, 'He has forgotten.'

The manager of the Rancho de las Sombras was no dilettante. He was a 'hustler.' He was generally up, mounted, and away of mornings before the rest of the household were awake, making the rounds of the flocks and camps. This was the duty of the major-domo, a stately old Mexican with a princely air and manner, but Teddy seemed to have a great deal of confidence in his own eyesight. Except in the busy seasons, he nearly always returned to the ranch to breakfast at eight o'clock, with Octavia and Mrs. MacIntyre, at the little table set in the central hallway, bringing with him a tonic and breezy cheerfulness full of the health and flavour of the prairies.

A few days after Octavia's arrival he made her get out one of her riding-skirts, and curtail it to a shortness demanded by the chaparral brakes.

With some misgivings she donned this and the pair of buckskin leggings he prescribed in addition, and mounted upon a dancing pony, rode with him to view her possessions. He showed her everything—the flocks of ewes, muttons and grazing lambs, the dipping vats, the shearing pens, the uncouth merino rams in their little pasture, the water-tanks prepared against the summer drought—giving account of his stewardship with a boyish enthusiasm that never flagged.

Where was the old Teddy that she knew so well? This side of him was the same, and it was a side that pleased her; but this was all she ever saw of him now. Where was his sentimentality—those old, varying moods of impetuous love-making, of fanciful, quixotic devotion, of heart-breaking gloom, of alternating, absurd tenderness and haughty dignity? His nature had been a sensitive one, his temperament bordering closely on the artistic. She knew that, besides being a follower of fashion and its fads and sports, he had cultivated tastes of a finer nature. He had written things, he had tampered with colours, he was something of a student in certain branches of art, and once she had been admitted to all his aspirations and thoughts. But now—and she could not avoid the conclusion—Teddy had barricaded against her every side of himself except one—the side that showed the manager of the Rancho de las Sombras and a jolly chum who had forgiven and forgotten. Queerly enough the words of Mr. Bannister's description of her property came into her mind—'all inclosed within a strong barbed-wire fence.'

'Teddy's fenced, too,' said Octavia to herself.

It was not difficult for her to reason out the cause of his fortifications. It had originated one night at the Hammersmiths' ball. It occurred at a time soon after she had decided to accept Colonel Beaupree and his million, which was no more than her looks and the entrée she held to the inner circles were worth. Teddy had proposed with all his impetuosity and fire, and she looked him straight in the eyes, and said coldly and finally: 'Never let me hear any such silly nonsense from you again.' 'You won't,' said Teddy, with a new expression around his mouth, and—now Teddy was inclosed within a strong barbed-wire fence.

It was on this first ride of inspection that Teddy was seized by the inspiration that suggested the name of Mother Goose's heroine, and he at once bestowed it upon Octavia. The idea, supported both by a similarity of names and identity of occupations, seemed to strike him as a peculiarly happy one, and he never tired of using it. The Mexicans on the ranch also took up the name, adding another syllable to accommodate their lingual incapacity for the final 'p,' gravely referring to her as 'La Madama Bo-Peepy.' Eventually it spread, and 'Madame Bo-Peep's ranch' was as often mentioned as the Rancho de las Sombras.'

Came the long, hot season from May to September, when work is scarce on the ranches. Octavia passed the days in a kind of lotus-eater's dream. Books, hammocks, correspondence with a few intimate friends, a renewed interest in her old water-colour box and easel —these disposed of the sultry hours of daylight. The evenings were always sure to bring enjoyment. Best of all were the rapturous horseback rides with Teddy, when the moon gave light over the wind-swept leagues, chaperoned by the wheeling night-hawk and the startled owl. Often the Mexicans would come up from their shacks with their guitars and sing the weirdest of heart-breaking songs. There were long, cosy chats on the breezy gallery, and an interminable warfare of wits between Teddy and Mrs. MacIntyre, whose abundant Scotch shrewdness often more than overmatched the lighter humour in which she was lacking.

And the nights came, one after another, and were filed away by weeks and months—nights soft and languorous and fragrant, that should have driven Strephon to Chloe over wires however barbed, that might have drawn Cupid himself to hunt, lasso in hand, among those amorous pastures—but Teddy kept his fences up.

One July night Madame Bo-Peep and her ranch manager were sitting on the east gallery. Teddy had been exhausting the science of prognostication as to the probabilities of a price of twenty-four cents for the autumn clip, and had then subsided into an anæsthetic cloud of Havana smoke. Only as incompetent a judge as a woman would have failed to note long ago that at least a third of his salary must have gone up in the fumes of those imported Regalias.

'Teddy,' said Octavia suddenly and rather sharply, 'what are you working down here on a ranch for?'

'One hundred per,' said Teddy glibly, 'and found.'

'I've a good mind to discharge you.'

'Can't do it,' said Teddy, with a grin.

'Why not?' demanded Octavia, with argumentative heat.

'Under contract. Terms of sale respect all unexpired contracts. Mine runs until 12 p.m., December thirty-first. You might get up at midnight on that date and fire me. If you try it sooner I'll be in a position to bring legal proceedings.'

Octavia seemed to be considering the prospects of litigation.

'But,' continued Teddy cheerfully, 'I've been thinking of resigning anyway.'

Octavia's rocking-chair ceased its motion. There were centipedes in this country, she felt sure; and Indians; and vast, lonely, desolate, empty wastes; all within strong barbed-wire fence. There was a Van Dresser pride, but there was also a Van Dresser heart. She must know for certain whether or not he had forgotten.

'Ah, well, Teddy,' she said, with a fine assumption of polite interest, 'it's lonely down here; you're longing to get back to the old life—to polo and lobsters and theatres and balls.'

'Never cared much for balls,' said Teddy virtuously.

'You're getting old, Teddy. Your memory is failing. Nobody ever knew you to miss a dance, unless it occurred on the same night with another one which you attended. And you showed such shocking bad taste, too, in dancing too often with the same partner. Let me see, what was that Forbes girl's name—the one with wall eyes—Mabel, wasn't it?'

'No; Adèle. Mabel was the one with the bony elbows. That wasn't wall in Adèle's eyes. It was soul. We used to talk sonnets together, and Verlaine. Just then I was trying to run a pipe from the Pierian spring.'

'You were on the floor with her,' said Octavia, undeflected, 'five times at the Hammersmiths'.'

'Hammersmiths' what?' questioned Teddy vacuously.

'Ball—ball,' said Octavia viciously. 'What were we talking of?'

'Eyes, I thought,' said Teddy, after some reflection; 'and elbows.'

'Those Hammersmiths,' went on Octavia, in her sweetest society prattle, after subduing an intense desire to yank a handful of sunburnt, sandy hair from the head lying back contentedly against the canvas of the steamer chair, 'had too much money. Mines, wasn't it? It was something that paid something to the ton. You couldn't get a glass of plain water in their house. Everything at that ball was dreadfully overdone.'

'It was,' said Teddy.

'Such a crowd there was!' Octavia continued, conscious that she was talking the rapid drivel of a school-girl describing her first dance. 'The balconies were as warm as the rooms. I—lost—something at that ball.' The last sentence was uttered in a tone calculated to remove the barbs from miles of wire.

'So did I,' confessed Teddy, in a lower voice.

'A glove,' said Octavia, falling back as the enemy approached her ditches.

'Caste,' said Teddy, halting his firing line without loss. 'I hobnobbed half the evening with one of Hammersmith's miners, a fellow who kept his hands in his pockets, and talked like an archangel about reduction plants and drifts and levels and sluice-boxes.'

'A pearl-grey glove, nearly new,' sighed Octavia mournfully.

'A bang-up chap, that McArdle,' maintained Teddy approvingly. 'A man who hated olives and elevators; a man who handled mountains as croquettes, and built tunnels in the air; a man who never uttered a word of silly nonsense in his life. Did you sign those lease-renewal applications yet, madama? They've got to be on file in the land office by the thirty-first.'

Teddy turned his head lazily. Octavia's chair was vacant.

. . . . .

A certain centipede, crawling along the lines marked out by fate, expounded the situation. It was early one morning while Octavia and Mrs. MacIntyre were trimming the honeysuckle on the west gallery. Teddy had risen and departed hastily before daylight in response to word that a flock of ewes had been scattered from their bedding ground during the night by a thunder-storm.

The centipede, driven by destiny, showed himself on the floor of the gallery, and then, the screeches of the two women giving him his cue, he scuttled with all his yellow legs through the open door into the furthermost west room, which was Teddy's. Arming themselves with domestic utensils selected with regard to their length, Octavia and Mrs. MacIntyre, with much clutching of skirts and skirmishing for the position of rear-guard in the attacking force, followed.

Once outside, the centipede seemed to have disappeared, and his prospective murderers began a thorough but cautious search for their victim.

Even in the midst of such a dangerous and absorbing adventure Octavia was conscious of an awed curiosity on finding herself in Teddy's sanctum. In that room he sat alone, silently communing with those secret thoughts that he now shared with no one, dreamed there whatever dreams he now called on no one to interpret.

It was the room of a Spartan or a soldier. In one corner stood a wide, canvas-covered cot; in another, a small bookcase; in another, a grim stand of Winchesters and shotguns. An immense table, strewn with letters, papers, and documents and surmounted by a set of pigeon-holes, occupied one side.

The centipede showed genius in concealing himself in such bare quarters. Mrs. MacIntyre was poking a broom-handle behind the bookcase. Octavia approached Teddy's cot. The room was just as the manager had left it in his hurry. The Mexican maid had not yet given it her attention. There was his big pillow with the imprint of his head still in the centre. She thought the horrid beast might have climbed the cot and hidden itself to bite Teddy. Centipedes were thus cruel and vindictive toward managers.

She cautiously overturned the pillow, and then parted her lips to give the signal for reinforcements at sight of a long, slender, dark object lying there. But, repressing it in time, she caught up a glove, a pearl-grey glove, flattened—it might be conceived—by many, many months of nightly pressure beneath the pillow of the man who had forgotten the Hammersmiths' ball. Teddy must have left so hurriedly that morning that he had, for once, forgotten to transfer it to its resting-place by day. Even managers, who are notoriously wily and cunning, are sometimes caught up with.

Octavia slid the grey glove into the bosom of her summery morning gown. It was hers. Men who put themselves within a strong barbed-wire fence, and remember Hammersmith balls only by the talk of miners about sluice-boxes, should not be allowed to possess such articles.

After all, what a paradise this prairie country was! How it blossomed like the rose when you found things that were thought to be lost! How delicious was that morning breeze coming in the windows, fresh and sweet with the breath of the yellow ratama blooms! Might one not stand, for a minute, with shining, far-gazing eyes, and dream that mistakes might be corrected?

Why was Mrs. MacIntyre poking about so absurdly with a broom?

'I've found it,' said Mrs. MacIntyre, banging the door. 'Here it is.'

'Did you lose something?' asked Octavia, with sweetly polite non-interest.

'The little devil!' said Mrs. MacIntyre, driven to violence. 'Ye've no forgotten him alretty?'

Between them they slew the centipede. Thus was he rewarded for his agency toward the recovery of things lost at the Hammersmiths' ball.

It seems that Teddy, in due course, remembered the glove, and when he returned to the house at sunset made a secret but exhaustive search for it. Not until evening, upon the moonlit eastern gallery, did he find it. It was upon the hand that he had thought lost to him for ever, and so he was moved to repeat certain nonsense that he had been commanded never, never to utter again. Teddy's fences were down.

This time there was no ambition to stand in the way, and the wooing was as natural and successful as should be between ardent shepherd and gentle shepherdess.

The prairies changed to a garden. The Rancho de las Sombras became the Ranch of Light.

A few days later Octavia received a letter from Mr. Bannister, in reply to one she had written to him asking some questions about her business. A portion of the letter ran as follows:

'I am at a loss to account for your references to the sheep ranch. Two months after your departure to take up your residence upon it, it was discovered that Colonel Beaupree's title was worthless. A deed came to light showing that he disposed of the property before his death. The matter was reported to your manager, Mr. Westlake, who at once repurchased the property. It is entirely beyond my powers of conjecture to imagine how you have remained in ignorance of this fact. I beg that you will at once confer with that gentleman, who will, at least, corroborate my statement.'

Octavia sought Teddy, with battle in her eye.

'What are you working on this ranch for?' she asked once more.

'One hundred——' he began to repeat, but saw in her face that she knew. She held Mr. Bannister's letter in her hand. He knew that the game was up.

'It's my ranch,' said Teddy, like a schoolboy detected in evil. 'It's a mighty poor manager that isn't able to absorb the boss's business if you give him time.'

'Why were you working down here?' pursued Octavia, still struggling after the key to the riddle of Teddy.

'To tell the truth, 'Tave,' said Teddy, with quiet candour, 'it wasn't for the salary. That about kept me in cigars and sunburn lotions. I was sent south by my doctor. 'Twas that right lung that was going to the bad on account of over-exercise and strain at polo and gymnastics. I needed climate and ozone and rest and things of that sort.'

In an instant Octavia was close against the vicinity of the affected organ. Mr. Bannister's letter fluttered to the floor.

'It's—it's well now, isn't it, Teddy?'

'Sound as a mesquite chunk. I deceived you in one thing. I paid fifty thousand for your ranch as soon as I found you had no title. I had just about that much income accumulated at my banker's while I've been herding sheep down here, so it was almost like picking the thing up on a bargain-counter for a penny. There's another little surplus of unearned increment piling up there, 'Tave. I've been thinking of a wedding trip in a yacht with white ribbons tied to the mast, through the Mediterranean, and then up among the Hebrides and down Norway to the Zuyder Zee.'

'And I was thinking,' said Octavia softly, 'of a wedding gallop with my manager among the flocks of sheep and back to a wedding breakfast with Mrs. MacIntyre on the gallery, with, maybe, a sprig of orange blossom fastened to the red jar above the table.'

Teddy laughed, and began to chant:

> 'Little Bo-Peep has lost her sheep,
> And doesn't know where to find 'em.
> Let 'em alone, and they'll come home,
> And——'

Octavia drew his head down and whispered in his ear.

But that is one of the tales they brought behind them.

R. MURRAY GILCHRIST

1867–1917

THE GAP IN THE WALL

It was a hot May forenoon and the sloping meadows were pied with anemones. Four cuckoos were crying against each other at the end of the hazy valley; a building magpie castanetted incessantly from the elm planting.

Keziah Unwin was going down to Hatherton Flat with a present of Rouen ducks' eggs for old Mrs. Pursglove. The produce of the poultry on her father's farm was Keziah's perquisite, and she was so accomplished in the art of rearing that her advice was sought by all the countryside. There was no need for her to save the money she earned, for she was the only child of a well-to-do man; so she spent it in the purchase of good and pretty clothes, such as raised the standard of the village taste.

She had donned a dainty gown of pale blue linen that clung without wrinkles to her slender figure. A little tippet of white lace covered her shoulders. Cousin Sarah, who had opened a milliner's shop in the country town, had sent her that Parisian hat which seemed like nothing but a tangle of apple-blossom that had broken off the parent tree and fallen prone on a cushion of emerald moss.

It was only natural that such a beautiful girl should be troubled with many suitors. Swain after swain strolled into the house-place at night, ostensibly for the sake of listening to her father's old tales, but really to give themselves the wild delight of making sheep's eyes at the young mistress. She had listened to numerous offers of marriage and had declined all, and now experience had taught her how to slay a would-be lover's courage with well-planted barbs of good-natured ridicule. Local history enshrines the story of young John Hancock's proposal. Keziah revealed it to none, but the discouraged youth wailed it out at the *Bold Rodney* whilst in his cups. By unlucky stratagem having been left alone with her for a while, he began to stammer his feeble declaration. She affected great terror, but still retained enough presence of mind to enable her to pour a bucket of cold water over his head. When he became normal again she prevented a repetition of his misdemeanour with the cruel words, 'Eh dear, I am glad! I thowt yo' were i' a fit!'

Once only had her heart been touched, and that was when Rafe Paramour of Rocky Edge had put the question. They had been school-mates together, and in later years had romped like hoyden and hobble-de-hoy seeking birds' nests in Milton Dale. She had begun to care for him without knowing it, but when he spoke she flouted him so mercilessly that he had withdrawn at once. The lad had attributed her refusal to the narrowness of his circumstances, and although since then his love had increased, he had never noticed her save in the coldest fashion.

At the curve of the highway where the hawthorns grow thickest, she paused to reflect. If she continued walking along the white, dusty road she would have two miles farther to go; but if she took a short cut, which necessitated slipping through hedgerows and climbing rough, loosely-built limestone walls, she could reach Hatherton Flat in less than a quarter of an hour.

'I'll risk et,' she said. 'They're Rafe Paramour's fields, but he wunna be abaat to-day. I'm welly sweltered wi' th' heat.'

So she laid the basket on the bank, and crept between the gnarled trunks. In another minute she was walking leisurely on the bank of a brook, where May-blobs and ladies'-smocks luxuriated. At the well-head, where the water leaped from under a block of sandstone, she turned and made for a gateway that opened to a field of green wheat, and skirting this she reached the first high wall.

It was a difficult place to climb, for the ground on the farther side was on a higher level and the loose coping overtopped the tallest flower in her hat. But she was young and agile, and she did not flinch. She placed the egg-basket on a safe stone and began to ascend. It was more dangerous than she imagined, and the scaly limestone crumbled beneath her feet.

She had almost reached the top when her heart gave a great leap, for the wall had begun to rock with her weight. She had only just time to fling herself on the soft turf of the higher field when more than three yards of masonry fell down into the green wheat.

She rose leisurely. Despite her alarm, her flushed face bore a pleasant look of malice.

'Et'll be a nice job for Rafe to build et up again,' she said. 'Ef et'd bin onybody else's I'ld hev towd as I'd done et, an' paid for et too, but sin et's his, et'll part work out my spite.'

Suddenly she gave a little scream of fear, for almost within touching distance was Rafe Paramour himself, seated beneath a full-bloomed crab and busily whittling thatch pegs. He was smiling wryly ; there was something ogre-like in his aspect.

She caught up the basket, which had escaped any harm, and ran, but he sprang to his feet and followed with great strides.

'I heerd what yo' said, Keziah,' he remarked firmly, 'an' I dunna think et were i' a kindly spirit. Haasoever, et's th' custom here for him as pulls daan a wall to build et up again. An' yo've got to do et.'

She turned and faced him defiantly.

'I wunna !'

'But yo' will, for I'll mek yo'.'

Her colour deepened. 'Yo'll be th' first man as hes e'er med me do owt I hedna a mind to,' she said. 'Stan' aside an' let me go.'

'That I shanna. Yo're trespassin'; dunna yo' see yon board wi' "Trespassers will be prosecuted" cn? Well, I'll prosecute yo' by mekin' yo' build the wall up.'

'I'll call aat, an' someone 'll come,' she said, half tearfully.

'Call till yo're tired, nob'dy 'll hear. Yo' mun just buckle to!'

'Yo're a brute, Rafe Paramour, to tek advantage o' me i' this way! I werena browt up to build walls.'

He gazed at her with whimsical tenderness. 'Et'll be a lesson for yo', Keziah: yo' humbled my pride, and I'll humble yo'rn. Them big stones go first; set to as quick as yo' like.'

For the first time since her refusal of his suit she looked full into his face. He instantly assumed an air of great firmness. It had never struck her before that he was very handsome, but as he stood there without jacket or waistcoat, and with snowy shirt all damp with perspiration, she became convinced that there was none in the neighbourhood half so worthy of the name of man.

She drew off her yellow cotton gloves. There was a suspicious quivering about her lips; she did not know which was nearer—laughing or crying—and her eyes were sparkling brightly.

'I hate yo',' she murmured. 'Ef I mun do et, I mun. I doubt et'll murder me!'

He laughed outright. 'I dunna want that sin on my conscience,' he said. 'I reckon I'll hev to let yo' off th' hardest part o' the job. Yo' may pick up th' least stones, an I'll pick up th' biggest.'

So they began to work in silence. He noticed, with delight, that the stones she brought were no larger than apples, and that it took her five minutes to bring each. Neither spoke until the first two rows were laid.

'Et'll tek us a day at this rate,' Rafe said at last, 'an' et's dinner time now. I've gotten bread and cheese an' beer under th' trees. We'll share et.'

'What 'ld fowk say ef they knew ?' she whispered. 'I wouldna do et for th' world.'

'Yo' will do et,' he replied, resuming his sternness. 'None'll know fro' me.'

So she was forced to obey. The bread and cheese stuck in her throat, and she scarcely drank from the horn. She was soon ready to return to her work, but he made her remain at his side.

'I always hev a pipe o' bacca after meals,' he said. 'Let's chat abaat owd times. D' yo' rec'lect me killin' a hern to get his beard for yo' ? I climbed up th' biggest tree i' Hassop Park to pick him off th' branch wheer he'd dropped.'

Keziah sullenly refused to notice his ingratiations. Soon she rose perforce, and began to collect the stones again ; this time working more diligently than before. But somehow, the more she hurried, the more he lagged, and it was four o'clock before the gap was half-filled.

She fell a-weeping in earnest. He heard the sound, and his breath came quickly.

'Keziah, wench,' he said, in a soft voice, 'I think I've tried yo' enow. Yo' can go, an I'll finish et mysen.'

She took no heed ; but, hastily drying her tears, brought the stones faster than ever. Seeing that she was in such deadly earnest, he put on a spurt, and in two more hours the wall was finished.

Then Keziah took up the basket and began to walk in the direction of home. She was quite speechless, and her head hung forward almost limply. He felt afraid that he had been too hard, and overwhelming pity swayed into his heart.

He hurried after her, reaching her side before she passed through the gateway.

'Keziah,' he cried, 'I ask your pardon.'

She set down the basket and showed him her hands. The skin was roughened, the finger-tips were bleeding. The sight made his eyes swim.

'My poor Keziah, wunna yo' forgie me?'

All the shadow left her face.

'Yo've been a wretch, but I will,' she faltered. 'I wunna pull yo'r walls daan again.'

He came nearer and caught her in his arms.

'I wouldna hev done et ef I hedna looved yo.'

'Et's all reet, Rafe. Yo'll be master, I reckon.'

And she kissed him, and he led her to the road.

A WITCH IN THE PEAK

It was the evening after old Johnny White's funeral, and Elizabeth sat by the low fire in the house-place, wondering how she could manage to exist for the remainder of her days without him who had never spent a whole day apart from her since their wedding, fifty years ago. The bitterness of her spirit was increased by the knowledge that at the end of the week the little farm must be sold to pay the money which the dead man had owed for standing surety for a dishonest cousin. The original sum had been thirty-five pounds; but the lender, Luke Flint, a shoemaker, who was known as 'the Milton Spider,' from his knack of wrapping a web about such unwary folk as craved aid from him, had stipulated on an interest of fifty per cent. until all was repaid. This interest had eaten up all the profits of the stony acres, and Johnny had died heart-broken because one year's payment was in arrears.

Elizabeth had dismissed all her neighbours. She desired to be left in solitude for such short time as she remained in the house, so that she might recall scenes of bygone happiness. She was quite alone in the world, so that there was none save herself to suffer; but still the outlook was so depressing that the source of her tears was dried.

'I can see yo' again, Johnny lad,' she murmured, 'walkin' wi' me fro' church on aar weddin' morn, as coomly a man as were i' th' whöal Peak. . . . But yo' looked just as coomly i' yo'r shroud, wi' all ets pratty gimpings, tho' yo'r cheeks hed lost theer red, and yo'r gowd hair were gone as white as snow. Ay lad, ay lad, I do wish I might hev gone wi' yo'! When I think o' all our good life together; how yo' thowt nowt were too han'some for me, an' as whate'er I did were th' reet thing, I'm like to go mad. An' now I'm to be turned aat o' th' place wheer aar wedlock's bin spent! Et's hard, et's very hard!'

As she lamented, the latch of the door was lifted and the creditor entered. He was a dark, squat man of middle-age, with a bullet-shaped head and blue, close-shaven jowls. His arms and legs were unnaturally long, and his broad shoulders were so much bent as to suggest deformity. He strode forward to the hearth, and without invitation plumped down in the arm-chair which Johnny had always used.

Elizabeth rose in excessive anger. Her thin face flushed crimson, her toothless lower jaw moved oddly from side to side.

'I'll thank yo' to get aat o' that!' she cried. 'Et's always bin set in by a honest fellow, an' I canna see ony other sort use et! Ef yo' mun sit, sit on th' sattle.'

He assumed an air of bravado; but her aspect was so threatening that he rose sullenly and took the corner to which she pointed.

'Yo' needna be so haughty, 'Lizbeth White,' he said, with an unpleasant sneer. 'This spot'll be mine soon, for I'm a-going to buy et, an' happen yo'll coom a-beggin' to th' door.'

'I'ld liefer starve nor beg o' yo'. What d'yo' want, a-coomin' rattin'?'

'I on'y want to mind yo' as yo' mun tek none o' th' things aat o' th' place. My papers 'low me to sell all, an' if yo' touch owt—off yo' go to Derby.'

She cracked her fingers in his face. 'I'll be more nor thankful to get aat o' yo'r debt,' she said. 'Et's yo'r cheatin' simple lads like my John as keeps yo' alive. Yo're none fit to be 'mongst decent livers. I do b'lieve as th' law wouldna favour yo'.'

His sallow skin grew white and then purple.

'Yo' try th' law, 'Lizbeth White, an' yo'll find as et canna touch me. Yo'r man signed th' agreement to pay me my money, an' ef he couldna pay et, I were to be at lib'ty to sell th' lond. Th' lond, say I?—et esna lond—nowt but three akkers o' stone an' moss, wi'aat a rëal blade o' grass! Et wunna fetch thretty pun', an' I'm certain sure as th' furniture esna worth ten. Yo'll still be soom pun's i' my debt. I reckon yo'll hev to go to th' Bastille, an' I may mek' up my mind to losin' some of the good money!'

'I'd go to th' Bastille forty times ower, sooner nor be behowden to yo' for owt. But as long as I'm stopping i' th' haase, I wunna stond yo'r jaw! Aat yo' go, yo' brute yo'!'

She unfastened the door, and held it wide open. It was a dark night, and the air was heavy with the scent of withered leaves. The prattle of the spring as it leaped from the moor-edge to the trough in the paddock was distinctly audible.

'Yo' owd wretch!' he muttered. 'I'll see as yo' suffer for yo'r brazzenness. Yo' beggar! When yo'r a-hoein' taturs i' th' Bastille garden, I'll set th' others laughin' at yo'.'

He moved leisurely across the floor; she sharpened his gait by picking up a besom-stale.

'Whiles I'm mistress here, I'll hev none o' yo'. John's paid yo' time an' time again. Be off, yo' skin-alouse! I beg an' pray God to punish yo' this very neet. Ef et hadna bin fo yo' theer'ld hev been no buryin' here for mony a year. I'm none one as es gi'en to cursin', but yo' deserve whatten yo'll get.'

He slunk out into the darkness. She closed the door and bolted it carefully, and when the clatter of his footsteps had died away, she returned to the chair by the hearth, where a choir of crickets was now singing cheerfully, and delivered herself to the melancholy satisfaction of meditating on past joy and present sorrow.

Meanwhile the Spider walked down the lane in some trepidation, for her violence had unnerved him strangely.

'I do b'lieve hoo's rëally a witch,' he said. 'Her eyes brenned that red! Ef hoo'd lived i' my greet-gran'-feyther's days hoo'ld hev bin faggotted, sure enow!'

His mumbling was suddenly cut short by some terrible thing catching the hinder-part of his waistband and plucking him up from the ground. When he recovered his senses in some measure he was on a level with the tree-tops. His voice rose in a harsh shriek.

'Help! All o' yo' help! Jack-wi'-th'-Iron-Teeth's gotten howd o' me an's draggin' me to Hell!'

But as it was late, and the Milton folk were abed, none heard. He flew swiftly through the air, his long arms and legs sprawling frog-like. Once he caught hold of the thatch of a barn and clung for a moment, but the rotten wisps came away in his hands. He gave himself up for lost. The demon was dragging him over the moor in the direction of the river.

'O Lord, forgi'e me, forgi'e me, an' I'll tek' advantage o' innocent fowk no more. I'll do my best to set things reet as I've set wrong, ef only Thou'lt let me off this time!'

He fell with a heavy splash into the marsh of the Wet Withins. For a long time he lay, half-swooning, on a tussock of bent-grass. Then, when his strength returned, he crawled blindly over the heath to the road.

Instead of making for home, he went straight to Crosslow Farm and knocked feebly at the door. Elizabeth was sleeping in her chair. She had been dreaming blithely of years of good crops. She rose, drowsily, and drew back the bolts. In the dim firelight she looked more like a witch than ever.

'Yo've coom back again!' she said sharply. 'Be off! I wunna hev et said as I let yo' in at this time o' neet!'

He was trembling like a paralytic.

'Gi'e me a bit o' paper, 'Lizbeth White,' he stammered, 'an' I'll write a quittance. Yo're a wicked woman, an' I'll hev nowt more to do wi' yo'. Yo're on'y fit to bren!'

'I reckon et's conscience,' she said, as she took paper and pen and ink from the corner cupboard. 'Write whatever yo' like an' go to——'

'Dunna say thatten, for Lord's sake!' he yelled.

He took the paper and wrote:—'*I, Luke Flint, do hereby forgive Elizabeth White her husband's debt as she owed me, and I trust as she will bear no further malice.*'

Then he hastened from the place, as though it held a creature accursed.

Two days afterwards he returned to Crosslow, in a cajoling, lachrymose humour.

'Gi'e me that quittance back again,' he said, with a painful giggle. 'Yo're an honest woman, I reckon. I thowt yo' were a witch, but et were a b'loon hook as picked me up an' carried me to th' wayter-holes. Soom chaps droppin' advertysements for gin an' whisky 'ld gone astray an' were tryin' to fix on a spot. Summat hed gone wrong wi' th' machine. Gi'e me et back, wench; yo're a reet-dealin' woman, an' I'm sure yo' wunna do but whatten's just.'

She laid hold of the besom-stale again.

'I'll breek yo'r back ef yo' dunna go,' she cried. 'Yo' thowt I were a witch, but yo' munna think I'm a fool!'

GERALD WARRE CORNISH

1875–1916

THE STOWAWAY

A BOAT was rowing quietly along the shore of the Sogne Fjord, near its mouth and looking toward the sea. In its stern sat the owner, holding the tiller, whilst a boy and a girl, his son and daughter, pulled at the oars. It was evening, and the mountains on either side of the Fjord were reflected for miles into the distance. Far away could be seen the edge of the open sea, with its strips of low-lying land and islands. Over these hung a golden haze, the day's last gift. The man in the stern was a robust and happy-looking bearded man. His daughter was a typical Norwegian girl, strong, broad-chested and broad-waisted, with a healthy, beautiful complexion. His son looked like an English boy. On the stern of the boat, just behind where the owner sat, were painted the words 'J. Holloway—Sandener.' The boat quitted the shore, and made across for the other side, where Sandener could be seen. It was a little wooden village, close beside a rushing river; it possessed a wooden hotel, and a wooden church and tower. Above it rose the mountains, with waterfalls streaming down their shadowy sides. J. Holloway was an important man in his town, and had a flagstaff in his garden. He could see his little house and flagstaff, somewhat separate from the rest, beyond the church tower. His eye wandered from this to the open sea and the golden light beyond. In that direction lay England and Hull. He became meditative. The still waters, the mountains, the sound of the oars, the evening light, and the occasional talk of the rowers—these things faded from his mind, and he journeyed back into the past, across the sea to Hull. This was what he remembered.

. . . . .

James Holloway had been out of work for ten weeks. During this period he had 'eaten nothing,' as we say of invalids or persons of abstemious temperament. He had not drunk as much as usual either; but he had drunk more than he had eaten. He had a theory that beer was as nourishing as bread to a man of his constitution. It was all a matter of constitution. Some men grew fat on the drink, others grew thin; this was proved in every walk of life. He was one of those whom it nourished; and he was grateful to Nature for this mark of her favour. As he stood this morning in the road outside the docks at Hull, in the company of several hundred others of his kind, this peculiar constitution of his did not mark him out as being above the general average. The average was not a high one. The men were waiting to be hired, standing together in groups. It was six o'clock in the morning, and drizzling. The circumstances were depressing, yet there was an air of composure about the crowd. They sucked their pipes of foul tobacco, with an early-morning relish; most of them had had some breakfast. They spat on the ground with decision, and when they did speak—for the most part they were silent—they spoke out loud and bold, or short and sharp, with a jest and an oath. The chins were bristly throughout. They all shaved once a week. There was not a collar amongst them, but a great variety of knotted neckcloths; and there were great-coats of some kind or another, procured somehow or other, on the backs of all. There had been a long period of slackness in the Docks, and a slump in trade all through the town. The greater part of the men had earned next to nothing for two or three months past. Most of them had wives and families at home. A specialist in sociology could have passed an interesting morning, inquiring how these men and their families had lived during this period. But the results would not have worked out on paper. For none of these men knew how he had lived; and even their wives could not have explained the secret. According to all reasonable statistics, they ought not to have lived at all. It was a most peculiar state of affairs.

James Holloway was a bachelor; but he did not thank his stars for it. He was not of a grateful mind, and he was too full of theories. If he had had a wife, he theorized, she might have picked up a sixpence or two, now and then, and the children might have got something out of the church, and after school hours; together, he thought, they might have got along better than he was doing singly. There were men who had found it so. He had a theory, too, that money was always money, however many there were to spend it, and that one and sixpence was always better than a shilling, whatever the company. This had been proved again and again to his satisfaction when clubbing together with his pals.

He waited and waited, with his hands in his great-coat pockets, now and then jogging his elbows against his sides. He had lived all his life, twenty-five years, in Hull, alternately working and loafing, either by inclination or compulsion. But he had a theory that his life had not yet really begun. Some day he was going to do better than he had done so far. That was quite certain. He never allowed himself for an instant to believe that the distressed and irregular condition was a permanent thing. It was merely temporary, and therefore supportable. He talked and laughed with two or three others, as they waited for work. There was a faint blueness and bitterness, a touch of solemnity, lingering round the corners of his mouth and eyes, but scarcely noticeable, owing to the strong look of life and sense which animated his countenance, and those of his friends, as they talked and laughed in their abrupt, rapid, jerky manner. Discontent appeared chiefly in the filthy adjectives with which every substantive was heralded.

After several hours of the morning had thus passed, it became apparent that no more work was to be had that day. He went off into the town, walking up the street courageously as if he were in regular employment and going home to dinner. He spent the middle of the day as usual; that is to say, he did not know how he spent it; it spent itself. As usual, he was busy with his thoughts and theories, thinking over his prospects. He must do something—that was certain. It would not do to go on living in this way any longer. This sort of thing must come to an end. It was time he made a new start, struck out a new life. He had said the same for years past; he had said it oftener and oftener, and now he said it once every ten minutes. When he was not talking to himself in this way, he was talking to his pals. They talked of every imaginable subject under the sun, but they arrived at no fixed opinions on any. At least the opinions were all fixed, but they were all conflicting. For instance, all were agreed that the life they were leading was a dog's life, not fit for a Christian man, and that something must be done to better themselves. This was one fixed conviction, and its friend and companion was that a man could not better himself, that there was nothing to do, and nowhere else to go. Both these opinions were clear and certain. Again, when politics came up for discussion, Jim Holloway was convinced that the Government were not doing their duty to such as himself; that they were allowing the blood and muscle of the country to be drained away; that they only talked, never did anything, and had got their posts through the influence of society women, and that the condition of the people in his town was a scandal to the country. Simultaneously, if properly aroused, he was always ready to swear by the good old British

Constitution, the Flag, the Throne, the Army, Navy, and the sporting Aristocracy. So, too, with religion, which was frequently discussed in the lodging-houses of an evening. He was perfectly convinced that it was all a humbug, a got-up affair—Noah's Ark and the Flood and all. The clergy and the bishops did it all for money. 'Religion was civilization.' This was the idea of one of the talkers in the lodging-house; and he had succeeded in making his meaning clear to all. God could not be good, if He sent evil and suffering. The whole thing was a lie; but civilization needed it. This was perfectly clear to the unsophisticated reasoning of all. Truth had only to be stated to be understood and believed. This was one opinion. The other was that something good, some fatherly power or destiny, which understood things, lay at the back of his life. This was also quite certain. Apart from the direct knowledge of the fact, it had been proved again and again. For he would certainly have died for various reasons, chiefly for lack of nourishment, long before, if life had not been constantly supplied him—and so would they all have done. All the middle of the day he spent outside a public-house, cogitating these contradictory opinions, but especially about what he was going to do. For some reason he asked himself this question to-day with greater frequency and with more vital emphasis than before. 'Must do something—this can't go on,' he reiterated. He ran through all his old rejected schemes again for the thousandth time—emigration, enlisting, tramping into the country, going round the town once more.

In the midst of these thoughts, impelled by the certain conviction that something must be done, he found himself wandering down the street again. It was afternoon, and during all the period of the last ten weeks he had never before felt so empty and cavernous within. A crowd of people were going into a public hall, off one of the principal streets. Admission appeared to be free, and Jim drifted in with them, pondering on what he was going to do—on what he had got to do—rather than on what he was doing. He found himself at a political meeting. The chairman, a small, fat, smiling gentleman, in a fur coat, was introducing the speaker. The chairman spoke with daintiness and grace, looking round on his audience and smiling, and clasping his two little hands together. He was enjoying himself. Then the speaker began, a gloomy man. James Holloway followed all that was said. He seemed to have two minds this afternoon. With one mind he followed the speaker, and understood all that he said; with the other mind he was still determining that something must be done, that he must enlist, emigrate, cut his throat, or do something. The gloomy speaker was getting a little warmer. He had reached the glories of the Empire, the necessity for building it up, and doing all in our power to preserve it, and hand it on to our children. We must even be prepared to make sacrifices for it. Though in his own private opinion no sacrifice would be necessary, still we must be prepared to make sacrifices. James Holloway, along with the rest of the audience, loudly indicated his readiness to make a sacrifice. As he cheered, his mind Number Two was saying that something must be done, that it could not go on, and that he must go up again to the paper mills to see if a job was to be had there.

The speaker was now threatening his audience. 'Was England to become a second-class Power?' he asked them. Before asking that question he had paused; and he asked it, not triumphantly, but with a deadly significance. His voice lowered itself. 'Was it possible that England might ever become a second-class Power?' He spoke as if alluding to one of those darker subjects which are not mentioned in polite society. A third time he repeated the question, in a grave and awful whisper. 'Was there any one in that room who had ever faced the possibility of England's becoming a second-class Power—a Denmark, a Sweden, or a *Norway*?' James Holloway felt faint. Then the speaker recovered himself, and brought out his emphatic Noes. He passed on once more to Empire, to Royalty, the Flag, and the Army and Navy, in a grand peroration. Holloway, who sat at the back of the room, rose to his feet with many of the audience, and shouted. As he rose, it seemed to him that he was indeed rising and rising. For a moment he thought that his spirit had left the body. Then he realized that he must be ill; and immediately fright seized him, and he turned sick and faint. He made for the door, and hurried out.

James Holloway had a theory that when a man was feeling ill and done-up, the best thing he could do was to go and work. This he had often proved in practice. He made up his mind on the spot, that he would go and work. Cost what it might, he would work before nightfall. He went down to the docks, and slunk along the wharves unobserved. Come what might, he would work somewhere, at something. It was the only way to cure himself. Heaven was propitious. In a quiet corner, against a lonely wharf, he observed a Norwegian schooner, unloading small baulks of timber. The baulks of timber were being thrown out by hand from the hold of the vessel. Two seamen stood on deck, catching them as they popped out of the hold, and throwing them with a clatter on a huge pile that had formed itself on the wharf. Two other seamen stood on this pile, throwing the wood slowly about, so as to build and shape the structure, and allow room for more. James Holloway slunk alongside this pile of wood. For some time he watched the men at work. He caught the eye of one of the seamen, and winked. The big Norwegian stopped work, and straightened himself with a slow, pleasant gasp. Jim scrambled on to the pile, and began to throw the timber towards its farther end, so as to make room for more in the centre. The Norwegian smiled, and went on with his own work. Jim worked away with a will. It was a luxury to put out his strength again; and he felt better and better. Every moment he expected the mate to come and warn him off. The mate came to the edge of the vessel, and leaned his arm on the bulwarks, smiling ironically at Holloway. 'You laike vurk?' he said. Holloway worked away in silence. The mate smiled a deeper smile. He remained lazily leaning on the bulwarks for a minute, and then returned to his post above the hold, catching the timber as it popped out. The vessel was being unloaded by the crew, without any outside assistance but this voluntary aid proffered by our friend. They worked on till late. Holloway ventured no questions; but they were evidently working overtime. Only one thought now occupied his mind. Would his services be recognized in any form? His unchartered work was against the rules of the docks; and they had not even asked for it. Yet he augured well from the mate's impassive look; they were evidently in a hurry, as they were working late, and his work was a gain to them.

Presently the mate made a peculiar sound in his throat; and they all stopped work. The mate leaned again on the bulwarks. The big seaman on the pile straightened himself once more with the same pleasant gasp. Slowly they all disappeared into the little fo'c'sle. Holloway stood on the pile in the gathering dusk, dismally watching them depart. The mate had now disappeared in the forward part of the vessel; and his last hope was gone. Suddenly the mate's figure reappeared on deck. He looked at Holloway, and nodded his head casually towards the fo'c'sle.

Jim Holloway scrambled on board and, lowering his head, joined the other seamen in the fo'c'sle, which was about six feet by eight feet. A beautiful smell greeted his nostrils, of frizzled onions and potatoes, along with tobacco and oil and tar. One of the men was frying a mess over a little stove. A table in the centre was prepared for the meal. Holloway jammed himself down by the table on a chest, trying to take up as little room as possible. The three other seamen lay in their bunks, enjoying the luxury of relief from toil. They grunted to one another in Norwegian, paying no attention to Jim. The cook glanced at him and laughed, as he stirred his pan. The cook could speak English. 'No work in Hull,' he said, 'very slack, all out of work.' He smiled affectionately at his onions. Presently the fry was served up on the table. The seamen came out of their bunks, and all fell to. Jim Holloway never enjoyed a meal so much. Two of the hands were scarcely more than boys. They had fair hair and blue eyes, and looked fresh and blooming, with enormous shoulders encased in blue jerseys. On Holloway's right sat an older man, in a pair of boots reaching above his knees, which he had not troubled to pull off. Opposite to him sat the cook. All five of them ate away with a relish; a small lamp burned against the wall, and the smoke of the food went up from the table. The Norwegians became more talkative as they ate. Holloway thought that never had he seen four such pleasant-looking fellows. It was a luxury to him to rest his eyes on their contented faces. They paid but little attention to himself, and talked and laughed quietly to one another. It was a pleasure to hear them speaking in a foreign tongue, to watch their smiles and laughs and gestures, without knowing what it was they were talking about. The fo'c'sle was very warm. The men got out their tobacco, and began to smoke. They looked at one another through the smoke, now talking volubly. The cook began to hum, drumming his fingers on the table. He hummed louder and louder, and presently his humming broke into words, which he sang over to himself. When he reached a certain point in the song, the others stopped talking suddenly and joined in. The cook had a pleasant voice, and he made the most of it. He came out now with the next verse in style, and the others all joined in again at the right moment. The song sounded very pleasantly and strangely in Holloway's ears; unlike anything he had heard before. Opposite him on the wall was a picture post-card, representing a waterfall coming down a mountain-side into the sea; and Holloway kept his eyes fixed upon it. As the song rose and fell, Holloway became aware of the country to which these men belonged. He felt the atmosphere of the land from which they came; and it seemed to make the fo'c'sle fresher and purer. It was a happy land they belonged to, and one that was dear to them—a small land far away north, far away from his troubles in Hull. 'Lucky chaps! Lucky beggars!' he thought to himself. He spat on the floor. He could scarcely restrain his emotion and envy. He had never been outside Hull himself, and yet he felt and understood, and knew that he understood, the sort of country these men came from. He watched the Norwegians with closer interest and delight. Another of the seamen began to sing. One of the boys reached down a cardboard box from his bunk, and turned over a few letters, and photographs done up in newspaper. He took out a photograph of a girl with large eyes wide apart, and fair hair parted on her forehead, and plaited down her back. He looked at it fondly and winked at Holloway. Then he kissed it and held it in his arm, and smiled at Holloway. Then he replaced it carefully in the newspaper. Holloway swore to himself. The cook told him to sing them a song. He gave them as much as he could remember of the last music-hall song. His voice was nasal. He hoped to have made an impression, but, to judge from their faces, they did not understand his style and tone. At last he had to clear out. 'Well, good night, mates, and thank ye kindly—much obliged, I'm sure.' Somewhat to his surprise they held out their hands; and he shook hands all round. On the dark deck outside, he paused for a moment, and looked back with a sigh at the bright, steaming interior of the little fo'c'sle.

Then he slunk along the docks. He had a full belly, but no money in his pockets. Passing a deserted part of the wharf, he slipped into a storage shed, and presently came across an enormous empty packing-case, with straw in it, into which he climbed, and nestled down at the bottom. He felt tired, comfortable, and happy; but he could not sleep. He was thinking of the Norwegian schooner, and the land she was bound for. They were off the day after to-morrow, he had gathered from the cook—lucky fellows.

All in an instant his mind was made up. He would go with them. Yes, this was what things had been working towards. He had got to do something, he must do something. Then he would go to Norway. His spirits rose wonderfully. Why, of course, it was just the thing. He would stow himself away somewhere in the hold. But what was he going to do when he got there? He cared not a jot. Let them send him to quod, let them do anything with him; he wanted to see that little harbour, and the mountain, and the young woman whose photograph had been kissed. What was there to keep him in Hull? When in doubt, do something, he said to himself, and fell asleep, and dreamed of the waterfall and the mountain. In his ear the music of the Norwegian song kept rising and falling rhythmically. He sat beside the waterfall, with his arm round the waist of a young lady.

In the grey of the morning he awoke again. He remembered his decision of the night before, and felt doubtful. He was only a fool to think of such a plan. 'Go to Norway, eh?' He laughed, and spat into the straw in which he lay. He lay there thinking for some time. Then he scrambled out and sloped along the wharf. It was drizzling, and just getting light.

Jim Holloway had a theory that no man could fight against Destiny. This had been proved again and again in his life. He had often thought of getting married, of finding a nice girl who would do him good; and he had remained a bachelor. That was Destiny. He had often thought of leaving Hull and making a fresh start somewhere else, making the most of himself, earning the respect of his fellow-men, and a regular wage; but he had remained at Hull, in irregular employment, or out of employment. This was Destiny. He was always on the look-out for Destiny. His great-coat had come to him by Destiny. He had found it hanging on a paling. Destiny had ruled his life. Destiny now carried him up to the town. It first of all pawned his overcoat, and bought him two loaves of bread, some cheese, and a large stone bottle of water. It acted with infinite caution, and waited two days and a night. It rested his mind, and healed the pain of the last many weeks. It bade good-bye to Hull, and the drizzle, and the dreary tramp from dockyard to dockyard, and from one mill to another. He spent most of the day outside his usual pub. 'Now what should make me think of going to Norway?' he kept saying to himself. And then he laughed to himself. He discussed a variety of themes, as usual, with a choice company outside the public-house. He felt his eyes twinkling as he spoke, and he kept smiling. He was wondering what they would say, if he told them he was going to Norway? Who could tell? It was just pure Destiny. He had seen it last night in the fo'c'sle, and it was a place which would suit him, it was a place which was meant for him. This day and the next, as he waited for his schooner to be loaded up, and ready to start, were the happiest of his life so far. He was at last going to do something. For ten years past he had felt that Destiny was on its way; it was coming, and something would happen. Now he knew it had come. He smiled benevolently on his poor companions. He took the lead in the conversation. He was full of confidence and cheerfulness; and the spirits of his companions rose, they knew not why. Jim Holloway was conscious again of his two minds. With one mind he talked and jested and swore with his pals; with the other he knew that Destiny was at work, that a new life had begun. With one mind he talked sound sense and reason to his companions; with the other he cognized a project, the meaning and sense of which he knew it was impossible for him to explain to any mortal man. But the knowledge of this only made him happier. He thrust his hands deep down in his breeches pockets. Yes, he was going away, going away the following night—where to he did not know, what to do he did not care—but he was going somewhere, and Destiny was taking him there.

He kept an eye on the schooner, until the loading-up for the home journey was completed. That night he went down to the docks about midnight. He had not the slightest doubt that he should be successful in stowing himself away. He had no difficulty in getting on to the wharves, and soon found his little schooner. There she lay, with her old-fashioned spars and rigging visible against the sky. Sure enough, he had nothing to do but drop quietly on board, and slip down into the hold. It was all as easy as possible. He met no policeman or dock-watcher anywhere on the wharves. A miscellaneous cargo had been shipped in the hold. Jim looked about for a comfortable corner. Doubts kept drifting across his mind. He was afraid, now and then, that he had perhaps gone off his head in doing such a senseless thing; but this doubt troubled him very little. He had a theory that when a man thought one thing, the opposite was usually the truth; and this comforted him. He groped about with circumspection in the hold, cautiously lighting matches until he found a snug little corner right down in the cargo, where he could stow himself comfortably.

There was even a shelf for his bottle of water, his two loaves, and his bit of cheese. He felt neither hungry, tired, nor thirsty, but perfectly normal. He curled himself up, with a sigh of satisfaction, and was soon fast asleep.

Bang, bump. . . . It was morning, and more cargo was being swung down into the hold. Jim had climbed down into the hold by the forward hatch, and he had scrambled aft. The stern hatch had been closed down, and he had had an idea that it was closed for good. Now to his surprise the light shone ; it had been opened again. He heard the rattle of the steam crane, and big boxes began to swing down above him. Jim sat still, his heart in his mouth. Bump came a large case of several tons weight right above his head, entirely closing the aperture at the bottom of which he sat. He was shut in a trap. For a moment his head swam, and he thought of shouting and disclosing himself. But in another moment Destiny presented itself to his reason. He was acting under compulsion ; this was only a friendly joke on the part of his guide. All was yet well—though pitch dark. He lay comfortably and quietly, penned in his little cabin. As soon as the hatch overhead was closed, and all sounds had ceased, he tried the strength of his prison walls. The cleft in the cargo which formed his prison was about four feet high and three wide. Consequently he could get his back against its roof, and use the whole strength of his body to lift. He put his hands on his knees, and put out his strength little by little. So great was the purchase that it seemed to him that nothing could possibly resist him. Yet the case never budged. It weighed tons. Again he put out the whole strength of his body. Its force appeared to him tremendous, but it was of no avail. Well, he had his bottle of water and his two loaves, and they would not be many days crossing the sea—then all would be well. He had tobacco with him, and lit his pipe and made himself comfortable.

Presently he knew they were moving; and before long they were out at sea. The ship was tossing and rolling; he could hear the waves crunching against her sides, and rushing past them. It never occurred to him to be sea-sick, as his thoughts were busy. He had become happy again, now that they were off, as he smoked his pipe in the dark. It was madness from beginning to end, and he knew it; but that was just the point. He could never have settled on such an expedition as this for himself—it had all been done for him. He had been waiting for years and years, and now his time had come. To think that Destiny should have taken him in hand like this, singled him out from his companions, and sent him on a voyage of faith. It was glorious. Of course it was all nonsense. What possible use was there in his going to Norway? What in the name of fortune was he going to do when he got there? What the devil had ever suggested it? But it was just these arguments which proved the presence of Destiny. For, in spite of them all, he was going.

In the midst of these thoughts he fell into a happy sleep; then he awoke and thought, then he slept again. Time passed. Between sleeping and waking, and thinking and sleeping again, days passed by. It seemed to him that weeks, even months had passed; but he decided that it was not more than a few days. Still, they must be already somewhere near Norway, he thought. So far, he had eaten and drunk nothing. He was saving his provisions up in case of bad weather and delays; and he had felt no need of them, lying there sleeping. On waking from a nap some days before, as the time had seemed to him, he had felt hungry, and a trifle thirsty. But he had resisted the temptation to eat and drink; and it had passed away again. Such a long while had passed since then, without his taking anything, that he began to look upon himself as a sort of fasting man. He had a theory that sleep was as good as food and drink, and he was proving it up to the hilt. Now, however, the time had come, he thought, to take a little food and drink. He began with a bit of bread, but found he could not eat it till he had drunk some water. He took a refreshing gulp, and applied himself to the bread. But he could not get on with it; it seemed to stick in his throat. He took a little more water, not enough to satisfy him. He lay down and slept again, and awoke feeling thirsty. He then recollected a theory of his that, in the treatment of appetites, half measures were no use, and it was best to satisfy them fully, and so let them be. So he had a real good drink, wiped his mouth and corked up the stone bottle. Five minutes afterwards he felt thirsty again. This time he had to deny himself, but he could not sleep for thinking of the water in the bottle. He was also puzzled by this feeling of thirst. He could not make it out. He had drunk a good half-pint or more, enough to last a man who was not working, but just lying idle, as long as you like. Why should he feel thirsty again at once? The right plan, the normal plan was, to quench his thirst, and then go comfortably for twenty-four hours without any more drink. So he took another pull at the bottle, to make sure that the thirst was satisfied, and laid himself down to sleep. In three minutes he was thirsty again. He saw now that he had a battle to fight, that an enemy had risen up against him. He could sleep no more, because this enemy grew. When he did drop off into a doze, the enemy took new and strange shapes. It was better to fight it waking than sleeping. It was not thirst merely that he suffered from, but fear.

Fear laid hold of him more and more; an unknown horror of darkness lay before him. He had never been afraid of death. Death at this moment, in the open air and with his thirst quenched, would have been bliss. But death where he was, and with his thirst unsatisfied. . . . Every now and then he put his lips to the stone bottle, and enjoyed a few moments of exquisite pleasure. The thirst was momentarily relieved; but the fear remained, and soon the suffering came back again. At last the water was all gone. His whole being became absorbed in one awful want. The very objects of his consciousness—the darkness, the walls of his prison, the empty bottle, the remains of the bread and cheese, his own body—these things ceased to be themselves, and became one unspeakable thirst. He began to shout at the top of his voice. He put his back to the roof of his prison, and strained against it with his whole force. He shouted and shouted for days, it seemed to him. A raging madness took possession of him; he flung himself about his prison, then he lay and wept and sobbed, sucking the salt tears into his mouth with his dry tongue. Then he cursed God, Creation, and Destiny, with every foul word known in Hull.

Sometimes there would come a lull in these paroxysms. Whilst lying in one of these calmer moments, half senseless, he suddenly noticed that the ship was steadier. The deafening sound of plunging and surging had given place to a loud cackling, as she rippled through quieter water. A wild hope sprang up in his breast. They must be reaching Norway. He had been weeks and weeks in his prison; and the end of the journey must be close at hand. For a time his sufferings vanished, swallowed up by hope. Every moment he expected to hear even the ripple cease, and to reach the stillness of the harbour side. Hour after hour the water cackled loudly past the ship's sides. He shouted again and again; but his voice was still drowned and powerless to carry. How many more hours of anguish before they reached the port? Time, as it passed, brought its inexorable answer. There was no end to the journey, there never would be any end to it. He would go mad and die long before the end ever came. The cackle of the stiller waters sounded everlastingly in his ears, and yet they never got to the shore. The ship was evidently moving, so there must be some breeze outside; yet the waves no longer rocked her, they only splashed and rippled round her. He argued and argued as to the meaning of this. Gradually hope gave way again to madness and despair. He went off his head once more, and raged about within his little tomb. Once more he found himself calm. It seemed to him that he awoke from a state of unconsciousness. The waters were still talking round the ship's sides, in the same loud and senseless manner. He found his mind strangely clear, and saw things in the light of reason. He had been a fool and a madman. It was all a lie, that nonsense about Destiny—all day-dreams. This was the real truth; this was his awakening to the facts of life. He had always refused to face the truth, liked to live in a little world of his own imagination, and this was the end of it . . . this was the real truth . . . darkness and suffering, awful suffering. . . . 'People would never believe what suffering is,' he thought, 'they would never believe it, not if you was to tell them, till you was black in the face, they could not believe it . . . it's worse than what anybody understands. . . . And this is truth, this is God's blessed truth. I believed a fairy-tale, and I've got what I deserve.' He began to shout and scream once more; and then he fell by degrees into a state of coma.

As he lay unconscious, the ship came into port, after a long journey up the land-locked coast of Norway. Half an hour afterwards, he came to his senses again. All was still around him. For a while he thought that he was dead. Then he heard a sound overhead, and a crack of light appeared in the roof of his prison. 'Help, help!' he shouted, in a strong triumphant voice. Joy overpowered him, and quenched his thirst. Even in his excitement he noticed that his thirst was gone for the moment. He heard men walking above him, and he shouted again, strongly and joyfully. The case above began to shift, and in a moment he was out of his hole. 'Water!' he cried, and scrambled on deck. He was struck blind by the light, and held out his hands, crying—'Water!' They brought him water and he drank, checking his greed with all his might. He did not wish to drown his life, now that he had just found it. He compelled himself to drink quietly. He kept his eyes tightly closed as he drank. An ocean of blinding light surrounded him, as though he were in the presence of God. His whole being was absorbed in joy, and intense, almost insufferable light, as he sipped the water of life. Presently he staggered to his feet. A hand was stretched out to help him; but he put it from him, and reached the bulwarks. The world began to appear to him, unfolding itself little by little out of a sea of glory. Overhead he became aware of a mountain, its sides and summit steaming with a dazzling mist. Out of a golden haze on either hand appeared more mountains, and the sea, or a lake, he knew not which, reflecting one another into the distance. His vision became stronger and clearer. Now he saw that the sun was shining, and that waterfalls were streaming down the mountain-sides; he could hear the fresh sound of them in the distance. The sky was blue overhead. At the foot of the mountain the corn was growing. The waterfalls dashed down the rocks, and tumbled into the fields, making rainbows above the corn. He staggered back again to his can of water, and sat down on the deck, with his back against the fo'c'sle wall. The seamen stood around him, smiling. He had his drink; but they now acted as bread and meat to him, as he looked at their tanned faces and stalwart figures, warm in the sun. He felt very dazed and helpless as he lay on the deck, and wondered what they would do with him. Though he had staggered to his feet, he thought he was too weak to walk. The cook kept talking to him in broken English. The seamen had not been able to do anything but smile so far; but now the cook's expression became more emphatic.

'What you want? What you doing here? What you come over for?' Jim Holloway remembered himself. He scrambled on to his feet again. His head swam, and his knees began to totter. The cook caught him round the waist, but Jim put his arm aside. 'Just give us a bite of something,' he said, 'and then I'll go and look for work,' and he gazed up at the mountain overhead, standing firmly without assistance on the deck. He felt that, whatever happened, he must not give Destiny away again, but play up to it manfully. The cook smiled. He bent over the bulwarks and talked to a girl who stood on the wooden quay. Then he walked up the ship, talked to the mate, and came back to Jim, who was leaning on the bulwarks again, looking at the mountain. 'You go 'long with her,' he said, pointing to the girl. Jim stepped on shore bravely, and walked off with the girl down the sunlit road. The girl had blue eyes and a softly glowing complexion, a shawl was tied over her flaxen hair, her sleeves were white, and she wore a blue serge skirt. Jim limped along beside her in his greasy green-black clothes. All his life at Hull he had never before felt so like a tramp and a ne'er-do-weel. In his excitement he kept explaining to her his condition and suffering in voluble English. They passed up a little stone path, through the hayfields, crossed a bridge over a rushing and roaring river, and came to a large substantial wooden hut. Here Jim was seated at a table, and given milk and bread and cheese, and a hundred comforts. His soul was fed with fatness. The mother of the household and her daughter attended to him, freely and kindly, and with a roughness which put him at his ease. He cracked jokes at them, and laughed as he soaked his bread in the milk and gained strength. The cook soon turned up from the ship. 'Now you in luck, my friend,' he said. 'There is the pier building over there at Sandener, two kilometres, all short of hands, the men busy, milk the cows in the saeters. You get work on the pier.' 'I thought so,' said Jim, and a smile of triumph lit up his face. He was shown some clean straw in a barn next door, and rolled up for a ten hours' sleep. Next day he was off early. His sufferings seemed to have left no effect whatever. He walked lightly along the coast; presently he turned a corner of the bay; and a small village with a wooden hotel came in sight. Sure enough, a wooden pier was being constructed. He walked straight up to a little wooden office, and applied for work. The manager could speak English. There was a considerable colloquy. Jim explained that he had taken a passage over from Hull in search of work. The manager raised his eyebrows in astonishment. Jim told a string of lies in answer to his questions; he had heard, he said, in Hull that work was to be found in Sandener. The manager was baffled. He put back his cap and stared at the draggled figure. Then he engaged his services as a pile-driver at eighteen krone a week. Jim had a hard day's work. Now and then he feared that he was going to faint. He worked with four Norwegians, heaving up the ton-weight hammer, and letting it fall with a bang on to the pile. He marvelled at his own powers of endurance after his sufferings. What refreshed him was the thought of Destiny. When he was on the point of giving in, the thought came to him, and a sensation of sweetness and happiness stole over him, renewing his strength.

. . . . .

The steersman came to himself with a start. They were close to Sandener; and the boat had entered the shadow of the mountain. The sound of the oars echoed louder. He steered towards the wooden pier. On it stood his wife, smiling and waving. They landed, made the boat fast for the night, and walked up all together to the house with the flagstaff. The mountain rose above his house, grey, vast, and barren in the gathering gloom. But it brought no chill or vague foreboding to his breast. For, in spite of his settled life and prosperity, he still loved Destiny.